Rainer Bauböck, John Rundell (Eds.)

Blurred Boundaries:
Migration, Ethnicity, Citizenship

Ashgate
Aldershot • Brookfield USA • Singapore • Sydney

© European Centre Vienna, 1998

All rights reserved. No part of this publication may be reproduced, stored in a retrieval system, or transmitted in any form or by any means, electronic, mechanical, photocopying, recording or otherwise without the prior permission of the publisher.

Published by

Ashgate Publishing Limited
Gower House
Croft Road
Aldershot
Hants GU11 3HR
England

Ashgate Publishing Company
Old Post Road
Brookfield
Vermont 05036
USA

Copy-editing and DTP: Willem Stamatiou
European Centre for Social Welfare Policy and Research
Berggasse 17
1090 Vienna
Austria

British Library Cataloguing-in-Publication Data. A catalogue record for this book is available from the British Library.

ISBN 1-84014-893-4

Printed by *teritéka*, Hungary

Contents

Preface 7

Part I: Migration and Minorities.
　　　　The Diversity of Experiences with Diversity

CHAPTER 1
The Crossing and Blurring of Boundaries in International Migration.
Challenges for Social and Political Theory 17
Rainer Bauböck

CHAPTER 2
Temporal and Spatial Aspects of Multiculturality.
Reflections on the Meaning of Time and Space in
Relation to the Blurred Boundaries of Multicultural Societies 53
Charles Westin

CHAPTER 3
Changing Representations of the Other in France: The Mirror of Migration ... 85
Catherine de Wenden

CHAPTER 4
Multiculturalism à la Canadian and Intégration à la Québécoise.
Transcending their Limits 95
Danielle Juteau / Marie McAndrew / Linda Pietrantonio

CHAPTER 5
The Israeli Experience in Multiculturalism 111
Eliezer Ben-Rafael

CHAPTER 6
Multiculturalism from Above: Italian Variations on a European Theme 143
Giovanna Zincone

CHAPTER 7
Egalitarian Multiculturalism: Institutional Separation
and Cultural Pluralism 185
Veit Bader

Part II: Groups, Rights and Citizenship in Multicultural Contexts

CHAPTER 8
Globalization and the Ambiguities of National Citizenship 223
Stephen Castles

CHAPTER 9
Cultural Pluralism and the Subversion of the 'Taken-for-Granted' World 245
Maria Markus

CHAPTER 10
Toleration as the Public Acceptance of Difference 259
Anna Elisabetta Galeotti

CHAPTER 11
How Can Collective Rights and Liberalism Be Reconciled? 281
Daniel M. Weinstock

CHAPTER 12
Bridging the Gap: Citizenship in Europe and Asia 305
Alastair Davidson

CHAPTER 13
Tensions of Citizenship in an Age of Diversity: Reflections on
Territoriality, Cosmopolitanism and Symmetrical Reciprocity 321
John Rundell

CHAPTER 14
Self-Representation and the Representation of the Other 341
Agnes Heller

List of Contributors 355

Preface

The underlying theme of this collection of essays are new forms of cultural diversity which result from migration and globalization. Historically, most liberal democracies have developed on the basis of national cultures – either a single one, or a dominant one, or a federation of several ones. However, political and economic developments have upset traditional patterns and have blurred established boundaries. Ongoing immigration from diverse origins has inserted new ethnic minorities into formerly more or less homogeneous populations. Democratic liberties and rights provided opportunities for old and new marginalized minorities to resist assimilation and to assert their collective identities. The resulting pattern of multiculturalism is different from earlier ones. Often cultural boundaries are neither clearly defined nor do they simply dissolve by assimilation into a dominant group – they have become fuzzy and a constant source of real or imagined hostility and anxiety. A proliferation of mixed identities goes together with stronger claims for cultural rights and escalating conflicts between ethnic minorities and national majorities. In many countries multiculturalism is today perceived as a challenge rather than as an enrichment.

Our book focuses on the question how institutions and policies of liberal democracies can cope with these trends. It addresses three main tasks:

1) To compare different national contexts and types of ethnic groups (immigrant and indigenous, linguistic and religious minorities) and to discuss how policies of multicultural integration have to be adapted in order to cope with such differences.
2) To evaluate the impact of common trends of globalization which link societies and encourage convergence between national models of multicultural integration.
3) To discuss whether the shared status and norms of liberal democratic citizenship can still provide for sufficient integration of heterogeneous political communities.

In the context of this interplay between identity and integration, a basic challenge for democratic nation-states is to reconcile the recognition of a multiplicity of ways of life, experiences and aspirations of different ethnic groups with the egalitarian structure of citizenship. This becomes all the more difficult when citizenship itself becomes associated with exclusive definitions of national identity or even with deeply felt chauvinism. This double-sided challenge of the contemporary democratic nation-state provides the book's unity of focus and intent, as well as the rationale for its division into two sections.

Part I – Migration and Minorities. The Diversity of Experiences with Diversity – examines the way in which the boundaries between ethnic, national and migrant identities have become irrevocably blurred in 'the age of migration' (Castles/Miller, 1993). Within the history of nation-state formation democracy has often been a catch-all word which has simply assumed the integration of a migrant population into the body politic of the receiving nation-state without the assertion of identity or rights for the migrant communities' particular ways of life. A basic challenge for contemporary democratic states is whether the traditional language of integration can become compatible with the recognition of a plurality of aspirations, social ties and ways of life in multicultural environments. While many discussions assume that the transformation of previously rather homogeneous societies into multicultural ones is mainly due to new waves and characteristics of postwar migration, a number of contributions in our book argue that multiculturalism had already been a salient feature of many destination and receiving societies before recent immigration flows. The Canadian, Israeli and Western European societies all have long-established experience with various forms of national, ethnic, linguistic and religious diversity. Paradoxically, this need not make the task of accommodating new diversity resulting from immigration any easier.

Rainer Bauböck's opening chapter considers how international migration crosses and blurs three kinds of boundaries: territorial borders of states, political boundaries of citizenship and the cultural boundaries of national communities. He first argues for combining macro-, micro- and meso approaches in migration research so that the process can be seen from the perspectives of states of individual migrants and of migrant networks and communities. Bauböck then suggests that political theories of nationalism help to understand why territorial and cultural boundaries have become more rigid in modern states whereas societies have become mobile beyond these limits. This tension explains why migration is perceived as such a disturbing phenomenon. In response to these worries, Bauböck pleads for liberal pluralist norms which would make both citizenship and dominant national cultures more open for the migrant experience.

Charles Westin discusses the various meanings of culture and multiculturality and the different phenomena which emerge from incongruities between boundaries of states, ethnies and cultures which he illustrates in a critical examination of Swedish multiculturalism. The main task of his chapter is, however, an analysis of temporal and spatial dimensions of international migration and diaspora minorities which he contrasts to other societal formations like the nation-state ideal, settler societies and autochthonous minorities. The chapter concludes with a multidimensional analysis of three types of culture (folk, high and mass culture) which challenges the assumption of cultural homogeneity at the level of nation-states.

Cathérine de Wenden gives an account of the various representations of the Other in daily life which she finds in recent French history. The question which troubles her is to which extent images and stereotypes about successive groups of immigrants have served to create a negative consensus about the shared identity of the community of French citizens. She shows how the instrumentalization of Islam for this purpose is of relatively recent origin and creates an amalgam which severely distorts the experiences and motives of the 'silent Islam' of old first-generation immigrants as well as a more politicized and ostentatious Islam among second-generation youths.

Danielle Juteau, Mary McAndrew and Linda Pietrantonio compare the Canadian conception of multiculturalism with interculturalism in the province of Québec and find these two approaches less different than is commonly assumed. Against recent critics which accuse multiculturalist policies of promoting segregation and group egoism the authors defend normative pluralism, i.e. the attribution of positive value to cultural pluralism.

Eliezer Ben-Rafael examines cultural diversity in Israel which presents a case of rapid transition from a melting-pot ideology to multiculturalism. He compares the situation of three minorities: Oriental Jews, recent immigrants from the former Soviet Union and Israeli Arabs. Alongside the criteria of class position and social mobility Ben-Rafael considers whether the dominant culture adopts a segregative or unifying attitude towards a minority group. The analysis is guided by the idea that Wittgenstein's notion of family resemblances can be usefully applied to differences between ethnic groups which, on the one hand, mutually impact on each other and, on the other hand, share a common environment.

Giovanna Zincone's contribution argues forcefully against some common assumptions in the debate on multiculturalism. One among these is that multiculturalism is a North American and Australian phenomenon which has only come to Europe with recent waves of immigration and is now threatening democratic stability there. Analysing mainly the Italian case, Zincone demonstrates that there are old traditions of political multiculturalism in Europe which articulate and represent ethnic, religious, linguistic and regional identities. The chapter also presents a comprehensive theoretical framework for distinguishing levels of multiculturalism (in civil society, political society, public policies and in the state) and emphasizes that multiculturalism is not merely a transformation of society from below (by new immigrants) but quite often initiated from above (as in the case of the Northern League's regional separatism).

Veit Bader's chapter takes a fresh look at debates within normative theory about the conflict between equality and difference. He argues that it should be possible to uphold both values simultaneously and that attention to contexts can help in this task. Distinguishing forms of inclusion and separation in institutional and cultural dimensions Bader presents a list of fields of incorporation and a comparative typology of four kinds of multicultural regimes. Finally, by discussing pluralistic solutions to problems of multiculturalism in public education he illustrates how the norms he defends can be applied in context.

If one of the challenges for democratic states is to recast the language in which the relation between integration and diversity is thought, another is to rethink the category of citizenship in more robust terms. This is the focus of Part II on 'Groups, Rights and Citizenship in Multicultural Contexts'.

The integrating mechanism for nation-states, at least formally speaking, has been their criteria of citizenship, and in democratic states the universalist and inclusivist assumptions of the democratic heritage assumed that this was enough not only for an integrated citizenry, but also one that was tolerant of its own internal diversity. However, as the history of democratic nation-states has shown, a formal universalism has not been the only criterion of citizenship; national identity, a sense of belonging, and a generalized tolerance towards cultural and ethnic diversity have also been important, but often unstated, criteria that may conflict with one another. Universalistic assumptions may conceal other bases of citizenship, such as the conflation of nationalism and democracy, or a concealed ethnicity which comes to be challenged and defensively acted upon once multi-ethnic communities emerge or become visible. The very experience of multi-ethnicity permanently challenges and tests the universalistic premises of democratic citizenship.

Stephen Castles argues that contemporary globalization processes have resulted in a crisis of national citizenship that has uncovered its implicit ambiguities. Castles discusses four recent books which present different responses to the crisis. Dominique Schnapper's defence of a republican conception of citizenship has exclusionary implications and raises the danger of a re-ethnicization of nations as emotional referents after the demise of national politics in globalized society. In contrast, Kenichi Ohmae fully embraces economic globalization and a borderless world of consumers and corporations, but ignores the undermining of democracy involved in these developments. For Yasemin Soysal it is the liberal human rights revolution which has weakened the importance of citizenship as legal mechanism for allocating rights, but in Castles' view she underestimates the exclusionary power of national as well as European citizenship. Robert Reich, finally, presents a sober analysis of the demise of national economies and of the successful secession of a class of analysts from the rest of society, but responds to this with a voluntaristic programme of reconstructing national solidarity. Castles ends by sketching alternative proposals for participatory membership at regional, state and transnational levels which reflect the shifting modes of territorial, cultural and political belonging.

The following three chapters address challenges of contemporary cultural pluralism for political theory and philosophy. Maria Markus distinguishes two layers of culture: an unreflective belonging to a way of life or everyday culture and a reflectively generated system of beliefs, norms and organized traditions. Markus shows how cultural pluralization results from a politicization of indigenous or migrant cultures which transforms prereflective ways of life into reflective identities. Modern states are not neutral towards such plurality because they themselves foster national cultures. Markus discusses Habermas's theory of constitutional patriotism as one response to this problem which attempts to uncouple the two forms of culture. She suggests that the blurring of cultural boundaries through hybridization could be a starting point for an alternative perspective. Hybridization can, however, also produce a siege mentality of cultural closure unless it becomes itself self-conscious and reflectively asserted.

Anna Elisabetta Galeotti discusses another core aspect of the traditional liberal solution to problems of cultural diversity: the norm of toleration. She points out that, in its standard version, toleration addresses clashes between religious creeds, moral values and ideological views and resolves these by establishing individual liberties and a separation between public and private spheres. However, contemporary non-trivial cases of toleration, such as the prohibition of racist hate speech on US campuses, the admission of gays to the US army or the wearing of headscarfs in French public schools are about equal respect, status and opportunities for groups rather than about individual liberties. In response to these claims she proposes a pluralistic model of toleration which goes beyond mere non-interference but need not involve recognition, in the sense of positive affirmation, of what remain essentially disputed differences.

Daniel Weinstock addresses collective rights which are another controversial issue in the liberal response to diversity because they appear to be incompatible with moral individualism, state neutrality and a procedural view of the political process. Weinstock discusses Will Kymlicka's theory of multicultural citizenship as the best liberal defence of group rights for cultural minorities so far. He identifies several problems in this approach, especially that it derives a justification for group rights from the value of secure cultural membership for individual autonomy which seems to exclude minority cultures that do not value autonomy in the same way as liberals. As an alternative, Weinstock proposes the broader value of individual well-being as a foundation for valuing group membership. He suggests that this move need not lead to a Pandora's box of endlessly proliferating collective claims. Collective rights can be tailor-made when they respond to a criterion of vulnerability of particular groups.

Alastair Davidson's chapter enters the normative debates about citizenship from a comparative angle. He looks at cultural differences at the global level and asks how they shape particular conceptions of citizenship. The presumed "clash of civilizations" invoked both by Western academics like Samuel Huntington and Asian politicians like Malaysia's and Singapore's prime ministers seems to imply that the Western concept of citizenship has no relevance outside of Western societies. Davidson shows that this claim misinterprets the evolution of citizenship which has already left behind the Rousseauean and Kantian notions of the citizen-warrior or the citizen as master of himself. Contemporary citizenship has to respond to blurred boundaries between societies and cultures and involves a shift towards norms of civility and civic virtue derived from the basic premise that no individual and no group or culture can be a judge in its own cause. This conception is no longer a particular Western one which would be inaccessible to Asian traditions.

For John Rundell citizenship is a concept which condenses notions of national and cultural identity, of sovereign state power, and of public activity and democratic participation. The tensions between these are never fully resolved. Rundell focuses particularly on the fault lines between territorial/national citizenship, on the one hand, and sovereign and democratic citizenship on the other. He argues that Habermas's discussion of this problem remains ambivalent between a linguistic/procedural approach and a more latent anthropological-cultural one which acknowledges the particularity of national political cultures. In Marcel Mauss's analysis of the gift relation and Agnes Heller's generalization of the underlying norm of symmetrical reciprocity Rundell finds a standard of intersubjectivity which could inform a more adequate understanding of common citizenship termed cosmopolitan citizenship, shared by different cultural groups both within societies, and at the global level.

The concluding chapter by Agnes Heller addresses another essentially contested norm in multicultural societies: the representation of group differences. Heller challenges the idea of self-representation of groups which presupposes that only a member of the group can represent it authentically. Playing on the double meaning of 'representation' she discusses the implications of this norm for the representation of groups in literature and in politics. While vigorously opposing any fundamentalism of difference in both areas, Heller suggests that what is worth preserving is the difference between self-representation and representation of the other. Self-representation may add something valuable to hetero-representation. In literature, autobiography and self-portrait reflect an important artistic experience. National or women's literature can contribute to world literature and elements of direct democracy can supplement the inevitable representation by others in politics. In both fields, the alternative is not between difference and universalism, but between closure and openness. Heller's vision is thus a pluralistic one like that of all the other authors in our volume.

Most of the contributions are based on papers presented at a conference held at the University of Melbourne in July 1996 and jointly organized by the European Centre for Social Welfare Policy and Research in Vienna and the Ashworth Centre for Social Theory at the University of Melbourne. We would like to thank all sponsors and co-organizers of this event:

At the Australian end, amongst others: Marianne Bodi who has done a lot to make the conference a success; Horst Imberger, Joanne Finkelstein, the Australian Centre and Ruth Fincher, the School of Languages, all at the University of Melbourne; the Australian Multicultural Foundation; Brian Nelson and the Centre for European Studies at Monash University; and the Office of Multicultural Affairs, Canberra.

In Vienna, Pia Trost has helped with the preparation of the meeting. The conference was co-sponsored by the following Austrian and international institutions: the International Organization for Migration, the Vienna Integration Fund and the Austrian Federal Ministries of Science, Research and the Arts, of the Interior, and of Education and Cultural Affairs.

In Melbourne, Danielle Petherbridge assisted with attentive and careful language editing of several chapters. In Vienna, Willem Stamatiou has very efficiently taken care of the copy-editing of this volume just as with the two previous books in our series.

June 1998   Rainer Bauböck (Vienna) / John Rundell (Melbourne)

Reference: Castles, S./Miller, M.J. (1993) *The Age of Migration. International Population Movements in the Modern World.* London: Macmillan.

PART I

Migration and Minorities.
The Diversity of Experiences with Diversity

CHAPTER 1

The Crossing and Blurring of Boundaries in International Migration. Challenges for Social and Political Theory

Rainer Bauböck

In this chapter I want to discuss the effects of international migration on political boundaries in modern highly industrialized societies. I will consider three different kinds of political boundaries: first, territorial borders of states; second, boundaries of the polity, that is, of membership in political communities which is defined by citizenship status and citizenship rights;[1] third, boundaries of cultural communities which have become politicized because they are associated with national identities or because states grant specific rights to minority cultures. In my view, all three kinds of boundaries are essential features of modern societies which are not about to be abolished in a unified global society. However, international migration is a phenomenon which causes considerable irritation. It affects the social meaning, the permeability, the spatial location or the temporal stability of the three kinds of political boundaries.

I want to explore this phenomenon of boundary crossing and boundary blurring in international migration from three different angles: first, a sociological one which argues for combining the macro approaches of studying the effects of migration on societies and states with the micro and meso perspectives of the migrants, their networks and communities; second, an evolutionary perspective in political science which emphasizes the specific territoriality of modern nation-states as the general context for understanding the profound social and political irritations caused by international migration; third, a political theory perspective which addresses the normative question whether or to which degree liberal democracies ought to open their citizenship and their national cultures for immigrants.[2]

1 Towards a 'Relativity Theory' of Migration?

A sociological analysis of migration faces a descriptive and an explanatory task. It is first concerned with describing migratory patterns by answering questions of the following kind: How many people and which kind of people have moved from A to B in a given time period? The explanatory task is then to find out something about the causes of such migratory movements or about their effects on sending and receiving areas. The great challenge for theories of migration lies in those questions where migration figures either as the phenomenon to be explained or as the cause of some broader social change. However, attempts to formulate a general theory of human migration which started more than 100 years ago with E.G. Ravenstein's search for the laws of migration (1885 and 1889) have not been successful since.[3] The basic reason for this failure is that it seems exceedingly difficult and at the same time pointless to make the kind of generalizations that would be required for a general theory. Human migration is not determined by either a single kind of purpose of the individual migrants nor by a single function which migration fulfils for social systems.

Migration is a human activity involving a shift in territorial residence. Micro theories focus on the individuals who move and their motives. People migrate to improve their income, to join their family or to establish a new one. They migrate because they prefer a destination society for cultural, religious or political reasons to their society of present residence or because they have been forced to flee as undesirable minorities. The emphasis on individual purposes and agency is essential for understanding these phenomena. Migration is never fully explained by structural forces. Not only voluntary, but also most kinds of forced migration involve migrants as human agents who take decisions whether, when or where to go. A sufficiently general rational choice approach may account for most of these motives. However, a comprehensive theory must not only adequately represent the diversity of reasons, but also the different specific cases where it is not the migrants themselves, but others who take the basic decisions.[4] The formation of some nation-states has involved organized population transfers or exchanges of ethnic minorities. Prisoners of war or slaves have been forcefully brought into another country rather than being forced to go there themselves. Refugees are driven out of their homes by their persecutors, but they may also be taken out of their country by international rescue operations. These are extreme cases. If we understand migration as a purposive human activity we could suggest to exclude them by definition. However, they serve to illustrate the broader problem present in most other forms of migration as well. We cannot simply assume that the motive of the individual migrant is the relevant *explanans* or cause while structural variables and decisions by other agents are merely constraining and intervening conditions.

At the other end of the spectrum of sociological theories we find structuralist explanations which see migration as the outcome of macro processes of functional adaptation or systemic requirements. In some neo-Marxist accounts, for example, migration is basically explained by the capitalist need for providing an ongoing supply of foreign labour for a broad industrial reserve army or for specific jobs shunned by natives. However, slave trade, indentured labour, guestworker recruitment and spontaneous chain migration may all serve this purpose. Any plausible theory will have to account for the differences of status and agency of migrants involved in these types of movements. Furthermore, the structural causes vary themselves strongly for different kinds of migration. Some are economic but others are essentially political. Germany's open door policy for ethnic German immigrants from Eastern Europe[5] cannot be explained by economic needs (neither of the German economy nor of the immigrants themselves). More generally, differences in wages, employment rates, social security and welfare provision are normally not sufficient to predict the direction and size of migrations. Historic ties between states and societies, cultural similarities, constructions of national identities, foreign policy interests and, last but not least, efforts to enforce political control over emigration or immigration are highly relevant for the transformation of latent migration potentials into actual flows.

What these cursory remarks want to suggest is that the study of migration is a genuinely interdisciplinary task in which one should deliberately avoid attempts to construct a unified theory or to establish migration studies as a discipline of its own with its particular methodology and leading paradigm. As a social phenomenon migration crosses and blurs the boundaries of societies; as an object of scientific enquiry it crosses and blurs the boundaries of academic disciplines. In order to understand migration we need, among others, theories of labour markets as well as of nation-building; but we probably do not need the theory of migration.

The descriptive task of migration research seems much easier to tackle than the explanatory one of migration theory. The former is concerned with finding patterns in the direction, size and composition of migratory movements. The first step is to collect demographic and geographic data which could categorize and compare different migratory patterns. In order to do this, one has to make some basic decisions about the spatial and time units over which individual movements will be aggregated. To a considerable extent the patterns we find will depend on the units we choose. In international migration it is obviously sovereign states which are the relevant spatial units.[6] This creates the problem that effects of size can be quite difficult to standardize for comparative purposes. While *ceteris paribus* larger countries admit larger absolute numbers of migrants, smaller countries generally have higher percentages of inflows and stocks of immigrants per head of their population. The reason for this phenomenon is that in a larger territory a larger percentage of the total amount of long-distance migration will be internal movement of citizens. It is therefore not difficult to explain why Luxembourg and Switzerland have such a high percentage of foreign populations and why many European states have long overtaken the USA in terms of their shares of foreign-born populations.

A second and more interesting complication is that in order to aggregate movements one has to assume that the units of aggregation themselves do not move. We therefore suppose that states are entities with stable borders and definitions of citizenship. But this is not always the case. State borders sometimes move, too. There are different ways how this can happen. In some rare cases like Poland after 1945 entire countries have been shifted on the map. More frequently states have expanded or shrunk in size due to acquisitions or loss of territories. In some cases borders have been fully abolished and states have disappeared through voluntary unifications or forceful annexations. Finally imposed division, unilateral secession or agreed separation can create new states and borders where none (or only provincial ones) had existed before.[7] Borders may also remain fixed in their territorial location but change in their significance for sovereign statehood. Colonialism was highly inventive in creating different grades of formal dependency which could be manipulated and changed in response to pressure for decolonization. French and British legislation on immigration and citizenship are still trying to cope with this legacy which creates all kinds of strange irregularities (such as holders of British passports not entitled to enter the country).[8] Finally, even when there are no changes with regard to the borders or status of territories, modifications in the legislation on naturalization and citizenship may have substantial impacts on the statistical data supposed to measure international migration. For example, comparing the percentages of resident foreigners between countries with *ius soli* or *ius sanguinis* legislation may be highly misleading because the latter include second and third generations of immigrant descent born in the country.

Even the accurate definition of immigrants as foreign-born populations can present problems when borders and definitions of citizenship have changed. An example that shows the impact of both is Austria in the inter-war period. The 25 years before World War I were a time of fervent migratory activity with large-scale immigration especially in the capital Vienna. However, international migration was negligible because virtually all of these migrants came from other parts of the Empire. The breakup of the dual monarchy transformed the immigrants of the previous period suddenly into foreign residents and thus redefined their internal migration *ex post* as an international one.[9] In 1934 12% of the population qualified as 'immigrants' by the common criterion that they were born outside the territory of the new Austrian republic. A greatly reduced movement between the successor states of the monarchy during the inter-war period led then to much more impressive statistics of international migration and prompted the first attempt to control the access of foreigners to the labour market.[10] Similar phenomena have occurred with the dissolution of the Soviet Union.

The assumption that states are stable and people move is not only indispensable for statistical aggregation of migration data, but it also dominates social perceptions. This may explain why people who stay are suddenly perceived as foreign immigrants if a movement of borders has redefined their origins as foreign. Let me use an analogy to illustrate this phenomenon. Imagine you sit in a train waiting in the station and there is another train on the rail next to yours. The other train fills the whole background of what you see when you look out of your window. If that train starts to move you will experience the irresistible impression that it is rather your own one which moves in the opposite direction. Our normal experience is that backgrounds do not move when foregrounds stay still. So we reinterpret such an event by experiencing it as if we had moved ourselves. State borders and the boundaries of citizenship form a similarly pervasive national background for the perception of migration. When they move this deviation from common experience is corrected by treating the people whose background has been shifted beyond the new boundaries as if they had just moved in the opposite direction, that is, as if they had entered from outside.

Once we have discarded the illusion of permanently stable backgrounds against which to register migration we might as well go a step further. When we begin to doubt the experience just described, we may look out of the opposite window and see the station. This will reassure us that it is not our train which has moved. And once the station seems to move we will immediately know that now our train is indeed departing. However, our previous disillusion might warn us to reflect on this new experience. Could we not as well say that the station has moved in relation to our train? In fact this is probably a quite accurate description of the experience of people like the ticket collector who live on the train for a large part of their daily lives. Could the migrant experience be described in these terms? From the point of view of resident populations migrants come and go; from the migrants' perspective states enter their lives and leave again.

This switching of perspectives informs an alternative descriptive approach in migration research. While the dominant method focuses on macro processes and chooses resident populations as reference groups, the alternative approach is oriented towards the micro level and studies the process from the perspective of migrant populations. This change involves also an inversion in the relation between time and space. In macro approaches the basic unit is a spatial one with regard to which we register incidents of individuals crossing its borders and aggregate them over any chosen period of time. The patterns of inflows, outflows and times of residence of migrant groups are aspects of the historical time as it is experienced by the society inhabiting a given territory. In micro perspectives the basic unit is a temporal one, the biography of migrants with birth and death as its ultimate limits. The crossing of territorial borders introduces spatial markers into the flow of time. For migrants biographical time is structured into periods marked by changes of places of residence.

For sociological purposes we will be interested in broader migratory patterns rather than in single biographies of individuals. So the task is then to aggregate individual migration itineraries into groups which allow for meaningful comparison. In his contribution to this volume Charles Westin describes three different ways how individuals may be grouped along the time dimension: by age, by period or by cohorts. What we should be specifically interested in is data about migration cohorts, that is, groups who have left their country, or have entered another one, in the same year. Many relevant questions, for example about patterns of return migration or naturalization, would require examining cohorts.[11] Unfortunately, such data are rarely available from official statistics which are generally collected from the 'macro perspective' of the receiving society. The most accurate data are those on stocks of foreign citizens or immigrant populations, data on flows are often much less reliable estimates and cohort data are often only available for small samples.

A migrant perspective need not, and should not, focus on individuals only. Often the relevant units are the family, the household, groups of common ethnic origins or immigrant neighbourhoods. This shift towards what Thomas Faist (1997) calls 'the crucial meso level', introduces a whole new set of problems how to describe migration patterns. First it removes the temporal limitation of a biographical perspective. Migrations can then be understood as events structuring the history of social groups and institutions which stretch across generations into an indefinite future. Secondly, it opens the choice between basic units of aggregation which are fixed in a territorial location (such as households and neighbourhoods) or units which can themselves move in space (like families and ethnic communities).[12] Unlike individuals the latter can also be located in different places simultaneously, can move in different directions, can expand or contract in space.

If we take the family as a unit migration decisions can be understood to affect both individuals who move as well as those who stay. The approach which has been labelled the 'new economics of migration'[13] emphasizes the family unit which pools resources for, and gains from, migration and is often motivated by attempts to diversify risks or to overcome relative deprivation rather than merely by income maximization. Critics of the shift towards the family and household as basic units have argued that this might lead to ignoring, once again, the independent motives and agency of women.[14] The proper approach seems to be a combined one. For most individual migrants the family is not only a social context within which they take their own decisions, but manifests itself as an agent who actively constrains or promotes their choices. However, while migrants invariably have to take into account how their decisions will affect other family members, this does not mean that they cannot pursue their own targets within these relations of mutual dependency. Women who want to increase their independence from their husbands who have gone abroad may thus, for example, prefer not to join them because they enjoy greater autonomy as heads of the household in the country of origin. Alternatively, they may themselves decide to follow their husbands when they see greater opportunities to find employment in the receiving society and can thus improve their status by contributing their own wages to the family income. In order to explore hypotheses like these we must be able to relate individual data to aggregate ones at the level of families and households.

Considering neighbourhoods or ethnic communities as units of aggregation makes the descriptive task even more complicated. Migration is then seen as a pattern of flows within a wider network stretching across several countries.[15] We know, for example, that urban neighbourhoods in a destination society are often populated by migrants who come from a single village or small region in a country of origin. Macro data in immigration countries which register only the countries of birth or citizenship do not give us clues about the relevant social units within which migrants are selected and channelled towards specific destinations. The task would be to match regional data in sending and receiving countries and to follow the itineraries of samples of migrants.

These remarks are just meant to show the enormous difficulties in specifying the relevant units of descriptive analysis in international migration. As I will try to show later on, adopting a single perspective at the expense of alternative approaches creates biases in perceptions, explanations and expectations. In descriptive analysis like in migration theory concerned with causes and effects of movements, the best practice may be one of shifting perspectives. Ideally, we should develop a comprehensive relativity approach which regards the train we sit in, the train on the next rail and the station all as potentially moving elements within a single integrated system so that the movement of each element can only be described in relation to the others. However, the complexity of this task is quite daunting. What can and should be done for practical purposes is to successively explore the macro and micro perspectives that emerge from regarding one of these elements as moving and the others as fixed and to enrich them further with the meso perspective of the migrant networks and communities which expand across societies and political communities as a result of their members' movements.

2 Transnational Migration and the Territorial Segmentation of the State System

While I have just challenged the exclusive focus on states as stable territorial units for descriptive analyses of international migration I want to emphasize now that territoriality is a deeply ingrained feature of modern statehood which explains why international migration is such an irritating phenomenon. This view contrasts with those of other authors who predict a new era of empires for whom territory is increasingly less important because their power is located in global markets and the cyberspaces of telecommunication (Guéhenno, 1994) or who think that migration itself creates territorially unbound nations stretching across political borders (Basch et al., 1994).

Following Ernest Gellner (1990) and many others we may distinguish three basic types of human societies: pre-agrarian societies of hunters and gatherers, agrarian societies and industrial ones. Each of these societies relates to territory in specific ways and each has characteristic forms of political organization. Pre-agrarian societies seem to have been generally stateless and nomadic; agrarian ones were sedentary and their states were essentially defined by military control over territory; industrial societies are mobile and states organize territorial populations by means of bureaucratic administration. These are of course crude generalizations but they are still useful for understanding the specific territorial modes of organization of societies and states in different eras of history. Let me make some brief observations first on territorial mobility of societies and then on the territoriality of states and how it structures migration.

Some post-modern authors have picked up the notion of nomadism in order to describe the migrant experience and what they see as a general tendency towards deterritorialization and uprootedness in contemporary society.[16] According to a standard definition, nomadism is a "way of life of peoples who do not live continuously in the same place but move cyclically or periodically. It is distinguished from migration, which is non-cyclical and involves a total change of habitat" (Encyclopedia Britannica, vol. 8: 753). This definition is clear enough with regard to the difference between migrants and nomads. Migration is a phenomenon which presupposes a sedentary society as a background. In such societies, households which are firmly anchored in specific locations form the basic institutions of economic and social life. Migrants move within or between such societies from one household, place of work or education to another. In nomadic cultures where the whole collectivity moves in search for pasture land or hunting grounds the societal structure moves along because it is not tied to the territory. The territory provides material resources (food) and spiritual ones (sacred places) both of which can only be collected by moving around.[17] Moving in space structures the time experience of nomadic society as harvesting seasons do in agrarian ones. This probably creates a very special image of space. In the metaphor discussed above nomads are really like people who never leave the train and see the stations move by. The train needs to be refuelled in the stations. However, for the passengers the structure of the train itself remains the static element in their lives whereas the scenery and the stations they see from their windows are the mobile elements. In such a way of life, territory and movement must be experienced in a manner which we can hardly imagine in our societies whose social geography is structured by durable human settlements and territorial borders. For our discussion the most relevant difference is that territorial movement in nomadic societies contributes to freezing the culture and the societal structure whereas modern migrations are a ferment for accelerated change. Migrants are people who leave the train and enter the cities. For them the train is no longer a self-sufficient social unit; they come in search for houses where they can stay for a while or forever. By leaving their societies and by entering others they introduce or reinforce all kinds of demographic, economic, social, political and cultural changes. What makes for this dynamic is the contrast between the territorial stability of states and households and the mobility of migrants.

Another category of territorial movement which should not be confused with either nomadism or migration is tourism. Unlike nomads tourists do not move along with their societies (although they often move in groups or crowds). Like nomads they move according to seasons, that is, periodically, and do not establish a stable residence where they go. Unlike migrants tourists move for the sake of moving. For them the subjective experiences of distance and cultural difference are not costs to be born for the benefit of a better income or security another society might offer. Like migration tourism affects the country of destination and may expose it to accelerated change, but it does so in a very special way. Tourism changes the 'receiving society' by making it adapt to the preferences of outsiders and temporary visitors. It turns local populations into providers of personal services and promotes the over-exploitation of scarce natural resources or the 'preservation' of local popular cultures for standardized mass consumption. Migration, however, changes societies by changing their membership. The most important impacts of immigration on societal development come from the immigrants' participation in the economy, in civil society, in cultural life and in politics.

Once these basic forms of territorial mobility have been distinguished we can take a closer look at the many kinds of migration and their specific impacts on societies. The national macro perspective has tended to split up all migration into two different, and indeed opposite, models. The model of permanent immigration assumes that migration is a one-way road from origin to destination and implies ultimate settlement and full integration into the receiving society. The other model is temporary migration which supposes that migrants come only for a limited purpose and a limited time and will ultimately return to their sending societies. The first model has been historically associated with the European transatlantic migration to North America. The second model underlies the European guestworker schemes as well as more recent policies of temporary protection for war refugees. It is also supported by many sending countries which emphasize their emigrants' ongoing membership in societies of origin.

While there are migration flows which fit either the one or the other type, the point is that more and more seem to fit neither or both at the same time. On the one hand, immigrants who settle in a destination country for good may still keep the citizenship of the sending society and travel there regularly so that the sending country rightly regards them as having retained strong ties to their origins (see Basch et al., 1994: 7). Temporary migrants, on the other hand, often find it difficult to return and to reintegrate. Some migrants become permanent residents in destination countries without being accepted as immigrants and without regarding themselves as such; others develop patterns of frequent movement between different countries in none of which they establish themselves permanently. The national perspectives of sending and receiving countries not only misinterpret these different experiences but often plainly ignore them. Until recently US-American historians wrote about the great transatlantic migration as if there had been no return movement back to Europe. From the perspective of building an American nation of immigrants these were simply lost populations who did not have a lasting impact. In my native country Austria politicians and media alike still use the label 'guestworkers' for immigrants who have arrived since the mid 1960s. Similarly, many countries of emigration, including Greece which is a member of the European Union, do not accept the voluntary expatriation of their emigrants and regard them as a temporary diaspora. Contemporary migration research should go beyond these narrow national views and conceive of migration as a genuinely transnational phenomenon, not only at the moment of border crossing but also with regard to the resulting social affiliations. International migration transnationalizes both sending and receiving societies by extending relevant forms of membership beyond the boundaries of territories and of citizenship.

One should carefully distinguish this phenomenon of societal transnationalization from the broader one of globalization in the realms of the economy, of transportation and information flows. The societal ties created by international migration are generally neither global nor deterritorialized. At the micro level they connect households located in different countries to each other, at the macro level they connect societies structured by territorial states. We may characterize movements of money, goods and information as increasingly globalized in the triple sense that (1) nearly all countries have become involved in these flows as senders and/or receivers; (2) national control policies have been normatively delegitimated and factually eroded or subverted; (3) territorial location has become increasingly unimportant for the production of many goods and services with general convertibility of currencies and growing external pressure on governments to stabilize exchange rates, with rapidly decreasing costs of transportation and with global information networks. There is also some globalization of such kind in the movement of people, although of a more limited kind. The movement of tourists, academic professionals, diplomats, or staff of international organizations and of transnational corporations is subjected to very little control of exit and entry and spans more and more the whole globe. However, while destinations have become globalized in these movements, origins have remained limited to a small number of wealthy countries or to small numbers of wealthy elites in a large number of states. The bulk of international migration follows very different patterns (1) because chain migrations develop along paths linking specific sending and receiving countries to each other; (2) because movement is subjected to a generalized regime of admission control which has become increasingly tighter rather than looser (with exemptions for privileged groups of migrants); (3) because place is of paramount importance in migration. The last point merits special emphasis. First, pull factors in economic migration are tied to specific places. Computer software can today be produced almost everywhere in the world. But economic activities in offshore production zones (Froebel/Heinrichs/Kreye, 1986; Cohen, 1987) or in global cities (Sassen, 1991), which attract an increasing number of today's labour migrants, are concentrated in certain locations. Second, migrants themselves are attracted to specific territorial locations not just because of economic opportunities but also because relatives, friends and members of their ethnic groups have settled there. Third, transnational households and migration networks involve the multiplication of territorial stakes and societal ties rather than their diminishing.

The transnationalization of societies through migration can be partly understood as a spillover effect of internal territorial mobility but is, paradoxically, to a large extent also a result of the process of nation-building itself. Without internal mobility the very notion of societies composed of the territorial populations of states would make little sense. In agrarian societies the borders of states were quite irrelevant for the boundaries of societies. The vast majority of the population was immobile both in the sense of territorial movement and in the sense of being unable to communicate in a standardized national idiom (Gellner, 1983). Political territory stretched as far as the military control of rulers went but was not experienced as a bounded social space. Only when entire populations are territorially mobilized by a market economy and culturally mobilized by compulsory public education can they come to conceive of nation-states as encompassing and representing distinct societies. This new mobility of the industrial era reshapes the micro structure of societies by breaking up the territorial and institutional unity of private households and workplaces and by pulling the former towards the locations of the latter. It transforms the macro structure by attributing a wholly new significance to the external geographic, political and cultural boundaries of states. Both these dynamics give impulses to migration which cannot be confined to internal mobility. When labour markets expand across national economies the movement of households towards employment opportunities does not stop at the borders. The other major source of international migration is the formation of nation-states. In the history of modernity attempts to make political and cultural borders congruent have probably forced just as many people to go abroad as the colonial expansion of empires and the industrialization of core economies. Transnationalization through migration does therefore not involve a dissolution of boundaries of distinct societies into a single global society but is, on the contrary, intimately linked to the same processes which shape these boundaries and attribute an immense social importance to them.

In agrarian economies the state system is characterized by rather well-defined and controlled borders of smaller units like cities or principalities, but diffuse and permeable frontiers of larger empires expanding around a stable core by the territorial acquisitions or annexations of peripheries and colonies. In this era migration as a social routine was an activity of specialized elites (such as traders or clergymen) or part of an educational programme in certain crafts and professions. The experience of moving borders was probably more common than that of moving populations. However, the movement of borders could not give rise to the illusion caused by the departure of the train on the neighbouring rail because state borders were not a highly relevant feature of the social background perceived by agrarian producers.

By contrast, frontiers become increasingly relevant in the age of industrialization and nationalism. I suggest to analyse this as a dual process of growing internal and external territorial rigidity. Internally, the emergence of a modern public administration with a professional bureaucracy creates a new hierarchical structure of territorial government. The abolition of local sovereignties, the uniform enforcement of law and a single status of national citizenship are preconditions for creating an open space where goods, money and people can move freely. This requires a unified structure of territorial administration which reaches down to the local level. In those states which have been formed from previously autonomous colonies, provinces and cities, federal constitutions and limited municipal self-government often integrate traditions of local autonomy into this single territorial hierarchy which is then not only structured by top-down flows of commands but also by bottom-up decisions that constrain the sovereign power of central authorities. However, both federal and centralized systems of government rely on a unified and hierarchical structure quite different from the diffuse, overlapping and perpetually contested internal territorial sovereignties characteristic for European feudalism. The development of democratic citizenship and its enrichment with social welfare rights[18] with its accompanying forms of localized social control by public administrations has further strengthened the importance and rigidity of the internal territorial structure of the modern nation-state. Enhanced mobility of populations thus goes along with, and depends on, a political homogenization of social spaces through territorial administration.

Increasing territorial rigidity is also a characteristic feature of the external environment of modern nation-states, that is, the international system of states. States and nations have become more and more entrenched in specific territories. Claims to territory must be well-defined. Dynastic or colonial legitimations of claims were typically expansive and imprecise. National claims are usually much more precise although they are not necessarily compatible with each other. Where they challenge existing borders they do so in the name of populations who are deprived of independent statehood or who involuntarily live as external minorities outside a national homeland. The nationalist dilemma is, of course, that in spite of these more limited and precise territorial claims no possible principle of allocating territories to states could satisfy them all. There are many more cultural groups which could strive for nationhood than there are territories which can be parcelled out into separate states (Gellner, 1983). Even with a gradual relaxing of 'viability conditions' of a minimum size of territories and populations and a corresponding increase in the number of states after World War II there is no possible solution in sight for states where ethnic and national groups live interspersed in the same territory. The Bosnian tragedy is the strongest possible illustration for the disastrous consequences of fighting out incompatible territorial claims between ethnic groups sharing a common territory.[19]

In order to achieve some minimum stability in the global state system the principle of national self-determination enshrined in international law had to be strictly limited in its application. After 1945 it became more or less confined to decolonization, a process for which the borders established by colonial administration were much more relevant than ethnic patterns of settlement among the colonized populations. In spite of the high number of wars the period since then has been one in which existing borders have been rarely successfully challenged. Not national self-determination but the inviolability of borders became the dominant norm in the international system of states and this principle continues to be strongly enforced against national groups like the Kurds whose claims to independence in their territories would affect the borders of four states. However, the entrenchment of existing borders in the international system does not prevent ongoing changes of the global political map. My hypothesis is that this entrenchment operates as an overriding norm which limits the opportunities for national self-determination. From this hypothesis we can derive an expected frequency distribution of various types of border changes, which by and large conforms to historical developments since 1945.[20]

The most important and durable changes result from the splitting up of colonial empires or multinational states into their components or from the secession of minority regions who form their own independent states. These are the most likely incidents both because at any given moment the number of potential nations is greater than the number of existing states and because separation is the least harmful violation of the norm that existing borders are sacrosanct. It multiplies frontiers rather than reducing or shifting them to a different location. When one state breaks up into several parts this does not affect the territorial integrity of other states.

Second in frequency is the unification of states which had formed a single political unit in the past and had maintained the idea of common nationhood during a period of separation. Unification is most likely to remain on the agenda where previously existing states with a common national tradition have been separated into ideologically opposed regimes (as in Germany, Viet Nam, Yemen and Korea). Unification is supported by the principle of national self-determination and it is not contradicted by the norm of externally protected territorial integrity if it is agreed between both regimes or if one of the regimes which opposes fusion is overthrown from inside. In the nineteenth century unification nationalism was a response to the *Kleinstaaterei* of German principalities and to the politics of *divide et impera* in the large multinational and colonial empires. Once the nation-state has become a dominant model there are simply very few candidates for voluntary unification. As long as their separation has not been externally imposed even those communities which had originally been imagined as belonging to a single nation will over time develop a sense of separate nationhood. The most important reason for this is that the ideological legitimation of state power as well as its daily activities inevitably foster such a distinct identity.

Relocations of existing borders will occur even more rarely, or be less stable in their outcomes, than separation or unification. One possibility how such territorial shifts of borders can happen is by simultaneous secession and fusion when a minority region which had been part of a multinational state joins a neighbouring one which is regarded as its national homeland. As this involves territorial gains of another state, consensual separation is quite unlikely and unilateral secession will be generally resisted. This is the only constellation where the principles of national self-determination and of territorial integrity directly clash with each other. If national self-determination is the overriding norm we should expect many such incidents. If these are in fact quite rare this shows that territorial integrity is in fact the overriding norm which constrains national self-determination.

Least frequent, or least stable, should be annexations of territories of other states without evidence of popular consent among the newly incorporated population which violates both principles. Whether or not in such cases the inviolability of borders is enforced by outside intervention with a mandate of the international community of states, as it was after the annexation of Kuwait by Iraq in 1990, certainly depends on other factors such as economic or strategic interests of great powers. However, the combination of the two norms seems to be pretty strong and to have had a tangible impact on the evolution of the global political map in the late twentieth century.

The hypothesis of increasing external territorial rigidity of states is thus not contradicted by those changes which have led to a multiplication of the number of states. The emergence of stronger forms of regional integration among highly industrialized states by the North Atlantic Free Trade Agreement (NAFTA) in North America or in the European Union might seem to be a counter-trend. However, we have to be clear what would count as evidence of 'deterritorialization' in these processes. A European Union which is functionally integrated rather than territorially is still quite difficult to imagine. One scenario suggests a flexible geography with different countries choosing different projects of integration from a menu. Economic-monetary integration would then become decoupled from security-foreign policy integration. A second scenario insists that these functions have to go together and suggests that the most likely development is a geographical core which is fully integrated and a periphery which participates in weaker forms of integration. The former scenario would come closer to the idea of deterritorialization at the supranational level but at the same time implies the maintenance of a much higher level of sovereignty for the member states. The latter scenario reduces the territorial sovereignty of the member states but involves strengthening the territorial rigidity of the European state system as a whole by reinforcing existing state borders both between the broader Union and non-member states and between the core and periphery within the Union itself. The Schengen Agreement is the most obvious test case. Initially it organized a core of five countries (Germany, France and the Benelux states) which were determined to go forward with abolishing internal borders. In the meantime all member states apart from Britain and Ireland have joined the Schengen club.[21] While the internal boundary between core and periphery was therefore a temporary and flexible one, this expansion was accompanied by a strong shift in emphasis from creating a zone of free movement towards a harmonization and reinforcement of external border controls. Through the very process of supranational integration territorial boundaries have thus gained a new significance and rigidity which they had not possessed before.

Contemporary social systems theory as developed by Niklas Luhmann distinguishes three basic modes of differentiation in social systems: segmented differentiation, hierarchical differentiation and functional differentiation. In this evolutionary view, the international state system appears to be stuck at the stage of territorial segmentation while the functionally differentiated market economy has become the leading system of modern society. Why politics is so resistant to functional differentiation beyond the state level is a puzzle which seems hard to resolve for systems theory. An alternative approach might start from the specific quality of the political as collective decision-making in a pluralistic world of distinct collectivities. Politics thus inevitably involves the creation and reinforcement of boundaries. In this view the territorial segmentation of political communities can be seen both as a counterweight and as a precondition for the weakening of segmented differentiation in other spheres of modern society.

3 Three Conceptions of Citizenship

When states become territorially more rigid while societies become mobile across state borders this obviously creates a tension. The tension manifests itself in the organization of membership at the level of states. The imperative of organizing populations into systems of membership becomes stronger in the transition to modernity. For states which are basically machineries of military control over a territory the very notion of membership of subjected populations does not make sense. In the premodern world only small republics and city-states could develop a collective sense and a legal system of membership resembling the contemporary conception of citizenship. In modernity the kind of social control exercised by states over their populations makes a mechanism for determining membership indispensable, independently of whether the regime is a democratic, authoritarian or totalitarian one. Formal membership is organized as the legal status of citizenship (sometimes also called nationality). Externally citizenship declares an individual to belong to a certain state and thus allocates populations to states as the basic units of the international political system. Internally citizenship is a status of basic equality declaring a person to be a full addressee of collectively binding decisions and a bearer of generalized rights and obligations. Each state develops a set of rules how citizenship can be obtained and lost by individuals and how it is transmitted across generations.

As I have argued elsewhere (Bauböck, 1994b), the legal status of citizenship can be allocated according to three different conceptions of the political community: a national, a republican and a societal one. In a national conception, the relevant community to be included in citizenship has a life of its own, independent from the state by which it is presently organized. This may be a community of language, of religion, of imagined common descent or of shared historical experiences. Citizenship ought to remain accessible for all those who can claim membership in such a national community regardless of where they live and whose state's citizens they are at present. Furthermore, the rules of transmission of citizenship across generations should ideally reflect the self-reproduction of membership in the national community for which, in most cases, a principle of descent (ius sanguinis) is the best approximation. By contrast, the republican conception of citizenship is self-referentially focused on the political community which takes priority over other affiliations such as ethnic, religious, or societal ties. It extols the virtues of patriotism and active participation in politics. Citizenship is thus seen as practice more than as a legal status. Self-referentiality makes it difficult to define the appropriate rules for the allocation of membership. In the ancient and early modern city states republican conceptions of citizenship have generally combined an ethnic with an elitist definition of political community. The elitist conception of recognizing only those as full citizens who are qualified, capable and willing to participate actively in politics is intimately tied to a hierarchical structure of society organized in estates and excluding slaves, women, labouring classes and foreigners from the polity. Today, neo-republicans often endorse some form of liberal nationalism which emphasizes that historical continuity and cultural homogeneity are necessary preconditions for participatory democracy (see for example Miller, 1995). A societal conception of citizenship is more inclusive. It refers to the population which is durably subjected to a state power and depends on this power for a guarantee of its fundamental rights. Because of the internal territorial organization of modern states, society so conceived is basically identical with the resident population of a state.

The three conceptions of citizenship have very different implications for how to resolve the tension between the territorial rigidity of the state system and the territorial mobility of societies. Nationalism always implies a claim to a territory where the community can rightfully exercise its political sovereignty. This territory need not be confined within existing state borders and nationalists may even raise historical claims to regions presently not inhabited by members of the nation. Finally, a national community may also stretch beyond the borders of its present or desired territory by including exile populations. In this way, a nationalist conception will introduce a strong distinction between different categories of non-citizens: on the one side those who can claim membership in the national community and enjoy a moral right to admission to the territory and the citizenship of their nation, and on the other side foreigners who can and should only be admitted on a temporary basis or for a limited purpose, but not for full membership. National conceptions of citizenship thus attribute a quasi-membership to those who are part of the wider community which can be transformed into legal status when the need arises. The same conception also allows to organize and instrumentalize exile communities for national purposes. Emigrants and groups of emigrant descent can relate to their homeland when they keep their original citizenship. Expatriation will be difficult or impossible and citizenship can be transmitted to generations born abroad when it is seen as merely a formal expression of membership in a community of descent. Exile groups can thus participate actively in the political decisions of their countries of origin, for example by absentee ballots. Even when they do renounce their former citizenship, emigrants and their offspring still remain members of their national community by birth or descent. In some cases their naturalization makes them even more valuable for the national cause as they may then try to influence the policy of their country of residence towards their state of origin. In a nationalist conception international migration thus creates communities which extend across borders of territory and of citizenship. Within such communities, political impact may go both ways: homeland governments try to control and instrumentalize their co-nationals living abroad, but emigrants may also attempt to change the policies, or even the regime of their countries of origin and may use the citizenship of their country of residence for that purpose (as for example many Cuban Americans do).

Republican conceptions of citizenship will be generally more open internally for naturalization. The will and capacity to contribute to the common good of the community can be documented through efforts of immigrants to assimilate. Republican conceptions allow thus for individual crossing of the boundary that separates citizens and foreign residents, but they are incompatible with a blurring of this boundary by extending more and more rights of citizenship to 'denizens', that is, permanently resident foreigners. Externally, republicans will be generally wary of transmitting citizenship to generations born abroad who have not been educated as citizens, have not participated in the public life of the polity and will not be affected by most of its political decisions. Republican patriotism may, however, be a strong motive in exile politics among refugees whose goal is to change the regime which forced them to go abroad.

A societal conception of citizenship will be the most open one within the territory. It will support both lower thresholds for crossing the boundary of citizenship and a blurring of the boundary itself. This model obviously favours transmission of citizenship by ius soli for native-born second or third generations. For first-generation immigrants acquiring citizenship depends on a period of residence more than on assimilation, although learning the dominant language should be certainly promoted and naturalization should still involve an act of will (documented by individual application) rather than being awarded automatically. At the same time, the boundary will become blurred by extending rights which had been a prerogative of formal citizenship to resident foreigners who have not yet naturalized or are unwilling to do so. The difference between denizens and citizens will thus be reduced to those core rights which might still distinguish the political community from the wider societal one (mainly active and passive voting rights at the national level). The societal conception allows also for quite extensive inclusion of citizens living abroad because it readily recognizes the ongoing relevance of their social ties to the countries where they have come from. However, respect for the basic right of voluntary exit prohibits regarding those who have renounced their citizenship by voluntary expatriation as still retaining a politically relevant form of membership. Finally, a societal conception is not only inclusive towards those who want to keep their citizenship abroad, but also respects the same kind of ties among immigrants who want to naturalize. Toleration for dual citizenship is a natural consequence. The tension between mobility across borders and the territorial structuration of societies at the level of states can thus be attenuated by an allocation of individual rights and citizenship status which acknowledges that societies linked by migration are not only interconnected but also increasingly overlapping in their membership. In this perspective migration expands the liberal polity through elements of external citizenship for emigrants living abroad and pluralizes it domestically by introducing denizenship rights and dual citizenship for immigrants.

In my view, the societal conception of citizenship must be the bedrock for a liberal answer to the challenge raised by international migration. The national and the republican versions should be rejected for two reasons. First, they rest on an unrealistic, or even mythical, description of societal boundaries in modernity which ignores the powerful forces of territorial structuration of societies by the state system. Secondly, by excluding from the political community and the rights of citizenship populations who are nonetheless subjected to political power of states these conceptions violate the basic liberal principle of equal concern and respect (Dworkin, 1977) for everybody who depends on a government for a guarantee of her or his rights.

Still, a liberal conception has to add something to the principle of societal inclusion. For example, a rule of voluntary application for naturalization rather than automatic attribution after some time of residence gives immigrants a choice between different legal statuses which leads to less formal equality and inclusion. This rule also acknowledges that the polity is not simply identical with the wider society but should indeed be conceived as a democratic community sharing in the collective decisions which apply to the society. On such grounds liberals may also justify excluding foreign residents from the franchise in national elections as long as they can easily acquire this additional right by naturalization.[22] Republican concerns can thus be taken into account without accepting the exclusionary implications of the republican approach.

4 Migrant Minorities and Cultural Boundaries

A more difficult question is whether and how a liberal conception could respond to nationalism in a similar way, that is, by acknowledging some of the nationalist concerns while developing an alternative response of its own. The concern worth considering is that liberal-republican conceptions of the relation between society and polity do not take into account that many people feel deeply attached to cultural communities which might not be identical with either of the two.

The traditional liberal response to this challenge is, of course, that governments should treat cultural differences like they have learned to treat religious ones, that is, in a neutral manner and by benign neglect. In this view, liberal states already guarantee the best possible conditions for the flourishing of cultural communities by protecting individual liberties and the freedom of association. Liberal democracies should neither promote or protect specific ways of life nor should they intervene into the internal affairs of cultural communities as long as these can be regarded as voluntary associations whose members are free to leave (Kukathas, 1992).

However, as Will Kymlicka (1989, 1995) and others have pointed out, such a response will not suffice if one acknowledges (1) that modern states are by their very nature not culturally neutral but organize the reproduction of dominant national cultures and (2) that cultural communities can be internally oppressive towards their members in a way which constrains abilities of individuals to fully enjoy the freedom and opportunities of democratic participation offered by liberal citizenship. These insights provide a justification for special rights of cultural minorities and simultaneously imply that in a liberal conception cultural group rights will have to be constrained by the requirement to secure basic individual rights of citizenship. Which kinds of rights and which kinds of constraints should be supported for which kind of cultural minorities is a matter of considerable controversy and the approach suggested by Kymlicka does not necessarily provide a specific answer to this.

My intuition is that at this point applied normative theory has to go beyond the assertion of foundational principles, such as liberty or equality, and beyond a purely deductive method of deriving more specific norms from them. No theory of cultural rights can do without a plausible account of how the modern state and economy structure cultural affiliations and produce cultural boundaries between groups. Liberal theorists too often seem to regard cultural difference either as an almost naturally given fact or as a freely chosen element of a person's conception of the good. Against the latter view I want to argue that the most important affiliations which identify citizens as members of intergenerational cultural groups are normally not chosen but ascribed. However, this process of ascription is not due to a natural self-reproduction of cultural communities independently of their specific societal environment. On the one hand, the allocation of material resources and political powers to groups in the economic and political systems is essential for their prospects to pass on their membership. On the other hand, cultural difference can in itself become a resource for socially disadvantaged and politically powerless minorities in their attempts to improve their lot. Liberal theorists should thus regard the claims of minority cultures not merely as an expression of a naturally acquired or freely chosen distinct way of life, but must also consider how these claims arise from social relations of dominance and disadvantage, of oppression and resistance. This does not imply that all such differences would vanish or become politically irrelevant in a more egalitarian society, but their social and political significance would certainly not be the same.

Instead of speculating about the significance of minority cultures in a society where cultural differences are less marked by social and political inequality we may also contrast 'symbolic ethnicity' (Gans, 1979) among groups which have become part of national majorities (such as Catholic or Jewish groups of European origin in the USA) with the kinds of claims raised by national minorities (like the Québécois, the Basks or Catalans), by indigenous minorities (like America's First Nations or Australia's Aborigines), by native 'racial' minorities (like African Americans), or by minorities of immigrant origin who are defined as fundamentally different from a national majority in terms of language, religion or 'race'. The claims of these minorities to specific rights cannot be answered by pointing out that if only liberal societies would be more liberal each of these differences could be freely articulated in civil society and none of these differences would matter much politically.

What such 'ideal theory' overlooks is that liberal societies do have a historical dimension which explains why internal and external boundaries do not simply vanish when these societies become more liberal. Liberal pluralism views the organization of the world into separate states and the internal devolution of political power within states to provincial and municipal levels as something which is in itself preferable to uniformity and the absence of political boundaries. However, the question where exactly state borders should run or which groups within a state can claim territorial autonomy cannot be decided by principles applying to ideal worlds. Answers emerge only from carefully considering the particular histories of particular polities. Once equal citizenship has been established and explicit legal discrimination of minority members because of their language, religion, 'race', or ethnic origins has been abandoned groups defined by past exclusion and oppression may already have learned to think of themselves as distinct political communities. This does not give them a *carte blanche* to redraw territorial borders by secession. But it may well support a view of the political community as composed of equal citizens and of distinct sub-communities which enjoy some autonomy and special representation. Once such rights have been granted they establish internal political boundaries whose justification no longer depends on proving that past discrimination still has not been fully redressed or has ongoing impacts. If the sub-communities fully guarantee their members' rights as citizens and if their internal procedures of decision-making fully comply with democracy and the rule of law these internal boundaries become self-justifying over time in the very same manner as the external borders of liberal democratic states. What requires then special justification is not their persistence but attempts to abolish them by abandoning special minority rights. We may call such liberal states plural polities composed of several constitutive groups.[23]

Obviously, not all minority rights are of this kind. Some, like affirmative action against racist discrimination, are meant to be temporary and would be difficult to justify when there is no longer any evidence of negative impacts of group membership on economic and educational opportunities. Also, racism is different from discrimination referring to cultural markers like language, religion or ethnic origins because it establishes an inherently vicious distinction. Yet groups which have been racially discriminated may still redefine and transform themselves into ethnic communities sharing a common past and a specific cultural heritage and may thus qualify for more or less permanent recognition as constitutive minorities.

Immigration presents a different set of problems for liberal pluralism. Immigrant minorities normally do not form constitutive minorities which require a reconceptualization of the political community as a plural one. Indigenous, racially oppressed and regional linguistic minorities pose the challenge whether existing cultural boundaries within a society should be translated into political ones; immigration challenges the existing structure of cultural boundaries by adding new groups, by processes of boundary crossing through assimilation and by boundary blurring through intermingling of populations and cultural hybridization. Migration pluralizes polities by transnationalizing their citizenship and it pluralizes societies by making them multicultural. In contrast with the segmented pluriculturalism of pre-modern and pre-liberal societies, such as the Ottoman millet system, liberal multiculturalism in societies of immigration has to keep cultural boundaries open for changing affiliations. In the rest of this chapter I will try to sketch how such an approach to cultural difference may fit together with the combination of macro, micro, and meso perspectives in migration research defended in the first section and with the liberal approach to citizenship and migration expounded above.

The cultural options most immigrants and refugees face when they settle in Western liberal democracies illustrate the inadequacy of the models of naturally given and of freely chosen cultural membership. The small group of privileged migrants mentioned above for whom global free movement has become already a reality may come close to the type of cultural choosers who integrate various elements of the cultures they encounter into their own particular cosmopolitan way of life. As Jeremy Waldron (1995) has pointed out the mere existence of such groups and the apparent satisfaction they receive from their cultural detachment disproves cultural primordialists who maintain that such a way of life is psychologically impossible or that it is undesirable.[24] However, as long as such ways of life depend on privileges which cannot be universalized liberals should focus on the cultural needs of those to whom such options are denied.

I want to suggest that meeting these needs requires fairly open boundaries of dominant national cultures in societies of immigration. This general requirement of openness cannot be applied to every kind of cultural community. Clearly, the specific degree of openness of religious or ethnic communities may legitimately vary with their particular beliefs and needs. The only universal norm for boundary crossing which liberals can defend with regard to any kind of cultural community is a right of exit, but certainly not a general right of access for outsiders. Yet more specific norms ought to apply to dominant national cultures and these include liberal principles for new admissions. The reason for this is that national cultures penetrate the public spheres of civil society and are maintained and reproduced through the working of the institutions of a liberal democratic state. This maintenance is different from mere external support which may also be granted to minority cultures. Public education, a democratic system of elections, a public administration which provides general services for the citizens, all these institutions inevitably create and reproduce dominant national cultures as a 'public good' for majority populations (see Kymlicka, 1989: Chapter 9). This monopolistic (or, in multinational states, oligopolistic) position of national cultures makes exclusion from them particularly harmful (just like exclusion from access to a life-saving medicine by a monopolistic producer would be). Norms which apply to national cultures directly sustained by a state are therefore different and more stringent than norms applying to cultural groups which are organized as associations in civil society and which compete for state support.

A second reason for special norms is that a political conception of liberalism is specifically concerned with justice of the basic political institutions in a society. According to Rawls (1993) such a conception ought to spell out the fair terms of cooperation in a society where people hold different and even incompatible conceptions of the good (including affiliations to particular cultural communities). Now if it is true that liberal democratic states cannot be culturally neutral because the working of their core institutions inevitably reproduces specific dominant cultures, then it follows that such national cultures cannot be allowed to undermine equal respect and concern for all citizens and the fair terms of cooperation in society. In a society where there is permanent immigration the rules of access to citizenship will be constrained by liberal norms so that they differ from membership in a club whose members can freely choose whom to admit. Much the same consideration supports analogous constraints on the closure of dominant national cultures.

In order to specify a general norm of fairly open boundaries of national cultures[25] I will have to introduce some further conceptual distinctions. The first one is between cultural beliefs or practices[26] and cultural membership. A person may believe in a religious dogma or speak a language without being a member of a cultural community which regards this language or dogma as its defining criterion. Only actual recognition by other members makes a person a member of a cultural community. The second distinction is between required practices which are regarded as minimum criteria for obtaining or retaining membership, supported practices which constitute the full range of a cultural tradition, and permissible practices which may deviate strongly from the tradition without being regarded as incompatible with membership. Further distinctions emerge from considering boundary crossings with regard to cultural practices and with regard to membership. We may use the term acculturation for a process by which an individual comes to acquire cultural practices belonging to the tradition of another group. Assimilation would then indicate a change of membership which makes an individual similar to a receiving community in the sense that its members recognize her as one of their kind. Finally, acculturation and assimilation may be subtractive or additive,[27] that is, earlier practices and memberships may be either abandoned or retained when new ones are acquired.

Let me now state a possibly not exhaustive list of liberal norms for the cultural integration of immigrants:

(1) *Required acculturation:* Acculturation required for recognition of full assimilation should only refer to those practices which are necessary for enabling newcomers to fully exercise their basic liberties, to participate in the democratic process and to use the general economic opportunities in this society. Acculturation may be required because the capacity to participate in a culture which dominates the public sphere is needed for full citizenship in a liberal nation-state. But acculturation requirements should therefore also be limited to those aspects of the culture which are essential for exercising one's rights of citizenship. The most important aspect is communication skills in a dominant language.

(2) *Disconnecting acculturation from formal citizenship:* Acculturation which is necessary for a full exercise of one's citizenship rights should be promoted among all permanent resident members of society but should not be turned into a demanding test for naturalization. The basic requirement for naturalization is not acculturation but societal membership acquired through continuous residence. Furthermore, a liberal state must be interested that all permanent members of society (and not just those willing to naturalize) have plenty of opportunities to acquire basic skills in the dominant national culture. Acculturation may thus be encouraged among the whole resident population but it is required only for those who want to be seen as full members of a national culture.

(3) *Impermissible practices:* Once required acculturation has been achieved only those practices should be regarded as incompatible with cultural membership which conflict directly with human rights or obligations of citizenship. Practices which are merely seen to undermine a certain national tradition should not be regarded as impermissible, that is, as incompatible with achieving or enjoying full recognition as a member of a national cultural community. Liberal states may legitimately support practices which continue a broad cultural tradition but they may not declare other practices to be impermissible merely because they fall outside this range.

(4) *Non-exclusive assimilation:* Nobody should be seen as being incapable of assimilating into a national culture because of her ethnic or 'racial' origins, her gender or other innate features, or because of her present affiliation to a particular cultural, linguistic or religious group. Denying the capability of members of such groups to assimilate into a national culture 'naturalizes' cultural differences and defines them implicitly in racial terms. A liberal con-

ception of citizenship maintains that no human group is a priori disqualified from citizenship because of its innate characteristics or because of its cultural affiliations. A national culture which penetrates the public sphere where people act as citizens may not define its own boundaries of membership in terms incompatible with the liberal conception of citizenship.

(5) *Acculturation as a sufficient condition for assimilation:* The kind of acculturation which may be required as a necessary condition for assimilation should at the same time be regarded as a sufficient condition as far as the receiving community is concerned. It should be up to the person who has acculturated whether she wants to see herself, and be recognized by others, as a new member of a national majority. If she wishes to assimilate and has shown her capacity to do so by acculturation, she should be accepted. Although, according to the distinction I have suggested, assimilation is different from acculturation in that the former requires some 'ratification' by the group, a national culture should tie its own hands by granting that ratification more or less automatically. This rules out a double bind which has been a nightmare for many minorities who were first told that they could not become full citizens unless they took an effort to shed their traditional culture and adopt the majoritarian one and then found that once they had transformed themselves as thoroughly as they could they were still not accepted but defined as unalterably different. The most notorious case is the assimilation of Western European Jews and the subsequent racialization of a boundary that had been previously defined in religious and cultural terms.

(6) *Voluntary assimilation:* Assimilation into a national culture should be regarded as a strictly voluntary decision, not only in the sense that it depends on an 'applicant's' choice whether or not to join a dominant national culture, but also in the sense that this decision cannot be required in the same way as some minimum acculturation can be. Individuals who do not want to see themselves as members of a national culture, although they have the necessary cultural skills to participate in it, should not be pressed or even encouraged to change their mind. This presupposes that non-assimilation does not entail a severe disadvantage, such as a diminished status of citizenship. What a liberal state cannot and should not guarantee for each group of newcomers is that their members will be able to resist assimilation. They may succeed in this resistance if there is a sufficiently large and supportive ethnic minority which wants to remain distinct from the national majority. Where such ethnic minority communities form out of their members' choices not to assimilate, they have a basic claim to public recognition. However, just as a liberal state should not impose or even encourage assimilation it should also refrain from imposing

multiculturalism from above by creating ethnic categories of immigrants defined by their origins or descent, and by distributing benefits and resources to them according to such assigned membership.

(7) *Additive acculturation and assimilation:* The norms proposed so far already imply that acculturation will generally be additive rather than subtractive. Individuals who do not want to leave their community of membership will be able to acculturate into a dominant national culture and those who assimilate will be able to retain previous cultural practices because these will not be defined as impermissible unless they conflict with human rights and obligations of citizenship. Going a step further we can also defend the possibility of additive assimilation, that is, of retaining a previous cultural membership while acquiring a new one. Most individuals may not want to find themselves in an ambiguous position of plural affiliation and identification, but for those living in mixed marriages or for children of mixed parentage this may be an obvious choice. Just as liberal pluralism should recognize the overlapping forms of societal membership which emerge from migration, so it should also acknowledge that multiple cultural membership is not necessarily only a short transitory stage but can be a way of life which is fully adequate for the cultural needs of certain groups and as valuable as a single affiliation.

Let me consider two relevant objections against this approach. A first objection might be that I have overstated the analogy with access to citizenship. Citizenship is a formal status and admission to membership is regulated in an explicit procedure. Even when we use a wider concept of transnational citizenship which covers multiple membership and the rights of foreign residents we can still determine easily for each single right whether a group of denizens is included in the system of citizenship or not. By contrast, cultural membership is mostly informal and implicit. Observers and participants may reasonably disagree about whether a certain person is or is not a member of a particular cultural group. Moreover, cultural membership is not directly ratified by the state nor by any other particular agent in society, but the requirements of open boundaries are clearly addressed to an agent who must have the power to change the rules of admission.

While I concede that these are relevant differences between the boundaries of polities and of cultures, I still think that in the age of modern nationalism it is useful and indeed necessary to conceive of the liberal nation-state as a cultural agent which shapes the boundaries between national cultures, on the one side, and minority or foreign cultures, on the other side. The reproduction of dominant national cultures through state legislation, institutions and policies implicitly defines other cultural groups as minorities or as foreign. Furthermore, such boundary definitions are also made explicit in political discourse in parliaments or in public speech. Certainly, such discourses are not only shaped by state institutions and political actors, but also by powerful agencies in civil society, foremost among which are the modern mass media. However, the role attributed to the media in this respect may sometimes be exaggerated – for example when Luhmann says that the mass media specialize in the task of self-description of modern societies (Luhmann, 1995: 38). I would like to suggest that self-description of society by the media cannot itself generate a description of the boundaries of societies, polities and national cultural communities. This remains fundamentally a political task. We may therefore attribute a primary responsibility for changing and opening cultural boundaries to the individual and collective agents operating within the political system.

A second relevant objection is that it may be misleading to use the term culture in such a broad way which covers language, religion and ethnicity. The inevitable involvement of modern state institutions in cultural reproduction primarily refers to language, not to religion. While a liberal state can therefore be fairly neutral with regard to religion, it cannot possibly be similarly neutral with regard to the languages used in public education or administration. Most of the norms which I have suggested (with the significant exception of impermissible practices) seem also to apply only to language. Does not required acculturation of immigrants boil down to learning the dominant idiom of the society where they settle? Is it not obvious that additive acculturation is only possible with regard to languages but not for religions? Furthermore, if the cultural boundaries at stake are those of language rather than religion we could eventually reassert that states can be culturally neutral in the sense relevant for liberalism. Religion inherently involves a particular conception of the good, but language can be seen as a medium for articulating any conception of the good. Many religions allow their followers to pray in their everyday language. And those which require that communication with God must be in a holy language do not force their adherents to speak only that language in their everyday lives. So a liberal state might after all remain perfectly neutral between different religions and conceptions of the good even when it promotes a particular national language.

This is, again, a relevant objection which cannot be easily dismissed. It is certainly true that the standardization and spread of national languages has been the most important way in which modern states have shaped cultural boundaries. However, two arguments can be advanced to defend my broader use of the term cultural boundaries. First, it may be impossible, or very difficult, for liberal states to be entirely neutral towards other aspects of cultures beyond language; second, the difference between language and religion may be historically contingent and relative rather than inherent and absolute, and national languages may not be a neutral medium for some important conceptions of the good.

Liberal states differ in the ways how they relate to religion. The French republic has strongly emphasized secularism and has tried to use its institutions in order to inculcate a sense of common belonging to the political community which may be seen as almost hostile rather than neutral towards manifestations of religious community in the public sphere. In the U.S. the tradition, whose primary interpreter was Alexis de Tocqueville, is one of state neutrality which at the same time relies on a vigorous religious pluralism in civil society. In many continental European democracies, the larger religious congregations enjoy certain privileges granted by the state such as religious instruction in public schools or state involvement in the collection of church taxes. In some Western European countries like Britain or Sweden there is still an established church officially linked to the state. All of these traditions of course subscribe to the principle of religious toleration but not all of them can be called neutral. While each of these traditions may be reasonably criticized, I do not think that any among them can be a priori ruled out as incompatible with liberal principles. Prudential arguments may justify certain arrangements which prima facie seem to violate liberal neutrality. For our discussion the more important point is that even those states which have officially embraced secularism and neutrality may still be rightly criticized by members of minority religions for being discriminatory. The allocation of religious holidays, regulations for working and closing hours, dress codes in public institutions, etc. may conflict with rituals of minority religions and may reveal how strongly the public sphere of liberal societies has in fact been shaped by a Christian tradition.

Moreover, modern states are also non-neutral with regard to elements of culture beyond language and religion such as the construction of historical continuities and identities. A polity is always conceived as a transgenerational community and this makes it imperative to interpret its history. The public culture shaped by states promotes certain interpretations of history which always exclude some groups (and especially recent immigrants) who have not shared this history. Liberals should respond to this dilemma by striving for more open and inclusive interpretations of national histories rather than for a 'presentist' conception of the polity which neutralizes its history (see Bauböck, 1998).

The contrast between religious and language boundaries and their relation to state power may be a historically contingent matter. Before the rise of Christianity and Islam, religions were not only mostly polytheistic, but also syncretistic and civic. In the ancient societies of Greece or Rome, religion was a marker of ethnic identity more than a profound expression of a person's deepest conceptions of the good. State religions were meant to provide legitimation for the system of political rule, but at the same time were seen as perfectly compatible with asserting other creeds alongside. Even modern political theorists have sometimes defended the idea of a civic religion as a necessary underpinning for patriotic loyalty and a sense of civic duties.[28]

Liberalism has emerged from religious rather than linguistic conflict and this explains why emphasis has been so heavily on religious neutrality while liberal thinkers have hardly ever considered requirements of cultural neutrality with regard to languages. However, the experience of violent national conflicts focusing on language communities should have taught the lesson that this may be a fatal neglect. In modernity language is not just a neutral medium which can be used to express any idea or conception of the good; it is also a marker of ethnic and national identity and thus serves to define the boundaries of groups which may raise claims to political autonomy. Endemic conflict in modern society does not only emerge from social inequalities and from the clash of political and religious doctrines, it also erupts over competing claims for autonomy and the definition of political boundaries marked by language. The openness of internal cultural boundaries with regard to language is therefore not something which is already inherent in the general human capacity to speak several languages, but has to be continuously reasserted against the tendency of nationalism to separate populations into mutually exclusive monolingual communities.

How would the norms of relatively open cultural boundaries correspond to cultural needs of immigrants and how would they affect receiving cultures? Immigrants will generally need acculturation more than those minorities concentrated in their historical homelands where they can create their own public spaces. For these minorities their particular culture may be a fully adequate medium for realizing equal citizenship in the larger political community. For immigrants access to the dominant culture is a more vital need in order to achieve a similar status of full citizenship. Many immigrants find themselves also exposed to conflicting social pressures with regard to acculturation and assimilation. The receiving society may either expect them to assimilate as quickly as possible, or may want to keep them apart from the native population as guestworkers or refugees who are meant to return to their origins. Sending states which regard their emigrants abroad as a temporary exile community will expect them to retain their culture of origin and will be wary of their acculturation attempts. Immigrant communities in the receiving country may, on the one hand, support the acculturation of their members to the dominant culture while at the same time opposing their assimilation in order to establish the community as a distinct ethnic minority which can claim support from the state. Immigrants themselves have to negotiate their cultural orientation within a family framework where there are often strong norms with regard to religious practices, the use of languages at home or intermarriage. Immigrants thus do not choose their cultural affiliation freely from a menu of available options but frequently experience their changing cultural practices and memberships as something that is imposed on them. For liberals, however, this very exposure to conflicting pressures provides the strongest argument for widening the range of choices by making the boundaries of national cultures more permeable for immigrants. The possibility to choose should therefore be seen not as a luxury like the abundance of various brands of cereal in a supermarket, but as a condition for regaining autonomy within a tight network of political and social dependencies. This normative argument relies on a descriptive analysis outlined in section 1 which combines expectations of cultural change that emerge from macro, meso and micro perspectives.

The relation between immigrant minorities and dominant national cultures in receiving societies which results from applying the norms of openness is characterized by a double asymmetry. On the one hand, immigrants clearly have to adapt more to the existing culture which is hegemonic in the public sphere than vice versa. While they can be expected, and should be encouraged, to take efforts to learn the national language(s) of the receiving country, the native population of that country cannot be expected to learn the immigrants' languages. Acculturation is thus not symmetric. On the other hand, the terms of admission implied in voluntary assimilation and additive acculturation do impose unilateral constraints on how a dominant national culture should conceive of its own tradition and practices. Ethnic minorities may legitimately fight for maintaining certain cultural traditions against the eroding effects of market economies and of a common democratic system. They can claim collective rights which enable them to keep cultural boundaries relatively closed and traditions relatively stable, as long as this is what their members want.[29] National cultures, however, which penetrate the public sphere and use the common institutions of the state to pass on their cultural traditions and practices, expose themselves to stronger normative constraints on how exclusive they may be. Rather than defending an illusory norm of neutrality or equality of resources for all cultures, liberal pluralists should welcome this trade-off between legitimate hegemony and legitimate exclusion. National cultures in liberal societies of immigration will thus have to transform themselves to become more open for the cultural traditions added by immigrants who would like to become full members of this culture. Furthermore, these national cultures will also have to accept that ongoing immigration from various origins pluralizes societies by creating new cultural communities which in some cases may form distinct and relatively stable ethnic minorities. Even where such minorities are only transitory phenomena and vanish because third or fourth generations want to fully assimilate, the overall structure of internal cultural boundaries may well be reproduced by successive inflows of new groups of migrants. In such a structure cultural boundaries are open for individual crossing, are constantly blurred because of their inclusive tendency, but nevertheless remain a permanent feature of a pluralistic society.

5 Conclusions

Migration research has long developed on two different tracks which hardly ever meet. One group is mainly concerned with the aggregate effects of migration on sending and receiving societies and with structural causes of migratory movements that might be influenced by policies of these states. The other group wants to understand migration from the migrants' point of view and studies their motives, decisions, and social networks. From the former perspective migration is registered against the background of stable borders and states. From the latter perspective this institutional reality almost vanishes from sight while a new social world of transnational and deterritorialized communities emerges. I have argued in this paper that both views are inadequate: the former because state borders themselves may change and states are often not the relevant unit for understanding migratory phenomena; the latter because it fails to grasp the impact of states on migration flows through their control policies and it does not help us to understand why the political irritation through migration and the efforts to control it have become one of the mega problems of the late twentieth century.

In this chapter I have, first, suggested that a comprehensive theory of international migration would have to relate the spatial structure of nation-states and the time perspectives of migrants' biographies and communities to each other. I have, second, defended the view that the political cause for the 'global migration problem' is that the modern state organizes societies as territorial units of population whereas international migration transcends these boundaries and expands societies beyond the polity. Finally, I have tried to link two normative proposals to these descriptive and analytical perspectives. Liberal democracies ought to respond to the transnationalization of societies through immigration by opening admission to their citizenship and to their dominant national cultures, while at the same time acknowledging that such access need not come at the expense of the migrants' previous political and cultural affiliations and that such integration will profoundly change perceptions of their own collective identities.

Notes

[1] Citizenship as a legal form of membership in a polity is an aspect long neglected by political theory (where the republican tradition has emphasized active citizenship as a practice stimulated by civic virtues) and by political and historical sociology (where T.H. Marshall's seminal essay of 1949 [Marshall, 1965] has established a view of citizenship as a bundle of universal rights). In legal theory the analysis of citizenship as state membership was always present but probably

never a mainstream concern. Two influential books by Bruce Ackerman (1980) and Michael Walzer (1983) reintroduced a notion of citizenship as membership into normative political theory. In comparative and historical political science the most important contribution was made by Rogers Brubaker who explicitly analyses citizenship as an allocation of persons to states (Brubaker, 1992: esp. 21-34).

2 The questions whether liberal states should also open their territories for immigration and to which groups of migrants they ought to open them is a more difficult issue which I will not address in this paper. For my tentative answers see Bauböck (1994a: 321-332 and 1997).

3 Comparative overviews over current theories of migration are provided by Massey et al. (1993) and Hammar et al. (1997).

4 The obvious case of minor children who come along with their parents can be taken into account by shifting the focus from the individual to the family as the relevant unit for migratory decisions.

5 A policy which has recently been constrained by setting yearly quota, reducing monetary and welfare incentives and by restricting the immigrants' free choice of initial settlement.

6 In this chapter I will be mostly, though not exclusively, concerned with spatial boundaries and boundaries of membership which are imagined as quasi-spatial limits of communities. I have tried to deal with time dimensions of migration in another paper (Bauböck, 1998). The most interesting descriptive tools for analysing human mobility in space and time have been provided by Torsten Hägerstrand's time geography (1975). For recent applications to problems of international migration see Charles Westin's chapter in this book and Malmberg (1997).
In his chapter in this book Charles Westin has combined both spatial and temporal aspects of migration.

7 I discuss these various possibilities at greater length in section 2 below.

8 see Dummett/Nicol (1990).

9 The reallocation of populations to the newly formed states was based on their home municipality which was normally determined by the place of birth. During a limited period of time individuals could opt for a different nationality than the one assigned to them by this rule if they were different in language and 'race' from the majority of that country and similar to the majority of the country for which they opted. The criterion of 'race' was used by the Austrian authorities to deny citizenship to Jewish immigrants.

10 The *Inländerarbeiterschutzgesetz* (law for the protection of native workers) of 1925.

11 For an example how cohort data can be used to analyse naturalization propensity see Hammar (1990: 92-96).

12 See Bjerén (1997: 232-238) for the relevance of distinguishing between households and families in migration research.

13 Stark (1991) see also Massey et al. (1993)

14 See Pessar (1996).

15 Arjun Appadurai (1996: 33) has described this process as the emergence of global 'ethnoscapes' through transnational migration.

16 See for example Guéhenno (1994: 72).
17 The Australian Aborigines' songlines are the best-known example of the spiritualization of territory in nomadic societies. For a literary and speculative account see Chatwin (1988).
18 See Marshall (1965), Parsons (1971), Dahrendorf (1974, 1992), Roche (1992).
19 The specific complication in the Bosnian tragedy is that no territorial division could possibly do justice to the claims of Bosnian Muslims which could only have been satisfied by maintaining a single state organized as a multinational federation on a non-territorial basis.
20 I have not managed to count and categorize all incidents of border changes since 1945. Somebody must have done this already.
21 In order to maintain free movement within the Nordic Passport Union, even Norway, which has refused to join the EU, had to enter the Schengen agreement.
22 For a more detailed argument see Bauböck (1994b and 1998).
23 I use this term here in a meaning which differs from that of 'constitutive communities' as suggested by Daniel Bell (1993). While Bell and other communitarian writers think of communities which are constitutive for an individual's identity, I refer to those which are constitutive parts of a political community.
24 One may, however, challenge some aspects of the empirical description underlying the image of a cosmopolitan lifestyle. Quite often such privileged migrants live in segregated neighbourhoods and narrow cultural enclaves. Cosmopolitan lifestyles with regard to cultural consumption (of food, music, high culture) may go together with self-isolation from participation in the polity and culture of one's society of residence.
25 I borrow this term from Veit Bader. See Bader 1997 and his chapter in this book.
26 I will not discuss the distinction between beliefs and practices here and will use the term practices as a generic one encompassing beliefs.
27 The term is borrowed and generalized from the linguistic distinction between subtractive and additive bilingualism (Lambert, 1983; Bodi, 1996: 271).
28 Most famously Jean-Jacques Rousseau in his *Contrat Social*.
29 The strongest claims of this sort can be raised by indigenous minorities.

References

Ackerman, Bruce (1980) *Social Justice in the Liberal State*. New Haven: Yale University Press.
Appadurai, Arjun (1996) *Modernity at Large. Cultural Dimensions of Globalization*. Minneapolis: University of Minnesota Press.
Bader, Veit (1997) 'Fairly Open Borders', pp. 28-61 in Bader, V. (ed.), *Citizenship and Exclusion*. London: Macmillan.
Basch, Linda/Glick Schiller, Nina/Szanton Blanc, Cristina (1994) *Nations Unbound. Transnational Projects, Postcolonial Predicaments and Deterritorialized Nation-States*. Amsterdam: Gordon and Breach Publishers.

Bauböck, Rainer (1994a) *Transnational Citizenship. Membership and Rights in International Migration*. Aldershot: Edward Elgar.

Bauböck, Rainer (1994b) 'Changing the Boundaries of Citizenship', in Bauböck, R. (ed.), *From Aliens to Citizens. Redefining the Status of Immigrants in Europe*. Aldershot: Avebury.

Bauböck, Rainer (1997) 'Notwendige Öffnung und legitime Schließung liberaler Demokratien', *Archives Européennes de Sociologie* No. 1.

Bauböck, Rainer (1998) 'Sharing History and Future? Time Horizons of Liberal Democracy in an Age of Migration', *Constellations* 4 (3).

Bell, Daniel (1993) *Communitarianism and its Critics*. Oxford University Press.

Bjerén, Gunilla (1997) 'Gender and Reproduction', pp. 219-246 in Hammar, Tomas et al. (eds.), op.cit.

Bodi, Marianne (1996) 'Models of Multicultural Education. The Dynamics of Pluralistic Integration and Social Accommodation', pp. 259-278 in Bauböck, R./Heller, A./Zolberg, A. (eds.), *The Challenge of Diversity. Integration and Pluralism in Societies of Immigration*. Aldershot: Avebury.

Brubaker, Rogers W. (1992) *Citizenship and Nationhood in France and Germany*. Cambridge, Ma.: Harvard University Press.

Chatwin, Bruce (1988) *The Songlines*. London: Penguin Books.

Cohen, Robin (1987) *The New Helots. Migrants in the International Division of Labour*. Aldershot: Avebury.

Dahrendorf, Ralf (1974) 'Citizenship and Beyond: The Social Dynamics of an Idea', *Social Research* 41: 673-701.

Dahrendorf, Ralf (1992) *Der moderne soziale Konflikt: Essay zur Politik der Freiheit*. Stuttgart: DVA.

Dworkin, Ronald (1977) *Taking Rights Seriously*. Cambridge, Ma.: Harvard University Press.

Dummett, Ann/Nicol, Andrew (1990) *Subjects, Citizens, Aliens and Others. Nationality and Immigration Law*. London: Weidenfeld & Nicolson.

Faist, Thomas (1997) 'The Crucial Meso-Level', pp. 187-217 in Hammar, Tomas et al. (eds.), op.cit.

Froebel/Heinrichs/Kreye (1986) *Umbruch in der Weltwirtschaft. Die globale Strategie: Verbilligung der Arbeitskraft/Flexibilisierung der Arbeit/Neue Technologien*. Hamburg: Rowohlt.

Gans, Herbert (1979) 'Symbolic Ethnicity: The Future of Ethnic Groups and Cultures in America', *Ethnic and Racial Studies* 2 (January): 1-20.

Gellner (1990) *Plough, Sword and Book. The Structure of Human History*. University of Chicago Press.

Gellner, Ernest (1983) *Nations and Nationalism*. Oxford: Blackwell.

Guéhenno, Jean-Marie (1994) *Das Ende der Demokratie*. München und Zürich: Artemis & Winkler.

Hägerstrand, Torsten (1975) 'Space, Time and Human Conditions', in Karlqvist, A. (ed.), *Dynamic Allocation of Urban Space*. Farnborough.

Hammar, Tomas (1990) *Democracy and the Nation-State. Aliens, Denizens and Citizens in a World of International Migration*. Aldershot: Avebury.

Hammar, Tomas/Brochmann, Grete/Tamas, Kristof/Faist, Thomas (eds.) (1997) *International Migration, Immobility and Development. Multidisciplinary Perspectives*. Oxford: Berg.

Kymlicka, Will (1989) *Liberalism, Community, and Culture*. Oxford University Press.
Kymlicka, Will (1995) *Multicultural Citizenship. A Liberal Theory of Minority Rights*. Oxford: Clarendon Press.
Kukathas, Chandran (1992) 'Are There Any Cultural Rights?', *Political Theory* 20: 105-139.
Lambert, Wallace E. (1983) 'Deciding on Languages of Instruction: Psychological and Social Considerations', in: Husen, T./Opper, S. (eds.), *Multicultural and Multilingual Education in Immigrant Countries*. London: Pergamon Press.
Luhmann, Niklas (1995) 'The Two Sociologies and the Theory of Society', *Thesis 11*, No. 43: 28-47.
Malmberg, Gunnar (1997) 'Time and Space in International Migration', pp. 21-48 in Hammar, Tomas et al. (ed.), op. cit.
Marshall, T.H. (1965) 'Citizenship and Social Class', in Marshall, T.H., *Class, Citizenship, and Social Development. Essays by T.H. Marshall*. New York: Anchor Books.
Massey, Douglas/Arango, Joaquín/Hugo, Graeme/Kouaouci, Ali/Pellegrino, Adela/Taylor, Edward (1993) 'Theories of International Migration: A Review and Appraisal', *Population and Development Review* 19 (3): 431-466.
Miller, David (1995) *On Nationality*. Oxford University Press.
Parsons, Talcott (1971) *The System of Modern Societies*. London: Prentice-Hall.
Pessar, Patricia (1996) "The Role of Gender, Households, and Social Networks in the Migration Process: A Review and Appraisal", paper submitted to the conference *Becoming American/ America Becoming*, organized by the SSRC, Sanibel Island, Florida, 18-21 January 1996.
Ravenstein, E.G. (1885) 'The Laws of Migration', *Journal of the Royal Statistical Society* 48 (2): 167-227.
Ravenstein, E.G. (1889) 'The Laws of Migration', *Journal of the Royal Statistical Society* 52 (2): 241-301.
Rawls, John (1993) *Political Liberalism*. New York: Columbia University Press.
Roche, Maurice (1992) *Rethinking Citizenship. Welfare, Ideology and Change in Modern Society*. Cambridge: Polity Press.
Sassen, Saskia (1991) *The Global City. New York, London, Tokyo*. Princeton, NJ: Princeton University Press.
Stark, Oded (1991) *The Migration of Labour*. Oxford: Blackwell.
Waldron, Jeremy (1995) 'The Cosmopolitan Alternative', in Kymlicka, Will (ed.), *The Rights of Minority Cultures*. Oxford University Press.
Walzer, Michael (1983) *Spheres of Justice: A Defense of Pluralism and Equality*. New York: Basic Books.

CHAPTER 2

Temporal and Spatial Aspects of Multiculturality
Reflections on the Meaning of Time and Space in Relation to the Blurred Boundaries of Multicultural Societies

Charles Westin

Culture, *Ethnie*, and Multiculturality

Culture has a variety of meanings. Its most central meaning comes from cultivation. To cultivate is:

- to plant, tend, improve or harvest crops or plants;
- to prepare the ground to promote the growth of crops or plants;
- to educate and train.

Cultivation, either of the soil or of the mind, is about growth and development, planned and ordered. In a general sense, *culture* is posited as an opposite to *nature*. Culture is that which nature is not. Culture is about the domesticated, nature about the wild. Culture is man-made and learned, in contrast to that which is given by nature and transmitted genetically. In a classic piece Alfred Korzybsky (cited by Rapoport, 1967) proposes that culture may be seen as time-binding. This is to emphasize the distinction between different forms of life – plants, animals, and human beings. The survival mechanism of plants is to capture and bind energy from external sources. Animals he regards as 'space-binders'. Their survival depends upon their ability to find food and refuge, and to seek out mates. Human beings are 'time-binders' because survival is distinctly related to the capacity to accumulate cultural capital. Rapoport puts it thus: "Time-binding is to culture what learning is to an organism, and what evolution is to a species" (Rapoport, 1967: 136).

Anthropological views on culture refer to patterns of organization of everyday life. Language, categorizations, myths, traditions, rites, self-understanding, and social relations that are common to and upheld by a collective, determined and delineated by some generally accepted self-definition, have all been traditionally regarded as elements of culture. Essential to the anthropological view on culture is a basic outlook and understanding of the world as it is given. Or, in other words, culture is about the expression and social distribution of meaning.

An influential definition of culture was given by the British anthropologist Edward Tylor in 1871: "Culture or civilization, taken in its wide ethnographic sense, is that complex whole which includes knowledge, belief, art, morals, law, custom, and any other capabilities and habits acquired by man as a member of society" (Tylor, 1958: 1). Within social anthropology two different understandings have come out of Tylor's interpretation.

Clifford Geertz is a representative of one approach. Culture refers to the system of common knowledge, beliefs, and values that are the foundation of society's social, economic, political, and religious institutions. As Geertz puts it: "(Culture) denotes an historically transmitted pattern of meanings embodied in symbols, a system of inherited conceptions expressed in symbolic forms by means of which men communicate, perpetuate, and develop their knowledge about and attitudes toward life" (Geertz, 1973: 89). What Geertz points to are not *differences* between civilizations but *commonalities*, that is to man's inherent capacity to exist as a cultural being, to his 'culturality'. Culture, like language, is something that all members of mankind have in common. It is part of the essence of being human, and thus should unite rather than divide.

In the second, and more restrictive interpretation, culture refers to that which is typical of meaning expressions of a particular people located at some distinct period in time and (usually) within some particular geographic region. Different cultures exist in the way that different tongues exist. Culture in this sense is often given as one of the determining characteristics of an *ethnic group* or *ethnic collective*. It refers to the pool of common beliefs, customs, values, meaning constructions, and ways of being that are shared by members of such a collective. A shared culture is seen as an essential ingredient for ethnic identification.

In English there is no appropriate noun denoting a specific category of people to whom we would apply the corresponding adjective *ethnic*. The term ethnic group is often used but *group* easily leads to underestimation of scale. On the one hand, groups are normally less extensive than collectives (in terms of numbers). On the other hand, the term *collective* doesn't capture the sense of belonging and commitment that accompanies a people's ethnic awareness and solidarity. The French noun *ethnie* has been adopted by writers such as Anthony D. Smith and

John Rex to refer to those wide and large-scale conglomerations of people that imbue the individual with a sense of belonging that is characteristic of the original small-scale community into which she was socialized (Smith, 1986; Rex, 1994). The socialization into an ethnic identity at a young age, and the correlation of ethnicity with first language, is taken as one possible explanation for the force of ethnic solidarity. An *ethnie* differs from other collectives to which an individual may feel a sense of belonging in that it also adds a touch of sacredness through the mythologizing of common origin.

Ethnies obviously vary in size and complexity. In many cases, but not all, there is attachment to a territory. The term covers an array of possibilities, ranging from territorially based bodies of people on their way to forming a nation and state, to communities in diaspora which may only have a myth of origin, a name, and perhaps some elements of culture in common (Rex, 1994). In his analysis of the ethnic origins of nations Smith distinguishes between two kinds of *ethnies* – *lateral* and *vertical*. His distinction refers mainly to premodern types of communities (Smith, 1986). A *lateral ethnie* is extensive in space but shallow in the social hierarchy, whereas the opposite applies to a *vertical ethnie*. *Lateral ethnies* are predominantly rural, *vertical ethnies* mainly urban. In conclusion we may argue that cultures are borne by *ethnies*, by peoples. However, the question of what people bear upon which culture is becoming increasingly difficult to answer in an age of migration, transnational communities, and diasporas.

A fundamental criterion of a culture in the sense of an *ethnie's* self-understanding is that some kind of continuity must be discernible. Although by the very nature of temporal existence cultures are in a process of development, change takes time to catch on. A given culture needs to be reproduced for each new generation. Society provides institutionalized settings for the transmission of culture through training and education – 'macrolearning processes' as Boulding puts it (Boulding, 1967). Thus, cultures are conservative in the sense that institutions represent inertia. To an external observer, continuity is usually more obvious than change.

Different cultures also face one another in space, thus allowing for the diffusion of ideas, the penetration of one culture into another, giving rise to processes of acculturation and assimilation. So while there is a certain degree of continuity, both in time and in space, discontinuities are always also present, challenging the predominant understanding. There are cracks in the façade where change may be born. Demographic and political changes, technological and social innovations, are some factors that may shape the course of a culture.

The most important vehicle of culture is language. It is the principal provider of concepts and conceptualizations by means of which the world is experienced and understood. It is the most powerful means of interpersonal communication, and it serves as a forging social cement within the community of speakers. Language is not identical with culture but there is certainly a close correlation. Nor is language identical with ethnicity. Not all *ethnies* have a distinct language of their own, but an *ethnie* practically always has its own way of speaking a language.

In modern anthropological discourse, *culture* is about the internal world of ideas, experiences, and feelings, but also about their external expression as they are made public (Hannerz, 1992). The cultural flow involves both the externalization of meaning and the interpretation of these expressions by others, in a continuous, interactional, meaning-producing process. Each and every individual externalizes her interior world of meaning and interprets externalizations of others. Meaning production is all over because people are constantly in each other's presence – in family life, in work, in leisure, in transactions of various kinds, and in casual and anonymous encounters in public spaces.

Hannerz outlines three dimensions as essential to culture:

1) ideas and modes of thought, that is to say, entities and processes of the mind;
2) forms of externalization, that is, how meaning is made publicly accessible;
3) social distribution, that is, how internal and external modes of meaning are spread in a population (Hannerz, 1992: 4-10)

Traditional social anthropology, as exemplified by Tylor's definition, has mainly been concerned with the first dimension, paying some attention to the second, but almost entirely disregarding the third dimension. It may be argued, however, that the three dimensions are inextricably bound together and that complexities of 1 are consequences of the complexities of dimensions 2 and 3. Hannerz' approach to culture is interactional. Social structures and meanings are shaped in the everyday interactions people have with one another. Societies emerge and cultures evolve as the aggregated outcomes of interpersonal exchanges. Thus, culture is reproduced and developed in response to changing conditions of subsistence and existence. In the contemporary world of rapidly developing technology, the media play an essential role for all three dimensions mentioned above – processes of mind and identity, externalization of meaning, and distribution of meaning.

A third point of departure I want to take is the concept of the multicultural. Today the concept is in vogue. How does it relate to culture? And where do *ethnies* enter into the picture? There is some confusion about the concept and to what phenomenon it refers. Actually it is used in several different senses.

Some writers emphasize an ideological and normative aspect. Multiculturalism is a democratic policy response to cultural and ethnic diversity (Inglis, 1996). It is about acknowledging cultural diversity. Ethnic identity, or membership of, or identification with any cultural group should under no circumstances serve as an obstacle for people to exercise their social, political, and constitutional rights. It should not prevent them from enjoying full access to societal institutions, or to participate in society as equal, worthy members. In other words, multiculturalism is about equal opportunities, the rule of law, and respect for human rights. It is incompatible with racism and ethnic or cultural discrimination.

Other writers stress discursive aspects and look at the ways in which power holders, politicians, and opinion moulders address issues of cultural diversity and social disintegration (Ålund/Schierup, 1991). Some analysts are highly critical of the way in which multicultural programmes are implemented. For example, Sweden adopted an immigration policy in the 1970s that was to reinforce the position of immigrant minorities with regard to social, economic, and political rights without forcing them to assimilate (Hammar, 1985). This policy was intended to bring out a society in which cultural diversity is seen as a strength. This, however, is not the way things have turned out. Instead there has been a marked increase in racist actions, discrimination, segregation, and unemployment. The foreign-born population has been especially hard hit. Among the Swedish-born majority there is also an increasing criticism of immigration and integration policies that are seen as too lenient.

According to a third interpretation, demographic and empirical in scope, the term 'multicultural' refers to the simultaneous presence of several ethnic cultures within one political, administrative, geographical, or otherwise accepted spatial unit. History provides numerous examples of multicultural societies in this sense. The simultaneous presence of several ethnic cultures within one territorial unit, however it is defined, is the outcome of various historical events – wars and peace treaties, the drawing of political boundaries, colonization, the slave trade, trading networks, migration, displacement, differential population development, etc.

Some of the confusion may be cleared by consistently using the term 'multiculturalism' for normative, programmatic approaches, and the term 'multiculturality' for empirical conditions of cultural plurality.

However we define and understand the multicultural side to society, it is here to stay. There is no turning back to some idealized, and in fact non-existent, cultural homogeneity. Multiculturality implies living with cultural diversity and blurred boundaries. External boundaries between different cultures have been incorporated as internal boundaries. Where? One answer would take the abstract locus of culture into consideration. As mentioned earlier, anthropological or ethnic culture is about modes of thought and meaning within our minds, and then about the externalization of this understanding. The implication is then, that blurred boundaries of multiculturality are in our minds.

Ambiguities of Swedish Multiculturality

A different answer to the question refers to boundaries *within* the modern state. At this point I will make a fairly lengthy digression and reflect upon Sweden's multicultural experiences. In a television interview for the news and broadcasted by one of the national channels, a young man in his late teens, born in Sweden to immigrant parents, and living in Alby, one of Stockholm's segregated suburbs, said that when he took the underground into the city centre he felt he was entering foreign country. Therefore he seldom left the neighbourhood although the centre of Stockholm with its culturally diversified night-life attracting many young people is less than half an hour from Alby by the underground. Blurred cultural boundaries are right there at the centre of power. To uncover the full meaning of this experience we shall have to look more closely at Sweden's historical experiences of cultural diversity and homogeneity.

Sweden is a small country of close to nine million inhabitants. It is an old state, one of Europe's oldest, formed when the Viking era was drawing to an end and Christianity was adopted by the ruling classes (around the year 1000). The core regions have never been subjected to foreign occupation or rule.

Ten per cent of the contemporary population of Sweden represents persons born in other countries (the first generation). If their children (the second generation) are included the population of *non-Swedish origin* is 17%. These figures suggest that Sweden has a multicultural condition. Racist organizations propagate these data on the Internet to emphasize the threat to Swedish culture and to the Swedish 'racial stock'. People within the immigrant resettlement business find support in these data for their own weight. But what do the figures actually represent?

Approximately one third of the *foreign-born* population is of Nordic origin (predominantly from Finland), having migrated to Sweden during the years of labour immigration in the 1960s and 1970s (Westin/Dingu-Kyrklund, 1997). Another third is of other European origins, consisting of labour migrants (Germans, Greeks, Yugoslavs), refugees from Eastern Europe (Estonians, Czechs, Hungarians, Poles), and, most recently, refugees from Bosnia and Serbia. The remaining third is of non-European origin (Chileans, Ethiopians, Iranians, Iraqis, Lebanese, and Turks to mention the largest groups).

Nordics represent a larger share of *the second generation* than Europeans. Non-Europeans represent an even smaller share. Nordic immigrants from the 1960s have had the time to raise families. To some extent the second generation of Nordic origin is the offspring of mixed marriages. Having one Swedish parent, these persons are normally Swedish by citizenship, language, and self-identification. Even the majority of this group, those with two Finnish parents, are well integrated, not to say fully, assimilated into Swedish society. Even a significant number of the second generation of European origin are integrated into Swedish society in terms of education and profession, less, though, in terms of self-identification. The second generation of non-Europeans represents an even smaller percentage because the first generation is still in the process of forming families. On an average first-generation non-Europeans are ten years younger than first-generation Nordics. The first- and second-generation non-Europeans are facing severe problems of establishing themselves in the labour market due to a subtle but nonetheless painful racial/ ethnic discrimination. People of non-European origin are the primary targets of a vicious racist propaganda that has caught hold of an alarming number of young Swedish working class males.

The current debate in Sweden on multicultural society is about open racism, unemployment, segregation in the housing market, and how to bring people from the immigrant sector in to full participation in the societal processes.

Multiculturality is geographically located in specific housing areas in the major cities. In some of these 75% of the residents are of non-European origin. To counteract these concentrations the authorities developed a dispersal policy, sending accepted refugees to smaller towns all over the country, in view of increasing the chances of integration into mainstream society. What this policy actually has led to instead is that segregation has been introduced on a national scale.

One of the nationalist myths is that Sweden used to be an ethnically homogeneous nation – one people, one race, one language, one church, one historically given territory, one common culture, and one recognized centre of power. Even those who refute nationalistic views usually accept this description. For nationalists, multiculturality is the result of uncontrolled and encouraged immigration of 'racially inferior' and culturally alien elements.

Historical data tell another story. If multiculturality implies the co-presence of different cultural groups, or *ethnies*, within the unit defined as the Swedish state, the truth is that it practically always has been a multicultural entity, although the distribution and location of the non-Swedish speaking population has changed over the centuries.

Reindeer-herding Samis have always existed within the boundaries of the Swedish state. They have been the victims of degradation, persecution, and internal colonialism. As other autochthonous peoples, the Sami identify themselves as belonging to the Fourth World. Sami history is one of displacement, unequal rights, and non-recognition. Even today the Swedish state refuses to recognize Sami territorial claims. In the north a Finnish-speaking border minority was denied rights to its language as late as the 1970s. Archaeological data, historical records, and place names indicate that ethnic Swedish presence in the northern hinterland is of a fairly recent date, that is to say, has developed over the past 200 years.

Looking back 300 years in time, the equivalent of about ten generations, plurality was obvious. Within the bounds of the state, Swedish speakers were a numerical minority. In addition to the Sami there were Finns, Russians, Estonians, Livonians, Latvians, Prussians, Poles, Germans, Danes, and Norwegians. These peoples inhabited regions that had been annexed by conquest in war. There was little intermixing. Internal migration obviously cannot compare to present-day mobility. The fact that 99% of the population was rural counteracted any large-scale migration. In Tilly's terms, spatial mobility was local and circular (Tilly, 1978). Yet in the numerous wars fought against Russia, Finns, Estonians, Livonians, and even Russians were drafted. In the Thirty Years War, the bulk of the Swedish armies consisted of drafted Germans. Within the commanding ranks the military organization provided for some social mobility. German, Baltic, and Russian aristocracy was introduced into the Swedish nobility.

Looking even further back in history to the Hanseatic trade of the fifteenth century and earlier, trading ports such as Visby, Stockholm, and Kalmar were virtually German cities. This massive German presence left a permanent imprint on the development of the Swedish language. Prior to the nineteenth century, immigration consisted of Finnish burn-beating peasants, skilled Walloon labour, Scottish military advisors, and Dutch city planners. The Finns and Walloons maintained their cultural identities for generations.

Three hundred years ago the spatial extension of the state was east-west, from the lakes of central Sweden across the Baltic into the Gulf of Finland. Today the axis has a north-south orientation. This is due to the losses of Finland and the Baltic possessions in wars against Russia, and to the incorporation of Danish provinces in the south and Norwegian ones in the north and west. A remarkable feature in historical self-reflection is the avoidance of discussing the brutal efficiency by which the former Danish and Norwegian provinces were brought under Swedish rule. Popular opposition was overrun and dissenters were punished.

My point is that multiculturality has many faces when we look at it diachronically. Visby on the island of Gotland is still a Hanseatic town in its architecture, in its street plan, and in its memories. The German heritage has been amalgamated into something Swedish. Similarly, towns in the province of Scania (Skåne) have maintained elements of a Danish atmosphere. The university town of Lund is a typical example. Many Scanians do not actually identify themselves as 'real Swedes' but jokingly refer to themselves as 'spare Danes'. Rinkeby, a Stockholm suburb dominated by an immigrant population, represents a different, complex, and possibly problematic aspect of multiculturality.

The conception of a lost cultural homogeneity is mistaken. What it stands for is a strong centralized power that did not hesitate to crush provincial or ethnic opposition. Power is still highly centralized, and this, I believe, is what so many 'denizens' in Sweden experience. It is not a coincidence that Tomas Hammar modelled his concept of *denizenship* upon Sweden's experiences of seeking ways to integrate its foreign-born population (Hammar, 1990). There is a strong egalitarian strain in Sweden. Its historical roots are to be found in the strong position of free peasants, one of the estates of the realm. The feudal system was never introduced in Sweden.

Neither is it, in my opinion, a sheer coincidence that an outstanding Swedish sociologist, Gunnar Myrdal, so brilliantly analysed the American dilemma of the coexistence of an ingrained racist ideology with a genuine adherence to the American democratic creed. Although it hasn't been formulated as such, there exists a corresponding Swedish quandary. I believe Myrdal must have been aware of it. It is about the coexistence of and conflict between the historically based and popular egalitarian tradition on the one hand, and, on the other, a subtle but bureaucratic and sometimes arrogant exercise of power, often full of good intentions but almost always streamlining solutions that don't take the common people's experiences and wishes into account, nor those of marginalized minority groups. The sterilization policy that was practised for 40 years right up until 1976 is one example of this Big Brother ideology. It was precisely the absence of a feudal system that laid the foundations of an exceptionally strong central power, in earlier centuries invested in the Crown, in modern times in an independent, powerful, and centralized bureaucracy. The difficulties that multiculturalism has faced in Sweden must be understood in terms of these historically rooted contradictions.

Time, Space, and Population Movements

This leads us to problematize some basic categories – continuity and change, time and space, mobility and immobility.

It is generally accepted that cultures are not rigid monoliths given once and for all, as National Romanticism of the nineteenth century would have it, but receptive and responsive ways of constructing meaning, continuously battered by requirements to change and develop, and by counter-forces stressing ideals of purism, opposing newfangled expressions and interpretations. In the grand historical perspective, cultures develop organically out of preceding ones. Thus a culture is never completely novel. It may incorporate specific innovations (technical, social, political), reshuffle elements into new combinations, gradually developing forms of understanding that did not exist previously. The paradox of the cultural flow is that it harbours both change and continuity at the same time. Although aspects of a *longue durée* may be identified as a *gestalt* that to some extent defies the ravages of time, there are beginnings and there are endings (Braudel, 1980; 1981-84). But who can say when a culture actually began? And who can say where it shades off into an adjoining one?

The boundaries in time between different cultures are blurred and indistinct. They are seldom, if ever, experienced by those who were around when the transition is said to have taken place. Rather, when we speak of boundaries in time, it relates to retrospective classifications made by scientists of the temporal past – archaeologists and historians. Cultural change is not, and cannot be instantaneous, but has to be understood as a gradual process of reorientation and acceptance.

Certain spectacular events may have had an enormous symbolic importance, such as the storming of the Bastille. This event was, however, only the beginning of the end of the old order. When we look at what appears to be fairly rapid cultural change in the distant past, one must put it down to unsatisfactory theorizing, the lack of data, the spacing in time of material evidence, and the illusions of temporal scale that can create the impression of a sudden change. Even such fundamental innovations as the transition to agriculture in prehistoric times, and the introduction of industrialization some 250 years ago, or the Christianization and Islamization of the Old World, were never instantaneous changes affecting entire peoples simultaneously. They were drawn-out processes influencing various segments of society at different times and with different consequences.

Because cultures are carried by peoples, collectives, *ethnies*, and these entities by the very nature of material existence must have spatial extension, cultures are extended in space too. The spatial distribution of cultures is complex, and possibly even more so in the contemporary world than in the past due to the radical development of modern communications by means of which spatial extension may be bridged. Moreover, the modern media have revolutionized our understanding of the distribution and spatial extension of culture. Culture as collective and shared meaning, externalized and interpreted, assumes local variations in ways similar to the distribution of regional and social dialects. In this sense, culture may be regarded as the distribution of the diversity of meaning. Boundaries between cultures in space are blurred and indistinct. When a cultural boundary coincides with the borders of the state, as it sometimes does, certain markers such as written language in public places (signposts, advertizing, etc.) may give a visual impression of cultural differences on either side of the state border. The concept of *boundary* tends to be seen as a more or less rigid line of division. This applies to the dividing lines between states but not between cultures. In many respects, the concept of a cultural *frontier* is a more appropriate way to designate the fact that one culture blends into another in space. Frontiers are not lines but spaces of transition.

How is cultural diversity socially constructed into something regarded as a whole? How do deviations from the norm survive? And where do cultural and ethnic minorities fit into this general framework? The nation-state claims to answer these questions by homogenizing cultural expressions of meaning, languages, forms of distribution, and ways of being. Outlying provinces and border regions where cultural and linguistic forms may deviate slightly are brought into accord with the cultural norms and practices of the power centre. The nation-state may employ harsh assimilation policies, oppression, displacement, resettlement, and colonization. It may also use more subtle methods such as to rewrite history, disregard uncomfortable facts that contradict its claims to supremacy, and emphasize historical feats of glory that support the myth of legitimacy.

States have extension. Territorial control is one of the most significant features of the state, and one of the criteria by which it is recognized by other states. The general rule seems to be that one state does not contain another independent state, although there do exist some exceptions (the Vatican, San Marino, and Lesotho). Normally a state controls a continuous stretch of territory. Islands, of course, provide special cases. Other exceptions are the Kaliningrad enclave and a small Belgian district entirely encircled by Dutch territory. Spatially, the closest two states can get is to touch each other, that is to have a common border. State boundaries may be disputed but they are not blurred. In Europe these boundaries are usually marked in the terrain – cairns, stone mounds, barbed wire, walls, minefields, or iron curtains.

A driving force of the nation-state is to consolidate the politico-territorial entity into one dominant culture (language), one dominant people (*ethnie*/nation), and one legitimate political system. The spatial distribution of cultures and *ethnies* is ever so much more complex than that of states. It is the aggregated result of historical factors that include migrations, power struggles, wars, economic competition, and just plain organic, uncontrolled population growth. Although cultures and *ethnies* may dominate continuous stretches of land, there are numerous examples of ethnic and cultural cohabitation. The *Census of India* shows tables and maps of the thousands upon thousands of villages that are entirely segregated in terms of religious groups and *jatis* (endogamous guilds). These villages represent one type of multicultural mix. The diversity and complexity of culture contrasts to the uniformity and simplification of the nation-state ideal.

The issues of continuity and change lead us to the fundamental categories of time and space. Time is given by the duration and change of things. The arrow of time is the perceived progression of things coming to pass, one leading to the other, from the past towards the future with no turning back. It is a conception that has evolved from observing the transition that all life forms make from birth to death (and similarly the withering down of more complex inorganic structures), in other words, a generalization with its roots in the human experience of identity. Social time is given by events following upon events in social interaction, ordered into timetables, agendas, and calendars. Cultural time is given by the *longue durée* of institutions, mentalities, and social structures, succeeding earlier formations and to be followed by others.

Social time pertains to the complex network of tasks that is to be accomplished for social structure to maintain and reproduce itself. Personal or individual time emerges from the individual's needs. The relationship between individual time and social time is complex. Societal projects of various kind structure personal time. Social roles constitute points of intersection of individual and social time, generating strains and conflicting temporal demands. Synchronization is one means of avoiding the conflicts that are embedded in the clash between individual and social time.

Pace and control are two aspects of social time. The pace of social time differs between cities and villages. It varies between cultures, regions, and countries. A common observation is that it also varies with seasons, hours of the day, stages of the life course, occupations, and social positions. Control of time pertains to the individual's freedom to act. Traditional industrial production implies a formidable external control of time (time clocks) with the conveyor belt and assembly line as the prototype of strict external control. Spare time, leisure time, and time-off all imply that the individual is free to organize her time.

Mobility is embedded in time. Movement of any kind always consumes time. There is no instantaneous transportation of persons or material goods. Time invested in voyages and land travel was much more extensive for the nineteenth century emigrant than it is today. Crossing the Atlantic was a matter of several weeks. Although physical transportation is much faster today, it is the social and political side to migration that is time-consuming. It involves waiting for decisions on residential permits and participating in resettlement programmes. Asylum-seekers may have to spend years in refugee camps before being accepted.

Psychological adjustment to the new situation, learning to communicate in the (new) language, acquiring a repertoire of social skills that are appropriate to the new environment and a basic understanding of how things operate in the new context so as to be able to provide for one's family take their toll of time. Adjusting to the new society involves increased participation and integration into its economic and political structures. Qualifying for citizenship follows a strict timetable. All these aspects connect migration with time.

Moreover, different conceptions of time and space are brought to the fore through migration. Every culture has its way of organizing time and space as revealed in landscapes and timescapes, architecture and organization, art and music. Migrating from developing to developed countries, or moving from rural regions to metropolitan conurbations, involves moving between different cultural conceptions of time, pace, and control. In agrarian cultures with a cyclical mode of production, time is experienced rather as a set of opposites than as a sequence of moments: day and night, spring and autumn, summer and winter, sunrise and sunset, birth and death, opposites which in their synthesis endow time itself a cyclical significance. Changes in life and in the world are not thought of as permanent conversions but as alternations between different phases of an eternal cycle. In these cultures, clocks have not primarily determined time, as they do in modern societies; it has been the task in which one is occupied, each matter being allowed to take its time. The meaning of this is thoroughness, not indolence.

This cyclical conception of time is not alien to man in post-modern post-industrial society. There are still the annual, weekly, and daily rounds by which life patterns are organized. Predominantly, however, time is conceived of as a linear progression of moments. This conception is consistent with the 'ever-expanding' industrial mode of production. It is obvious in digital time-giving. Exploitation of physical resources also means exploitation of time. Man's life is divided into years of work and years of retirement, hours of work and hours of leisure. The hours of work, and consequently the hours of leisure, are by and large controlled by the clock. Time thus becomes equivalent to money. One never seems to have enough. Migration from developing to developed countries or from rural provinces to industrialized regions implies moving towards an increasingly elaborate external control of time. Time control is possibly one of the most obvious determinants and markers of power. Throughout history power holders have structured and controlled time – the Christian Church, the capitalists and industrialists, and today, significantly, the media.

Multicultural societies may have problems of synchronizing different social and cultural timescapes. Different conceptions of time have repercussions on how people structure their engagements, commitments, work, social life, and religious worship. In a tolerant, pluralistic society this may not be a big deal. In an intolerant society, on the other hand, time that is taken off for cultural and religious needs from what members of other communities may regard as working hours may create great strains and pressures.

Industrialization is about organizing time, controlling the work process, and concentrating the workforce in space. It presupposes mobility. Industrial society separates places of residence from places of work, thus giving rise to the phenomenon of commuting. Migration of manpower may be seen as a form of large-scale commuting, greater distances are covered, longer times are involved, and international borders are crossed. On the other hand, only some return. Like the linear progression of clock-time there is no turning back for most migrants.

Mobility is intimately related to the process of economic development. It increases in volume as modern society with its linear time infringes upon the traditional worlds of cyclical time. Migration serves as one of the links between these two worlds, drawing people from one to the other, then sending back images of modern life, implanting hopes of bettering one's situation. It follows the international flow of capital and goods, but in the reverse direction. One solution to the mounting immigration pressure that is currently being considered by Western governments is to direct development aid specifically to regions of large emigration. What is not realized, however, is that economic development elicits mobility and migration, it doesn't contain it.

In a general sense space is given by the trajectories of mobile persons or objects. The building of the railroads in the nineteenth century was a truly dramatic reorganization of cultural space. Space was conquered and time standardized. If geopolitical space is given by the existence of states bordering to states, the geo-cultural and ethno-territorial dimensions of space are given by the existence of cultures beyond and within cultures, and *ethnies* beyond and within *ethnies*. Migration is a phenomenon taking place in this context. It is embedded in political, cultural, and ethnic space.

The individual migrant moves from point A to point B. After some period of time she may decide to continue to C, remain in B, or return to A, depending upon the unfolding structure of opportunities. Migration involves the crossing of boundaries. Even cases referred to as local migration, moving from one village to another, or from rural districts to cities, involve crossing municipal, parish, or provincial boundaries. Boundaries are an inherent element of the grained structure and packaging of space (Hägerstrand, 1991). In most cases migration also involves crossing an existential boundary within – between the familiar and the unfamiliar, the known and the unknown. Some boundaries are easily crossed. Others are virtually impenetrable if not regular entrances or exits are used. Yet others are legally impermeable but in actual practice porous (the US-Mexican border). All mediaeval European cities of importance were bounded by walls. Their gates of entry still exist as place names, as for instance in London and Paris. Today the categorical and unambiguous boundaries are no longer the city walls but the national borders of the state. The gates of entry are situated at the airports and harbours. It is in the nature of things that these gates are controlled.

If points A and B (or B and C) lie on either side of a national boundary, we speak of international migration. Crossing national boundaries and settling in another state entails issues of differential rights, participation in the political process, and access to power. Quite frequently international migration involves moving across linguistic and cultural boundaries, boundaries of a sort that are not imprinted in the terrain. Nevertheless, these subtle boundaries are highly compelling. These issues make international migration a distinctly different undertaking from spatial mobility within the state.

Western societies may have entered the so-called post-industrial era as some analysts claim (boundaries in time are hard to see). Be that as it may. These societies are still basically under the influence of the enormous restructuring of social time and space that was brought about by industrialization. Post-industrial societies in the future will be likely to organize time and space differently. This is possibly what we are witnessing in the globalization and media developments. One thing is certain. Mobility will hardly decrease. Although restrictive immigration policies are currently being enforced by many states, international migration is also likely to increase as a side-effect of a generally increased readiness to move.

Theories about migration have been developed within several academic disciplines. Few attempts have been made to synthesize terminologies and frameworks that are employed into coherent statements about the subject matter. One principle is to organize the approaches in macro (structural, socio-economic) and micro (individual, motivational) perspectives.

One comprehensive macro approach concerns the overall demographic development and its relationship to modernization. In the process of modernization, during which countries progress from low to high stages of economic development, a parallel shift from an initial situation of high birth rates coupled with high death rates to a situation of low birth rates coupled with low death rates will take place. Population growth is low at these two stages because birth and death rates more or less cancel each other out. During the intermediate transitional stage death rates decline as a result of improved living conditions and nutrition, inoculations, health care, etc. while birth rates are still comparatively high because behaviour patterns, norms, and values with regard to mating, marriage, and sexuality take much longer to change. This leads to a phase of rapid population growth that is referred to as *demographic transition*.

Demographic transition is the outcome of a complex set of factors relating to the dissemination of knowledge, changing social organization and production, rising demands and economic development mixed with a good deal of ideological justification, ultimately affecting general living conditions. Today death rates are going down in many developing countries while birth rates are still high, especially in Africa. The world population is increasing rapidly. Almost half of the present Third World population is under 15 years of age. Mobility is regarded as one response to increasing population pressures.

A distinction needs to be made between *spatial mobility* and *international migration*. There is always a certain amount of mobility within the boundaries of a given state. Moving from a country's peripheral backward regions to its economically and politically dynamic centre resembles international migration in some psychological and social respects; the individual migrant experiences a loss of social networks, lack of recognition, and hardships of establishing himself.

In other respects, however, mobility within a given state differs from international migration. A free democratic state does not prevent its citizens from resettling elsewhere within the country. Neither does the state object when citizens wish to emigrate. By way of contrast legal restrictions exist to the in-migration of noncitizens. Of specific importance are the consequences of state *boundaries*, *border control*, *citizenship*, and *political rights* when it comes to categorizing individuals and groups with regard to their rights.

The root causes of migration are complex. They involve conditions in the sending as well as receiving countries. Moreover, migration is selective. Therefore analyses of migration need to take individual as well as structural factors into account.

At the individual level of analysis, people's motives to migrate, their aims and objectives, their beliefs and access to information, as well as their economic and social means to carry out their intentions are of essential importance. An underlying assumption is that the individual makes rational decisions about migrating and integrating into the receiving society. The individual migrant weighs the pros and cons on the strength of available information (which need not necessarily be correct). Migration may present a means to reach one's goals.

At the structural level immigration policies, labour market requirements, public opinion, discrimination and segregation, the existence of immigrant communities in the receiving country, and the general structure of opportunities awaiting would-be migrants need to be considered. Macro-structural approaches focus on processes which trigger, direct, and sustain migratory flows. Structural analyses generally assume that the economic differentials of the sending and receiving countries determine the overall pattern of migration. If significant income differentials exist between two countries, the flow of migration will be to the country with the higher income levels, all other factors being equal. Economic models of this kind are generally too simplistic. Factors such as regulation policy, border control, and transport facilities confound and disturb the 'free' passage of manpower from one country to another.

Two central concepts of migration theory are push and pull factors. *Push factors* apply to conditions in the sending country that induce people to engage in migratory endeavours. Thus, push factors may refer to unemployment, unsatisfactory educational opportunities, unequal career opportunities, discrimination, and racism. Push factors pertain to lack of democracy, authoritarian rule, political oppression, and violation of human rights. Poverty, overpopulation, and environmental disasters are other push factors. Generally speaking, push factors imply that significant numbers are prepared to pay the cost in money, discomfort, and effort to seek better opportunities elsewhere.

In a sense *pull factors* are the opposite. If migration is about improving one's lot, receiving countries must be able to offer the migrant such opportunities. Higher wages, lower taxes, and career opportunities will always attract a mobile labour force. Social welfare, educational opportunities, and public health care in a receiving country are other attracting forces. A majority of the nineteenth-century European migrants to the United States were peasants. The availability of free land to till was a most important pull factor. Nowadays there is no free land to claim. Instead jobs in industry, public services, and, in some countries, in the agricultural sector, are the options.

In a world of increasing ethnic conflict, civil war, and political oppression, democratic government and safe havens will always draw people who are subjected to political persecution, coercion, and abuse.

Established immigrant communities in the receiving country represent another pull factor, providing members with various cultural services and attributes to their sense of identity and belonging. Most importantly, an established immigrant community provides its members with an organizational infrastructure. The community may organize schools, community centres, and religious sanctuaries. The newcomer may seek guidance and support, temporary shelter, and advice. Agencies may direct newcomers into an unofficial labour market.

An immigrant community depends upon an influx of newcomers since there is always a loss of members to mainstream society. Numbers are important if the community is to serve as a pressure group. Numbers are also important for endogamy to be maintained. Since immigration regulations are tight in most target countries today, new members will claim refugee status or apply for family reunification.

Migration is a *two-way traffic*. Individuals move in one direction. Images, information, know-how, parcels, and remittances are sent in the other, thus building up a readiness to join friends and relatives who have gone the whole way. Entrepreneurs in the immigrant community may actively persuade members of their social networks to migrate. In this way processes of chain migration are established.

A considerable share of the emigrants return within the space of a few years, serving as personal conveyors of impressions and ideas. Some commute back and forth for personal as well as business reasons. Kinship and friendship ties are an essential element of these networks which may be seen as a kind of social capital. Receiving and sending countries thus get increasingly entangled into each other through family networks. Over space and time flows acquire both stability and structure. Countries that are drawn into a flow need not be geographically close. Rather, migration flows reflect economic and political, in some aspects also cultural, proximity.

Migration theory may be criticized for its lack of coordination of different explanatory models. Attempts to synthesize various disciplinary approaches are rarely made. For some theoretical statements the empirical foundations seem to be of questionable value. Some economic models don't really apply to the current refugee migration. Many models lack historical depth. Nor do they seriously consider the impact of linguistic, cultural, and religious factors.

It has become increasingly difficult to distinguish between economically and politically induced migration. Whereas democratic welfare states of the North are restrictive about labour migration from the South, these same states have political obligations to grant individual refugees asylum. Instruments of control affect the types and flows of immigrants. Control and regulation policies also bear upon public opinion, ethnocentrism, and the process of integration. All these dimensions need to be incorporated into the theoretical models. Hammar et al. have recently made a valuable contribution to this end (Hammar et al., 1997).

A central task of migration research is to theorize about why migration takes place. Why do people move, and what are the socio-structural conditions that promote or reduce immigration? Kubat and Hoffmann-Nowotny, however, have suggested that the key issue is not why people migrate but rather why so many in fact are sedentary (Kubat/Hoffman-Nowotny, 1981). Hammar et al. have raised the same question (Hammar et al., 1997). How does migration theory explain immobility which is a test case, because it is after all the most common response to the conditions that migration theorists point out as explanatory factors? For instance, the theory of demographic transition would lead one to expect much more migration than one can actually observe. It does not explain immobility.

Theories of international migration need to deal with these complex issues in a systematic way. Most theories and models are simplistic and one-dimensional. The historical dimension and time factor needs to be taken into account. This can be done in terms of *generative models* of the interplay between economic, political, and individual factors. Moreover, general migration theory seems to lag behind the rapid developments towards a global society. Nor does it fully recognize the role of the media when it comes to disseminating images of what Henri Tajfel once called *cognitive alternatives to status quo*. The spatialization of transnational communities in a global context needs to be spelt out.

The Spatialization of *Ethnie* and Culture in a Global Context

People have always had to be prepared to move at some stage of their lives – to colonize and cultivate new land, for purposes of trade, in search of jobs, or to flee oppression. In pre-industrial society moves were basically *local*. People journeyed short distances, on an average seldom more than a few days by foot. Much of all this mobility was seasonal and *circular*, adapted to the yearly round of rural society. Workers would return to their points of departure after harvest. Although international frontiers would be crossed at times, most movements took place within the borders of one state.

The industrial revolution, starting in eighteenth-century England, led to a headlong restructuring of society. Power configurations changed. The rural working classes were uprooted, exploited, and victims of widespread poverty. This had profound and lasting effects on the organization of social time and space. In time, however, as the economic benefits of the industrial mode of production were reaped, gradual improvements of living conditions led to a reduction in infant mortality, in turn giving rise to an immense population increase. Industrialization led to an exodus of labourers from rural villages to growing industrial cities. Some of these movements spilled over into other countries. Overseas migration was one effect of the restructuring of rural into industrial society. Mass migration to the Americas started as a trickle, but it grew by degrees to the largest population movement in history. These moves were *long-distance*, rather *permanent*, and predominantly European.

Population movements that followed from the parallel processes of industrialization and colonization thus differed from earlier forms of mobility in covering greater distances, and as a consequence thereof, having a more permanent nature. For a long time the mass migration from Europe to North and South America served as a conceptual model for theorizing about population movements in geopolitical space. Demographic transition and its relation to migration potentials is one example. The Eurocentric perspective is also evident in the melting pot metaphor which served as a conceptual model for policies of integrating migrants into the receiving society.

A leap forward in time brings us to post-World War II developments and an economy of growth that lasted some 25 years. All important industrial countries were short of manpower at this time, despite the fact that women were joining the labour force in greater numbers than ever before. The solution was to recruit migrant workers from abroad, mainly from former colonial possessions and from the European periphery. Thus people from Third World countries – the South – were drawn into the global economic system resulting in an increasing mobility in general, and a growing out-migration from these regions to the First World – the North – as one of the results. What observers in the developed world are not always aware of, however, is the tremendous volume of South to South migration (Adepoju/ Hammar, 1996).

Today, conventional notions of geopolitical space are being eroded. Economic and technological developments over the recent decades have given rise to an efficient global communications network linking all nations to one another. Commodities and capital, tourists and emigrants, ideas and popular culture cross modern state boundaries and ancient cultural, religious, and linguistic borders in a constantly increasing flow. We have a world economy with quicker and denser transactions and a new international division of labour. Practically every part of the globe can be reached by modern transportation within a few days from any given starting point. One way of interpreting this change is, then, that migratory movements that take place in the context of globalization once again qualify as *local* if we consider the *time and effort involved* in travelling rather than the *distance covered*, but also the fact that stays are more intermittent and not necessarily aiming at permanent settlement.

Inevitably this development has led to a range of cultural encounters of a magnitude never witnessed before in history. Satellite-based TV-broadcasting and Internet are highly efficient conveyors of Western popular culture, currently penetrating into traditional African and Asian cultures, implanting images of living conditions and lifestyles in affluent Western societies. If we accept that world space has shrunk to such an extent that any part of the globe actually qualifies as being just about next door, we must also recognize the temporal effects. For the first time in the history of human kind we may speak of a *global present*.

Obviously, these changes of the very infrastructure of communications, not only of persons and material goods, but also of ideas, information, and popular culture have repercussions on the bounded and almost monolithic political entities of sovereign states, on cultural development, on power relationships, and economic transactions. The ease of travelling from airport to airport facilitates movements across national boundaries. Young people from affluent Western societies may spend months, sometimes even years, on touring the world. For migrants heading for the West the difficulties are not primarily related to transportation from one place to another, but to the control of national borders and ports of entry. For despite the virtually free flow of capital, goods, and ideas, migration is highly restricted.

Officially the migration of unskilled labour to the Western world has more or less stopped. There is also a common understanding that refugee crises involving mass flight situations can really only be solved by concerted international efforts in the region. Western countries are in agreement that migration and permanent (or temporary) settlement in Europe or North America is not a durable solution to refugee problems in Third World countries. Restrictive refugee policies are therefore being enforced. Economic motives are not recognized as sufficient grounds for permanent residence. Refugee status and family reunification have been the only valid reasons for granting resident permits. Until the collapse of Soviet hegemony in Eastern Europe in 1989, and the fall of the Soviet Union itself in 1991, several Western European states (among them Germany, Austria, and Sweden) had reasonably liberal refugee policies as one element of the Western strategy *vis-à-vis* Soviet totalitarianism. Refugees and asylum-seekers from other parts of the world (the Middle East, Latin America, South-East Asia) could benefit from these policies. The joint effect of stopping labour migration in the early 1970s and only accepting refugee grounds has had a sorting effect on prospective migrants. Those who believed they stood a fair chance of qualifying for the refugee category had a go at it. I am not implying that the asylum institution was, or is, misused, although obviously such cases also exist. Considering the violation of human rights, ethnic cleansing, political persecution, torture, and traumatization of civilians for which a great number of regimes are responsible, many persons have perfectly valid reasons to flee and apply for asylum in countries that are willing to accept them. Other migrants have chosen to sneak in illegally. So despite the massive control of migratory movements, political and illegal economic refugees from countries of the South are establishing themselves as new minorities in the metropolitan areas of major receiving countries.

One response to these developments is the rise of new kinds of creolized culture. Syncretic cultural forms are evident among youth groups who have been raised in the multicultural urban ghettos of the receiving countries. A different response to these developments is the emergence of political movements that totally reject the multicultural and transnational sides to modern society. In many countries these movements are being drawn to nationalistic and racist ideology.

In non-Western cultures we find movements, some in power, others in opposition, that are re-establishing conditions and rules of authority that are associated with traditional religious institutions. They may be seen as reactions to the development of secular society modelled upon Western examples. These movements have been especially militant in some Muslim countries – Iran, Algeria, Egypt, and Lebanon – but not only there. Similar movements are found among the Hindus and Sikhs of India, Buddhists in South-East Asia, Catholics in Latin America, and Protestants in North America. The rise of these movements seems to be a global phenomenon, more malignant in some countries and cultures than in others.

Politics is becoming increasingly internationalized. Conflicts in one country will inevitably have repercussions in others, even quite distant ones. Internationalization and globalization are paving the way for reawakened forms of nationalism and chauvinism. Multiculturalism and globalization are bringing out fundamentalism.

The phenomenon of ethnicity has been brought to the attention of social scientists basically through three approaches. It first entered the social sciences through the study of traditional, often autochthonous cultures, frequently situated in non-European settings. This used to be the main focus of cultural anthropology. The second approach pointing to ethnicity is represented by studies of migrant societies, above all the USA, but in recent times also European countries of immigration. This work has mainly been carried out by sociologists. The third approach is the study of nation-states and their territorial minorities, power relations, and political conflict. Historians, political scientists, and peace researchers have mainly been responsible for this approach.

Most theorists regard territoriality as a determining criterion of ethnicity. Other criteria that are frequently mentioned are joint culture, language, religion, and the belief in a common origin. In many, though not all cases, *ethnies* have a strong attachment to a territory. But there are two sides to it. As John Rex points out, "ethnic communities are often concerned precisely with their detachment from a territory" (Rex, 1994: 211). Globalization, however, is changing much of the conventional wisdom about ethnicity. New kinds of bounded entities with complex relations to the older constructions of territoriality are emerging, and Cohen points to the fact that social identities are in effect being deterritorialized (van der Veer 1995; Cohen, 1997). Communities of interest (professional, business, artistic, religious etc.) are developing that bind people together across various kinds of borders. These communities which are not new in themselves but have received renewed significance are gradually replacing the conventional, and in some respects more immediate or even 'natural' communities of place as foci of identifications. Communities of place are local. Interaction is face to face and what takes place in the local setting is what we refer to as everyday life. Face to face interaction is not a necessary condition for the maintenance of a community of interest, although it does help which the conference industry testifies to. Communities of interest rely upon other kinds of communication. Today the electronic media are of great importance.

The study of international migration and ethnic relations in the era of globalization has been enriched with the concept of *diaspora*. Although the concept was coined by the ancient Greeks, and thus hardly represents a novel experience, it has acquired a new significance in this age of globalization. Safran defines diasporas as expatriate minority communities that are characterized by a dispersal from an original centre to two or more peripheral locales (Safran, 1991). The diasporic community experiences a real or believed feeling of not being accepted in the host community. It cherishes a myth of the original homeland which is seen as a place of return, and it is committed to the restoration of this homeland. This commitment and continuing relationship with the homeland is essential to group solidarity and identity within the diasporic community.

The classic diaspora traces the origins of its displacement to some past catastrophe which is maintained in collective memory. Perhaps the most typical example is the Jewish dispersal. It is certainly the most cited example, tracing its displacement to the Babylonian captivity. Even modern catastrophes can give rise to diasporas, as in the case of the Armenian genocide staged by the Young Turks 1915-1920. For people of African origin in the Americas slavery was the cause of dispersal. To my knowledge neither oral history nor written documents record the original displacement of the Roma peoples from their ancestral homeland which most scholars believe is India. Disrupting events at the time of the Islamic penetration of India could have led to the displacement of the Roma.

Robin Cohen broadens the concept of diaspora and applies it to a larger range of exiled communities (Cohen, 1997). He identifies a typology of diasporas which besides the victim category also includes dispersals resulting from labour migration, trade, and imperial colonization. According to Cohen the following features usually apply to a diaspora:

1) dispersal from an original homeland – sometimes traumatically; or
2) the migration from a homeland for reasons of work, trade, or colonization;
3) a collective memory of the homeland;
4) the idealization of the ancestral homeland;
5) the development of a return movement;
6) a strong ethnic consciousness and a sense of distinctiveness;
7) a troubled relationship with host societies;
8) a sense of solidarity with co-ethnics in other countries;
9) the possibility of a distinctive, creative life in pluralistic host societies (Cohen, 1997: 26).

Diasporas are of importance for understanding nations and nationalism. They are test cases that defy the nationalist image of one state, one territory, and one history. As Clifford puts it: "Positive articulations of diaspora identity reach outside the normative territory and temporality (myth/history) of the nation-state (Clifford, 1994: 307). Diasporas are not nation-building communities but operate in transnational, horizontally organized networks.

Diasporic communities have benefited greatly from the communications revolution in the sense that people now are much closer to each other. Post Cold War developments have also made it possible for some diasporic groups (for instance Armenians, Circassians, and others) to visit, and even return to their 'homelands'. Diaspora is a question of *roots* and *routes*, or in other words, solidarity outside national time and space. It is about the struggle to maintain identity and community in a context of displacement (Clifford, 1994).

If the nation-state is about *here* and *now*, diasporas are about *there* and *then*. By this I am not implying that nation-states don't have a past or future, or that diasporas don't live in the present. What I am driving at is that the nation-state emphasizes the boundedness of its populations in time and space. It is in control of its territory, it totalizes its history, and it looks to the future in its development plans, reform policies, and economic investments. Its past as well as its future are seen as inherent parts of the present. The present reaches out to encompass the past and articulate those aspects of it which reinforce the legitimacy of the nation-state. Likewise, the future is seen as a matter of evolution and improvement, but still essentially as a continuation of the present. In other words, the future of the nation-state is seen as a realization of the present. For an established nation-state there is little place for revolution.

Diasporas, on the other hand, don't control territory. Although exceptions exist, many of the classic diasporas have been denied ownership of land in countries of residence. Diasporic communities live in the present no doubt. People work, raise families, and go about their business of everyday life. But in a mythic sense their identities are tied to events outside the temporality of the nation-state. Past events of great significance explain their present situation and their difference. Some future event may bring about a change of things. 'Next year in Jerusalem'. When space is not *here*, time (myth) becomes all the more important.

Nationalism needs the diaspora of others to establish the rootedness of the nation (van der Veer, 1995). If outsiders are not available, nationalists will invent them. In this respect it makes little difference how long a diasporic community has been present. It continues to fulfil the nation-state's need for outsiders. But nationalism may also fear diasporic communities because they are seen to represent alternatives, and thus potential subversion. The observation has frequently been made that revolutionaries quite often come from, or find their base in marginalized, sometimes diasporic communities.

Diasporic groups challenge the hegemony of the nation-state, but so do also autochthonous or First Nation peoples (Clifford, 1994). Autochthonous peoples stress their original attachment to the land, their natural right to the land, and the continuity of their attachment to the territory. Thus tension may arise between conflicting interests of recognition between First Nations and diasporas. Many First Nation peoples have suffered displacement through colonization and land acquisition by powerful settler communities. Many have been dispersed to reserves, and to the lowest ranks of the settler society. In a sense, then, First Nation people represent an internal diaspora, and classic diasporas may represent a kind of First Nation people in exile.

For many diasporas 'return to the homeland' is not a viable option, realistically speaking. The plural societies of the Caribbean for example may trace their historical origins to European colonizers, African slaves, and Asian-indentured workers of Indian and Chinese origin. The future of these peoples, however, has to be carved out in that region. Return to the African roots takes on cultural expressions, an example being the mythical significance given to Haile Selassie (Ras Tafari) by the Rastafarians of Jamaica. It is when the idea of the 'return to the homeland' is actually realized that exceptionally violent and irreconcilable conflicts may arise because there will invariably be people 'in the promised land' for whom it by no means is right or obvious to give up their claim to the land. The 'return' to Israel of Jews from the diaspora has given rise to a Palestinian diaspora.

In terms of the proposed temporal and spatial dichotomies autochthonous minorities would seem to be represented by the categories *here* and *then*. They are *here* by virtue of being in the land of their ancestors. However, this land is now in the hands of others. The full authentic meaning that the land once had in the past – *then* – cannot be recaptured. There is no return to the homeland of the past. For autochthonous peoples whose lands have been colonized by powerful settler communities it has proved to be extremely difficult to find viable solutions to the problem of their futures as autonomous peoples.

The remaining pair of categories are *there* and *now*. Colonial societies at an early stage of settlement fit in with this description. In settler societies such as Australia and New Zealand, to take an example, the colonists tried to reproduce the culture and society of the mother country. This was obvious in almost all domains of social life from place names, traditions from the mother country, institutional infrastructure, and also the fact that the landscape was domesticated by the introduction of familiar plants, trees, and animals. In Cohen's typology settler societies represent one form of diaspora.

The spatial and temporal typology proposed in the preceding paragraphs may be summarized in terms of the following matrix:

Table 1: Space and Time Coordinates of Societal Formations

	here	there
now	nation-state ideal	settler society
then	autochthonous minority	classic diaspora

Diasporas represent one type of transnationally interconnected communities. Globalization and international mobility lead us to re-evaluate the temporality and spatiality of *ethnies*. In countries of immigration ethnic minority communities are now forming that no longer need be entirely dependent on conditions in the host society. Established cultural networks are being transformed into international economic networks. Transnational communities, the new forms of diaspora, can manage much of their interconnectedness by means of the electronic communications. Information, knowledge, and skills can readily be exchanged electronically. Business and trade, a second domain of exchange, can be handled by means of e-mail, phones, and faxes. Capital is readily transferred this way. In a third crucial domain of exchange, that of partners for marriage, modern technology is also employed. Prospective marriage partners may for instance view and listen to each other on video tapes before a relationship is actually commenced. But there are some limits set by biology. Actual family formation can never be managed solely by electronic means. If families are to form and children be born, partners will have to meet face to face, and more than that, for some period of time. This has implications on movements across international borders.

The meaning of multiculturality is the empirical observation that several cultures, here understood as *ethnies*, reside within one bounded political, regional, or geographic entity that is separated from other entities of the same kind. The most important bounded entity is the state. It monopolizes violence. Membership of the state is given through citizenship.

The nation-state is a European construction that mainly formed in the nineteenth century. Quite a few European states regard themselves as nation-states. According to the ideal, one nation (or *ethnie*) forms one culturally, linguistically, and religiously uniform and autonomous state. This ideal seldom corresponds with empirical reality. Iceland and some midget states such as San Marino are the only entirely monocultural states. Countries like Belgium, Spain, and Switzerland are telling examples of the opposite with both historically established national divisions as well as large populations of immigrant origin. But even recognized nation-states such as France, Germany, Italy, the Netherlands, and the Scandinavian countries have indigenous ethnic minorities and large immigrated populations.

In many respects the 'nation-state' has been a highly successful project. It has managed the transformation from rural to industrial society. It has organized the welfare state. Despite the fact that many 'nation-states' are liberal democracies, not all have been consistently successful in defending equal and democratic rights for marginalized ethnic and cultural minorities. On the contrary, it appears that many 'nation-states' have pressurized minorities to adapt to standardized cultural expressions and language norms. 'Nation-states' tend to be centralized. Basically two strategies may be identified by which 'nation-states' can achieve cultural and linguistic uniformity. One is to alter people, the other is to alter territory. Altering people is done through education, persuasion, and example, or through more coercive methods of forced assimilation, punishment, relocation, and the banning of cultural expressions that go against the national strain. Altering territory means changing boundaries. This is problematic because it affects other states. Normally states do not voluntarily concede part of their territory to other states. Altering territory usually means demanding territory from other states. This strategy will easily lead to conflict. It took three major wars to settle the contested boundary between France and Germany.

The format of the nation-state is a model that many young states established after decolonization have tried to follow. For quite some time the nation-state has been regarded as a norm of state formation, that is to say, as the final stage of an *ethnie's* political autonomy and achievement. Currently, however, in the age of globalization and transnational connections, the nation-state ideal may be regarded as a special case of the relationship *ethnie* – state. The nation-state ideal represents the specific situation of *one* nation (or *ethnie*) and *one* state. In the matrix below the nation-state is related to various multicultural formations.

Table 2: Relations between State(s) and Ethnie(s)

		STATE	
		one	*several*
ETHNIE	*one*	nation-state ideal	transnational diasporas
	several	multi-ethnic state	supranational communities

The multi-ethnic state is represented by one state but several *ethnies*. Most states are multi-ethnic. A third category is represented by diasporic communities (one *ethnie* in several states) which stretch over national boundaries but have developed intense interdependence with co-ethnics residing in other states. The fourth category is represented by several ethnies in several states. Supranational communities such as the European Union would seem to fit into this box. What do these different formations mean in terms of membership, participation, empowerment, and influence?

When we speak about the space of multiculturality we must recognize that the same space will be invested with a range of different meanings. But what about the time of multiculturality? A reasonable conjecture is that we will have more culture everywhere, more diversification, and more change. The *longue durée* of mentalities is likely to be replaced by increasing generational divergences. Cultural differences that previously were spatially organized will be less marked. Instead cultural distinctions between generations are likely to become more noticeable. Time in the guise of age cohorts (vintages) is supplementing space in the guise of bounded entities as a principal arena of cultural difference.

The Facets of Multiculturality

Let us now return to the question of culture and its relation to multiculturality. An anthropological understanding is that culture is about the *constitution* of meaning in thought and emotion, the *expression* of meaning in public, and the *social distribution* of meaning. This is also what the multicultural in the demographic and empirical sense is about. In the accompanying matrix I group a number of aspects of culture in multicultural contexts departing from these three conditions (see Table 3). These aspects are given in the rows of the matrix.

Multiculturality refers to a situation of many cultures coexisting and influencing each other, but also carving out their distinctiveness in competition with each other. I will distinguish between three domains in which meaning is developed – folk culture, high culture, and mass culture. These domains are given in the columns of the matrix, below. They form a triad that some readers may recognize as an instance of the dialectical logic of thesis, anti-thesis, and synthesis. This, however, is coincidental. It is important to note that people, groups, organizations, and *ethnies* are part of, and take part in, all three domains. Thus the domains are different but not mutually exclusive. It goes without saying that the boundaries between them are blurred.

Temporal and Spatial Aspects of Multiculturality

Table 3: Meaning, Externalization and Distribution in Three Cultural Domains

	Folk culture	High culture	Mass culture
Meaning	explicit, unproblematic	implicit, subtle	multiple, ambiguous
Setting	situational and interactional	contextual and conventional	contextual and interactional
Arena	everyday life	intellectual life	post-modern life
Time and space	now and here	then and there	nowhere, anytime, anywhere
Situation	face to face	separation in time and space, time lag	separation but connectedness
Receiver	someone (special)	everyone	anyone
Understanding	interlocution	interpretation	deconstruction
Externalization	speech	writing (art, music)	talk shows, home pages
Structure	homogeneous	multi-layered	heterogeneous
Medium	language	the arts	electronic images
Style	intrinsic, private	artistic, elaborate	extrinsic, public
Communication	personal, devoted	general, committed	advertizing, exposure
Product	direct, ephemeral	fixation, eternal	cumulative, short lived
Relation to sender	dialogue, social responsivity	analysis, criticism	idolatry, detached admiration
Distribution	conversation, rumour	print	Internet, broadcasting
Range	local	national, universal	global
Depth	intimate	deep but restricted	broad but shallow
Flow	natural and spontaneous	convention-bound and creative	lax and unsophisticated
Storage	human memory	libraries	data banks
Community	*Gemeinschaft*	*Gesellschaft*	global ecumene
Moral values	traditional	inner-directed	other-directed

Folk culture and everyday life is characterized by being local, face to face, personal, spontaneous, intimate, and traditional. People are just there in each other's presence. Meaning arises in this context of interaction. It must be understood in terms of the relationship between the persons engaged in dialogue. But as soon as the situation dissolves the meaning vanishes, only recorded in the memory of those actors who participated in the situation. Meaning in this context is thus invisible and inaccessible to others. Folk culture represents roots. It is archaic.

High culture and intellectual life is often national with regard to media of externalization and distribution. On the other hand, it is often universal with regard to the questions with which it is concerned and the meanings and values that are conveyed. The written text is the principal mode of externalization and serves as a model, though other media (art, music, film, etc.) are also employed. Characteristic of the written text is that it is elaborated, its meaning is not necessarily related to or dependent upon the author as a person. Meaning is usually multi-layered. Understanding may require acts of interpretation.

Mass culture and post-modern life (in lack of a better term) are global. The media and electronic communications are essential conveyors of meaning, images, stereotypes, and beliefs. Meanings are ambiguous and diversity is a virtue. The range of mass culture is extremely broad reaching out to the whole world (an effect of media technology) but at the same time, and because of this, it is rather shallow and short-lived. Deconstruction is the mode of understanding.[1]

Different folk cultures will coexist in a multi-ethnic state but not always be accessible to one another. Many products of high culture will transcend ethnic divisions, but because high culture depends heavily upon the written text there will be language barriers making certain aspects of high culture inaccessible to those who don't speak or understand the language in question. Mass culture is dependent on the *lingua franca* of popular music, aviation, electronic communication, and social anthropology – English. Multiculturality involves all this diversity.

Concluding Remarks

Cultural differences of a kind have probably existed ever since Palaeolithic man moved out of his original East African homelands. It is reasonable to assume that cultural frontiers are as old as cultural differences, and, furthermore, that multicultural societies at least have been in existence in frontier regions.

The main argument of this chapter is that the speeding up of technological and social change, and the shrinking of the globe through modern communications technology have given rise to new and complex forms of multicultural relationships. Traditional, elaborate and post-modern cultural expressions interact in previously unforeseen ways across time and space. The movement of people, capital, and ideas challenges ingrained conceptions of the nation-state.

Note

1   I have tried to assemble some ideas about meaning and understanding from various thinkers, among them Johan Asplund (1987), Ulf Hannerz (1992), Paul Ricoeur (1981), David Riesman (1961), and Ferdinand Tönnies (1974).

References

Adepoju, Aderanti/Hammar, Tomas (1996) *International Migration in and From Africa*. Dakar: Population, Human Resources and Development in Africa.
Ålund, Aleksandra/Schierup, Carl-Ulrik (1991) *The Paradoxes of Multiculturalism*. Aldershot: Avebury.
Asplund, Johan (1987) *Det sociala livets elementära former*. Göteborg: Bokförlaget Korpen.
Boulding, Kenneth (1967) 'The Learning Process in the Dynamics of Total Societies', in Klausner, Samuel Z. (ed.), *The Study of Total Societies*. Garden City, N.Y.: Anchor Books.
Braudel, Fernand (1980) *On History*. London: Weidenfeld and Nicolson.
Braudel, Fernand (1981-84) *Civilization and Capitalism. 15th-18th Century*. London: Collins. First published in French 1979.
Castles, Stephen/Miller, Mark J. (1993) *The Age of Migration. International Population Movements in the Modern World*. London: McMillan Press.
Clifford, James (1994) 'Diasporas', *Cultural Anthropology* 9 (3): 302-338.
Cohen, Robin (1997) *Global Diasporas. An Introduction*. London: UCL Press.
Fraser, Julius T. (1990) *Of Time, Passion, and Knowledge*. Princeton: Princeton University Press.
Friedland, Roger/Boden, Deirdre (eds.) (1994) *Now, Here. Space, Time and Modernity*. Berkeley: University of California Press.
Geertz, Clifford (1973) *The Interpretation of Cultures*. New York: Basic Books.
Giddens, Anthony (1984) *The Constitution of Society*. Cambridge: Polity Press.
Hammar, Tomas (ed.) (1985) *European Immigration Policy*. Cambridge: Cambridge University Press.
Hammar, Tomas (1990) *Democracy and the Nation-state*. Aldershot: Gower.
Hammar, Tomas/Brochmann, Grete/Tamas, Kristof/Faist, Thomas (eds.) (1997) *International Migration, Immobility and Development. Multidisciplinary Perspectives*. Oxford: Berg.
Hannerz, Ulf (1992) *Cultural Complexity. Studies in the Social Organization of Meaning*. New York: Columbia University Press.
Hannerz, Ulf (1997) *Transnational Connections. Culture, People, Places*. London: Routledge.
Hägerstrand, Torsten (1991) *Om tidens vidd och tingens ordning*. Stockholm: Byggforskningsrådet.
Inglis, Christine (1996) *Multiculturalism: New Policy Responses to Diversity*. MOST Policy Papers 4. Paris: UNESCO.

Kern, Stephen (1983) *The Culture of Time and Space. 1880-1918*. Cambridge, Mass.: Harvard University Press.

Kubat, Daniel/Hoffmann-Nowotny, Hans-Joachim (1981) 'Migration. Towards a New Paradigm', *International Social Science Journal* 33 (2): 307-329.

Rapoport, Anatol (1967) 'Mathematical, Evolutionary, and Psychological Approaches to the Study of Total Societies', in Klausner, Samuel Z. (ed.), *The Study of Total Societies*. Garden City, N.Y.: Anchor Books.

Rex, John (1994) 'The Nature of Ethnicity in the Project of Migration', *Innovation. The European Journal of Social Science* 7 (3): 207-217.

Ricoeur, Paul (1981) *Hermeneutics and the Human Sciences*. Cambridge: Cambridge University Press.

Riesman, David (1961) *The Lonely Crowd*. New Haven: Yale University Press.

Safran, William (1991) 'Diasporas in Modern Societies: Myths of Homeland and Return', *Diaspora* 1 (1): 83-99.

Smith, Anthony D. (1986) *The Ethnic Origin of Nations*. Oxford: Basil Blackwell.

Tilly, Charles (1978) 'Migration in Modern European History', in McNeill, W./Adams, R. (eds.), *Human Migration. Patterns and Policies*. Bloomington: Indiana University Press.

Tylor, Edward B. (1958) *Primitive Culture. Researches into the Development of Mythology, Philosophy, Religion, Art and Customs*. Gloucester, Mass.: Peter Smith.

Tönnies, Ferdinand (1974) *Community and Association*. London: Routledge and Kegan Paul. First published 1887 as *Gemeinschaft und Gesellschaft. Abhandlung des Communismus und Socialismus als empirischer Culturformen*, Leipzig.

van der Veer, Peter (1995) *Nation and Migration. The Politics of Space in the South Asian Diaspora* Philadelphia: University of Pennsylvania Press.

Westin, Charles/Dingu-Kyrklund, Elena (1997) *Reducing Immigration, Reviewing Integration*. Stockholm: CEIFO Press.

CHAPTER 3

Changing Representations of the Other in France: The Mirror of Migration

Catherine de Wenden

Introduction

The presence of the Other is often not well accepted. Meanwhile, the Other attempts to construct a distinct identity contrasting the national identity of an opponent by whom he feels rejected. What emerges from these oppositions is a re-territorialization of identities based on reconstructed ethnic or religious solidarities. Frontiers are being erected in this European context, inside the French nation-state and within the daily life of everyone (Badie, 1995). Paradoxically, this occurs at a time when immigration has become transnational through its references, choices and through European citizenship. This generates a strange dialectic – the imaginary of the Other both shares in the definition that the political community makes for itself and sometimes creates plural allegiances in a renewed definition of citizenship.

Images of the Other

The Other has been at the centre of French society's questioning of itself throughout the nineteenth and twentieth centuries, when it increasingly came in contact with foreigners through colonization and decolonization, wars, the collapse of great empires and the coming of refugees, stateless people, new French and new foreigners, the development of mass migration and family reunion. In more recent times immigrants have participated in the life of the city and are no longer simply workers. The globalization of exchanges and migratory flows has meant that the daily and private life of the Other has entered more general public life, when in the past she/he was confined to an exoticism and a cultivated curiosity, or restricted to the public world of work, associations and trade unions.

This 'otherness' in daily life, which existed before and did not attract any attention, is not well perceived and accepted because today it has become politicized. Today, politics is meant to be in charge of daily life, of the apparently 'trivial' dimensions such as 'exclusion', 'smells', housing, school, religion, and marriage. Since the 1980s and its politicization, the discourse on immigration has been used as a dividing-line between political parties (Cavanna, 1978; Chirac, 1991).

It is in this politicized and oppositional context that the Other has built an identity for himself, which is a reconstructed one made on the basis of a rejection by an opponent who also builds an identity in opposition: those who declare themselves as 'Arabs' or 'Muslims' are confronted by the 'authentic French' (*Français de souche*). Two processes thus appear simultaneously – a differentialist racism, as Michel Wieviorka terms it, and daily integration (Wieviorka, 1995; Tribalat, 1995).

One can observe a re-territorialization of identities based on ethnic or religious solidarities, which are often reconstructed, according to Bertrand Badie (1995), while immigration is becoming transnational through its references, choices and through European citizenship. The imaginary of the Other contributes to the definition the political community is making of itself, sometimes creating an allegiance through opposition.

Today, in contexts of unemployment, a crisis of class allegiance, and of European unification, frontiers are being set up within the nation-state and inside its social texture, because they have disappeared – for Europeans – in the external world. A century ago, the image of Germany had an influential role in the construction of the French myth of national homogeneity, in the making up of memory as it has been described by Alfred Grosser (Grosser, 1971). Between the World Wars, the stereotype of the Jew, who was distrusted as far as his allegiances were concerned, contributed to the negative construction of an exclusive nationalism of withdrawal against a universalist citizenship. Today, the Arab-Muslim is the one who is the target of the worst myths.

The Other, Close and also Far-away

Who is the 'Other'? The definition of the Other is plural, because definitions and solidarities vary throughout the years, destroying the traditional frontiers and setting up new ones, especially if the Other resembles oneself or is a neighbour, a frontiersman or a half-breed.

Since the mid-nineteenth century, representations of the Other have succeeded one another as the migrant categories have changed. However, despite these changes in representation the criteria of otherness have almost been invariable: religion (be it Christian, Jewish or Muslim), health (syphilis, AIDS), politics (traitors, dubious allegiances, military service) and communitarianism which distances one's group from universalistic values, assimilation and integration.

Up until World War I the frontiersman, who was often a worker, represented the Other in everyday life in a country which was in need of manpower and soldiers: Italian or Swiss painters, German shoemakers or tailors, Savoy workers in all small trades. As early as 1848, violence was growing: French workers saw them as dangerous competitors, Proudhon started a campaign against them, and anti-Italian feeling spread all over the Isère department, the 1849 law dealing with the expulsion of foreigners who were characterized by some as "dangerous and a nuisance". In 1883, in the weekly *L'Economiste Français*, Paul Leroy Beaulieu became alarmed at the progressive 'invasion of France by foreigners' (Leroy Beaulieu, 1883). He supported the nationalist target to 'make Frenchmen out of foreigners', that is, mainly soldiers. Great industry, however, was in favour of a mobile migrant labour force, against protectionists and workers. In Leroy Beaulieu's view, Italians were the most undesirable immigrants because of their tendency not to mix with the population and to live together "like soldiers who camp in enemy land".

Some observers were already anxious about the assimilationist theory, when faced with the dilemma of demographic loss or the collapse of national identity (Blanc, 1901). The foreigner was viewed as the wrongly assimilated, the one who was most ready to profit from the national wealth without paying anything in return, especially the blood tribute in military service. He was also viewed as a competitor (as testified by the 1893 Aigues Mortes' carnage of seven Italians) and sometimes the delinquent. When the Great War was immanent, the image of the traitor became prominent, with the foreboding collective fear that a foreign state may use its nationals in France to organize or prolong strikes in order to gain a competitive advantage over French industry. In 1889, the Painters' Union of Nancy refused access to 'foreigners and Jews'. The Dreyfus Affair also revealed another round of such suspicions of foreign interference and of a lack of loyalty on the eve of a major war.

World War I accentuated these fears: the 2 August 1914 decree compelled all foreigners to declare their nationality to the local administration where they resided. German and Austro-Hungarian nationals were encouraged to leave the territory and if they refused, they were under obligation to evacuate North-East and South-East France.

The Other as a Danger: the Silent Invasion and the Social, Political and Health Risks

The interwar period was marked by a tightening of policies towards foreigners. In 1931, France had 3 million foreigners and became the first immigration country in the world (with the immigrants' share in the total population reaching almost 7%), overtaking even the United States. But, the crisis brought about a virulent xenophobic wave, entailing the repatriation of foreigners and protective measures for the national labour force. A feeling that foreigners were a danger for public health spread in public opinion, especially concerning syphilis, a stereotype about immigration from Algeria, although tuberculosis was more frequent and the Messali Hadj's *Etoile Nord Africaine* was trying to mobilize around Islam. Islam was rarely perceived as a danger and the conservatives thought that the population's submission to it could distract them from political and social activism.

The image of the delinquent was also quite widespread. In the classical work of Georges Mauco, the North Africans were described as fifteen times more criminal than the French, followed by the Polish and the Italians, whose Catholic traditionalism was seen as a major obstacle to their assimilation (Mauco, 1932; Schor, 1985). Others were developing the thesis of surreptitious invasions: sexual (the rape of women), political (plotting within the Popular Front), social (the undesirable competitors) and sanitary (France as Europe's cesspit). Some like Dr Martial (1934) advocated the selection of foreigners according to four criteria: race, nation, family and health. Some denounced the Popular Front as 'the consecration of the allogeneous' reign' and others finally perceived the reception of Spanish refugees as a risk for internal security and the financial balance, all these issues being marked by a virulent anti-Semitism (Oualid, 1939).

From Immigration to Islam

The 1945-1974 period was marked by the relative absence of the Other in public and political discourses, as she/he was mainly confined to his/her world of work (consisting of immigrants' residences, workplaces, coffee shops, trade unions and associations). The other of everyday life was mainly a single man, a foreign worker, with regard to whom the dichotomy of the class struggle seemed to transcend any other categorization to the point of forgetting that immigrants had a religion, a culture, a family, an emotional life (Ben Jelloun, 1985). Sociological surveys and press coverage were mainly interested in the 'revolutionary vanguard of advanced capitalism' or contrary to that, in the alienated lumpenproletariat. This somewhat monolithic view of immigration hid the other dimensions of foreign presence in France for many years (de Wenden, 1987).

The 1980s and the definitive settlement of immigrants gave rise to other imaginaries in the irresistible move of immigration to the centre of political debates. The 1983-1984 car industry conflicts suddenly revealed to French public opinion that a part of the immigrants had a religion – Islam – that in the past had been private, hidden and shameful, but was now being collectively and publicly negotiated in French society. Immigrants and their children, the 'second generation', had by now gained a greater daily visibility in urban neighbourhoods, in the housing estates, and in schools. Their presence was reflected in new debates on citizenship, multiculturalism, integration, identity, civic behaviour, and political allegiances.

However, some people became worried about basic French identity and values in this fast-changing context. After some insidious questions had been brought forward by the extreme-right about the new French 'despite themselves' 'without knowing or wishing it' who 'were not deserving it', a first (and then unsuccessful) attempt was launched to reform French nationality law in 1987. According to Bruno Etienne this debate "revealed more about French society than about Islam" (Etienne, 1990). Mosques and prayer-rooms, believers crouching down in the streets, religious militants and trade unionists, arranged marriages, polygamy, headscarfs at school all conferred a huge variety of images of Islam in daily life, and as such they were carried by the media and became the predominant representation in political debate. Islam, the second religion of France, appeared as a poor people's religion, dominated and still embedded in traditional and rural practices and cults. Henceforth immigrants have been identified with Muslims: earlier visions of an exotic Islam give way to the images of a daily Islamic presence built on a few shock images, perceived as anachronistic and dangerous and very unlike the pacific Islam of the majority of immigrants.

In certain episodes such as the Rushdie affair, headscarf affair, and the Gulf War, Islam appeared as a cultural and a security challenge: politics and daily life, private and public, the internal and international issues were all conflated together. The fear of a fifth column with dubious allegiances takes shape. The Muslim (that is, the Maghrebian, or more specifically Algerian) becomes the ideal-typical foreigner, often defined as a fundamentalist or represented as a terrorist fighting against French and Western identity. Attempts to build a community identity appear as an alternative solution: a denial of citizenship. However, large-scale surveys show that Algerians and their families are the most integrated in France with regard to language, schooling, marriage, and religious practice, even though they tend to be strongly discriminated against in entry to the labour and housing markets (Tribalat, 1995). But being built on mediatized stereotypes and imaginaries of a static Islam which appears unchangeable even in a migratory context, public opinion is only distantly aware of such an evolution. Other stereotypes add to those of 'invasion'

(Valéry Giscard d'Estaing, 1989), 'smells' (Jacques Chirac, 1991), and deficits in family allowances and social security: the proselyte bearded Islamic fanatic, the terrorist, and the home-confined Muslim woman. In short, the Islam of the Other in everyday life is 'the opium of the people'.

Living with the Other

In the early 1990s, the belated awareness that the populations of extra-European origin – a new dividing line which has replaced the earlier one between nationals and foreigners – have definitively settled is still widely resented. A strange amalgam confounds first-generation immigrants, who have grown older and are often unemployed and who have sometimes lost their workers' identity, with the youth born out of immigration, who are more often French citizens, and with the asylum-seekers and illegal immigrants. An increasing feeling of both internal and external insecurity and individualism feeds this imaginary.

The Illegal, the Muslim and the Excluded: a Suspicious Combination

Although there is a progressive shift of the boundaries between 'them' and 'us', three social figures come to the forefront in mediatized everyday life: the illegal immigrant, the fundamentalist and the excluded. The immigrants' image still mentally conserves the attributes defining them in the 1970s, with some discrepancies between representation and facts. But present reality is quite different. While the immigrant populations were, in the past, sociologically and economically more homogeneous, today we witness a diversification of populations and trajectories which involves the arrival of new immigrants, the development of elites or semi-elites who are often transnational actors in search of a double positive insertion, asylum-seekers resulting from the globalization of migration flows and networks, and, in spite of prevailing unemployment and exclusion, a progressive access of youth of immigrant origin into the middle class. Still, others are committed to a quest for a collective ethnic and religious identity, as today it is better to assert oneself as a Muslim rather than an unemployed, especially when it concerns an identity which disturbs. It is the Maghrebians who suffer most from the contemptible images portrayed above, who at the same time seem to be most smoothly integrated in daily life. The frontiersmen who act as mediators between the various groups best exemplify the combination of localism and transnationalism (economic, cultural, religious, matrimonial, Mafioso) which characterizes contemporary immigration.

Being economically desired but politically undesirable the illegal often assumes rapidly changing features. She/he is at the same time familiar and close, because she/he is usually employed in the domestic services or the building industry, and unfamiliar and distant, because she/he has come from far-away countries less well known than the traditional sending states. Even though the illegal seeks to remain socially and politically invisible she/he accrues several negative and contradictory representations with his economic function. Many settled immigrants, which today are viewed incorrectly as 'well integrated', such as the Portuguese, have started as illegals.

The Muslim represents a different version of the 'Other' in daily life, although the identification of immigration with Islam is quite recent. Neither the privately hidden Islam of the foreign workers of the growth years or of World War I soldiers, who had been thanked for their engagement by the building of the Great Mosque in Paris, nor the demand for Islam's legitimacy during the long Sonacotra strike (1976-1981) left a strong image of immigrant Islam. What has changed since is that Islam is now perceived as a collective force with a political vocation proselytizing in a secular state, defying local citizenship in the socially excluded urban neighbourhoods and manipulated from abroad creating a risk of foreign interference in French affairs. A return to a quiet Islam among the old generation is confounded with the visible and public manifestations of a reconstructed Islamic identity among the youth who have failed in their school careers. These practices are often ostentatious rather than emotionally based in faith but are interpreted by public opinion as an insurmountable barrier for the acquisition of citizenship and French identity.

The excluded, defined as living outside the margins of mass society, has caused a rupture in recent socio-economic debates. The evocation of this figure is often accompanied by another discourse on the collapse of class society and the classical institutions of the workers' movement. This marks another frontier, that of the poor and dangerous rather than working classes, who are responsible for urban violence, delinquency, insecurity, suburban disorder and neighbourhood-based tribalism. The figure of the excluded was already present in the sociological literature on the Fourth World present in the immigrants' slums of the 1970s, but it has for long been overshadowed by that of the illegal, of the asylum-seeker (suspected to be phoney) and of the Muslim. The collapse of civic associations and movements in the suburban peripheries, the destructuring of families which is certainly a cost of integration, and the emergence of drugs, youth gangs, unemployment, and anomie illustrate the landscape of ordinary exclusion in the 1990s. Other forms of exclusion, such as that of the immigrants growing old in the collective hostels, or that of the rejected asylum-seekers who are barred from employment remain less visible.

Other stereotypes, developed on either side of politics, also represent the Other in everyday life, not as an individual but as a collective symbol: the invasion syndrome, tinted with security concerns (linked to fast demographic growth), presumed social costs, polygamy which is considered as uncivil, a breach of the social contract and a cultural danger (but is a practice only among a very small group of black African Muslims in France). Islam is thus seen as the new geopolitical challenge after the fall of the Berlin Wall.

Other confusions have also a long life, such as the amalgam between the illegal, who is really a foreign worker, and the suburban youth, who is really a French citizen but has been recently harassed by questioning his allegiance to French society on issues such as the reform of nationality law, the Gulf War, military service or terrorism (de Wenden, 1995).

The Other as Another Self

Faced with these troubled images, does the Other in daily life symbolize a deadlock in which the community of citizens (Schnapper, 1994) has become unable to define itself, and instrumentalizes for that purpose a partly fabricated otherness of immigrants? In the United States, it is the language question which has served to define the Other in everyday life; in France it seems to be religion, which is somewhat paradoxical in a secular state. The Other has contributed to create a negative consensus: in the past, it was the Other as a neighbour, the German or the Jew, which has helped in fabricating the myth of national unity by blurring the other cleavages between regions and social classes. Today, the extreme right is trying to constitute a *tricolore* community of blue, white and red, in opposition to the Maghrebian, but also the European. However, the Other in everyday life, can also be the rich (the capitalist), the poor (*'la misère du monde'*), women, children, the old, the sick. Beyond one Other there always hides another one, who allows the former to become more legitimate, more 'equal'. Every society defines itself in the Other's mirror whether in dialogue, in love or in hate, but always painfully. This is the lesson of 150 years of immigration in France.

References

Badie, B. (1995) *La fin des territoires*. Paris: Fayard.

Ben Jelloun, T. (1985) *La plus haute des solitudes*. Paris: Seuil.

Blanc, A. (1901) *L'immigration en France et le travail national, thèse de droit*. Université de Lyon.

Cavanna, F. (1978) *Les Ritals*. Paris.

Chirac, J. (1991) Public speech at a RPR gathering, 7 May 1991.

de Wenden, C. (1987) *Citoyenneté, Nationalité et Immigration*. Paris: Arcantère.

de Wenden, C. (1995) 'Minorités immigrées: la question de l'allégeance nationale', in Remond, René (ed.), *L'Etat Nation et son avenir*. Paris: FNSP.

Etienne, B. (1990) *L'Islam en France*. Paris: Editions du CNRS.

Giscard d'Estaing, V. (1989) *Figaro Magazine*, 25 November 1989.

Grosser, A. (1971) *Germany in our Time*, translated by Paul Stephenson. New York: Praeger.

Leroy Beaulieu, P. (1883) *L'Economiste Français*.

Martial, R. (1934) *La race française*. Paris: Mercure de France.

Mauco, G. (1932) *Les étrangers en France*. Paris: A. Colin.

Oualid, W. (1939) *Esprit*, 01.07.1939.

Schnapper, D. (1994) *La Communauté des Citoyens*. Paris: Gallimard.

Schor, R. (1985) *L'opinion française et les étrangers, 1919-1939*. Paris: Publications de la Sorbonne.

Tribalat, M. (1995) *Faire France*. Paris: La Découverte.

Wieviorka, M. (1995) *Le racisme en France*. Paris: La Découverte.

CHAPTER 4

Multiculturalism à la Canadian and Intégration à la Québécoise. Transcending their Limits

Danielle Juteau / Marie McAndrew / Linda Pietrantonio

Introduction

Multiculturalism or Integration? is the question which defines the terms of the current debate in Quebec and in Canada as a whole, a public debate which extends far beyond the walls of the academy. It is by no means a new one and raises normative issues concerning what is 'desirable' with respect to the integration of minoritized populations as well as the society as a whole.

The terms of this debate are often presented in an oppositional, antithetical way. In English Canada, multiculturalism as policy is criticized in the name of equality, the latter being contrary to the promotion of distinction or differentiation. Such a criticism advocates a unity that is impossible to reconcile with the constant insistence on the population's ethnic diversity (Bissoondath, 1994). In Quebec, the debate has taken the form of a mega-objection which presents this policy as negating the special status of Quebec within the Confederation and as being completely different from Quebec's policy of integration. Moreover, while it is common practice in Quebec to intrinsically link the emergence of Canadian multiculturalism and 'the Quebec Question', in English Canada there is a tendency to reduce intercultural relations to linguistic policies and to affirm that Quebec imposes assimilationism on all immigrants.

The antithetical formulas characteristic of these debates simplify the complexity of the issues surrounding relations between majorities and minorities, just as they reduce complex social phenomena, namely national policies and ideologies, to a single factor, a powerful and Machiavellian actor such as the prime minister or the government. In both cases, however, these criticisms, which often have opposite goals and are formulated as much by the left as the right, as much by immigrants as non-immigrants, tend to conceal the rejection of an ideology espousing the desirability of pluralism, which we call normative pluralism.[1] These issues are not something to be ignored. They are fundamental not only for Quebec and Canada as a whole, but also elsewhere in the world, in the United States, Australia, Great Britain, France and Germany, not to mention Bosnia-Hercegovina or Rwanda.

Our analysis first includes a succinct review of the historical context that gave rise to multiculturalism as ideology and policy and an overview of its development since 1971. Multiculturalism is conceived as a field of struggle opposing various forces and actors, as a site of power relations between differentiated and hierarchized groups which are constituted into ethnic and/or national collectivities. This will be followed by a comparison between *'multiculturalism à la Canadian'* and *'intégration à la Québécoise'*, drawing out their similarities and differences. We will then present recent critiques of these policies as well as some of the emerging responses. Finally, we will examine the appropriateness of the opposition between multiculturalism and integration as well as the relevance of the new criticisms which are linked to the political and ethical debate over the so-called limits of pluralism.

The Struggle for a Pluralist Model

Homogenizing Canada

The British North America Act of 1867 had implemented a certain level of structural pluralism in Canada, which resulted from the struggle between competing national groups. The federal government developed a national policy guided by an assimilationist orientation. In its symbolic and cultural dimension, the process of nation-building was oriented toward the constitution of a British society in Canada. Immigrants establishing themselves in the country, largely in western Canada, were expected to become Canadians; i.e., to speak English within an institutional system modelled along British lines (Breton, 1984: 127-128). Anglo-conformity and nativism were dominant ideologies, and the project of constructing a 'white' Canada, based as much on the marginalization of aboriginal peoples as on the selection of 'white' immigrants, occupied the political scene from the mid-nineteenth century until the late 1960s. Aboriginal peoples (called Indians) were placed under state tutelage by the 1876 Act, the long-term hope being that they too would be assimilated. The French fact would be restricted as much as possible to Quebec, and a series of legislative measures, namely the abolition of French schools in Manitoba and in Ontario as well as the abolition of French as an official language in Manitoba represent steps in that direction.

Clearly then, the increase in cultural pluralism in Canada had little to do with the existence of a pluralist ideology nor was it the outcome of a formal political will. But, as we will see, normative pluralism would develop in Canada despite a clear preference for an assimilationist world view.

Assimilationism in Question

Following World War II, several factors combined to disturb the homogenizing vision provided by the assimilationist ideology and to undermine this specific process of nation-building in Canada: the growing flow, at the international level, of labour and capital, the breakup of colonial empires, and the emergence of a specifically Québécois nationalism. The delegitimation of ideologies central to colonialism was accompanied by a critique of Eurocentrism and a rejection of economic, political and cultural forms of domination. Fanon's *Peau Noire Masques Blancs* (1952) explores the devastating consequences of cultural domination, that is, of the imposition, by dominant groups, of their cultural models upon subordinated groups. The assimilationist model was also under siege in the United States, where an emerging social movement claimed that 'black is beautiful'. Franklin Frazier suggests that *The Failure of the Negro Intellectual* (1962) too readily accepted assimilationism as a means, as a pathway to integration. In doing so, 'Negro' Americans had been cut from their roots and saw the destruction of their identity. The critique of assimilationism was even taken up in France, the bastion of jacobinism and republicanism, as exemplified, in the wake of May 1968, by claims voiced by the left to the *'droit à la différence'*.

Canada did not escape this movement which went beyond its borders as exogenous factors combined with endogenous ones to destabilize former models and old compromises. Demands for greater autonomy formulated by the new political and intellectual elites in Quebec led to the Royal Commission on Bilingualism and Biculturalism (1969), mandated to propose a new model for Canada and a new entente between the two 'founding' peoples. Quebec's claims incited ethnic groups to formulate their own demands, namely the recognition of their material and symbolic contribution to the construction of Canada, while 'native' leaders were also increasingly discontented. It is in the context of these diversified pressures that the passage from assimilationism to normative pluralism occurred, when Canada's prime minister announced in 1971 a policy of multiculturalism within a bilingual framework.

This emerging pluralism remained embedded in a liberal conception of formal equality between individual citizens. Equal partnership between the two 'founding' peoples was defined in linguistic and cultural terms. The 'Official Languages Act' adopted in 1969 (Government of Canada, 1969b) consecrates the equality between two languages and not between two linguistic communities. The 1969 White Paper of the Government of Canada on Indian Policy (Government of Canada, 1969a) proposes a vision of Canadian society founded on the equality between individual citizens. The Official Languages Act, the White Paper, and the multicultural policy each deal with a specific group: French-Canadians, Indians, and 'ethnics'; put together, they constitute an ensemble of integrated solutions based on a liberal view of society. But the ethnically neutral vision such as the one proposed, does not take into account the existence of economic, political, and cultural inequalities.

Early Criticisms and Transformations

Among the many criticisms of this policy as a myth, a hoax, a cynical policy aimed at buying the ethnic vote, a tool for ideological inculcation reproducing the power of the Anglo-Saxon elite, a representation of the Canadian nation that masks the relations of power upon which it has constructed itself, a policy more conducive to division than to unity (Juteau, 1997), two are worth singling out. First, some observers such as J. Porter (1975) argued that the maintenance of cultural diversity was contrary to the liberal principle of equal opportunities, foreshadowing today's debate which opposes 'equality' and difference. Second, this policy was defined by Quebec intellectuals and politicians as sabotaging the idea of Canada as a partnership between two nations or, at least, between two equal partners. The policy was also later criticized by a new 'ethnic' leadership which claimed it was geared to 'white' ethnics and did not deal with the material problems they were facing.

In response to these many criticisms, the policy has undergone many transformations since its inception in 1971, adapting to "demographic change, new political pressures from ethnocultural minorities, and shifting state priorities" (Stasiulis, 1991: 84). Even though the newly-created administrative units were criticized for insisting too much on reconciliation and not enough on the demands being made, new and different interests were acknowledged. As a result, objectives and budgets shifted towards issues related to heritage languages, racism and discrimination. Despite all its imperfections and continuing criticisms, the policy enjoyed considerable popularity outside Quebec in the late-1980s, the height of which was in 1988 when the policy became law. This Act incorporates a new **Multiculturalism** policy based on three principles: (1) multiculturalism is a central feature of Canadian citizenship; (2) every Canadian has the freedom to choose to enjoy, enhance and share his or her heritage; (3) the federal government has the responsibility to promote multiculturalism throughout its departments and agencies (*Multiculturalism Canada*, 1989: 17). In 1989, a separate Department of Multiculturalism and Citizenship is created in order to strengthen: "(...) the solidarity of the Canadian people by enabling all members of Canadian society to participate fully and without discrimination in defining and building the nation's future" (*Multiculturalism Canada*, 1989: 9).

Redefining Boundaries and Identities in Quebec

While the Quebec 'question' constitutes one of the factors which brought on multiculturalism, the adoption of normative pluralism in Canada will in turn exert a determining influence on the process of nation-building in Quebec, by enhancing the value of diversity and questioning the ideal of cultural homogeneity. Defining a nationalist project in Quebec without asserting a commitment to pluralism became increasingly difficult.

In its publication *Autant de façons d'être Québécois* (1981), the Quebec government had already proposed a vision that rejected the American model of the melting-pot and the Canadian model of multiculturalism. It wanted to avoid the pitfalls of cultural homogeneity without adopting the principles of multiculturalism, perceived as the static juxtaposition of diverse groups. This document also states that the development of Quebec's various cultural groups requires the vitality of Quebec as a French society. In other words, cultural pluralism will be encouraged within the context of a French-speaking society but its acceptance would not preclude the adoption of measures ensuring the strengthening of the French language in Quebec.

In that document, individuals are differentiated into two mutually exclusive categories: members of the '*Québécois*' nation and those belonging to 'cultural communities', which include all ethnic minorities, such as the British, the Italians, the Greeks, etc. The members of the cultural communities, although residing in Quebec, were thus not defined as *Québécois*. Ten years later the boundaries of the *Québécois* nation were officially redefined in more inclusive terms; in the document *Au Québec pour bâtir ensemble. Énoncé de politique en matière d'immigration et d'intégration* (1990), the expression *Québécois des communautés culturelles* replaced *communautés culturelles*. All residents of Quebec, irrespective of ethnic origin, are now defined as *Québécois*. Furthermore, the use of '*communautés culturelles*' is presented in a very critical light, as a necessary evil acknowledging two sociological facts: the persistence of an attachment to one's ethnic group by some Quebecers of non French-Canadian background and the persistence of obstacles to full participation linked to ethnic 'origin'. The statement is also very clear on the rejection of any perspective that would postulate a necessary and automatic link between ethnic origin and ethnic identity.

This tentative redefinition of national boundaries nonetheless remains an uncompleted process. Although less and less used publicly, the expression *'Québécois de souche'* (authentic Québécois) indicates the persisting existence of internal boundaries, which define a core of real nationals, surrounded at the periphery by culturally diverse circles of subordinates. One must also recognize that this boundary is maintained in part by the ethnic groups themselves – especially older groups who are traditionally linguistically assimilated to the anglophones – who sometimes even resist pluralistic discourses or interventions emanating from the francophone majority (McAndrew, 1995). In addition to the debate concerning the degree of pluralism that should be allowed within a framework provided by a common citizenship, a debate which it shares with Canada and other societies, Quebec must also deal with an unresolved conflict of allegiance between groups.

Nonetheless, the early 1990s did witness a flurry of activities and debates around the ideology and practice of interculturalism in Quebec, which were often couched in terms of the management of diversity and reasonable accommodation. Quebec and Canada as a whole seemed to be articulating a civic type of nationalism, transcending both the ethnic and jacobinist-assimilationist models.

Multiculturalism à la Canadian and Intégration à la Québécoise

Similarities and Differences

When we compare the *Québécois* policy of integration to the policy of multiculturalism (which is not officially an integration policy, even if it presupposes integration practices), one must take into account the changes undergone by the federal policy adopted in 1971.

At the time of writing the *Énoncé de politique du Québec*, the dominant vocabulary at the federal level had shifted: 'participation' was spoken of as a synonym for 'integration', and institutional adaptation was emphasized. Maintaining cultures was out while valuing and acknowledging diversity was in. There was talk of a feeling of belonging and loyalty, but little left of identity. These themes are echoed in *l'Énoncé de politique en matière d'immigration et d'intégration* (Gouvernement du Québec, 1990).

In spite of rhetoric to the converse, multiculturalism and interculturalism share many similarities (Pietrantonio/Juteau/McAndrew, 1996). Both policies celebrate pluralism and reject old-fashioned assimilationism as a mode of managing relations between majorities and minorities. They entertain similar relationships to linguistic pluralism to the extent that the latter is more and more presented as offering economic and political advantages in light of globalization. In both cases, language and culture are subsidized with a view to integration or to national interest. Both give priority to social and cultural issues, and focus on racism, participation, *rapprochement* and the reduction, as much as politically possible, of cultural maintenance programmes. Both recognize that the actualization of equality requires more than formal equality; that is, they recognize that there are differentiations in the practice of equality. There is also a gradual shift in subsidies to communities towards public institutions, as well as a willingness on the part of the Quebec *Ministère des Affaires internationales, de l'Immigration et des Communautés Culturelles* (MAIICC) and Heritage Canada (the federal department) to develop wider horizons in response to accusations that they were serving specific clienteles.

However, these similarities should not mask their differences. The Quebec Policy Statement pays less attention to anti-racism than does the multiculturalism policy, in spite of promises that such issues will be addressed. For the moment, however, there is nothing in that direction, not even in the *Projet de Loi no. 18* establishing the *Ministère des Relations avec les Citoyens et de l'Immigration*. Indeed, it only reaffirms its general commitment in favour of equal participation. A second difference concerns the fact that the Policy Statement in Quebec is seen as more clearly liberal, in the philosophical sense of the term, in its relationship to the individual and the community than the wording of the Law on Multiculturalism adopted by the federal government in 1988. This trend has paradoxically gained support for the *Énoncé de politique* from those citizens – especially elite and intellectual – who resist their potential confinement within the boundaries of a community that multiculturalism, so they argue, imposes on them (Bissoondath, 1994). The Quebec Policy Statement also deals more explicitly than the Multiculturalism Act with the possible contradictions between human rights and the acceptance of pluralism, since it identifies the respect for democratic values, sexual equality, non-violence and children's rights as non-negotiable elements of the pluralist consensus. Nevertheless, it must be understood that the Canadian ambiguity lies more in its discourses than in its practices, for the latter are embedded in the same legal framework.[2] Finally, the Canadian policy on Multiculturalism emphasizes there is no official culture in this country while the Quebec statement reaffirms the pluralism of *la culture québécoise*. This is more than a simple nuance. The difference is crucial, since the existence of a *culture québécoise* is here posited.

Notwithstanding these differences, one clearly notes that both attempt to shift from a cultural paradigm to one that is more civic and social in nature. In both cases, this shift has met with similar resistances from older communities who often regret the culturalist paradigm and from some members of the dominant groups (Francophone and Anglophone) who are not eager to share their power with disadvantaged minorities. Such misgivings have been expressed in Quebec in terms of the 'limits' of pluralism. One thinks here of the passionate response to the French 'headscarf affair' in Quebec, while in English Canada the need to define core Canadian values has received considerable support.

Multiculturalism in Question

New Criticisms

The barrage of criticisms which have been formulated with regard to multiculturalism since the early 1990s may seem surprising. Above and over former critiques, what now emerges is a feeling that too much diversity is anti-egalitarian, divisive and responsible for breaking up the country. Such views are expressed by public opinion, ethnocultural groups, political parties and some academics (Abu-Laban/Stasiulis, 1992).

Mosaic Madness by Bibby (1990) provides a good example of the new criticisms. Normative pluralism, perceived as promoting relativism and heightening divisions, is now under siege. This rejection of pluralist models has been supported by public opinion, the dominant feeling being that Canada must define a national vision and identify its core values, that it must search for commonalities rather than differences. As Abu-Laban and Stasiulis point out (1992: 370), the *Citizen's Forum on Canada's Future* (known as the Spicer Commission) recommended a refocusing of official multicultural policy so as to "welcome all Canadians to an evolving mainstream" (1991: 129). Pluralism, construed as more centrifugal than centripetal, should be replaced. Here, the meaning of integration is shifting backwards, and is conceived more in terms of a melting-pot, which has after all always implied the idea of an evolving mainstream.

While not all ethnic minority groups and associations reject multiculturalism, some individuals and groups do. Some feel the policy still over-emphasizes ideal interests at the expense of discrimination and exclusionary practices, others, whose most famous advocate is Bissoondath (1994), affirm that stressing differences hardens hatreds. The emphasis on ethnic diversity is incompatible with the promotion of unity and equality. This position resembles the critiques voiced by academics who originally felt that multiculturalism reinforced an essentialist view of ethnicity and culture (Moodley, 1983).

The more traditional criticisms of the promotion of 'differences' over equality are now coupled with questions about the compatibility of pluralism or multiculturalism with liberal (understood as egalitarian) democracy. These questions, as mentioned previously, were originally posed by sociologist John Porter (1975). Since he attributed social inequalities to cultural and ethnic variables (1965), he envisaged, not surprisingly, assimilationism as a means to eradicate them. The problem with this analysis resides in its blindness to the social relations structuring inequalities, which are more rooted in economic and power differentials than in cultural differences. Today's questions continue to focus on desirable forms of integration, both for ethnic groups and the society as a whole, and on the relation between pluralism and the actualization of equality. Some critics wonder whether such policies subordinate individual liberty to control by the community, while others argue that we should accept the preference for difference and particularism over universalism expressed in the name of authenticity by some collectivities.[3]

Governmental Fears and Responses

In the face of mounting criticisms, the political parties present on the federal scene have wavered in their support.[4] The populist Reform Party, in its 1991 statement of principles, demands the abolition of the Multiculturalism department and affirms that it "stands for the acceptance and integration of immigrants into the mainstream of Canadian life" (Reform Party of Canada, 1991: 35, in Abu-Laban/ Stasiulis, 1992: 373). The Progressive Conservatives, who had strengthened the administrative structure of the policy during their stay in power (1984-1993), saw the passing of a number of resolutions at its August 1991 convention. One called the Progressive Conservatives to "abandon the policy of Multiculturalism and foster a common national identity for one people living together in harmony as equal citizens, loyal to the Canadian ideal" (Abu-Laban/Stasiulis, 1992: 374). The left of centre New Democratic Party, during a convention also held in 1991, did not find it necessary to counter the new wave of criticisms. Finally, some deputies from the Liberal Party, which created the policy in the first place, are strongly against multiculturalism, arguing that it is divisive, ghettoizes ethnic groups and relegates them to an inferior rank. At its convention in 1992, the Liberal Party nonetheless reaffirmed its support of multiculturalism while endorsing Canadian citizenship.[5]

Stressing that we are all Canadian reminds one of a former Conservative prime minister, John Diefenbaker, who argued, in the late 1950s, for unhyphenated Canadians, a vision that led to the impasse of the 1960s. What is noteworthy is the incapacity, for many people, to recognize the existence of many identities, some of which are more inclusive than others. They find it difficult to conceive ethnic identities not only as multiple, contextual and changing, but also as functioning, sometimes, like a set of Russian dolls.

Both levels of government also responded to these pressures by articulating a new discourse on citizenship. When the newly-elected Liberal Party modified some of the administrative structures of the federal government in 1993, citizenship was linked to immigration rather than to multiculturalism and a new department, "Citizenship and Immigration Canada", was formed. Multiculturalism, although keeping a Secretary of State, no longer constituted a separate department and it became part of a wider department symbolically renamed Canadian Heritage. Furthermore, inside the federal bureaucracy, there has been a clear shift of influences and resources from the former Department of Multiculturalism towards the Department of Citizenship and Immigration whose preoccupations, due to its mandate, are much more centred on the integration of newcomers than on structural or cultural pluralism.

In Quebec, the law creating the new *Ministère des Relations avec les Citoyens et de l'Immigration* was widely supported and was applauded by the ethnic and the Anglophone press as well as by the Francophone one. Nonetheless, the reorganization of the former *Ministère des Affaires Internationales, des Communautés Culturelles et de l'Immigration* had many shortcomings. First, putting interculturalism at par with solidarity between the generations, defining pluralism in terms broader than its ethnic dimension,[6] and giving the new department responsibility for family matters, elders and youth, raised concerns about the specific problems of minorities being neglected. Moreover, the shift towards citizenship remains incomplete, since women, Anglophones and Aboriginals have been excluded from the mandate of the new department. Although this move is understandable from a political point of view, it gives the impression that real issues deserve specific agencies, while other clienteles do not. Finally, the department has kept its traditional functions of integrating immigrants to Quebec society. This juxtaposition reveals the ambiguity[7] of a commitment to a pluralist form of citizenship which also stresses the necessity of socializing newcomers to some core values. The debate that surrounded the rephrasing of the 1969 article stating the responsibility of "favouring the linguistic, social, and economic integration of immigrants to Quebec society, in particular to its francophone majority" (our translation), is most revealing. Indeed, what is required seems more than learning French and functioning in that language, but participating in the institutions of the majority. Although the words "in particular to the francophone majority" were dropped, the original presence of these words indicates the fragility of normative pluralism in Quebec, and, more so, of structural pluralism.

Finally, although both the Quebec and the Canadian states acknowledge the sociological existence of communities and their potential contribution to integration and participation, they (though less so in the wording of the 1988 Multiculturalism Act) supplement this acknowledgement with warnings about the limits, if not dangers, of what they call communitarianism. The latter is often rejected in terms of its ghettoizing effects which impede integration. Their critique of 'communitarianism' often masks their fear of demands voiced by certain groups which would lead to greater levels of structural pluralism, that is for greater control over institutions. While Canada for example is incapable of dealing adequately with claims of equal partnership coming from Quebec, so in turn Quebec cannot cope with many of the demands stemming from the Anglophone community. This is also exemplified in their respective treatment of First Nations. To move beyond the recognition of diversity and the celebration of difference, to achieve full equality between various ethnic and national collectivities coexisting within the boundaries of a given nation-state, remains a formidable challenge. It does imply treating the existence of ethnic neighbourhoods and schools, enclave economies and internally organized services as means of integration and pathways to equality rather than as factors of non-integration.

Post-Assimilationist Universalism?

The fact that so many individuals, groups and organizations have jumped on the bandwagon of multiculturalism-bashing requires serious consideration.

The accusations of ghettoization and maintenance of social inequalities do not stand up to the facts. This would be tantamount to attributing to multiculturalism phenomena that clearly precede it. The essentialization and naturalization of ethnic groups existed prior the policy of multiculturalism. Furthermore, if multiculturalism cannot abolish social inequalities, it is surely misguided to claim that it creates them.[8] One cannot help but remark that lurking behind these criticisms there seems to be the idea that the counter-models or the old models were and would be better. They evoke a nostalgia for a golden age in which majority/minority relations appeared to be much simpler, before multiculturalism, bilingualism, Aboriginal land claims, and turbans.[9] This is essentially the same nostalgia that ones finds in the longing for the relations between men and women, which were apparently much more harmonious before the arrival of feminism.

The problem with this approach, of course, is that the good old days were not so good, after all, as attested, among other things, by the tutelage of Aboriginals (Wotherspoon/Satzewich, 1993), the oppression of French-Canadians (McRoberts, 1988), the definition of racist immigration policies and the exploitation of immigrant labour, the constant presence of antisemitism (Abella/Troper, 1986) and other forms of racism and sexism.

Finally, as certain cynics have argued, if multiculturalism had ghettoized groups and maintained inequalities, it would not be as contested as it is today. In hindsight, one can also see that multiculturalism served as a mobilizing ideology for a heightened participation in public institutions. It allowed for the definition of a more inclusive discourse on the participation of minoritized groups within the political community (Abu-Laban/Stasiulis, 1992) and provided an ideological space for the erosion of the myth of national homogeneity.

We should, of course, remain vigilant with regard to unwarranted uses of the notion of difference as well as to an essentializing politics of difference. Culture must not be seen as static, as an unchanging baggage with which immigrants first arrive. It must be considered as process, as constantly transformed in the context of experiences related to immigration and insertion. Ethnic groups are continually engaged in the construction and transformation of their boundaries. Furthermore, multiculturalism and interculturalism must keep on addressing the issues of political, cultural, and economic inequalities. These two policies should not be defined only in terms of the 'others', that is the 'ethnics', neglecting the dominant group and the society as a whole. This requires questioning the very core of the society, of what is and wants to become, so that it redefines itself constantly, in such a way that boundaries are traversed and transcended, not reinforced. What is at stake here is the ethnocentrism of the dominant group (Moodley, 1983: 327); mainstream culture, both Canadian and *Québécois* must become 'multiculturalized'.

Thus, one cannot escape the uneasy feeling that much of the recent critiques are really directed at the pluralist model itself. Underlying such critiques of pluralism runs an underlying thread, which constructs an opposition between liberalism and communitarianism and between universalism and particularism.

Rather than debating the relative merits of universalism versus the recognition of difference, it is more fruitful to critically examine the foundations upon which this opposition is constructed. This would bring us to reflect on the construction of what Bader has called 'chauvinistic universalism', that is, a universalism of the dominant groups which in fact constitutes a pseudo-universalism (Bader, 1995). We would then discover that the dominant group identifies itself with universalism while it defines the minority in terms of its difference. The dominant group sees itself as *embodying the norm while the minoritized group is conceived as incar-*

nating la différence (Guillaumin, 1972). In other words, the dominant group does not see itself as different, as specific or particular. So when it articulates an ideology of universalism, it actually defends its specificity which it then imposes upon others. It then legitimized its policies, quite perversely we may add, in the name of egalitarianism, which would require that all citizens be treated equally.

When the social relations constitutive of dominant and subordinate groups are uncovered, we begin to see how they shape the very definition of what is universal and what is specific, and we discover that the politics of universalism and the politics of difference (Taylor, 1994) are indissociable and form a whole. Rather than opposing specificity to universalism, we can now acknowledge that universalism is a specificity, and specificity a universalism.

Thus, we do not propose that universalism as norm and ideal be rejected, but that it become more embracing than the pseudo-universalism it often is. Its pursuit must rest on the recognition of the power relations which constitute majorities and minorities. Questioning and making visible the basis upon which the latter are constructed would help dispel the confusion which still obscures the distinction between the right-wing defense of natural difference and the pluralist one of constructed historical diversity.

Notes

[1] While the presence of normative pluralism refers to the acceptance of pluralism as a desirable state, cultural and structural pluralism refer to what is, whether it is desired or not (Schermerhorn, 1970). Van den Berghe (1967) also differentiates cultural pluralism from structural pluralism. The latter involves institutional duplication, the differentiation of a society into analogous and parallel structures, such as religious and educational ones. Cultural pluralism, which can exist with or without structural pluralism, is not only produced by ethnic diversity, but also by class and gender.

[2] In fact, both the Canadian and Quebec Charter of rights are very similar.

[3] In the Canadian context, Taylor (1994) and Kymlicka (1995) represent two defenders of the claim of some groups to difference and particularism.

[4] The analysis of the reactions and responses of political parties at the federal level is based on Abu-Laban and Stasiulis' excellent and thorough analysis (1992).

[5] Although the Bloc Québécois sometimes attacks multiculturalism on the traditional basis that it jeopardizes the status of the Francophones in Canada (a curious preoccupation for an independist party), it has been the more systematic ally of the Liberal Party in this regard.

[6] As indicated by: 'il [le ministère] est chargé de promouvoir la solidarité entre les générations, en tenant compte des besoins des familles, des jeunes et des aînés, l'ouverture au pluralisme et

le rapprochement interculturel, favorisant ainsi l'appartenance à la société québécoise' (Gouvernement du Québec, 1996: 8).

7   More so than in the Canadian case where the laws governing Multiculturalism and Citizenship and Immigration are separate.

8   Also worth mentioning, are the difficulties in rigorously comparing the pluralist model with the Jacobin model and its resistance to the use of ethnicity in any attempted statistical 'performance' measure of integration.

9   This example refers to the struggle led by orthodox members of the Sikh community, who in the late 1980s fought to obtain permission to wear their turbans as headgear, rather than the traditional stetson so characteristic of the Royal Canadian Mounted Police (RCMP).

References

Abella, I.M./Troper, H.M. (1986) *None is too many: Canada and the Jews of Europe 1933-1948*. Toronto: Lester & Orphen Dennys.

Abu-Laban, Y./Stasiulis, D. (1992) 'Ethnic Pluralism under Siege: Popular and Partisan Opposition to Multiculturalism', *Canadian Public Policy* 18 (4): 365-386.

Bader, V. (1995) 'Benign Liberal Neutrality vs. Relational Ethnic Neutrality. Part I: Dilemmas of Affirmative Action', Conference Paper, Berg en Dal, The Netherlands, November 1995.

Bibby, R.W. (1990) *Mosaic Madness: The Poverty and Potential of Life in Canada*. Toronto: Stoddart.

Bissoondath, N. (1994) *Selling of Illusions. The Cult of Multiculturalism in Canada*. Toronto: Penguin Books.

Breton, R. (1984) 'The Production and Allocation of Symbolic Resources: An Analysis of the Linguistic and Ethnocultural Fields in Canada', *Revue Canadienne de sociologie et d'anthropologie* 21: 123-244.

Citizen's Forum on Canada's Future (Spicer Commission) (1991) *Report to the People and the Government of Canada*. Ottawa: Le Forum.

Fanon, F. (1952) *Peau Noire Masques Blancs*. Paris: Éditions du Seuil.

Frazier, F. (1962) 'The Failure of the Negro Intellectual', pp. 267-279 in *On Race Relations. Selected Writings*. Chicago and London: University of Chicago Press.

Gouvernement du Canada (1989) *Le multiculturalisme (...) être Canadien*. Ottawa: Ministère du Multiculturalisme et de la Citoyenneté.

Gouvernement du Québec (1996) *Projet de loi no 18. Loi sur le ministère des Relations avec les citoyens et de l'Immigration et modifiant d'autres dispositions législatives*. Québec: Éditeur officiel.

Gouvernement du Québec (1990) *Au Québec pour bâtir ensemble. Énoncé de politique en matière d'immigration et d'intégration*. Québec: Ministère des communautés culturelles et de l'immigration.

Gouvernement du Québec (1981) *Autant de façons d'être québécois*. Plan d'action du gouvernement du Québec à l'intention des communautés culturelles. Ministère des communautés culturelles et de l'immigration. Québec: Bibliothèque du Québec.

Government of Canada (1969a) *Statement of the Government of Canada on Indian Policy*. Ottawa: Queen's Printer.

Government of Canada (1969b) *Official Languages Act*. Ottawa: Queen's Printer.

Grosz, E./Probyn, E. (eds.) (1996) *Sexy Bodies: the Strange Carnalities of Feminism*. London, New York: Routledge.

Guillaumin, C. (1972) *L'idéologie raciste. Genèse et langage actuel*. Paris, La Haye: Mouton.

Juteau, D. (1997) 'Beyond Multiculturalist Citizenship. The Challenge of Pluralism in Canada', in Bader, Veit (ed.), *Citizenship and Exclusion*. Houndmills: Macmillan Press.

Juteau, D. (1996) 'Theorizing Ethnicity and Ethnic Communalizations at the Margins: from Quebec to the World System', *Nations and Nationalism* 2 (1): 45-66.

Juteau, D./McAndrew, M. (1992) 'Projet national, immigration et intégration dans un Québec souverain', *Sociologie et Société* 24: 161-180.

Kymlicka, W. (1995) *Multicultural Citizenship. A Liberal Theory of Minority Rights*. Oxford: Oxford University Press.

McAndrew, M. (1995) 'Le procès actuel du multiculturalisme est-il fondé? Une analyse de la politique ontarienne d'antiracisme et d'équité ethnoculturelle', *Education et Francophonie* 13 (1): 26-33.

McRoberts, K. (1988) *Quebec: Social Change and Political Crisis*. Toronto: McClelland & Stewart.

Moodley, K. (1983) 'Canadian Multiculturalism as Ideology', *Ethnic and Racial Studies* 6: 320-331.

Multiculturalism Canada (1989) *Rapport annuel (1988-1989): L'application de la Loi sur le multiculturalisme canadien*. Ottawa: Supply and Services Canada.

Pietrantonio, L./Juteau, D./McAndrew, M. (1996) 'Multiculturalisme ou intégration: un faux débat', pp. 147-158 in *Actes du colloque Les Convergences culturelles dans les sociétés pluriethniques*. Québec: Presses de l'Université du Québec.

Porter, J. (1965) *The Vertical Mosaic: An Analysis of Social Class and Power in Canada*. Toronto: University of Toronto Press.

Porter, J. (1975) 'Ethnic Pluralism in a Canadian Perspective', pp. 267-304 in Glazer, N./Moyhnihan, D. (eds.) *Ethnicity: Theory and Experience*. Cambridge: Harvard University Press.

Probyn, E. (1995) *Sexing the Self. Gendered Positions in Cultural Studies*. London, New York: Routledge.

Royal Commission on Bilingualism and Biculturalism (1967-1970) *Report*. Ottawa: Queen's Printer.

Schermerhorn, R.A. (1970) *Comparative Ethnic Relations: A Framework for Theory and Research*. New York: Random House.

Stasiulis, D. (1991) 'The Symbolic Mosaic Reaffirmed: Multiculturalism Policy', pp. 81-111 in Graham, K. A. (ed.), *How Ottawa Spends 1988-1989: The Conservatives Heading into the Stretch*. Ottawa: Carleton University Press.

Taylor, C. (1994) *Multiculturalism: Examing the Politics of Recognition*. Princeton, N.J.: Princeton University Press.

Van den Berghe (1967) 'Ethnic Pluralism in Plural Societies: a Special Case?', *Ethnicity* 3: 242-255.

Wotherspoon, T./Satzewich, V. (1993) *First Nations: Race, Gender, and Class Relations*. Toronto: Nelson.

CHAPTER 5

The Israeli Experience in Multiculturalism

Eliezer Ben-Rafael

Family Resemblances in Multicultural Societies

Since the 1970s, various social researchers have explored the problems emerging in society from the absorption of mass immigration. These studies turned comparative by focusing either on the developments of a particular group in different settings (see for a classic example, Van den Berghe, 1978), or on various groups situated in the same setting (see for a no less classic example, Glazer/Moynihan, 1970). They led to a view of society first depicted as 'pluralism' (Kuper, 1965), and later as 'multiculturalism' (see Taylor, 1994). The former term points to the socio-cultural diversity that one may find in contemporary society; the latter indicates that this diversity has become an essential attribute of society itself. Concomitantly, one speaks of a multi-cleavage setting to designate a setting that experiences several types of socio-cultural divisions simultaneously (see Horowitz/Lissak, 1989).

These conceptual elaborations coincide with general theoretical developments in the social sciences, especially the expansion of discussions about postmodernism (see, for instance, Apter, 1987) and late modernism (Giddens, 1990) that describe social reality in terms of chaos and fragmentation and set the 'subject' and his/her particular allegiances at the centre of their preoccupations. Against this background sociologists have found in the socio-cultural diversity of contemporary societies the ground to ask if, effectively, ethnic groups and communities have made society irremediably fragmented (see Wieviorka, 1996). Some, like Touraine (1997), do not hesitate to speak of the existence of communities as an existential threat to society itself, questioning how it can remain integrated when it is constituted by socio-cultural groups of the most diverse kinds.

It is, indeed, undeniable that in many contemporary societies, a diversity of groups assert their existence by retaining distinct symbols and tokens of identity which posit their autonomy and difference from society as a whole. Yet, whatever the strength of this tendency, it necessarily concretizes through contact, communication and contingence with the group's own environment – including other cohabiting groups. This very co-presence of the group and the non-group raises the question: how is it possible to distinguish 'something' they share, which binds them together, despite the differences which separate them? I suggest that the notion of 'family resemblances' as used by Wittgenstein (1961) may be useful to explain this capacity of groups to simultaneously differentiate themselves from, yet identify with a given society.

Wittgenstein speaks in these terms of the similarity one finds among what he calls *language games* which, notwithstanding their semantic and structural differences, make up a same linguistic system. This similarity is depicted by him as 'family resemblance' because of its equivalence to the familiarity that binds relatives to each other in a variety of modes and degrees of closeness which by no means excludes tension and conflict. This notion might apply to multiculturalism to indicate resemblance, if among particular groups imprints can be found which reflect their confrontations with the language, modes of behaviour and cultural symbols of the surrounding environment. It refers to any cultural trait that makes individuals who belong to different groups feel *familiarity* with each other. This feeling does not necessarily depict the same degree of closeness nor does it exclude antagonisms and it need not recognize a supreme authority either. Rather, it indicates the existence of common references at the same time as differences between the cultures and perspectives of groups fragment society.

It is in this respect that achievements of the sociology of language may be recalled. On the one hand, Giles (Giles, 1985; Giles/Johnson, 1987; Giles/Coupland, 1991) and many others have shown that members of groups articulate and assert their social boundaries and cultural particularisms through a wide variety of possible linguistic markers – from full-fledged languages to lists of tokens, down to mere intonations – (Garmadi, 1981; Myers Scotton, 1983; Laverand Trudgill, 1979; Helfrich, 1979). On the other hand, and borrowing from the sociolinguistic notion of inter-language (Adjamian, 1976), the exposure of group cultures to the environment may also result in developing *intercultures;* that is, original cultural patterns and modes of behaviour which tend to undergo change, perhaps even transformation, by borrowing numerous tokens and symbols from the culture that predominates in their environment. Among other factors, this influence of the culture of the environment on groups is, obviously, quite unavoidably bound to the very insertion of the group into a wider society and its facing the latter's public agenda, sociolinguistic norms and specific endeavours. It is under these conditions that one might perceive the reality and diffusion, within the group, of family resemblances with outsiders. Multiculturalism is thus to be viewed as dynamic and diversified, providing a space where groups tend to acquire new symbols and cultural tenets and retain distinctiveness at different degrees and according to different patterns. (Myers Scotton, 1983; Gumperz, 1982). They may then exhibit a capacity to alternate their use of the different cultural codes they master, according to situations and interlocutors, while their original language and culture is itself necessarily influenced by acquired ones and gradually becomes an interculture. This interculture de-marks and re-marks the group's social boundaries at the same time as it articulates its familiarity with the environment.

Against this background, the notion of multiculturalism raises an additional question, which relates to Touraine's query: How do various cultural entities in society, both different from and familiar with each other, imprint themselves on the development of society as a whole? This question, we will argue, focuses on multiculturalism from the perspective of politics. The same groups, indeed, which fragment society are themselves political actors which participate in power relations and societal decision-making; they are not only constituted *by* society but are also constitutive *of* society and take part in the daily formation of society's culture and identity (Orans, 1971; Olzak, 1983; Ben-Rafael, 1994). Hence, the question of their imprint on society asks how groups tend to influence the shaping of society in ways that express their being a part of it. Obviously there would be strong links between these two aspects; that is, how groups emerge and crystallize within and beyond society, whilst simultaneously acting as constituent parts of the society. From the viewpoint of the researcher, however, these two aspects require different analytical perspectives. Analysing the development of different groups in society demands a conceptual framework able to account for the emergence and practical expressions of groups, in a way systematic and structured enough to illuminate both their differences and congruities. In contrast, the question of how groups shape a given society refers to the political dimension, that is, their power, action and influence as political actors in the polity.

The following discussion elaborates and illustrates this perspective by analysing three groups in Israeli society: Mizrachi Jews, Arabs and Jews from the former Soviet Union. Israeli society is a major example of contemporary multiculturalism. Until the late 1990s, about 43% of its Jewish population were foreign born. It was only until the mid-1940s, that its Jewish population (about 650,000 in 1948, in contrast to nearly 5 million, and close to 6 million when including the Israeli Arabs, in 1997) retained a relative ethnic homogeneity with Eastern Europeans comprising 85% (Eisenstadt, 1985). With mass immigration in the 1950s and 1960s

Israel witnessed a large influx of Middle Eastern and North African Jewish (or Mizrachi, that is, "Oriental" in Hebrew) immigrants, who, thanks to a high birth rate, have numbered 43-45% since 1984 (ICBS, 1989: 75-79). No single group of origin, however, is demographically dominant – Moroccans, Poles, Russians, Rumanians, or Iraqis all number between 8 to 10% of the Jewish population; Germans, Hungarians, or Yemenites between 4 and 7%; many others around 1% or less. Recent Soviet immigration (about 750,000 from 1989 to 1997 – including 75% Ashkenazi from former European USSR territories) (Gitelman, 1997) forms around 14% of the Israeli population and 17% of the Jewish population in 1997. Moreover, the Arab population constitutes another segment of 18% consisting of 77% Moslems, 13% Christians and 10% Druzes (ICBS, 1995). These demographic data effectively illustrate the extent of multiculturalism in Israel. Moreover, it is also clear how far the three groups studied below, i.e. Mizrachi Jews, formerly Soviet Jews and Israeli Arabs, are important in this multicultural reality. Together they comprise, indeed, no less than 71% of the Israeli population; 40% of Israelis are Mizrachi Jews, 14% are formerly Soviet Jews and 17% Arabs. In what follows, this highly complex reality will be examined as an example of multiculturalism. The three cases will first be considered comparatively with respect to each of the facets of the conceptual framework developed below. In a second phase, these cases will also be reviewed in the frame of a structural political analysis of Israel's version of multiculturalism, with the aim of examining how groups may imprint themselves – through interaction – on the development of society as a whole.

A Comparative Framework

Society, we contend, is composed of its divisions. By division, we mean differences between groups distinguished by particular socio-cultural characteristics. This approach is close to Tajfel's perspective which takes the notion of 'ethnic' in its widest sense as referring to any form of social solidarity (Tajfel, 1978 a,b,c). Milroy's *Language and Social Networks* (1989) is another example of this perspective, relating language and culture to the crystallization of groups emerging from specific social conditions. Following Dorian and Hauge, however, we know, that although cultural singularity may be elaborated it is by no means definitive. Dorian (1981) shows the difficulties groups may experience in preserving their cultural-linguistic personality when circumstances press them to relinquish their particularism; Haugen (1989) illustrates the ways social and cultural processes may lead to the disappearance of socio-cultural groups.

As part of a larger society, the group necessarily experiences some degree of acculturation in the sense that it is influenced by its environment and becomes increasingly similar to the strata that embody the values and norms predominant in society. Eventually, the group might even undergo assimilation, which means that acculturation comes to include identity (Orans, 1971; Olzak, 1983). The theoretical significance of acculturation and assimilation resides in their constituting possible criteria of comparison between groups that, otherwise, can hardly be related to each other considering the endless diversity of their particularisms. Moreover, measuring acculturation and assimilation constitutes, in itself, a major interest of the study of multiculturalism, questioning the extent to which groups remain, or do not remain, *different* from the rest of society.

The literature here suggests three major conditions. Firstly, there is the dimension of stratification, that is, the class positioning of the members of the group and the scope of their social mobility. This dimension is of particular importance in a modern setting because here more than anywhere the individual's social status or class widely determines his or her social position as a whole, the class or status distribution of the members of a group, and the latter's location in society. The second condition, it is suggested, consists of the influential models, beliefs and definitions exhibited by the political centre; the dominant culture which largely dictates the action of social institutions towards a group's insertion in society. Finally, the third factor consists of the group itself; referring to the group's own original orientations, perspectives, and legacies which influence its velleities and ambitions regarding its insertion in the setting. These three factors, when seen both individually and in their mutual relations, can be considered primary determinants of the development of socio-cultural groups, and thereby, of a society's multiculturalism. Using each of these parameters we will examine the three Israeli cases under consideration in the context of the space they structure together.[1]

(1) The Dimension of Stratification

Many conditions determine a group's location on the stratificational map. These include the control, or lack of control, by members of human capital assets (such as education, professional training, and cultural predispositions for social mobility) which may strengthen or weaken individuals' competitiveness on job markets (Blau/Duncan, 1967). Moreover, groups may be encouraged or discouraged to enter mobility tracks by the cultural (individualistic or traditionalist) values and models of social life – including versions of ideal types of family life – which they identify with. Last but not least, there are the opportunity structures and features of labour markets, including discriminatory or non-discriminatory practices, that outline the trajectory of advancement (Bonacich, 1980).

Whatever the causes of the group's privileged or underprivileged position, the very fact of its positioning is, in itself, a factor of its development in society. It may, indeed, be assumed that, all other factors being equal, the more a socio-cultural group remains concentrated on the underprivileged side of the social barrier, the more feelings of deprivation fuel the identification of members with their group in the face of outgroups, and the stronger their tendency of blaming society for discriminating against them, on the ground of their particularism. Moreover, the more the members of a group are characterized by a low status in society, the less they constitute a desirable target for social relations on the side of the outgroup, and the more such relations may effectively be of stigmatizing effect. Hence, this relative isolation tends to strengthen the effect deprivation has *per se* on group identification.

In the context of the importance of stratification, it is also evident that the social mobility of members carries major implications. Whether partial and involving a minority, or more general and concerning the majority, the very experience of mobility signifies for the members concerned more relations with outgroups and more exposure to the environment. As A.D. Smith suggests: "ethnicity persists most strongly among lower classes who are less exposed to acculturation" (Smith, 1981: 153). This is variously illustrated by the three cases under study.

Mizrachi Jews

The Mizrachi Jewish immigrants who arrived during the late 1940s and the 1950s came from traditional or modernizing settings where they formed religious communities which generally eked out a living from small shops, peddling and craftsmanship (Ben-Rafael/Sharot, 1991). In Israel, these groups joined the lower class as many had little formal education – particularly women – and retained their longstanding traditions – including the value of large families. Poorly equipped to meet the requirements of competitive labour markets, they soon concentrated in sectors of the working class, elevating earlier generations of European immigrants to the middle class. The fact that the traditional culture of Mizrachi Jews contrasted with the secular, even anti-religious horizons of the predominantly European elite, was also to account for the diffusion of prejudices among the latter *vis-à-vis* the former, and their tendency to give them less preferential treatment than immigrants who came from Europe.[2] Ever since, Israeli society has been characterized by a relation between class and origin. However, educated and wealthy families from Bagdad, Aleppo, Alexandria or Casablanca have been able to integrate into the middle class and all groups have experienced progress and mobility over time (Smooha, 1972; Swirski, 1981).[3] Hence, in recent years, the correlation between ethnicity and inequality is visible mainly at the peripheries: there are four times more Europeans in the highest-income tenth, and the proportion is reversed in the lowest-income tenth (ICBS, 1988).[4] In brief, 35%-38% of Mizrachi Jews belong to the middle class, compared to two-thirds of Europeans. Large communities of Mizrachi Jews have long remained quite isolated in the periphery and have only gradually acculturated to their environment.

Formerly Soviet Jews

The Russian immigrants of the 1980s and 1990s have not only immigrated to a more developed Israel than Mizrachi Jews in the 1950s, but are themselves characterized by a higher level of education representative of the whole range of white-collar professions.[5] Formerly Soviet Jews share ambiguous notions of family that, on the one hand, emphasize solidarity with parents and grandparents, but are, on the other, reluctant to have large numbers of children themselves. Hence, these immigrants possess all attributes for successful insertion and social mobility. After six to seven years of living in their target country, a majority of these immigrants are unable to find jobs equivalent to their former positions in the USSR and have to make do with working-class positions – in factories, on building sites or in the supermarket. However, in the early 1990s already 35% of the employed formerly Soviet Jews held professional positions and tended to expand throughout all layers of the setting. Despite the downgrading of their human capital assets connected to the very fact of immigration and change of milieu, formerly Soviet Jews display a tendency for social mobility. This can be explained by their readiness to find initial employment in sectors which offer underqualified jobs until they are able to find more suitably qualified positions (see Lerner, 1993; Raday/Bunk, 1993). Hence, this group is potentially a middle-class group, even though it still tends to congregate in lower strata in the first decade after settling in the country. It is thus reasonable to expect rapid acculturation to the predominant models of culture among this group proportionate to their ambitions and achievements and growing relations with outgroups.

Arabs

Like the former cases – and especially the Mizrachi Jews – this group displays a particular identity and an underprivileged condition. Less than 20% of Arabs now work within their own village or town, in agriculture or in local services and retail business. The large majority are employed in the all-Israeli economy. There, Arabs are principally employed in construction, industry, or low-class services and comprise an underclass of unskilled or semi-skilled workers (Semyonov/Lewin-Epstein, 1987).[6] Moreover, the high birth rate of Arab families is another factor that widens the Jewish-Arab gap, notwithstanding the general improvement of the living standards and the expansion of education and health services among Arab communities (Layish, 1981; Makhou, 1982). These conditions are due both to weaknesses in human capital and to discrimination (Smooha, 1976). The Arab population constituted a mostly illiterate peasant society in 1948, dominated by a few strong families. At the time, many were encouraged to leave their villages and towns to seek employment in areas of greater development. Yet, as the dominant party, Jews are reluctant to allow Arabs to achieve positions of authority, therefore undercutting the range of opportunities available to them. Many Jewish employers would prefer to employ equally competent Jews in place of Arabs. Furthermore, in light of Israel's security situation *vis-à-vis* the Arab world, Israeli Arabs are rarely employed in the weapons industry and diplomacy, and are exempted from the military. However, after the introduction of compulsory elementary education, the number of students completing secondary education increased and subsequently, the number of university students, too. A sector of mobile individuals crystallized within the community, who often had to explore ways to capitalize on their assets – as teachers, officials or politicians.

In Conclusion

All three groups show a concentration in lower class positions. The Arabs are the most underprivileged, followed by Mizrachi Jews, while the formerly Soviet Jews, still numerous in the working class, are a potential middle class. The importance of mobile elements in these groups also runs in the same order. All other factors being equal, and considering that the formerly Soviet Jews have been in the country for less than ten years, stratification should encourage more Arabs, then Mizrachi Jews, and less Soviet immigrants, to retain their particularistic identification. In reverse, the trend of acculturation should be stronger among Soviet Jews, less so among Mizrachi Jews and weakest among Arabs.

(2) The Dominant Culture

While all three cases illustrate forms of inequality, socially mobile elements have also appeared in each of them and might become a threat to the cohesion of the groups. The extent to which social mobility leads to the disappearance of particularistic identities and mitigates the salience of cultural characteristics is, however, to be attributed to additional factors. One major factor is whether or not assimilation is considered a legitimate course of action in society, that is, whether or not assimilation is encouraged by the dominant culture. The dominant culture is important in the current discussion of multiculturalism because it conveys general orientations towards the location and roles of groups in society and the reality of cultural heterogeneity. According to Grillo (1989) and Wardraugh (1987), dominant cultures tend to display either segregative or unifying attitudes towards sociocultural groups in general, or in relation to specific groups. A *segregative* dominant culture recognizes the social distinctiveness of the group and tends to institutionalize pluralism in relevant respects of the social order. This kind of dominant culture encourages the group, including its mobile elements, to retain its cultural identity. In contrast, a *unifying* dominant culture is less tolerant of group particularism, and discourages pluralism. This kind of dominant culture encourages both acculturation and assimilation.

The Israeli Version of Dominant Culture

For decades the dominant culture in Israel has emphasized two principal themes – Jewish nationalism or Zionism, and social democracy. In an attempt to duplicate nineteenth-century European nationalisms, Zionism had drawn much of its impetus from the idea of a new secular solution to the problem of a religious definition of Jewish identity, that is, the definition of the Jewish diaspora as a condition of 'exile' (Katz, 1960; Avineri, 1981). The Zionist solution consisted of the resettlement of the Jews in the Land of Israel, the culturally and religiously defined home of the Jewish People, and the creation of a secular and culturally unified nation-state (Buber, 1973). Zionists thus called for an *ingathering of the exiles*. Attaching themselves to a cultural revolution – marked by the revival of the ancestral Hebrew language as a spoken language – they intended to transform the Jewish legacy, but maintained Jewish solidarity as a basic tenet of a new kind of Jewishness (Ben-Rafael, 1982).

The founders were also moved by strong socialist convictions (Horowitz/Lissak, 1978); they created welfare services, a General Federation of Labour in control of key industries and cooperative and collectivistic rural settlements. Later on, the sons and daughters of these so-called veterans developed a nativistic style (Katriel, 1986) which was to be mitigated over time by the growing importance of another major tenet of the dominant culture, namely, the Western version of modernity. This focus accounts for stronger cosmopolitan outlooks – including the adoption of English as a de facto second language – and a reference to market economy and high consumerist and educational expectations (Horowitz/Lissak, 1989). Cultural bearings grew to emphasize meritocratic differentiation (Lissak, 1967).

This dominant culture shares very different orientations in relation to Jews or non-Jews (Ben-Rafael, 1982). As far as Jewish groups are concerned, the definition of Israel as the Land of the Jews by the 1948 Declaration of Independence, warrants the granting of citizenship upon arrival and special aid in lodgement and job searching.[7] In return, Jewish immigrants learn Hebrew in the *ulpanim* (accelerated courses of Hebrew) in ways that infuse new self-definitions together with the language (Ben-Rafael/Geijst, 1993). Immigrants are expected to conform to models of a *new Israel*, as embodied by first-generation immigrants and their offspring, and it is in this vein that ethnic parties among Jews were, as a rule, harshly opposed by Zionist parties for whom they undermined the ideal of a unified nation.

This approach has guided the establishment's absorption policy *vis-à-vis* all Jewish groups, though over time, it has received different formulations. Until the late 1980s, the Ministries of Absorption, Housing, or Labour were directly in charge of providing relevant services to immigrants, which created a strong dependency of the latter on the state bureaucracy. Beyond the late 1980s, this policy was replaced by what is called the *absorption basket*. Immigrants are now given a sum of money which they may use according to their own preferences, buying services independently. This model was used for formerly Soviet Jews and accounts for the freedom this group enjoyed, even in the political realm, from the beginning.

However, the dominant culture takes a very different approach in the case of Arabs. In keeping with the fundamental tenet of the state to maintain its Jewish character, Israeli Arabs have been relegated to the status of a national minority. There are no expectations of blurring group boundaries between Jews and Arabs, and consequently, in this respect, Israel is considered an openly pluralistic society (Gorny, 1986; Landau, 1970). Besides Hebrew, Arabic is an official language in the country while the Arabs' social and cultural autonomy is encouraged by the support of an Arab-speaking education system (spanning from kindergarten to teachers' colleges) as well as traditional religious courts in the realm of personal status. The dominant culture does not object in this case to sectorial parties which effectively emerge and crystallize as a political power in their own right. In brief, while the dominant culture belongs to the unifying type and encourages assimilation in relation to Jewish groups, it is pluralistic – almost to the point of segregation – and sustains particularism, in relation to Arabs.

(3) The Group's Perspective

A socio-cultural group crystallizes where individuals develop a group identity and a social boundary signalled by cultural and linguistic markers. It is from its location in society, through its images of the dominant culture and the culture and notions of identity that it conveys, that this group develops its present symbols, collective images and intellectual concepts which will influence its efforts to completely assimilate to society or to retain some aspects of its particularism and a degree of inner solidarity (Ben-Rafael, 1996). This process may take on different forms in different groups and among diverse milieus within the group itself. As stated by Hamers and Blanc: "A communal group may not wish (...) to assimilate (...) [while] some members will strive to achieve a more positive identity by 'passing' into the majority [and others] come to realize that status enhancement lies in [raising] the group consciousness of its members" (Hamers/Blanc, 1989: 159-160). Moreover, insofar as members hold views of the dominant culture which bring them to preserve some particularism, they concern themselves with their collective identity in relation to their additional commitment to the societal identity, and this may explain the divergences within the group.

On the other hand, once elaborated, an identity has its own effect on the behaviour of individuals (Geertz, 1965). Group boundaries are necessarily less precise in socially mobile subgroups, let alone where social mobility is general within the group. Even then, however, at least symbolically, social openness on either side may still be limited and create twilight zones. Whether acculturation, which is the primary outcome of social mobility, conditions assimilation depends on the dominant culture's attitude and the extent to which it makes itself accessible. However, even where assimilation is sustained by the dominant culture, and where class circumstances are also favourable, its concretization is still dependent on the attitudes of the group itself. Mobile elements are then in a position to exploit their closeness to the privileged groups – enabling them to detach themselves from their own group. If mobility is effectively widespread within the group this means nothing less than a general tendency for assimilation into a dominant culture. Even then, however, individuals may still find it advantageous to retain their particularism symbolically, and come to form a *middle-class ethnic group* (see Glazer/Moynihan, 1970).

Yet, where mobility is not general and many members of the group remain low-class, the assimilation of mobile elements among outgroups and their distance from their community, signify that the latter remains characterized by deprivation, not because mobility is non-existent, but despite its very reality. It is mainly where the group insists on the retention of its particularism and/or the dominant culture is pluralistic that one may expect those more advantaged elements to remain bound to their group – whether under the influence of the group's retentionism, or because of the constraints imposed by the dominant culture. Either way, mobile layers tend to constitute a potential leadership, badly needed by a predominantly weak and thus isolated group. Let me illustrate this once again by examining the characteristic patterns of Mizrachi Jews, formerly Soviet Jews and Israeli Arabs.

Mizrachi Jews

The insertion of Mizrachi Jews into Israel is characterized by a persistent tendency to congregate according to country of origin (Ben-Rafael/Sharot, 1991). These widely low-class Moroccan neighbourhoods, Yemenite villages or Kurdish quarters, are strongly marked by religious parochialism to the present day. All have synagogues holding their services in their own style and practice customs associated with legacies of the past.[8] This phenomenon is related to the fact that for Mizrachi Jews Zionism, the creation of the Jewish state and their own immigration to Israel have always been perceived in the light of the Scriptures' promise of Redemption from Exile. A redemption regarded as the fulfilment of the Jews' long-standing dedication to the faith and its commands. It follows that once in the Promised Land, Mizrachi Jews could not justify any disloyalty to, or rejection of, Judaism's values and norms which they believe had delivered them to the Return. This attitude was behind the rebuilding in Israel of the diasporic communities around traditional synagogues. It is true, the younger generations have been influenced by the national school, army service, the spirit of the workplace and exposure to the media. However, by taking place in compact communities, this transformation was gradual and eclectic, and by no means instigated a generational change of split.

Ideologically, Mizrachi Jews accept the Zionist concept of the *fusion of exiles* which accords with their understanding of the Redemption. However, because they have undergone secularization after immigrating to Israel and not before, they find it difficult to conceive of the encompassing identities – Jewish and Israeli – as beyond their own legacy. Hence, while strata at the upper levels of the class hierarchy are mostly Ashkenazi and endorse nationalist, secular, social-democratic and cosmopolitan perspectives, at the lower levels where Mizrachi Jews are a majority, one finds a variety of traditionalist communities. Interestingly enough, in these communities where loyalty to religious rites symbolizes the particularistic identity, one meets no few individuals who experience the expanding secularization impelled by the dominant culture as moral degradation. Over time, such individuals have been attracted to ultra-Orthodox religious studies and after completing rabbinical education have often come back to their community to constitute a new religious elite. There they have created religious academies of their own to assert the vitality of their own traditions of religious learning and lifestyles.

Language is a major area where these peculiar contours of the Mizrachi Jewish experience can be traced. In Dimona, for example, a small working-class town of 25,000 in the Negev Desert where the large majority of the population is Moroccan (Ben-Rafael, 1994), informants report that people express their particularism by using Moghrabi (Jewish Moroccan Arabic) in a variety of speech situations –

despite the fact that they know Hebrew and now use it as their principal language. The young know Moghrabi less fluently than their parents but still speak it with grandparents. Moreover, the general familiarity with the language accounts for the popularity in Dimona of films and video cassettes in Arabic. The fact that some young adults have recently become very religious, has further strengthened their ties to past traditions, and thus to Moghrabi. Furthermore, French can also be heard here among the middle-age generation originating from Meknes, Fez, or Casablanca, where French was the principal language of the Jews, and, as informants stress, the Moroccan Hebrew accent denotes both French and Arabic backgrounds.

Another example, Rosh Ha'ayin is also a low-class town (close to Tel-Aviv) of 12,000 Yemenite Jews, and like Dimona, very traditionalist. Children read the Bible and learn with the *mori* (the traditional teacher) who teaches *Yemeniteness* after regular school hours. There are about 120 synagogues in Rosh Ha'ayin and the intense religious practice of the Yemenite Jews explains the strong imprint in *their* Hebrew of quotations from the Bible and traditional poems. Hebrew, moreover, is unique here, with its distinguishing characteristics of close consonants and guttural vowels. This accent is understood as the true and *original* Hebrew. Jewish Yemenite-Arabic is also used on certain occasions – for example, when chanting traditional poems and songs in the synagogue. Even though many young adults confirm that Yemenite linguistic particularism is waning together with Yemeniteness, as in Dimona, parochialism recently received the support of new groups of young men that return to more rigorous parochial religiosity.

However, the fact that both the dominant culture – in its secular nationalist formulation – and the groups' perspective – in a quasi-messianic vein – emphasize the importance of a unified Jewish society and thus define Jewish particularisms as a *temporary* reality, is of special significance when it comes to the impact of social mobility on the community. Indeed, despite the wide concentration of Mizrachi Jews in lower social strata, many individuals are socially mobile,[9] whether through small-scale economic entrepreneurship or through educational-professional paths. These elements might now constitute a stronger basis for their groups and a reservoir of leadership; however, research suggests, that, in the case of Mizrachi Jews, the very endeavour of social mobility results not only in acculturation but also assimilation to predominantly Ashkenazi milieus (Ben-Rafael/Sharot, 1991). Indeed, for the privileged, who best represent the dominant culture, the unifying perspective of this culture prevents them from legitimately restricting access for individuals of culturally different backgrounds who, by their social achievements, are entitled to positions in upper strata. The Mizrachi community as well ultimately sustains the *fusion of exiles*, thus mitigating any sense of betrayal it might feel towards offspring entering new social strata.

This signifies that the ethnic problem represented by the Mizrachi Jews as a whole continues to be strongly related to the issue of inequality, not because of the absence of mobility, but in spite of this mobility. Furthermore, by leaving their community, secular mobile elements do not merely preserve the lower-class characteristics of their group. They also leave the group in the hands of emerging religious elites who due to their parochial calling view the community as their natural area of activity.

The formerly Soviet Jews

As for the potentially mobile Soviet immigrants, research shows that the very fact of their immigration has generally been motivated by instrumental interests more than by aspirations to join the historical and cultural *homeland* of the Jews (Ben-Rafael/Olshtain/Geijst, 1996). Jews who rapidly left the USSR in the late 1980s, were mainly motivated by the fear of anti-Jewish violence in an era of political disarray and economic crisis, and were also interested in immigrating to the USA, or at least to Western Europe. It is only when these countries implemented low quotas of Soviet Jewish immigrants that those who remained behind without any other destination accepted the offer of immigrating to Israel. When they arrived, however, the weight of their number in a small country and population became, in itself, a major aspect of their insertion.

Accepted in Israel as Jews, these immigrants probably came to feel more Jewish than they had in the USSR. The group is hardly characterized by any parochial cultural legacy. After 80 years of Marxist-Leninist regime, one finds among them only 1% of very religious people and merely 10% of individuals who declare themselves as religious at all. The two largest segments, at least as yielded by the random sample of Ben-Rafael, Olshtain and Geijst's work (1996), consisted of those who stated that they do have some feelings for Jewish tradition (44%), on the one hand, and those who stated they were alien to religion and tradition (45%), on the other. Formerly Soviet Jews are strongly motivated by the ambition to succeed and move into upper strata and, therefore, eagerly acquire Hebrew and elements of Israeli culture. By any standard, their level of achievements in the special Hebrew-teaching programmes for immigrants is remarkable (Ben-Rafael/Geijst, 1993). The language is important to them because it represents a key to the job market and all other areas of social participation.[10]

At the same time, however, the group evaluates its own original culture and language higher than the Israeli culture and the Hebrew language. On nearly all counts, and particularly when comparing Hebrew to Russian as international languages, they grade the latter higher than the former. Concomitantly, formerly Soviet Jews express the wish to retain their language and culture of origin and to transmit them to younger generations. In practice, they develop institutions which express their desire to form a speech community of their own, within the Israeli society. Hence, newspapers, magazines and annuals are published in Russian in Tel-Aviv for Israel's formerly Soviet Jews. Russian cultural and social centres have multiplied demonstrating an opposition to thorough assimilation – as openly or tacitly advocated by the dominant culture – and an ambition to create, for themselves, a new bilingual and bicultural reality. Interestingly enough, dozens of writers continue to produce works in their original language and to publish them with Israeli publishers, with an intended audience of both Russian-speaking Israelis and the Russian-speaking world as a whole. Yet, it is also worth noting, that Russian, as a spoken language in the group, tends (unavoidably) to be tainted with Hebrew words and concepts that express the influence of participation in Israel's daily life and institutional setting and individuals' interactions with others.[11]

In this respect, this group is very different from the ideologically-motivated Eastern European immigrants who preceded them by nearly one century and who made up the pioneer and founding immigrations. Compared to the formerly Soviet Jews, these pioneers aspired to nation-building and fought against the retention and use of diasporic languages in favour of Hebrew and Jewish nationalism (Ben-Rafael, 1994). On the other hand, the formerly Soviet Jews differ also greatly from the Mizrachi communities whose immigration has been motivated by a traditionalist nationalism. In brief, the former Soviet Jews show hardly any reference to a Jewish nationalism, whether of the secular and quasi-secular kind of the founding Eastern Europeans or of the traditionalist and quasi-religious mode of the Mizrachi Jews. At the same time, they are no less secular than the founding Eastern European Israelis and attached to their original culture like the Mizrachi Jews.

Formerly Soviet Jews are actually reminiscent of the German Jewish immigrants of the 1930s (Ben-Rafael, 1994). These middle-class immigrants were also generally secular and remote from Jewish nationalism and Judaism and, at the same time, strongly committed to the German language and culture. German immigrants and their offspring attempted to maintain a distinct German-speaking language community. German and its culture would have strongly influenced Israel's culture and society, had they not been tainted by the Holocaust which destroyed the prestige of anything German in the Israeli public. Moreover, Zionism in the 1930s and 1940s was triumphant – it led to the creation of the State of Israel in 1948 – and youth movements and para-military organizations were able to overcome the influence of parents and draft the support of the youth. These circumstances have made Israel's German-Jewish speech community a one-generation phenomenon that found only feeble continuation in the younger generation.

When comparing the cases of the formerly Soviet Jews and the German Jews, it seems that, in contrast with the conditions of the latter, Zionism today is much less vigorous than it was 50-60 years ago, and youth movements can no longer compete with the influence of parents on children. Moreover, nothing comparable to the memory of the Holocaust overshadows Israel's relations with Russia and its attitude to the Russian language and culture. Hence, at least in these respects, the formerly Soviet Jews should not experience the same difficulties as German Jews in creating and perpetuating their language community. If they succeed in opposing the unifying dominant culture and its open or latent condemnation of separate group identities, they may come to be the first middle-class secular ethnic group of (mostly) European origin able to retain an allegiance to a diasporic non-Jewish culture. It is to be expected that many former Soviet Jews will succumb to the temptation of assimilation as a consequence of their own social mobility and of encouragement by the dominant culture. Others, however, might successfully combine their original Russian-Jewish identities with the Israeli one they have acquired.

Arabs

Confronted with a pluralistic dominant culture (in contrast to the Jewish groups who face a unifying dominating culture), Arabs take pluralism for granted, and display a self-definition allying nation and culture which refers to a whole that excludes the Jew (Nakhleh, 1975). If one adds to this the tendency of Arabs to concentrate in lower strata, direct contacts between Jews and Arabs outside the workplace are rare (Levy/Guttman, 1976), even though in places like boarding schools where Jews and Arabs live together on an egalitarian basis, intergroup friendships may emerge (Kraemer, 1978). In recent years, mutual exclusion is evinced by the tendency of Arabs to insist on the Palestinian component of their identity. Hence, when Israeli Arabs are requested to define themselves in order of identification, they often designate themselves as *Arab* first, then *Palestinian*, followed by *Muslim* or *Christian*, and only finally, *Israeli* (see Al-Hadj, 1993).

On the other hand, as a minority and despite their relative isolation, Arabs are susceptible to the influence of the Jewish society. Induced to acquire the first national language, they have experienced modernization in the frame of the Israeli society and have generally become active bilinguals. It is through their knowledge of Hebrew that they have been widely exposed to the dominant styles and culture, up to the point that one is entitled to speak of a genuine cultural convergence; a convergence which, to be sure, by no means signifies a rapprochement of Jewishness, at the level of identity. Arabs, in fact, clearly draw the line between their attitude towards Hebrew as a means of communication and a conveyor of modernity and their perceptions of the Jews who are above all, in their eyes, Israel's dominant group (Ben-Rafael/Brosh, 1995). Notwithstanding all these factors, one still may speak of a kind of *Israelization* of Israel's Arabs, clearly evident in linguistic activity.

These statements are confirmed by a research in sociology of language in Tira (Ben-Rafael, 1994), a Muslim town of 13,000 inhabitants, where, as is usually the case in Arab towns and villages, the majority of men work outside the village, in blue-collar jobs. In all schools of the town (three elementary ones, one junior high, and one regional senior high) Arabic is the language of instruction and Hebrew is studied – from the third elementary grade on – as a second language. Modern literary Arabic which is taught at school, is used outside school for cultural consumption – newspaper or book reading, entertainment or listening/watching media – and public speech. In the street and daily speech, vernacular Arabic is predominant but Hebrew is also widely and quite perfectly known (especially among young adults). Hence, many watch or listen to Israeli broadcasts in Hebrew and also often prefer the Hebrew newspaper to the Arabic because they find it more informative.

The data about the influence of Hebrew on spoken Arabic is also provided by Koplewitz's research (1990) which indicates the penetration of Hebrew elements in vernacular Arabic particularly pertaining to institutions (*kupat holim* for health clinic, or *monit* for taxi), patterns of social organization (*ramzor* for traffic lights, or *hofesh* for vacation), or typically Israeli-Hebrew forms (*shalom* for hello). Koplewitz emphasizes that such borrowings from Hebrew include professional and technological terms, or names of new products. Arabs themselves confess they often use Hebrew extensively – at work, in the shopping centre or in business – and no longer consider it a foreign language. However, this does not weaken the Arabs' consciousness of being part of Arabic civilization. The fact that they make up a subordinate minority obviously contributes to their alienation from the dominant culture but this alienation does not prevent cultural convergence.

(4) Different Profiles

The above analyses of three Israeli cases from the perspective of the structural parameters of socio-cultural groups can be summarized in the following statements and is further illustrated in Table 1 below.

1) Many Mizrachi Jews continue to experience social deprivation in terms of social stratification. This deprivation remains salient in the context of the mutually unifying attitude of the dominant culture and of the Mizrachi groups whose mobile elements tend to assimilate out into the dominant Israeli cul-

ture at pace with their secularization. These communities exhibit eclectic influences of the modern environment and traditional versions of Jewish symbols; their markers are drawn from original vernaculars and their interlanguage shows a penetration of Hebrew by characteristic expressions and intonations of those vernaculars.

2) The formerly Soviet Jews are also over-represented in the lower class, ten years after beginning to immigrate to the country. Their human capital warrants, however, rapid mobility while their past accounts for their middle-class ambitions and culture. The dominant culture which also shares a unifying perspective is confronted by the group's determination to retain – concomitantly with its acquisition of Hebrew and the Hebrew culture – the Russian language and culture. However, at the pace of their insertion, the formerly Soviet Jews also allow Hebrew elements to penetrate their Russian. On the other hand, the secularism of the group and its upward social mobility create the expectation that a substantial number will assimilate into the non-ethnic middle class. Those who sustain their community exemplify a type of middle-class ethnic group.

3) Israeli Arabs, who also widely concentrate in lower strata, categorically differ from the Mizrachi Jews and the formerly Soviet Jews by the fact that in relation to them the dominant culture clearly emphasizes plurality rather than unity. The group itself, moreover, is determined to retain its national and religious identity – despite its cultural convergence with the Jews. Socially mobile elements remain an integral part of the group and, in effect, play a leading role in the public sphere. This kind of boundary is symbolized both by the retention of the original language, Arabic, and Arab culture, and the acquisition of Hebrew. The exposure to the influence of Israel's modernity shows in the emergence of an interlanguage that allows a strong penetration of Hebrew into spoken Arabic.

The following table formalizes this analysis by dichotomizing the values of the structural parameters. It considers the profiles obtained with respect to the contours of social boundaries and linguistic marking. Table 1 also shows that Mizrachi Jews and formerly Soviet Jews represent different models of a similar level of acculturation/assimilation where only one structural parameter is *negative* (that is, hinders the acculturation/assimilation process), while the two others are *positive* (that is, encourage acculturation/assimilation). On the other hand, the Israeli Arab case belongs to those cases which close the space of possibilities, at the *negative* end with *negative* values on all three parameters.

Table 1: Structural Parameters, Profiles of Social Boundaries and Linguistic Marking

socio-cultural groups	structural parametres* $\rightarrow$ social boundaries**	linguistic marking***
Mizrachi Jews	S-, D+, G+ $\rightarrow$ $(g_1) + (D_G+g_2)$	(LL marked by OL) + OL elements
Ex-Soviet Jews	S+, D+, G- $\rightarrow$ $(g_{2a}) + (D_G+g_{2b})$	LL + (OL marked by LL)
Israeli Arabs	S-, D-, G- $\rightarrow$ $(g_1+g_2) + (D_G)$	(LL_2 marked by LL_1) + LL_1

Notes:

*	S	Stratification	**	g_1	low-class members of the group
	S-	deprivation of the group		g_2	mobile elements of the group
	S+	social mobility of many members		g_{2a}	mobile elements remaining in g
	D	Dominant culture		g_{2b}	mobile elements assimilating out
	D-	pluralistic *vis-à-vis* the group		D_G	group in society best embodying D
	D+	unifying	***	LL	Legitimate (official) language
	G	Perspective of the group		LL_1	principal legitimate language
	G-	retentionist		LL_2	second legitimate language
	G+	assimilationist		OL	original language

The Political Dimension

Questions about the impact of socio-cultural groups as factors of change in society are especially pertinent in democracies where groups of nearly any kind are entitled to confront the political centre with their claims. Hence, whether this is legitimized or condemned by the dominant culture, and whether it is practiced openly or latently, religious communities, ethnic minorities or regional sectors invariably constitute political actors of a democratic regime. According to circumstances, they operate as political parties in their own right, as constituents of wider parties or simply as interest groups. This political dimension is especially relevant for retentionist groups who want to remain distinct and articulate their claims independently and where the dominant culture is also pluralistic and accepts that the group may have specific claims. In contrast, when it faces an assimilationist dominant culture, a retentionist group which utilizes the political opportunities offered by democracy to forward its claims and demand recognition enters into conflict with the dominant culture. By its very nature this conflict is not purely political but attacks the very premises of the dominant culture (see Wieviorka, 1996).

In any case, from the moment that a socio-cultural group enters the political realm, as for any political actor, success primarily depends on both the group's power and the political conjuncture. Larger groups able to draft strong support are, of course, in a better position to impose exigencies. But the effectiveness of this power also depends on the structure of power in the centre, and the role the group's actors might play. Moreover, the more potentially profitable the political game, the more it attracts groups – or at least, political entrepreneurs within groups – to participate and work towards crystallizing political power. Whether multiculturalism represents a dynamic force of the transformation of society as a whole will then depend on how far the various socio-cultural groups which participate in this power game want to, and are able to, imprint changes in the social order, perhaps even in the dominant culture itself, be it by collaborating among themselves or with other forces. This is a query which moves the analysis from the comparative development of groups to the specifics of the political scene and its power processes.

The Israeli case illustrates, in these respects, complex tensions on the side of the groups investigated; but in spite of the unsystematic character of the pressures involved, all tend to promote multiculturalism.

Israel's Socio-Cultural Groups as Political Actors

To begin, the fact that both Mizrachi Jews and the dominant culture share a unifying perspective widely accounts for the fact that the former have been politically silent for decades and that ethnic parties were unsuccessful until the late 1970s. These communities were also too weak to avoid supporting the establishment and the then dominant Labour party (*Mapai*). However, once they established themselves and became less dependent on the centre, these communities could express more freely their feelings about their relative deprivation in society. Many did so by switching their political preference to the right. Because the right had been the parliamentary opposition continuously for about 50 years, voting for it indeed satisfied the Mizrachi Jews' drive to express dissatisfaction with their underprivileged condition, which they blamed on the social-democratic establishment. Moreover, the traditional religiosity of the Mizrachi Jewish communities was closer to rightist nationalism than to social democracy.

The consequences of this switch were, however, most unexpected. The political right now established itself as an equal contender to the left, and this new balance literally transformed the rules of the political game. The Mizrachi Jewish vote was now crucially important to all parties and, as a result, became the constituency most courted from all sides. To be of Middle Eastern or North African origin became a political asset of primary importance, and in nearly all parties

Mizrachi politicians rose to prominent positions. The taboo against ethnic parties as 'divisive of the nation and anti-Zionist' long defended by the unifying dominant culture melted away and an ethno-religious party like *Shas* was able to emerge,[12] gradually strengthening its position and obtaining up to 11 seats in Parliament (out of a total of 120) in the 1996 elections. The number of Mizrachi members of Parliament jumped from 12 to 45 between 1977 and 1996. At the same time, welfare programmes became more generous while new school programmes acknowledged the role of non-Ashkenazi judaism in the history of Jewry. The late 1980s also witnessed the development of a special school system controlled by *Shas*. Last but not least, non-Ashkenazi music gained legitimacy and got more broadcasting time on TV and radio. These achievements by no means reverse the social hierarchies. Nor have they brought about any decline in ethnic awareness among these groups – on the contrary. Yet, they represent a significant change: one may speak of a rephrasing of the tenets of the dominant culture in a manner which leaves more room for tolerance and recognition of cultural differences.[13]

The formerly Soviet Jews thus found in the 1990s a new sociopolitical reality where groups organized according to origin achieved political power thanks to both their numerical importance and the political conjuncture. They soon comprised a significant percentage of society (about 14%) held together by their attachment to their language and culture. Moreover, the particular difficulties they experienced as immigrants including the hostility directed towards them by socially deprived strata,[14] convinced their leaders that they ought to organize as a political force. This was further influenced by the power-oriented political culture that immigrants conveyed from the USSR. Last but not least, their immigration was not strongly marked by ideological motives and thus gave little consideration to the imperatives of indiscriminate integration which the dominant culture still proclaimed. Above all, however, the example of the Mizrachi Jews guided the political entrepreneurs of the *Israel Be-Alyah* party. This party too, like *Shas*, was to enjoy the high profitability of political action of a strong group not committed a priori to a general ideological line.

The 1996 general elections, when *Israel Be-Alyah* first ran candidates, bluntly confirmed this strategy. Seven formerly Soviet Jewish MPs were elected on the party's ticket – in addition one more Soviet Jew was elected as representative of the group's caucus within the Labour Party. Hence, about seven years after their mass immigration began, the formerly Soviet Jews were able to obtain about 7% of the national vote – and later even two seats in the government, including the portfolio in charge of the absorption of immigrants. As a consequence, formerly Soviet Jews actually became a major factor of socio-cultural and political pluralization within the setting. The way was now open to the recognition of communities of immigrants as foci of multiculturalism. Among other expressions, the Russian language became an optional subject of study for high school graduation, while Russian programmes appeared on national TV.

In comparison, the situation of Israeli Arabs, within the complex political and conflictual context of Israel's relation with the Palestinians and the Arab world, is precarious indeed. As a recognized minority, however, they are allowed to set up their own autonomous parties and community institutions, and they effectively accumulate assets at the municipal level. At the national level, they are also permitted to create a roof organization under an agreed leadership – this is the role of the Supreme Committee of Coordination (*Vadat Ha-maakav Ha-eliona*). This body speaks on behalf of the whole sector with respect to local as well as all-Arab interests. Their parliamentary force itself is by no means insignificant. In the 1996 election, for instance, eleven Arab MPs were elected, eight of them on independent Israeli Arab lists and three of them with Zionist parties, as representatives of the Arab constituency. Yet, because of the political conjuncture of the Israeli-Arab quarrels,[15] the Zionist parties try to avoid a situation where Arab parties would hold the balance of power in matters of major national interest. Hence, Israeli Arabs are rarely given a genuine share in government.

On the other hand, the Arabs are often divided among themselves between the desire to exploit the opportunities still offered by the regime, and the natural aspiration as a subordinate minority to express virulent resentment of the establishment. For decades Israeli Arabs were quite an isolated element in parliamentary life dominated by Zionist parties strongly marked by a national Jewish orientation. The only other force which spoke on behalf of a particularistic sector in the polity were the ultra-Orthodox Ashkenazim whose parties embodied the perpetuation of traditional Eastern European non-Zionist religiosity, and who had always represented the antithesis to the Zionists' nation-building ambitions.[16] The emergence of the Mizrachi *Shas* party, and later the formerly Soviet Jews' *Israel Be-Alyah* party, created together with the ultra-Orthodox parties a situation where the representation of particularisms became most salient among Jews themselves. This multiculturalization of Israeli society means Arabs no longer face one Jewish block divided only by social or national ideologies and political programmes. Furthermore, in the early 1990s the increasing polarization of the polity over security conceptions and the Israeli-Arab quarrel reached a point when the Zionist leaders could not ignore the Arab parties as a parliamentary force anymore and, *nolens volens*, started to take them into consideration, whether as a partner in parliamentary support of the ruling coalition or of the opposition. These new circumstances worked, all in all, to facilitate and improve the political status of Arabs and bestow more power on them. This power has been translated, with different degrees of success, into a stronger recognition by the centre of the Arabs' material claims as well as, and this is the major achievement, a readiness to view the Israeli Arabs as a link, perhaps even a bridge, to the Palestinian non-Israeli population and the Arab world.[17]

It follows, that multiculturalization in Israeli society and the departure of the dominant culture from its original unifying definitions are now widely taken for granted. As a consequence, beyond central political problems, the polity has become absorbed by sectorial exigencies – with all the incoherence and tension which these imply.

What this development shows is that in a democratic regime where the political game is open to anyone, a dominant culture may lose its determination amidst attacks from different sides which exploit the divisions of the polity as well as each other's achievements, in view of obtaining advantages for themselves. These circumstances encourage the politicization of socio-cultural groups and *multiculturalize* society. They also increase the fragmentation of society and decrease its systemic coherence.

The Dynamics of Multiculturalism

We have seen that *multiculturalization* is a process of transformation of society where national politics play a determining role. More specifically, but hardly exceptionally, the Israeli project of nation-building through cultural homogenization has been widely mitigated by the growth and increasing saliency of multiculturalism. This development took place at the detriment of the dominant culture's influence which appeared unable to curb the growing strength of socio-cultural groups. Presently, however, this development raises the crucial question of the impact on society of the void left by this weakening of the dominant culture and the fragmentation of power exemplified by the development of socio-cultural groups.

There exist many ways to confront these issues but the above analysis points to specific elements which should be included in any answer. Beyond the fact that each socio-cultural group has confronted the dominant culture by asserting its contrastive particularism, it has, at the same time, also been widely exposed to that culture, through its very confrontation with it. In the cases reviewed, the analysis has evinced the importance of Hebrew as the legitimate language. Hebrew, it is true, has different connotations within different groups, and has had to share the space of linguistic activity with different partners – Judeo-Arabic among the Mizrachi Jews, Russian among the formerly Soviet Jews, Arabic among Arabs. In each group, it has also been granted a different status: for the Mizrachi Jews it is the language of Judaism; for the formerly Soviet Jews it is simply the language of the target society; and for Arabs it is a second language. Yet, the fact remains; its generalized use still creates a reference to a common set of symbols as well as the possibility of significant communication.

Furthermore, regarding each of the groups under study, the analysis has also pointed to the undeniable convergence of the perspective of groups and of the dominant culture. The dominant culture and the Mizrachi Jews understand Zionism in different ways but both see in *Israeli Jewishness* a form of Jewishness made a national identity. In a similar vein, while the orientation of the formerly Soviet Jews is much more pluralistic and ethnic than the dominant culture finds acceptable, both sides share the definition of those formerly Soviet Jews as a *returning diaspora*. Last but not least, their fundamental contention notwithstanding, Israeli Arabs are exposed, through the acquisition of Hebrew, to *Israeliness*, that is, the Israeli version of modernity.

These notions – Israeli Jewishness, Return and Israeliness – also exhibit the relative closeness of the various socio-cultural groups to each other. It is these similarities which unveil what binds together the constituents of this setting. Like threads of different colours which keep pieces of material together, through the evincing of their distinction, those tokens warrant the cohesion – but by no means the systemic consistency – of the setting by retaining both common and differentiated allegiances among segments. This is best observed through the variety of interlanguages that develop in the various groups. Among Mizrachi Jews the notion of interlanguage applies to their versions of Hebrew itself which is the target of many elements and intonations drained from the original Judeo-Arabic vernaculars. Among the formerly Soviet Jews, this notion refers rather to their original language. Russian, indeed, is gradually permeated by Hebrew vocabulary and forms of speech that express the very insertion of the group in Israeli reality and their parallel acquisition of the legitimate language and culture. As for the Israeli Arabs, their bilingualism and their interlanguage shaped by the deep influence of Hebrew on their spoken language clearly show that Israeliness is not, for them, just a matter of geography.

We maintain this perspective when, after comparatively tracing the different profiles of socio-cultural groups, we have focused on the politics of Israel's multi-cleavage setting. Multiculturalism is, in a democratic regime, a powerful factor of change within society at large. It is evident that in appropriate circumstances socio-cultural groups may even cause a dominant culture determinedly assertive of its unifying ambitions to recognize contrastive particularisms. The latter are then able to profit from each other's success – notwithstanding the fact that their interests eventually point to different, if not divergent, directions. Though specific historical and political conjunctures can hardly be encoded a priori in comprehensive models of social transformation, one learns even from the analysis of one case of multicultural setting the importance of the political dimension. In this sense, multiculturalism may effectively be a major force of social change in terms of the recognition and legitimization of cultural diversity as an attribute of the social order.

It is in this light that one may go back to the issue of what keeps socio-cultural groups *together*, as constitutive parts of a society, at the hour when its dominant culture is waning. Each group, we have seen, forges its individuality by selecting and devising its symbols, not only drawing them from its legacies but also through contacts with, and exposure to the influence of, the dominant culture. Each group is thereby led to invent its own interculture and interlanguage carrying the trademarks of both its own and the dominant culture's enterprise. Hence, whatever their essential differences, the various socio-cultural groups which belong to the same setting actually come to share common features. It is this closeness which we want to illustrate with Wittgenstein's notion of family resemblance. This term, we now well know, appropriately applies to multiculturalism to indicate *resemblance among particularisms which pertain to the same setting*. Through this analogy one may come to understand, at the moment of multiculturalization, how the dominant culture gradually tends to be identified with one specific constituency among others. Though, even then, it is still a major *ingredient* of the intercultures and interlanguages that groups elaborate at the pace of their social insertion when efforts to retain an allegiance to legacies have been concurrent with newly acquired and adapted codes and symbols. This is the kind of *adhesive* that apparently helps restrain those who share a setting but who, by themselves, also fragment it. This could be at least a part of the answer to the question which Alain Touraine (1997) asks in the title of one of his last books: *Pourrons-nous vivre ensemble?*

Notes

1   For an expanded presentation of the typology see Ben-Rafael (1996).

2   Polish Jews, for instance, who arrived in the late 1950s at the same time as Moroccans, were settled in the central area of the country while the latter were offered housing mainly in peripheral areas (Ben-Rafael, 1994).

3   In terms of the average income of Mizrachi Jewish families as a percentage of the average income of European families, the figures show a rise from 65% in 1956-1958 to 80% in 1978-1980. Per capita, inequality is somewhat greater, because of the larger average size of Mizrachi Jewish families, but the decline in family size has also meant greater equality. For instance, in 1956, the average number of persons per room of residence was 4.5 for the Mizrachi Jews and 2.7 for the Europeans; in 1987 the figures were 1.2 and 0.8 (Nahon, 1981; 1987).

4   In terms of occupations, in the late 1980s about one-third of all employees of European origin, but only 12% of those of Mizrachi origin, were professionals, academics, and technological experts. A similar gap exists among administrators and managers (ICBS, 1988).

5   On the basis of a random sample (see Ben-Rafael/Olshtain/Geijst, 1996), it was found that 33% of the individuals of age 35 and older had no more than 12 years of schooling, while 67% had 13 years and more. Nearly all respondents (97%) stated that they held a professional occupation in their country of origin and, which is of the greatest importance, this included women.

6   Sixty-two per cent, compared to 29% among Jews, are employed in industrial and agricultural blue-collar positions; 13% of the Arab manpower is employed in professional jobs, as opposed to 31% among Jews (Semyonov/Lewin-Epstein, 1987).

7   Israel is not unique in this respect. Germany is another country which also includes a diaspora in its definition of the nation. The well-known case of *Aussiedler* (*resettlers*), that is, of those ethnic Germans originating from Eastern Europe and who 'come back to the homeland', is also characterized by many features that one finds in Israel with respect to Jewish immigrants: citizenship granted on arrival, as an a priori right of German ethnicity; material assistance for getting settled and in finding lodgement and work; special programmes for learning the language, etc. (See Knapp, 1991; Braun/Bulten/Freser, 1990). China is another 'homeland' with a special relation to diasporas and aspires to strengthen its links with the 'Chinese abroad'.

8   One example is the North African *hillula*, the pilgrimage to the tomb of holy men, practiced with growing fervour throughout Israel at special dates of the year (Weingrod, 1990).

9   In 1993 it was estimated that about 45% of the Mizrachi Jews belong to the middle class (Ben-Rafael, 1994).

10 One example among many: A new theatre, the Gesher theatre, has been created by formerly Soviet Jewish artists in view of performing for the general public. The members of the theatre have learned Hebrew sufficiently well to become, in a couple of years, a leading theatre in Israel.

11 See Ben-Rafael (1994) for the 1970s' immigrants from the USSR.

12 Before *Shas*, another successful attempt was the case of *Tami*, a splinter of the national-religious party, which, in 1981, succeeded to have three members elected on a moderate national-religious list of Mizrachi Jews. *Tami* was to lose any foothold, however, with the rise of *Shas*. This latter party was sponsored by a genuine religious elite with ultra-orthodox leaning; it had gradually emerged over the years in the Mizrachi Jewish communities against the background of their fundamentally traditionalist orientation. Moreover, among the *Shas* leadership and followers one also finds many rabbis that fill the positions of Mizrachi Rabbi in the national rabbinical hierarchy. This institution is, indeed, dual and one finds Ashkenazic alongside non-Ashkenazic rabbis at every level from the chief rabbis to town rabbis. This duality is justified by the long-standing recognition of differences in cult and religious traditions.

13. The peace process with the Palestinians that started in the early 1990s was another major factor in this picture. It created an unprecedented polarization between right and left in the Israeli polity over the cessation of Palestinian territories and the eventual creation of a Palestinian state. The competition among parties on these issues touched upon matters that each side considered as of overwhelming importance, far beyond any other issue. This strengthened a priori the bargaining power of any political force that was available for support of either of the two sides regarding those central issues. Under these conditions, a party like *Shas*, which is sensitive to the social difficulties of its constituency and to the status of religion in society, responded better than any other force to these requirements for an optimal bargaining position on the political scene. Hence, it became a member of the coalition of both Itzhak Rabin who concluded the Oslo Agreements and of Bibi Netanyahu who fought against these agreements.

14. The massive character of the formerly Soviet Jewish immigration caused many mobile elements originating from Mizrachi Jewish communities to fear a shrinking of their opportunity structures. There have been even minor but frequent expressions of hostility and tension against the immigrants – at school, in the army or in workplaces.

15. The Israeli-Arab and Israeli-Palestinian quarrels also account for the fact that Israeli Arabs do not have to perform compulsory military service in Israel, with the exception of the Druzes (10% of Israel's non-Jews) and volunteers, among whom one mainly finds members of Bedouin tribes.

16. For decades and with the exception of the most extremist *Naturei Karta* sect, the ultra-Orthodox have been ready to support any government which responded positively to their material claims and their exigencies of strengthening the status of the religious law in the national legislation. They themselves were never ready to personally participate in governments. It is remarkable that with the increasing polarization of the polity, ultra-Orthodox parties became more aggressive against the left on the ground of a lack of confidence regarding the attitude towards religion on the part of the liberal left (see Friedman, 1986).

17. We think here of the rapprochement of Israeli Arab leaders and the Palestinian official leadership as well as the links that develop between populations. Contacts of Israeli Arabs with non-Israeli Arabs are often exploited by the Israeli authorities in bartering over the peace process. For example, in 1997 an Israeli Arab delegation (including members of Zionist parties) was received in Damascus, after having been okayed by the Israeli government.

References

Adjemian, C. (1976) 'On the Nature of Interlanguage Systems', *Language Learning* 26: 297-320.

Al-Hadj, Majid (1993) 'The Changing Strategies of Mobilization among the Arabs in Israel', pp. 67-87 in Ben-Zadok, E. (ed.), *Local Communities and the Israeli Polity*. NY: SUNY.

Apter, D.E. (1987) *Rethinking Development: Modernization, Dependency and Postmodern Politics*. Newbury Park: Sage Publications.

Avineri, S. (1981) *The Making of Zionism*. New York: Basic Books.

Ben-Rafael, E. (1982) *The Emergence of Ethnicity: Cultural Groups and Social Conflict in Israel*. Westport, Conn: Greenwood Press.

Ben-Rafael, E. (1994) *Language Identity and Social Division: The Case of Israel*. Oxford: Clarendon Press.

Ben-Rafael, E. (1996) 'Multiculturalism in Sociological Perspective', pp. 133-154 in Bauböck, R./Heller, A./Zolberg, A.R. (eds.), *The Challenge of Diversity. Integration and Pluralism in Societies of Immigration*. Aldershot, UK: Avebury.

Ben-Rafael, E./Brosh, H. (1995) 'Jews and Arabs in Israel: The Cultural Convergence of Divergent Identities', pp. 18-34 in Nettler, R.(ed.), *Medieval and Modern Perspectives on Muslim-Jewish Relations*. London: Harwood Academic Pubs.

Ben-Rafael, E./Geijst, I. (1993) *The Role of the Ulpan in Immigrant Absorption: Russian and English Speakers*. Summary Report Presented to the Jewish Agency, Report 16. Tel-Aviv: The Institute for Social Research (in Hebrew).

Ben-Rafael, E./Sharot, S. (1991) *Ethnicity, Religion and Class in Israeli Society*. Cambridge: Cambridge University Press.

Ben-Rafael, E./Olshtain, E./Geijst, I. (1996) 'The Socio-Linguistic Insertion of Russian Jews in Israel', in Lewin-Espstein, N. et al. (eds.), *Russian Jews in Three Continents*. London: Frank Cass.

Blau, P.M./Duncan, O.D. (1967) *The American Occupational Structure*. New York: Academic Press.

Bonacich, E. (1980) 'Class Approaches to Ethnicity and Race', *Insurgent Sociologist* 10: 9-23.

Braun, C./Bulten, J./Freser (1990) *Diskussion und freie Rede für deutsch lernende Aussiedler mit akademischem Abschluss*. Düsseldorf: Internationales Institut für Kommunikation.

Buber, M. (1973) *On Zion*. Bath, UK: East and West Library.

Dorian, N. (1981) *Language Death: The Life Cycle of a Scottish Gaelic Dialect*. Philadelphia: University of Pennsylvania Press

Eisenstadt, S.N. (1985) *The Israeli Political System and the Transformation of Israeli Society*, pp. 415-427 in Kraucz, E. (ed.), *Politics and Society in Israel*. New Brunswick: Transaction.

Friedman, M. (1986) 'Haredim Confront the Modern City', *Studies in Contemporary Jewry* 2: 74-96.

Garmadi, J. (1981) *La Sociolinguistique*. Paris: Presses Universitaires de France.

Geertz, C. (1965) *Old Societies and New States*. New York: The Free Press.

Giddens, A. (1990) *The Consequences of Modernity*. Cambridge: Polity Press.

Giles, H. (1985) 'Social Psychology of Language', *Social Science Encyclopedia:* 783.

Giles H./Coupland N. (1991) *Language Contexts and Consequences*. Milton Keynes: Open University Press.

Giles, H./Johnson, P. (1987) 'Ethnolinguistic Identity Theory: A Social Psychological Approach to Language Maintenance', *International Journal of the Sociology of Language* 68: 69-99.

Gitelman, Z. (1997) 'From a Northern Country: Russian and Soviet Jewish Immigration to America and Israel in Historical Perspective', pp. 21-40 in Lewin-Epstein, N./Ro'i, Y./Ritterband, P. (eds.), *Russian Jews on Three Continents: Migration and Resettlement*. London: Frank Cass.

Glazer, N./Moynihan, P. (1970) *Beyond the Melting Pot: Negroes, Puerto Ricans, Jews, Italians and Irish in New York City*. Cambridge, Mass.: M.I.T. Press.

Gorny, Y. (1986) *The Arab Question and the Jewish Problem*. Tel-Aviv: Am Oved (in Hebrew).

Grillo, R.D. (1989) *Dominant Languages: Language and Hierarchy in Britain and France*. Cambridge: Cambridge University Press.

Gumperz, J.J. (1982) *Discourse Strategies*. Cambridge: Cambridge University Press.

Hamers, J./Blanc, M. (1989) *Bilinguality and Bilingualism*. Cambridge: Cambridge University Press.

Haugen, E. (1989) 'The Rise and Fall of an Immigrant Language – Norwegian in America', pp. 61-74 in Dorian, N. (ed.), *Investigating Obsolescence: Studies in Language Contraction and Death*. Cambridge: Cambridge University Press.

Helfrich, H. (1979) 'Age Markers in Speech', pp. 62-107 in Scherer, K.R./Giles, H. (eds.), *Social Markers in Speech*. Cambridge, Paris: Cambridge University Press, Editions de la Maison des Sciences de l'Homme.

Horowitz, D./Lissak, M. (1978) *Origins of the Israeli Polity – Palestine under the Mandate*. Chicago: University of Chicago Press.

Horowitz, D./Lissak, M. (1989) *Trouble in Utopia: The Overburdened Polity of Israel*. Albany: State University of New York Press.

ICBS (Israel Central Bureau of Statistics) (1986; 1988; 1989; 1995) *Statistical Abstract of Israel*. Jerusalem.

Katriel, T. (1986) *Talking Straight in Dugri Speech in Israeli Sabra Culture*. Cambridge: Cambridge University Press.

Katz, J. (1960) *Between Jews and Gentiles*. Jerusalem: Bialik Institute (in Hebrew).

Knapp, A. (1991) *Das schwere Miteinander. Aussiedler in Deutschland*. Frankfurt am Main: Fischer.

Koplewitz, I. (1990) 'The Use and Integration of Hebrew Lexemes in Israeli Spoken Arabic', *Multilingual Matters* 71: 181-195.

Kraemer, R. (1978) *Intergroup Contact Between Jews and Arabs in an Israeli High School*. Tel-Aviv: School of Education, Tel-Aviv University.

Kuper, L. (1965) *An African Bourgeoisie: Race, Class and Politics in South Africa*. New Haven: Yale University Press.

Landau, J.M. (1970) *The Arabs in Israel: A Political Study*. London.

Laver, J./Trudgill, P. (1979) 'Phonetic and Linguistic Markers in Speech', pp. 1-32 in Scherer, K.R./ Giles, H. (eds), *Social Markers in Speech.* Cambridge: Cambridge University Press.

Layish, A. (1981) *The Arabs in Israel – Continuity and Change.* Jerusalem: Magnes (in Hebrew).

Lerner, M. (1993) *New Entrepreneurs and Entrepreneurial Aspirations among Immigrants from the former USSR in Israel* (Research Report). Tel-Aviv: Tel-Aviv University, Faculty of Management, The Israel Institute of Business Research, Working Paper no. 25.

Levy, S./Guttman, L. (1976) *Values and Attitudes of Israeli Youth vols. 1 and 2.* Jerusalem: Institute of Applied Social Research (in Hebrew).

Lissak, M. (1967) 'Stratification Models and Sources of Mobility Aspirations', *Megamot* 15 (1): 62-82 (in Hebrew).

Makhou, N. (1982) 'Changes in the Employment Structures of Arabs in Israel', *Journal of Palestinian Studies* 11: 77-102.

Milroy, L. (1989) *Language and Social Networks.* Oxford: Basil Blackwell.

Myers Scotton, C. (1983) 'The Negotiation of Identities in Conversation – A Theory of Markedness and Code Choice', *International Journal of the Sociology of Language* 44: 115-136.

Nahon, Y. (1981) *Trends in Occupational Status – The Ethnic Dimension.* Jerusalem: The Jerusalem Institute for Israeli Studies (in Hebrew).

Nahon, Y. (1987) *Patterns of Educational Expansion and the Structure of Occupational Opportunities – The Ethnic Dimension.* Jerusalem: The Jerusalem Institute for Israeli Studies.

Nakhleh, K. (1975) 'Cultural Determinants of Collective Identity – The Case of the Arabs in Israel', *New Outlook* 18 (7): 31-40.

Olzak, S. (1983) 'Contemporary Ethnic Mobilization', *Annual Review of Sociology* 9: 355-374.

Orans, M. (1971) 'Caste and Race Conflict in Cross-Cultural Perspective', pp. 83-150 in Orleans, P./ Russel, W.E. (eds.), *Race, Change and Urban Society.* Beverly Hills: Sage.

Raday, F./Bunk, E. (1993) *Integration of Russian Immigrants into the Israeli Labour Market* (Research report). The Harry and Michael Sacher Institute for Legislative Research and Comparative Law. Jerusalem: The Hebrew University,

Semyonov, M./Lewin-Epstein, N. (1987) *Hewers of Wood and Drawers of Water.* Ithaca NJ: Cornell Institute of Labor Studies.

Smith, A. (1981) *The Ethnic Revival.* Cambridge: Cambridge University Press.

Smooha, S. (1972) *Israel: Pluralism and Conflict.* London: Routledge and Kegan Paul.

Smooha, S. (1976) 'Arabs and Jews in Israel', *Megamot* 22 (4): 397-424 (in Hebrew).

Swirski, S. (1981) *Mizrachi Jews and Ashkenazim in Israel.* Haifa: Makhbarot Lemekhkar (in Hebrew).

Tajfel, H. (1978a) 'Interindividual Behaviour and Intergroup Behaviour', pp. 27-59 in Tajfel, H. (ed.), *Differentiation between Social Groups.* London: Academic Press.

Tajfel, H. (1978b) 'Social Categorisation, Social Identity and Social Comparison', pp. 61-75 in Tajfel, H. (ed.), op. cit.

Tajfel, H. (1978c) 'The Achievement of Group Differentiation', pp. 78-98 in Tajfel, H. (ed.), op. cit.
Taylor, Ch. (1994) *Multiculturalism: Examining the Politics of Recognition*. Princeton: Princeton University Press.
Touraine, A. (1997) *Pourrons-nous vivre ensemble? Egaux et différents*. Paris: Fayard.
Van den Berghe, P. (1978) *Race and Racism: A Comparative Perspective*. New York: Wiley.
Wardraugh, R. (1987) *Languages in Competition*. Oxford: Oxford University Press.
Weingrod, A. (1990) *The Saint of Beersheba* Albany: State University of New York.
Wieviorka, M. (1996) 'Culture, Société et Démocratie', pp. 11-60 in *Une Société Fragmentée? Le Multiculturalisme en Débat*. Paris: La Découverte.
Wittgenstein, L. (1961) *Tractatus Logico-Philosophicus, suivi de Investigations Philosophiques*. Paris: Gallimard.

CHAPTER 6

Multiculturalism from Above: Italian Variations on a European Theme

Giovanna Zincone

PART ONE: A FRAMEWORK FOR THE EMPIRICAL ANALYSIS

Aims and Arguments of this Chapter

The main aim of this chapter is to falsify some dangerous commonplaces about multiculturalism. In fact, we intend to contrast the prevailing opinion, whereby (i) democratic regimes are challenged by multicultural threats brought about by *new* waves of immigration, (ii) the cultural homogeneity of European nation-states is threatened by the settling of immigrants forming new minorities, and finally (iii) European countries will *become* multicultural because of immigration and will consequently have to deal with the same difficult problems that traditional countries of immigration are already having to cope with.

We try to demonstrate that many democratic regimes in Europe are already characterized by a high degree of multiculturalism due to *old* minorities, and that traditional countries of immigration are often less multicultural than they claim. It used to be believed that the impact of immigration and multiculturalism would be less strong in those democratic systems which had already experienced high levels of immigration and cultural variety.[1] Europe, especially Continental Europe, was not generally considered multicultural and was therefore assumed to lack political and institutional expertise in dealing with cultural minorities.

The vision of European countries as homogeneous nation-states, contrasting with the culturally fragmented traditional countries of immigration, has recently been criticized,[2] but perhaps not strongly enough. If we want to increase the opportunities for 'intercontinental' learning in the field of multiculturalism, we need first of all to get rid of the idea of culturally homogeneous European nations being undermined by new waves of immigration.

We shall try to demonstrate that the deepening of multicultural features – at least in Europe – is due largely to demands and moves coming from old, and mostly rich, minorities (the higher strata, groups and regions).[3] To put this thesis in a less radical way, we could suggest that whereas the degree of multiculturalism promoted by the new poor immigrant minorities (lower strata, underprivileged groups) tends to be overestimated, multiculturalism promoted by high strata is underestimated.

In Part One we present a theoretical framework, explaining its heuristic potential. Some empirical support to this framework is provided in Part Two, referring to both European and non-European cases. Lastly, in Part Three, we examine in detail the current Italian situation.

Multiculturalism: A Framework

In order to support the hypotheses stated above, we attempt to build an empirical framework that will enable us to detect different degrees of multiculturalism (see Figure 1), to understand the different nature of the main multicultural moves and trends (Figure 2), and finally to observe their impact on citizenship rights (Figure 3).

The conceptual framework shown in Figure 1 can help to clarify the hypothesis of non-homogeneous European countries. It argues that *social diversities* and *social markers* (such as religion, race and language) are not relevant unless they produce identities and structural segregation. When this happens we have *multiculturalism* in civil society (that is, a fragmented society), but this does not necessarily imply the presence of *multiculturalism in political society*, that is, the formation of ethnic lobbies, parties, unions or factions within parties and unions. Similarly, *multiculturalism* in political society does not always affect the *production of policies* aimed at culturally protecting minorities, nor does it imply a *multicultural organization of the state*, bodies and institutional devices representing minorities as separate entities. We can therefore identify four levels of multiculturalism: civil society, political society, public policies and the state whereas the mere existence of social markers and diversity would create a situation of *pre-multiculturalism*.[4]

Our suggestion is that multiculturalism can be positioned at different levels of the socio-political system. It would also seem reasonable to hypothesize that the higher the political level at which *multiculturalism* is located (with civil society being the lowest and the state the highest level), the stronger the degree of multiculturalism in the system. Unfortunately, this hypothesis does not match empirical reality. For instance, the presence of *multiculturalism* at a medium level (political society) does not necessarily imply a medium degree of multiculturalism. Let us consider the Christian Democratic parties in European countries. They should score quite high in terms of *multiculturalism*, since they are positioned at the level of political society and also involve relevant actors, but we know that Christian Democratic parties attract secularized voters, too, and that, vice versa, Catholics are voting increasingly for secularized parties.

Figure 1: Multiculturalism Dimensions and Degrees of Intensity

STRONG	−	*Porosity*	+	WEAK
	Social markers and diversities *(race, language, religion, custom)*			
Below (a)			society	l
M	Multiculturalism in civil society *(structural segregation and/or cultural identity)*			e
O	Multiculturalism in political society *(associations, union branches and party factions, parties)*			v
V	Multiculturalism in public policies *(policies of recognition, segregation)*			e
E	Multiculturalism in the state *(collective representation, federal reform, secession)*			l
Above (a)			state	
				STRONG

This case illustrates that other dimensions, such as the rate of *porosity* of cultural barriers, the degree of ascription and duration of the allegiances are relevant in evaluating the 'multicultural score' of a political system. We need two axes (more versus less porosity and society *versus* state) to properly assess the degree of multiculturalism of a political system. To score a high degree of *multiculturalism* requires more than a move from society up to the state, it also needs a shift from *loose and ineffective* forms of multicultural organization to more *secluded and effective* ones.

The framework presented in Figure 1 contests another apparently reasonable statement – that *multiculturalism* is the consequence of demands coming from below, that is, from members of the communities making up civil society. We suggest that *multiculturalism* does not necessarily go upwards from society to politics or from politics to the state, but that it can also operate in the opposite direction. In fact, multicultural policies sometimes come from above, that is, from the state, when it fosters the formation and consolidation of cultural groups. Cultural identities have been created, or at least reinforced, by a colonial definition of states and regions or by the symbolic representation of cultures, as in the former Yugoslavia and Soviet Union.[5]

We would suggest, in addition, that when there is a movement towards multiculturalism from below, it is not always the result of a move from low social strata (see Figure 2). It is possibly more often the result of a move from the high social strata. In other words, multiculturalism is not just a device to empower weaker groups, it can also be a weapon to reinforce strong ones. When referring to the classic distinction between moves from above and moves from below, it is therefore important to distinguish between *above (a)* (the state) and *above (b)* (high strata) as well as between *below (a)* (society) and *below (b)* (low strata). Organized civil society can promote high strata interests, as demonstrated by the classic oligarchic liberal models, and the state can protect the low strata that are too weak to get organized and become influential.

Figure 2: Multicultural Moves and Trends

Above (b)		
M		Culturalization of territorial economic cleavages
O	High strata	Deepening of traditional domestic cultural cleavages
V		Deepening of the national cleavage against immigrants
E	Low strata	Rise of cultural cleavages from new immigrant minorities
Below (b)		

In order to analyse the impact of *multiculturalism* on citizenship rights (see Figure 3), we have singled out the main dimensions of civil, political and social rights: inclusion, relevance and differentiation, which we now examine in turn.

a) *Inclusion* when applied to civil rights implies the free access to public spaces and social roles, to positions, to occupations and jobs, as in the case of the abolition of segregation of the Jews, black people or women, or lifting a ban on women's and minorities' access to certain professions and jobs. As far as political rights are concerned, it implies not only the extension of suffrage, but also the equalization of the weight of votes (for instance, the abolition of the plural ballot). The introduction of proportional electoral systems will generally make political representation more inclusive and equal compared to majoritarian systems. As far as social rights are concerned, inclusion implies not only the extension of entitlements and provisions to new categories and strata of the population, but also the equalization of the amount and quality of the provisions.[6]

b) *Relevance* of civil rights means the ability to eliminate serious social barriers and to liberate numerous groups constrained by them. With regard to political rights it implies the power of people to vote to form bodies that are crucial in the decision-making process. We could observe, for instance, that the increasing prominence of technical bodies and opacity in decision-making tend to drain power from popular suffrage and make political rights less relevant. In social rights, we could accept Esping-Andersen's suggestion and consider relevant those rights that emancipate people from the market and economic subordination. We can also widen this spectrum[7] and classify as relevant those rights capable of emancipating women, cultural and ethnic minorities from social segregation and marginalization.

c) *Differentiation* is the propensity of citizenship rights to accept and foster diversity of opinion, custom, language, religion, political organizations and social provision. The third dimension is not in contrast with the first. All citizens can receive, for instance, the same amount of money or the same value of vouchers and be free to spend them in different ways. The entitlement to vote can similarly be used to choose different parties. The equalization of the vote through the introduction of proportional systems reinforces the multiplication and differentiation of parties.

Figure 3: Dimensions of Citizenship and Culturalization Processes

REGIMES	RIGHTS	INCLUSION	RELEVANCE	DIFFERENTIATION (pluralism vs. multiculturalism)
liberal	Civil rights	access to roles and positions	liberation	cultural freedom vs. *identity*
republican	Political rights	extension and equalization	influence	competition vs. *segmentation*
social-democratic	Social rights	extension and equalization	protection	autonomy vs. *cultural assignment*

The real contradiction lies not between the three dimensions of citizenship rights, but within the dimension of differentiation. It consists of the contrast between pluralism and multiculturalism, plurality and separation, although this contrast is less clear than we are tempted to believe.

Let us start by distinguishing between pluralism and separation, between *pluralism* and *multiculturalism*.[8] Both provide differentiation, but while *multiculturalism* tends to separate, building barriers to the free circulation of people and rooting individuals in their original creeds, languages, cultures and roles, *pluralism* breaks down discrimination and barriers based on religion, gender, ethnicity and increases individual opportunities to opt out and choose. The distinction was first introduced by Dahrendorf (1979) when he contrasted 'ligatures' with 'life chances'. He underlined the importance of both dimensions of differentiation in reaching individual achievement. We need freedom *and* roots, discontinuity *and* consistency, doubts *and* truths to build an 'harmonious self'.

Furthermore, the difference between opinions and values is not as neat as we would be tempted to believe: creeds can change through questioning and hybridization and may be abandoned. The same single religious party, union, club, and school can represent a life chance *and* a ligature, a platform and an anchorage, an instrument of pluralism and an outcome of culturalism.

It is difficult in real life to draw a clear-cut distinction between pluralism and multiculturalism, between chances and ligatures. This is why problems arise when we want to intervene with regulations. How much can we allow ligatures to impair individual chances? How much can we allow cumulative individual wills to destroy ligatures, traditions and belonging? Can opting out be considered an appropriate solution for liberal multiculturalism? Are there situations in which some constraints could be exercised – as in preserving languages – without departing from usual liberal practices, though contrasting with abstract liberal principles? And vice versa, is opting out an appropriate and sufficient guarantee for individuals living in groups where human rights are repressed? Can we leave women and young girls free to 'choose' a condition of slavery or should we force them to accept our interpretation of freedom?

These are fortunately extreme cases and rare within democratic political systems. Political philosophers have focused attention on them because of the ethical challenge they present. However, as social scientists, we must be able to *empirically* analyse *multiculturalism*. To do so, we need to identify dimensions and indicators that enable us to detect different levels of multiculturalism in Western societies and therefore to understand whether strong degrees of *multiculturalism* are a real novelty for European countries.

Political science has already invented the concept of subcultures, and segmented society in order to single out strong cultural aggregation characterized by *low porosity*, that is, strong reluctance to accept messages and contact from outside and high intensity of internal communication (endogamy included). In Italy we used to identify two relevant subcultures, Catholic and social-communist regions (Galli, 1966). In the Netherlands political scientists have noted the presence of 'pillars' (Daalder, 1966; Lijphart, 1977). Multiculturalism in political society used to be strong in many European democracies and, in some, it still is.

We are thus starting to draw distinctions. As far as civil rights are concerned, we can allow and foster the plurality of associations and denominations, and thus widen the organizational 'offer' to individuals in civil society. The offer is wider only if individuals can choose freely and move from one association to another. The discrimination between liberal pluralism and illiberal multiculturalism is supposed to reside precisely in this freedom to move through different cultural memberships. Organizations and associations are free to exist and must be defended against the repressive majority, but they should not oppress their own members. Should we therefore ask fundamentalist religious organizations to adopt democratic institutions and practice? Or should we simply require a community to leave its members free to leave?

Kymlicka (1996a, b) identified a similar[9] *discrimen* when he distinguished between 'internal restriction' and 'external protection'. Unfortunately, in theory as well as in practice, it is difficult to reconcile a strict liberal interpretation of pluralism with the preservation of cultures. In fact, in theory it is impossible even to conceive of non-compulsory protectionism – in economics as well as in anthropology, protection implies compulsion. As Galeotti (1994) remarked, external protection cannot be implemented in the absence of internal restrictions. If you want to protect the community against pressure from the outside, but refuse to impose constraints inside (for instance, if you do not forbid children of the French Canadian minority to attend English schools, but do not make it compulsory for them to attend French ones), you must be prepared to see this linguistic group disappear (Kymlicka, 1996).

If we decide that culture should be freely chosen (Taylor, 1992, 1994; Dworkin, 1992) in order to nurture the Self – and this could be the right stance to take (that is, to place individual freedom under all circumstances before the preservation of the group) – we must simply be aware of the consequences of this option.

On the other hand, we must understand that, from a political point of view *what is at stake here is not so much a matter of individual freedom but of collective sovereignty*. All nation-states impose their dominant values, practices and language.

We take it for granted that no individual is free to refuse to learn and speak the official language(s) of the country, unless he or she decides to emigrate.[10] It is a share of this kind of sovereignty that organized minorities want to hold.

How far can the devolution of state sovereignty to internal minorities go? We allow foreign states to speak their own languages and apply their own alien values, we are not concerned when individuals are forced to learn useless languages or conform to primitive customs. We just demand the respect of human rights. Following the same principle, we can consider *human rights* as the moral boundary that cannot be crossed by domestic minoritarian cultures either.

It should not be very difficult to defend this stance. Taylor believes this set of non-negotiable values to be common to all human cultures. He observes that the right to survive, not to be mutilated or tortured, the right not to be imprisoned without fair trial are recognized by all religions. Furthermore, they are better conceptualized and accepted when the same general principles are nourished by each specific local tradition (Taylor, 1994).

However, Taylor's thesis is not completely convincing. We unfortunately know that the interpretation of basic human rights varies from culture to culture. Are foetuses entitled to survive? Can clitoridectomy be considered mutilation? Should the case of women locked in the home or caged in 'oppressive' clothes be judged as a breach of the habeas corpus principle? Until quite recently, it was considered quite normal for suffrage to exclude women. In France they were excluded from political rights till 1945 and in Switzerland and Luxembourg until even more recently. Why did no Western democracy take the initiative to put these countries under embargo for not allowing all their women citizens to vote?

If we were able to give a common transcultural definition of human rights, could we consider it a sufficient boundary that group rights should not cross, or do we need to strengthen it?

If we consider communication between members an essential requisite for a political community, then we must add other obligations which minorities should comply with, such as learning the official national language(s) or being acquainted with basic constitutional principles.

Within these boundaries *multiculturalism* is compatible with our traditional notion of international tolerance and with the survival of our political communities. By contrast – as we shall see later – *multiculturalism* is incompatible with all the major modern theories of democracy: liberal, republican or social-democratic. In fact, all these political ideologies were moved by the opposite aim, that is, they intended to break separation, the encapsulation of individuals into parochial cultures, institutions and allegiances. Separation and ligatures can be considered a premodern legacy. The main modern democratic ideologies, liberalism, republicanism and social democracy, have all contested the seclusion variant as a relic of the past and a challenge to their universalistic attitude.

To clarify our thesis, we suggest a very simplified conceptualization of the relationship between citizenship rights and modern Western ideologies. Each of these ideologies recognizes a category of citizenship rights which it considers more essential than others:

- For *liberalism* these are *civil rights*, that is, those rights aimed at emancipating individuals from religion, occupation, place and clan. *La Liberté des Modernes*, conceived by Constant, is precisely that – freedom from traditional constraining membership and from intrusive state activity. The liberal concept of freedom contrasts with serfdom (Skinner, 1996), and implies not depending on anybody's will but on the Law.[11] Liberal anthropology imagines man to be interested in self-determination and involved in his own private and economic life (Gianni, 1994).
  We must remember that liberalism was not conceived in opposition to republicanism, but against the *ancien régime*, it was not the refusal of the merchant to waste his time in politics, but a quest for freedom addressed to guilds and villages, to clans and churches. That is why liberalism fitted quite well with the creation of nation-states, because nation-states, too, wanted to break out of narrow memberships, widen spaces and standardize rules.
- For *republicanism* the core of citizenship rights are *political rights*. The republican feels it his duty to act in the public sphere, taking part in public decision-making but, in doing so, he must divest himself of his social membership. Whereas the liberal is free to keep his creed, provided that it does not contrast with a secularized attitude towards politics and market, the republican must believe in republican values. Neither liberalism nor republicanism are compatible with the survival of premodern allegiances. The same can be said for social democracy.
- For *social democracy* the core rights are *social ones*. They aim to materially emancipate the worker from the employer, a wife from her husband, the minority from the majority, and to enable citizens to become competent in controlling public life (Habermas, 1994), freeing them from urgent material needs.

The very idea of citizenship rights is based on the emancipation from particularism and on common access to equal legal status. Multicultural citizenship is a contradiction in terms. The liberal, republican and social-democratic ideals are incompatible with multiculturalism defined as separation, *but in practice actual regimes inspired by these doctrines (or more often by a mixture of them) all adjusted to multiculturalism*, and have come to terms with communitarian practices. Furthermore, the process of social separation or encapsulation in Europe may have had *non-cultural sources*, but it has always ended in a *culturalization of conflict*. Our historical expertise in dealing with multiculturalism is greater than we are accustomed to believe. When the working classes decided to gain power, not only did they build separate organizations (to which the bourgeois were not admitted), but they also invented an identity, a sense of belonging to a 'new humanity'. We should not forget that in doing so the workers were reacting to a degrading culturalization of the working classes by the upper strata (Zincone, 1997).[12] The same was true for the Afro-American 'black is beautiful' slogan in the 1970s.

Seclusion can be an answer to exclusion coming from above, that is, from stronger cultures and classes. Even today, democratic citizenship is more likely to be modified by moves by the privileged, that is, moves from above than by moves from below, that is, by the underprivileged.

We can single out and classify the main multicultural moves and trends (see Figure 2): *the culturalization of territorial divides* against the less wealthy regions, *the deepening of domestic cultural cleavages* and *of the national cleavage against immigrants* are classified as 'moves from above (b)', that is, moves by high strata. The mobilization of new immigrant minorities, that is, *the rise of new cultural cleavages by the underprivileged* is classified as a 'move from below (b)', that is, by low strata. Although the latter is generally considered the main factor behind multicultural processes, at least in Western Europe, we shall try to demonstrate that the first three are having a stronger effect in reshaping our political systems and citizenship rights. Furthermore, we suggest that the willingness to *react* to margin-alization and contempt[13] can be considered a relevant factor in the rise of new cleavages stemming from the low strata.

The impact of all these cultural moves on citizenship is not just multicultural. These demands are already changing and will probably have an even greater impact on *all dimensions of democratic citizenship* in the future. The moves by the upper strata have not just affected multicultural differentiation, generating new identities, new political movements, new regional autonomies and even threats of secession, they have also lowered the relevance of social citizenship, demanding reduction in fiscal and tax transfers and in taxes and social expenditure.[14] Multicultural upheavals fall, at least in part, in the wider category of the 'rebellion of the well-off',[15] like the fiscal revolt in Britain and the United States in the 1980s. Driven by post-modernism, we tend to underestimate the spread of what we could define the *culture of interests*,[16] the legitimization of the pursuit of selfish material goals, and the consequent reshaping of the status of individuals, regions and nations in terms of their capacity to achieve these goals.

Our hypothesis is that there is a *cultural* resistance to the spread of the dominant Western culture of interests, a genuine religious and traditional resistance to globalization, secularization and capitalism. We suggest, however, that this is not the only aspect of the phenomenon, nor possibly the most relevant.

It is also possible that the losers in domestic and international competition in the dominant arena of material interests could tend to readopt or reinforce the symbolic use of traditional identities as political tools to resist social marginalization.[17] We must also consider the fact that the winners, under pressure from the globalization of the economy, are tempted to free themselves of the losers' burden. They are supported in this strategy by the radical neo-liberal culture of interests, and are also readopting or reinforcing traditional cultural divides, or even inventing new ones, to morally justify their behaviour.[18] *Weak and strong social minorities are both turning economic divides into cultural ones.* This process may be due, as some authors maintain, to the crisis of traditional channels of representation, such as working-class parties and unions (Kepel, 1996) or, in the case of Italy, the Christian Democrats (Diamanti, 1996a). However, the cultural 'rebellion of the well-off', that is the protest of the high strata, is producing more serious effects than the resistance of the marginalized themselves and is likely to continue to do so in the future.

PART TWO: SOME EMPIRICAL EVIDENCE. RESTATING THE DIMENSIONS OF MULTICULTURALISM

In this part of the paper we shall try to reinforce the arguments presented in the first part of this chapter, in order to underline the operational nature of the dimensions of multiculturalism, before applying them to the Italian case. The reader with a good knowledge of the European situation, could skip directly to Part Three if the explanation in the previous section appeared clear enough.

Social markers and diversities: Societies can be characterized by differences in somatic features, nation of origin, language, religion, civil tradition and so on. This kind of variety is unlikely to produce socially relevant events, unless the individuals characterized by these social markers feel and/or are felt to be different from others. If no such processes of seclusion-exclusion, or appreciation-devaluation of cultures occur, then these sets of individuals do not become what we can define as *identity groups*.

Multiculturalism in civil society: Real cultural differences, on the other hand, may not exist or may have disappeared, but this will not prevent the members of the group from believing they hold common cultural traditions (Keyes, 1976;

Martiniello, 1995).[19] As stated by Weber "Ethnic community diverges from lineage group, because it is just a believed community" (Weber, 1961: 398). Ethnic groups are, in a sense, social and political constructions. Friedrik Barth (1969) pointed out that they are not necessarily characterized by a consistent common culture, but by social and symbolic frontiers.

We do not find multicultural societies in nature. The process of culturalization can be more or less advanced and more or less successful. As Carlos Barbé (1997) noted, various indicators reveal a far stronger cultural identity in Spanish Catalonia than in the territories referred to as 'Padania' by the Italian secessionist party Lega Nord (the Northern League), that is, the Po valley in the north-east of the country. It will be interesting to see whether the political action of the Northern League will succeed in the future in giving rise to a widespread 'Padanian' identity.

Identity groups become even more interesting for a social researcher when they also happen to be *structural groups*. Religious, linguistic or somatic groups become structural groups only if the members of the group do not freely circulate in all social roles of the social structure (Zincone, 1982). Roles with high social status tend to be assigned to members of the dominant groups and access is either formally forbidden or made difficult for others. On the other hand, the roles naturally or socially assigned to certain marginalized groups tend to be devalued. Perhaps the most striking and simple example is the function of reproduction, performed necessarily by women, which has a very low status in modern society compared with the function of production.

A crucial sociological question concerns the relationship between cultural seclusion (that is, identities) and structural seclusion (occupational, economic, residential segregation). Can cultures be considered in some way super-structural? Should Islamic associations be considered as new organizational opportunities that marginalized minorities are adopting after the disappearance of radical working class parties (Kepel 1996a and b)? Should they be considered as new ways of resisting capitalism (Wieviorka, 1996a)? Or is it true, as Pizzorno (1993) maintains,[20] that cultural identities dominate interests and are the real basis of political conflict? We would prefer to avoid entering this debate[21] by limiting the alternatives and examining specific issues, as we have already done in Part One. We therefore focus on a phenomenon that has been little aired in the present multicultural debate, but seems likely to have a strong impact on the transformation of our democracies, that is, the structural and territorial divide of culturalization as a move by *high strata and strong interests*.

A strong pre-existing and widespread cultural identity is not a necessary precondition for organizing cultural political movements and for producing *multiculturalism in political society*. The case of the Italian Lega Nord which wants secession from Southern Italy shows the possibility of turning regional economic differences into cultural divides, even in a country which is comparatively homogeneous in terms of religion, language and race. In other words, we can have weak identities and strong demands.

Vice versa, strong identities can give rise to weak demands. For example, cities and towns are sources of strong identification, but do not always raise strong localistic demands. Structural and/or identity groups do not necessarily become *political groups* and are not necessarily willing to make challenging political demands. The formation of a political group requires an agent and leadership which is willing and able to establish a cleavage towards the outside, diluting internal cleavages, constructing a shared creed, and setting up a stable organization (Zincone, 1982; Bartolini/Mair, 1990). Even if politically organized cultural groups do exist, their main goal is not necessarily to achieve differential treatment, that is, *multicultural policies,* or *multiculturalism in the state*. The main political goal of such a group can be integration.

A survey by the Australian Office of Multicultural Affairs in 1988 showed scarce interest in multicultural policies by the minorities that would have benefited from them (Betts, 1995). At present the new minorities brought to Europe by recent waves of immigration also have to fight for de-segregation and respect of their identities, at the same time. The first goal is often more vital than the second. Along with the fact that their numbers are still too small, this could explain why they have rarely been able to form parties, except at the local level, and even here they have not been able to obtain large and consistent support.

By contrast, old and new cultural divides created by high strata, well-off social groups and regions have already been able to form political groups and are having a strong impact on institutions in European countries. The culturalization of strong territorial interests is of course not the only source of multiculturalism in Europe. Corsica, for instance, which has made very strong demands, could not be defined as a rich region. And the high density of ethnic groups in certain 'areas' of the social structure is obviously a relevant phenomenon and potential source of multiculturalism, even though it is not always located in a specific territory. However, I suggest that we pay specific attention to the case of *territorial* cultural and structural diversities, because it appears to be currently the main potential factor of transformation of citizenship rights. In the case of some European countries, and also of Canada, the 'territorial division of labour' and regional differences in wealth and economic performance overlap with differences in language and/or religion and have produced important cleavages that have led to the establishment of institutional borders within the state (*state multiculturalism*) and have come close to becoming institutional borders between new states through secession.[22] In Europe and Latin America, in the past and present, as well as in India in the present, non-territorial cultural cleavages have already played, and seem likely to play in the future, a crucial role in shaping the political systems, provided that they are exploited by entrepreneurial political agents.

We can distinguish between *light* and *heavy multiculturalism in political society*, taking into consideration the fact that sometimes highly relevant cultural organizations are no longer very cultural. Catholic organizations, for instance, were often born with radical anti-system attitudes, since they tried to contest secularized policies of modern states. They were repressed in past centuries by liberal as well as by modernizing authoritarian regimes. At that time they were strong and cultural, now they are possibly stronger (having achieved political power), but less cultural. The numerical strength, low porosity[23] and radicalization of organizations should therefore be taken into consideration when evaluating the degree of 'multiculturalism' at this level. We could point out that neither the electorate nor the elite of the Christian Democratic Party 'DC' (Democrazia Christiana) in Italy were open only to Roman Catholics – many moderates supported the party against the risk of Communism or simply as a channel for a political career.

At the social, political and institutional levels there can, of course, be intermediate and high degrees of multiculturalism as well as *extreme cases*. Should we consider native reserves protective institutional devices? Can slavery and apartheid be considered extreme forms of structural multiculturalism enforced by law? In concentration camps, the use of human beings as guinea pigs is a dramatic demonstration that *the identity* of some groups can become so alien as to deprive their members even of the status of human beings, down-grading them to the condition of animals.[24] Banned from the social structure, they enter the economic structure as mere objects of physical exploitation. These extreme cases fortunately fall outside the limits of democratic citizenship and are not the subject of this paper, but they can help to illustrate the risk of triggering processes of alienation. Multicultural policies may be introduced even when people with the same social marker do not desire to reinforce their identities or when they have a low capacity for organizing themselves or make strong demands. Privileged groups (above b) can use the state (above a)[25] to impose identities and differentiated policies *from above*, as a way of marginalizing deprived structural groups.

Black cultural identity in the United States, for instance, has been and is still now in part an identity imposed from above, in a coercive way. This does not exclude a further and subsequent process of rebellious identification. In France, immigrant associations and claims for recognition of identity are stronger in those regions where previously the 'National Front' achieved a strong vote, that is, where an anti-immigrant, anti-'new minorities' culture had entered political society.

As suggested by Martin Schain (1996), this could be described as a 'reactive' culturalization. On the other hand, deculturalization has often been intended as a progressive stance. That is why, for instance, the Democrats in the United States, during the 1960s, and the Labor party in Australia, during the 1970s, supported provisions to favour underprivileged minorities by fostering their escape from 'cultural' stigmas through de-segregation and equal opportunities policies (Castles, 1992b; Castles/Vasto/Lo Bianco, 1992a).

Having established the focus of our analysis, we can begin by arguing in favour of our initial hypothesis: that multiculturalism is also, and possibly mostly, a European experience.

Countries of long-standing immigration, like Australia and the United States, were intended to be places of relatively homogeneous culture and did not seek diversity, neither did they pursue the objective of a multicultural society. They became so, quite unwillingly, at a certain point in their history. Despite this, they did not immediately nor necessarily have to become multicultural political systems. The United States, for example, was quite reluctant to adopt multicultural policies – publicly funded programmes for immigrants to preserve their mother tongue started only in the 1970s.

Even Australia, which is now considered a virtuous example of multicultural policies, had 'White Australia' policies in the recent past. This is just one of many examples of single-culture (mono-cultural) attitudes and policies through which dominant cultures have tried to obstruct an increasingly multicultural society. The United States has often introduced immigration quotas and Australia has pursued incentive/disincentive policies towards certain groups to protect the Anglo-Saxon cultural pre-eminence.[26]

By contrast, we must remember that many European countries have been and are still characterized by strong social multiculturalism and sometimes by strong political and institutional multiculturalism. The same countries which once resisted 'new cultures'[27] brought by immigration, now have quite advanced multicultural practices and attitudes towards new minorities. Belgium, for instance, is one of the few countries where the Islamic religion is taught in state schools. In the Netherlands, immigrants have formed a sort of additional 'pillar' in a system where different religions and cultures were used to having their own schools, radio broadcasts, social security structures and parties (Cross/Entzinger, 1988). In Europe, languages and cultures, as well as independent religions, like the Catholic Church, have contested nation-building and state-building processes, giving birth to political cleavages that offered a social platform for the formation of linguistic, regional or religious parties and/or encouraged federal institutions (Rokkan, 1970, 1998). Switzerland, and to a certain extent also the Netherlands and Belgium, represent rather different cases. The situation cannot be considered the consequence of an incomplete process of political modernization, since these states, from the very beginning, grew out of a plurality of cultures and 'nations'. Canada is an important example of a non-European state which was 'born' multicultural. Thus we are not maintaining that Europe is the only multicultural continent, but just that it is possibly the richest in multicultural experience and the least perceived as such.

The Netherlands, Belgium and the Swiss Confederation were institutionalized cartels of religions, languages, cultures and nations. They were kept together by the desire to maximize the economic benefits deriving from the control of commercial passages (across the North Atlantic or the Alps), the need to resist imperial military attacks or the claim for freedom of cities, guilds and leagues.

Europe has experienced a high degree of social multiculturalism and provided 'heavy' political and institutional solutions to promote it. For instance, federal institutions officially set up to protect the autonomy of places and territorial entities (states, cantons, regions) were often drawn up on the basis of cultural divisions. The Swiss political system has always claimed to represent territories rather than languages and cultures, but regional units were sometimes just disguised cultures.

This overlapping of institutional and cultural units can never be perfect and tends to become even less so over time, not only because of *physical changes* in cultural borders (people move), but because of the *identity changes* of the cultural borders. The secession of Catholic Belgium from the Netherlands in 1830 still left a multicultural country (including Flemish, Walloon and German groups).

Traditional cultural cleavages can be exacerbated by the unbalancing or even reversal of traditional economic primacies, as in Belgium. The lack of connections between social and political-institutional multiculturalism and the fact that the administrative units no longer coincided with cultural ones, brought renewed conflicts and eventually made it necessary to revise the constitution. Institutional reforms in Belgium, which started in the 1970s and went on into the 1980s, culminated in a federal reform of the state achieved in July 1993. This kind of constitutional settlement is rather unusual, as it claims to represent not only regions but also, quite openly, cultures.[28] It can be considered an uncommon combination of territorial and cultural federalism.

European scholars, like the Dutch Arend Lijphart (1977) and Hans Daalder (1966) both born in small multicultural countries, have identified a specific model of democracy characterized by heavy multicultural (so-called *segmented*) societies and heavy political and institutional (so-called *consociational*) solutions. According to these scholars, countries characterized by strongly perceived cultural cleavages that produce subcultures, tend to find unusual political solutions in order to avoid disruption. They generally adopt electoral systems with proportional representation, large coalition governments and proportional allocation of political positions. Switzerland is an extreme case of politico-institutional multiculturalism and consociationalism, where conventionally the major parties and the major cultures have to be represented in the seven-member executive, the Federal Council. Present tensions between the German and Romande (French) parts suggest that even these extreme consociational solutions are fragile, although Switzerland in fact shows a strong capacity to resist disintegration.

The differences between multicultural Switzerland and Belgium can be traced back to the fact that whereas the former opted immediately for a federal solution and counterbalanced it with transcultural parties, the latter chose a unitarian state and then moved towards federalism, passing through a phase of multicultural political society with traditional parties split into Walloon and Flemish sub-parties. The Netherlands is characterized by non-territorial religious cleavages: in this case, the divide between Protestants, Catholics and the secular population can only be represented by parties. The outcome has been far less disruptive than in Belgium.

The general decline in religious attitudes in the Netherlands was particularly marked. Combined with a lack of overlap between interests and cultures, this seems to have preserved the country from the rising wave of reinforced traditional cleavages. It leads me to suggest that the territorial settlement of cultures, that is, the overlap between place and culture, does not necessarily produce more explosive situations. Paradoxically, in these cases, institutional solutions are more easily found and function better, provided that they are taken in due time and that the cultural borders are clear enough. One of the problems in former Yugoslavia was the presence of enclaves and the lack of clarity of ethnic boundaries (Elazar, 1993). Unfortunately, the heaviest forms of institutional multiculturalism are not viable when there are too many ethnic enclaves.

If we compare the treatment of old subcultures already settled at the time of nation-building with that of newly established minorities, we can rephrase and repropose Castles' (1994) suggestion and ask: 'to what extent are the political solutions adopted by European countries also applicable for countries of traditional immigration?' The answer would seem to be: 'to a very limited extent', if we look at multicultural trends (see Figure 2). Except for Canada, other traditional immigration countries are not concerned with traditional minorities. They are affected mostly by demands from indigenous groups and new minorities, with very few phenomena similar to the European ones, such as:

a) the development of new cultural cleavages based on territorial divides (which we define as the 'culturalization of territorial economic conflicts') and the quest for new institutional responses to these conflicts;
b) a deepening of traditional domestic cultural cleavages and sometimes a crisis in their institutional settlements;
c) a deepening of the national cleavage, the rise of anti-immigrant attitudes and the consequent political reactionary dilemma between nationalist mood and regionalist demands;
d) cultural demands from new minorities that must be accommodated despite neo-nationalist moods.

Among New World countries only Canada is experiencing a similar combination between:

a) renewed conflicts within old dominant cultures that come close to secession;
b) the revival of protests by old repressed minorities (like the Indians);
c) weariness and diffidence towards newly settled minorities.

Differences nevertheless prevail over similarities when we compare Europe and traditional immigration countries, and within the European situation, Italy represents a special and rather unusual case.

PART THREE: ITALY AS A PURE CASE OF 'REBELLION BY THE WELL-OFF'

In this part I refer specifically to the Italian case, although I am aware that this may mean over-proving my point. New immigration minorities in Italy are much smaller, more recent and less organized than in Central and North-Western Europe. But, as we have already said, one aim of this paper is to shift the focus of multicultural analysis to processes whose importance has been underestimated,[29] that is, multiculturalism brought about by traditional, strong minorities and the culturalization of territorial interest conflicts. The latter is peculiar to the Italian case. I shall try to detect the impact of these processes on citizenship rights in order to demonstrate the strong influence of 'multiculturalism from above'.

I examine the Italian case not only for the good reason that it is the one I know best, or because it is relatively unknown abroad, but because it can be considered a sort of *casus mirabilis*. Firstly, it is one of the political systems most severely affected by the fall of the Berlin Wall, since it used to house the biggest[30] Communist party in the West. Alongside the crisis of the traditional working-class parties, the clean-up by the judges involved in the *Mani Pulite* (clean hands) trials, have also destroyed the other main channel of political representation, the Christian Democratic party. In addition, because of its large public debt, Italy has been forced to increase fiscal pressure very rapidly in order to come in line with other European Union countries of the Euro currency group. Traditional class and religious cleavages lost relevance and a new fiscal and territorial cleavage was set 'free' to appear.

The creation of the Lega Nord (Northern League), has made Italy the most striking example of the culturalization (and ethnicization) of territorial economic divisions. This party campaigns against Southern Italy claiming to represent a superior North-Italian culture, based on the values of industry, dignity and independence. Furthermore, to this day, strong old cultural minorities have been kept quiet by being granted remarkable privileges. By contrast, Italy, although it has only recently become a country of immigration, took little time to produce anti-immigrant attitudes. The recent introduction of measures that give priority to foreigners born of Italian descent indicate a reinforcement of the national cleavage that separates Italian nationals from new immigrant minorities.

The Italian case reveals:

- a *culturalization of territorial economic conflicts*, and hence the rise of multiculturalism at the level of political society and eventually the state;
- a *slight deepening of traditional domestic cultural cleavages* due to the *established privileges* enjoyed by strong linguistic minorities, which has already provoked multiculturalism in political society, in public policies and in the state;
- *the traditional hegemonic culturalism* due to the influential presence of the Catholic Church in Italy, which gave rise in the past to culturalism in political society and public policies, has started to decrease;
- a *reinforcement of the national cleavage opposing new minorities* that has fostered *new privileges* reserved to aliens of Italian origin;
- a *very low degree of multiculturalism* caused by recent immigration waves, especially if compared to *multiculturalism* promoted by old strong minorities through the culturalization of economic territorial conflict.

Culturalization of Territorial Economic Cleavages

I begin by singling out the exogenous factors that made the current changes possible. The first is the attenuation of the class cleavage and the democratization of the

Communist party. It is perhaps useful to briefly recall the factor that is normally identified as being responsible for the decay of traditional class cleavage. This is *economic globalization*, it increases competition, fosters labour-saving technologies and lean production, that is, the breaking up of big plants into smaller ones at local level and delocalization at international level. It also increases competition within the labour force, encouraging workers to identify with their company. Unemployment, discontinuity in working life, the growth of the tertiary sector and of jobs with a traditionally low rate of unionization are all factors which decrease the feeling of identity as members of the working class and weaken workers' organizations, causing a decline in unionization. The political salience of class cleavage was further diminished after the fall of the Berlin Wall and the clear failure of Communist experiments. The diminished weight of the class cleavage left room for the rise or reinforcing of other lines of conflict, such as cultural and territorial divides.

The impact of these restructuring factors was particularly strong in Italy because of its exposure to international economic competition (25.1% of its GDP goes into export) and the special position of the PCI, the Italian Communist Party, which used to be the largest in Western Europe. The PCI peaked in the 1976 elections (with 34.4% of the vote) and still gained 26.6% in the 1987 elections, the last before the break-up of the communist regimes.[31]

Furthermore, the pressure to meet the requirements for the European Monetary Union and to reduce the huge public debt[32] has led to a rapid increase in taxation (roughly 10% in ten years)[33] and offered reasons for fiscal rebellion. The industrial structure, with many small, often marginal, enterprises has emphasized the perception of economic precariousness and hence created a desire to lighten the fiscal burden, especially in regions exposed to economic competition and penalized in public redistribution.

The fading of dominant cleavages[34] was reinforced in Italy by a process of secularization, which stabilized around the mid-1970s.[35] This process also reduced the role of the cleavage opposing Roman Catholicism to secularism and was accompanied by an increasing cultural disconnection between religious creed and political behaviour. At the same time, the collapse of the traditional enemy deprived the DC of its anti-Communist glue.

The Catholic, Socialist, and the smaller social-democratic and liberal parties were finally destroyed by the activities of *Mani Pulite* judges. All these factors 'set free' a considerable part of the voters. The mobility of the Italian vote was as high as 53.6% between 1992 and 1994, and 34.6% between 1994 and 1996 (Segatti, 1997: 227; Cartocci, 1996: 631).

It is particularly interesting to examine the situation in the north-east of Italy, the main Northern League electoral basin. This area is characterized by small industries, and hence by face-to-face relations between employer and employee, promoting a sense of shared 'company destiny' depending on success in the market rather than on state assistance. The regional economy is also strongly export-oriented. Although the area represents only 11.4% of the total population its share in Italian exports rose from 16.2% in 1988 to 19.9% in 1994.

These regions used to be called the 'white area', since they were the stronghold of the Christian Democratic Party. The collapse of the DC deprived these peripheral regions, once under its control, of an important channel of patronage by the centre and thus favoured alienation from the government in Rome and demands for autonomy (Fabbrini, 1996).

A large share of the vote 'set free' from the DC was captured by the new Lega Nord Party. This can be considered an outstanding example of multiculturalism led by the well-off. This rebellion by the wealthy strata, like other rebellions from above, may have some ground in terms of fairness. In fact, it has occurred mainly in areas that objectively lose out in terms of income redistribution. The League proved successful in an area characterized by economic growth, high international competition, and unfair redistribution of public resources. The per capita fiscal loss of each resident in a Northern region like Lombardy is the equivalent of US$ 1,400 per year, Venetians lose US$ 485, and Piedmontese US$ 670, whereas residents in southern regions like Molise and Basilicata gain US$ 4,390 and US$ 4,100 respectively. In fact, Northern League voters show the highest concentration of fiscal discontent and anti-welfare attitudes and, what is more important, they also present the highest rate of hostility towards territorial redistribution from rich to poor regions (62.7% of its electorate as against 27% of the total Italian electorate). This 'anti-solidaristic' autonomy stance (Ferrera/Piazzini, 1996) is in general more widespread in north-eastern regions (42%).

The 'white area' had already started a silent secession from the state. The rate of tax evasion has always been incredibly high in this region (Mongeri, 1996) and the recent call to tax disobedience can be considered a formalization of an already widespread behaviour. Italian fiscal rebellion could be considered a late case of Thatcher-Reaganism, were it not associated with cultural claims. The Northern League adopted symbolic ethnic resources that were already present in civil society.[36] They were backed by social thinkers of the last century (Salvadori, 1963) and US immigration statistics, which used to distinguish between northern and southern Italians (Franzina, 1995) as belonging to different races.

We could say that an identity existed at the social level, but that it had not been transferred to political society. For this to happen, previous identities had to disappear, and a leadership capable of combining the symbolic resources of identity and material interests had to emerge.

It may be useful to give some examples of the culturalization and ethnicization of this territorial divide by the Lega Nord's leaders. Firstly, let me quote a few lines from a speech by one of the main ideologists of the new party, Professor Gianfranco Miglio: *"What was essential to the southern population was precisely the idea that respect is deserved by those who excel in living off someone else. This is the backbone of classic culture. Ulysses was nothing but a thief, a robber, a person who lived through extortion, claiming other people's wealth through cunning and the sword"* ('Viaggio nel Sud', RAI-1, 2 October 1992 in Costantini, 1994). Talking to a gathering of no less than 70,000 supporters in Mantua, the Secretary of the Lega Nord, Umberto Bossi, recently stated: *"There are two different cultures and civilizations in Italy, the Northern Padanian and the Southern Mediterranean."*

The political task of culturalizing the North-South economic conflict achieved striking results in the periphery of the north-eastern regions, in small towns and villages, where the perception of *'Heimat'* is still strong. In this 'Deep North' the League received 40.4% of the votes and 96.8% of seats (Diamanti, 1996a).

Northern culturalism, already transferred from society to political society, may change policies and institutions and eventually modify the very profile of Italian citizenship. The culturalization of territorial divides has already produced significant consequences for citizenship rights, and there could be even more dramatic effects in future. I shall attempt to make a rapid survey of present and foreseeable impacts.

In order to assess the transformation of *political rights* we can recall the three dimensions outlined in Figure 3 above: (1) extension-equalization, (2) influence, (3) competition vs. segmentation.

The existence of a new option (the Lega Nord) has widened both the competition and the segmentation of political rights in Italy's northern regions. Furthermore, multiculturalism in political society is likely to move to the institutional level and could have an impact on all dimensions (not only those listed in the 'cultural' column of Figure 3).

The possible introduction of a federal reform will increase the *influence* of the vote, since many decisions now taken at central levels and by administrative bodies will be de-bureaucratized and devolved to local elective bodies or to local administration agencies more strongly controlled by elective bodies. On the other hand, this same process is likely to decrease the *extension-equalization* (equal weight) of the vote. Federalist models usually adopt a two-house system in which one Chamber represents single states or regions not in proportion to their population. Even the least federalist solutions that have been proposed in recent constitutional debates in Italy,[37] foresee that a minimum representative quota would be guaranteed to small regions – and consequently to the vote of their inhabitants. (I do not intend to take the hypothesis of successful secession into consideration here.)

In order to evaluate *social rights* let me again consider the three dimensions of (1) extension-equalization, (2) protection, and (3) cultural assignment vs. autonomy. At present, social provisions in Italy are to some degree differentiated at regional and municipal levels, depending on governing parties, on the efficiency of local administration and on the local voluntary sector. All things considered, however, Italy is a centralized welfare state (some two-thirds of the social expenditure is controlled by the centre). The impact of multiculturalism on an institutional level – in so far as it will foster some form of federalism – is likely to introduce a localistic syndrome into Italian social rights. Federalism tends to increase autonomy and differentiation and reduce equality. Some scholars (Leibfried/Pierson, 1992) maintain that thanks to the veto system it also tends to lower welfare spending, and thus the degree of protection. The general reduction of social protection can be the outcome of economic, institutional and cultural changes that go hand in hand.

The culturalization of distributive conflicts can be seen as an application of Pareto's theory. Pareto maintained that we reach a condition of optimality when the position of an actor improves without worsening the position of another. Although the postulate clearly favours the status quo, it nevertheless allows for some redistribution. "The most common Paretian justification for welfare lies in the claim that the relief of indigence actually increases the well-being of the donor, since the existence of such deprivation is a kind of 'public sin'" (Barry, 1990: 53-54). The well-being of the one who gives grows when donor and recipient are joined by a bond of affection or sympathy.[38] The propensity to give is thus correlated to familiarity with the receiver. We could consequently maintain that, vice versa, the reluctance to give increases in cases of disaffection and non-familiarity. The reluctance to give is also correlated to scarcity and uncertainty of assets. Thus in situations of growing uncertainty and decreasing resources, we may seek cultural justifications for not giving and initiate a process of alienation from current and potential receivers, transforming them into undeserving poor and undeserving regions.

The Slight Deepening of Traditional Cultural Cleavages

The religious cleavage in Italy has lost its political influence. Two small parties which grew out of the dissolution of the Christian Democratic Party, the CCD[39] and the CDU, have joined the centre-right electoral coalition and a third one, the Popular Party, joined the centre-left, thus diluting the impact of Catholic identity on party alignment.

As far as religion is concerned, Italy ceased to be a pluralistic country after the Concordat or Settlement between the Fascist regime and the Catholic Church on 11 February 1929. The Concordat, which re-established the status of Catholicism as the state religion, was included in the republican constitution after the fall of Fascism. A mutually agreed reform of the Concordat on 18 February 1984, revoked the status of state religion and introduced a higher degree of tolerance towards non-Catholic religions (for instance, exempting pupils in secondary schools from having to attend religion education classes). But even after the 1984 reform teachers of religion had to have Church approval. Unlike France, where any kind of special legal recognition or financial support to religious congregations has been forbidden (Bastenier/Dassetto, 1991: 145), the Catholic Church has always received state support.

Traditional religious minorities in Italy, like the Waldensian Church, the Lutherans or the Jewish Communities,[40] were only recently allowed to join the Catholic Church in benefiting from the possibility of receiving the eighth-thousandth of the amount paid by income taxpayers. The Waldensian Church was able to raise a considerable amount of money due to support from a large number of non-believers and liberal Catholic taxpayers. The agreement with the Jewish community was signed only in 1997 and it is still not known how successful they will prove in fundraising. On the other hand, the opening of a Mosque in the holy city of Rome provoked strong reactions from conservatives.[41] The higher public status of traditional religious groups was thus confirmed.

Likewise, Italian border regions with traditional linguistic minorities (as well as Sardinia and Sicily) enjoy many fiscal and legislative privileges. Because of their special constitutional treatment as 'Special Statute Regions' (Art. 116), they can legislate in ways other Italian regions cannot. It creates a sort of *selective federalism*,[42] a federalism for the few, or constitutional privilege which could explain why Italy is not facing a deepening of traditional linguistic cleavages at the institutional level.

The Eva Klotz movement, which preaches a United Tyrol across Austrian and Italian borders, received around 10% of the local vote. However, its influence greatly exceeds its numerical strength. In fact, at the election it challenged and blackmailed the large SVP (Südtiroler Volkspartei) that traditionally holds an absolute majority in the province, but could not profit from a spread of discontent.

When the second Statute of Autonomy was approved in 1971, the Trentino / Alto Adige region became a federation of districts (provinces), which enabled it to grant further privileges to the German-speaking minority. The Bolzano (Bozen) constituency was redrawn giving it an overwhelming German-speaking majority (around 70%). Fixed quotas of jobs in public administration, the judiciary and public services are reserved for bilingual applicants (which rarely benefits the Italian local minority, since they are prevented from learning German at primary school, whereas German children must study Italian). Bilingual teaching was experimented with only recently in the Bozen district. Italian, German and a third language are compulsory for everybody in the region only at secondary school. As well as introducing cultural rights aimed at preserving the languages of dominant minorities, this situation generates inequality in access to jobs, roles and positions (column 'inclusion', row 1 in Figure 3), thus confirming the hypothesis that *multiculturalism* affects all dimensions of rights.

In Italy, parties produced by linguistic cleavages have not only been pro-system parties, but pro-government parties: the SVP in Trentino / Alto Adige and the UV (Union Valdotaine) in the Aosta Valley have backed government majorities in the past, and supported the winning Ulivo centre-left coalition in the last election.[43] In a way, they are closer to the Catalan strategy (using extremism as a way of dealing with the government) than the recent Lega Nord strategy (escalation of demands without bargaining). The increasingly aggressive Lega Nord was beaten in local elections (10 June 1996; 11 May 1997) when it lost votes in all large cities and many mayors in the North-West (Pavia, Mantua, Vigevano) and was rewarded in November 1997, when it managed to keep towns such as Varese and Alessandria and the important districts of Como, Varese and Vicenza.

In conclusion, traditional linguistic cleavages have sometimes deepened, as elsewhere, at the level of civil and political society (the new pro-Tyrol movement), but they have been kept quiet through the concession of privileges. Strong minorities in Italy were given selective rewards, including autonomy and important fiscal benefits, at the right time. These wealthy minorities did not need to rebel any further, which does not mean, however, that they will not do so in future.[44]

The impact of this trend on the *differentiation* of citizenship rights is strong. Here again multiculturalism affects all dimensions of democratic citizenship: civil rights (quotas for access to jobs in public administration), 'social-civil rights' (retaining minority languages and having them taught, preventing others from learning them) and political rights (the opportunity to vote for linguistic parties, the autonomy of the territory).

On the other hand, traditional religious cleavages have softened, Italian Protestant and Jewish minorities are now enjoying cultural rights (funding of their congregations) on an equal footing with Catholics. In this respect, there has been a slight rise of *multiculturalism*, since more groups are recognized. However, these organizations have a high porosity. They are open to non-members of the community, who can enter Catholic, Jewish, or Evangelic schools and be admitted to their hospitals.

Irrelevance of Multiculturalism Based on Cleavages Arising from New Minorities; Relevance of Dominant Culture Reaction against Immigration

I prefer to treat these two trends jointly, since they are often detectable from the logic embodied in the same public provisions and from the same statistics.

Immigration began in Italy in the mid-1970s after the oil shock, when the more 'attractive' European countries started to close their borders. It began with an influx of domestic labour and a return flow of people of Italian descent pushed by economic crisis in their adopted countries and pulled by Italian economic growth.

This was first detected in the 1981 census, when 210,937 foreign residents plus 109,841 other foreigners were recorded. Foreigners with legal residence permits now number 1,095,622 (31 December 1996), that is, less than 2% of the total population. 152,092 are citizens of European Union member states, and of the remaining 943,530 are non-European Union citizens, 852,588 come from developing countries.

The national composition of Italian immigration is extremely fragmented and many communities score around 1-2% of the total immigration. Following the typical 'globalization' syndrome, recent flows tend both to reinforce the regional character of immigration (the two top and the fifth largest sending countries being located in the Mediterranean area) and to widen the scope of the flows (Filipinos, for instance, rank third).

I should now like to illustrate the thesis that besides some minor and rhetorical measures, the new minorities are more an object of discrimination than agents of multicultural change.

Entry and Naturalization

The granting of a residence permit or naturalization is not usually considered as part of 'citizens rights', but in fact they decide who will enjoy those many rights connected with the status of legal resident and citizen. They represent the gates to citizenship in our democracies, but the criteria determining access are changing. In Italy, the principle of patriality, combined with a budding European citizenship is widening the gap between non-European Union citizens, on the one hand, and European Union citizens and foreigners of Italian descent, on the other.

The first screening starts with the access to the country. According to the Schengen Treaty (June 1985, ratified by Italy in June 1990 and implemented on 26 October 1997), European Union citizens are entitled to cross each other's borders. The Schengen agreement also includes the commitment of states to reach agreement on visas for third countries. Selective access to the territory can be considered a first measure in favour of those aliens perceived as culturally more homogeneous with the dominant national culture.

Access to naturalization rights further discriminates against non-European Union foreigners. A regular permit holder used to be able to apply for naturalization after five years (by Law no. 555, 13 June 1912). Law no. 91, 5 February 1992[45] raised this time limit to ten years for non-European Union aliens and decreased it to four for European Union citizens and to three for citizens of Italian origin. In 1996 there were only 6,961 naturalizations, of which 87.1% followed marriage with an Italian citizen.

We can consider the great reluctance of aliens to naturalize as a first rough indicator of a perceived condition of exclusion-seclusion. It is fair to add that Italy, unlike other European countries, does not submit applicants to assimilation tests (like being fluent in Italian or having knowledge of the Italian constitution) and allows dual citizenship.

Civil Rights

Free circulation of individuals in the labour market, a 'must' of liberal civil rights, does not apply to foreigners.[46] The first of Marshall's civil rights (freedom of labour) is not easily granted to aliens. In Italy, Laws no. 943 of 30 December 1986, no. 39 of 28 February 1990, and Decree no. 489 of 18 November 1995, give priority to Italians and European Union citizens in access to the labour market.

The free circulation of European Union citizens enacted by the Maastricht Treaty also implies equal access to work for Europeans, excluding people from non-European Union states. Art. 8 of Law 943, 1986, linked the regulation of immigration to an annual quota to be established according to labour market needs, and making it explicit that non-European Union labour can be hired only when no Italian or European Union citizens are available for the job. The new bill foresees the possibility for those foreigners able to find a sponsor, who guarantees their maintenance, to reside in Italy for a period of six months while seeking work.

The third decree on migration flows (1991) made an exception for domestic workers, but was overruled by the 1995 decree. Family reunion programmes are one of the few gates still open to immigration to the European Union and, in particular, to Italy. Spouses and children entering Italy on the basis of such provisions (Law 943/1986, art. 4) could not work during the first year of stay, and parents never. This rule was reformed by the new law on immigration (no. 40, 6–3–1998).

Summing up, immigration of non-citizens tends to create new strata of non-citizens who are excluded[47] from equal access to roles and positions (column 'inclusion' of Figure 3).

Associations can be considered a sort of bridge between political and civil rights. Strong cultural associationism among immigrants is bound to affect the profile of democratic citizenship. But, is this associational life in Italy strong and is it cultural? Unlike Belgium and France, Italy has never limited foreigners' rights to establish associations. This has eased the birth of immigrant clubs and leagues in our country. 739 such associations have recently been registered (Ministry of Labour, December 1994), 113 are Italian organizations concerned with immigration, 40 are intercultural associations.

When evaluating the degree of culturalization a distinction has to be made between national and continental associations. 31 out of 242 African associations accept only members from the African continent. Similar restrictions affect 10 out of 49 of the Latin American associations, but none of the 91 Asian associations. If we look at membership, we see that Italian unions and ancillary associations of leftist parties score much higher (Zincone, 1994) than immigrant associations. Until now, immigrants and new minorities in Italy have been targets of national associations rather than the tools of ethno-political associations and cleavage. As we shall see when referring to social rights, immigration is becoming a growing commitment for the national voluntary sector. The most interesting tool of multiculturalization, though, can be found among the ethnic and cultural associations that subcontract public services.

In cities like Turin and Bologna a relevant and innovative role is played by *mediatori interculturali*, the cultural mediators whose job it is not only to inform immigrants of their rights and to help them[48] deal with bureaucratic procedures and linguistic problems, but also to smooth frictions between Italian and alien cultures. In practice the position of *mediatori interculturali* often puts them in conflict either with the public administration or the alien receivers.

Political Rights

All the above – access to the territory, residence permits and naturalization – can be considered steps towards full citizenship and political rights. Those who are allowed to enter and stay, become potential future members of our political community.

Given the low rate of naturalization even in a virtuous European country like Sweden, the political rights of long-term residents should be a concern of European democracy, but they are not. Part Two of the new Treaty of the European Union on 'European Citizenship' introduced the right to vote in local elections (art. 8b1) and European elections (art. 8b2)[49] for European Union citizens residing in a member state. The EU Council adopted a convention (5 February 1992) to invite member states to foster the political participation of non-European Union citizens resident in the union through local vote and special consultative committees.

The convention had few practical consequences, except in Italy. The Scandinavian countries and the Netherlands had in fact already extended local suffrage, but the others either ignored the convention or delayed its adoption, waiting for the implementation of art. 8b 1 of the Maastricht Treaty. In Italy, the bill on immigration (no. 3240, 17 February 1997, now Law no. 40 , 6 March 1998) had envisaged granting voting rights in local elections to immigrants who have held regular permits for over five years (art. 38), but this article was temporarily put aside because it was feared to give rise to constitutional problems.[50] Articles 2 and 7 of the law still refer to political participation and local vote 'in accordance with our legal system', thus devolving the provision to a constitutional reform. They were both opposed through raising 'preliminary constitutional questions' by the Alleanza Nazionale (previously the MSI neo-fascist party) and the Lega Nord, backed by all the opposition parties.[51]

The reluctance of the Italian Parliament to extend the local vote to long-term resident immigrants contrasts with the propensity of the Italian Parliament to enfranchize Italians abroad, by not just permitting absentee ballots by mail or at an Italian consulate, but allowing them even to form their own constituencies abroad and to vote for candidates representing them there. These provisions have already passed the first step of constitutional review.[52]

Following the 1992 European Council Convention, some countries have introduced consultative bodies. Italy had already introduced this kind of body before. Art. 8, Law 943, 1986, had established a consultative committee on immigration attached to the Ministry of Labour and another one attached to the Cabinet Office (Presidenza del Consiglio). The same law also introduced committees at regional level. In some regions committees were simply not appointed, in others they were appointed, but never convened. The two main National Committees were supposed to include a limited number of immigrant communities but, in order not to displease any community or association, the number was enlarged and they became impossible to handle. After three years both were abolished. The committee attached to the Ministry of Labour was reinstated on 26 February 1996, together with a new Consultative Council on 11 July 1995, attached to the CNEL (National Council for Economics and Labour). Neither is politically relevant. For instance, Decree 486, issued on 18 November 1995, introduced major changes reinforcing the expulsion procedures, establishing educational and health rights even for illegal immigrants and it also introduced a new legalization provision for undocumented persons. This decree was neither suggested nor discussed by the Council.

In the past a proposal for new comprehensive legislation on aliens was drawn up by a small group of experts and public administrators (the so-called Commissione Contri, October 1993 – March 1994) and was discussed only afterwards, with, among others, members of the two old official committees. The same happened with Bill 3240: the committee of the CNEL approved the bill (3 October 1997), but it was actually prepared by a small group of experts and then discussed with voluntary associations.

These consultative activities can be seen as a strange kind of political right (Bauböck, 1994a), since it does not involve collective action by the cultural groups concerned, but on their behalf. The individuals appointed are selected from above, co-opted, and the right is exercised corporately. Furthermore, it scores a very low degree of relevance.

Other tools of political participation so far offered to immigrants in Italy can also be judged as rather irrelevant. Taking advantage of the autonomy granted to municipal governments by Law 142, 8 June 1990, town and city councils governed by progressive majorities voted for various forms of representation for immigrants. Bologna, Naples, Catania, Modena and Nonantola introduced one additional (co-opted) city councillor. In Turin, there is an extra councillor at district council level. Turin, La Spezia and Modena have also adopted consultative bodies elected by non-EU foreign residents. Despite their democratic investiture, these bodies were not provided with great influence. For instance, the Turin committee was not consulted before taking provisions for the explosive San Salvario district. Since this neighbourhood houses not only the 'new wave' immigrants – here, unfortunately characterized by high rates of criminality – but also the Evangelical Church and the Synagogue, an informal intercultural council that included the local head of the Catholic parish, the local Waldensian Minister, the Head of the Jewish Community and a local Imam was established and in fact worked quite successfully in calming down the situation, even though the Neo-fascists and Northern League proved much more effective in heating it up.

Turin, Rome and Bologna have extended to alien residents the right to participate in local referenda. We could conclude, however, that influential participation (in trade unions, for instance, and maybe in future local elections) is not segmented, and segmented participation (in committees, for instance) is not influential. Summing up, there cannot be any extension, relevance and significant segmentation of political rights in Italy, unless and until the local vote for immigrants is introduced.

Social Rights

On the one hand, as customary during the first phases of immigration, the *extension* of social rights tends to exceed differentiation and cultural assignment. On the other hand, *differentiation* in provision is accompanied by *autonomy* of the providing agencies through a sub-contracting of welfare functions to national and ethnic associations. These associations often play roles of *mediatori culturali*,[53] explaining the functioning of Italian social services and smoothing access to them. Furthermore, they provide mother-tongue teaching to immigrant children, meeting places, catering facilities, customary baths and massage parlours. These places, such as the Alma Mater in Turin, also welcome Italians.

Differentiation does not (yet) combine with segregation, although so far the 'mediation' has been one-way, consisting of explaining and translating Italian social services to foreigners, rather than helping Italian services also to understand and learn the needs and practices of immigrants.[54]

For the time being, access to social rights does not discriminate between immigrants and nationals (Law no. 943, 1986, and Law no. 39, 1990). But, unfortunately, the general level of protection of Italian welfare has shrunk due to the need to control public debt. Some social spending restrictions have in fact affected immigrants' access to welfare.

For instance, the financial reform of Public Health (Delegated Law no. 421, 23 October 1992) gave the Local Health Units the status of self-managed trusts, making it compulsory for them to certify all expenses and to comply with budgetary constraints. Many hospitals therefore had to give up the practice of informally treating illegal immigrants. To avoid leaving illegal immigrants without health care, Decree 18 November 1995, no. 489, art. 13, allowed not only for emergency and pregnancy care, already provided by law, but also for treatment of serious illness and accidents, as well as free prescriptions and medical examinations in preventive health care. The new Law no. 40 (6 March 1998) confirms such provisions.

As the issue has come to the surface, immigrant welfare has become less informal. Immigration policies (flows, permits, expulsion of illegal immigrants, etc.) have been tightened in keeping with the growing concern about law and order shared by a conspicuous part of the leftist, as well as the rightist, electorate. At the national level, however, the access of immigrants (even of illegal immigrants) to welfare has possibly been increased.

Italy is following the twofold line of 'equal opportunities' and cultural recognition in public education, too. The limited number of foreigners in schools discourages the provision of classes in native languages, whereas the teaching of Italian as a second language is more widespread (Operti/Cometti, 1992).

Equal opportunity practices started in 1989 (circular 301, 8 September), on the request of the Ministry of Education, which instructed headmasters to try to organize classes avoiding age discrepancy between immigrants and nationals, and by adopting special help (support teachers) for foreign students. The same principles were embodied in a series of circulars (no. 400 of 31 December 1991 and no. 119 of 6 April 1995) that invited education authorities to enrol the children of illegal immigrants and to issue school-leaving certificates. These circulars, which were preceded by local experiments, especially in Turin and Bologna, were temporarily enacted by the decree of November 1995, and became law no. 40 of March 1998. The Ministry suggested adopting intercultural programmes, even in schools without foreign students, in circular no. 200, 5 July 1990.

In conclusion, legal immigrants formally enjoy the same social rights as nationals, though possibly not in practice. For instance, due to discontinuity of employment, they have more difficulty in completing a retirement programme, and due to linguistic difficulties, they have higher drop-out rates from school. All things considered, however, the level of access and equalization is fairly good, and we can detect the first signs of 'differentiation without seclusion'.

The extension of political and social rights in Italy contrasts with prevailing trends in other countries. The explanation is political: unlike the vast majority of industrialized Western countries, Italy has not experienced, with the exception of the short-lived Berlusconi coalition government, a right turn in government. But it is not clear how long this uncommon condition can last.

Anti-immigrant cleavages have already entered political society supported by the Lega Nord and the Alleanza Nazionale. In the last general elections (1996) the right achieved an electoral majority, but was not able to transform this into a parliamentary majority, since the Lega Nord ran alone against the Polo delle Libertà. We do not know what policy changes a right-wing government would produce, or what policy changes the fear of the right winning could bring to a centre-left government. Law no. 40 of 6 March 1998 has simply introduced measures which make the expulsions of clandestine immigrants and criminals easier. The Northern League has already proposed referenda in order to abrogate articles of the law judged too liberal.

I hope this illustration of the Italian case has helped to corroborate the hypothesis that deep multicultural traditions already exist in Europe, and that high social strata and richer regions have a stronger impact on culturalization and on reshaping our democracies than the new immigrant groups themselves.

Notes

1. "Most European countries have much less ethnic and cultural diversity and populations with much deeper historical roots than the countries of immigration" (Carens, 1994: 153). Similarly Michael Walzer (1992) singled out cultural plurality as a marker of American citizenship. By contrast, in his last book (1997) Walzer appears aware of the dominant role played by the Anglo culture within the United States. His book is very much in tune with the arguments of my article.

2. The claim that 'immigration countries' are 'melting pots' has been falsified (Parillo, 1994; Martiniello, 1995). The United States policies were considered assimilationist till after World War II (Schain, 1996). Similarly, Australia introduced multicultural policies in the past few decades (Castles, 1993). On the other hand the most assimilationist country in Europe, France, adopted all sorts of multicultural policies alongside its republican rhetoric (Schain, 1996; Wieviorka, 1996).

3. Anomic behaviour, even terrorism, by marginalized minorities seems to falsify this hypothesis. Their capacity to reshape democratic regimes has to be proved and some authors have suggested to consider them as alternative deviant forms of social and political action in the absence of legal channels of incorporation and influence (Kepel, 1996).

4. I am adapting and integrating some of the five classes proposed by Stephen Castles (1992b).

5. Weber himself underlined the role of public action, i.e. of the state, in establishing and reinforcing ethnic identities. "Community, political community in particular, engenders a belief in ethnic belonging, even though the political entity was at the beginning extremely artificial" (Weber, 1961: 398).

6. This could be achieved, for instance, by tax-funded and flat-rate allocation. I do not want to enter the theoretical dimensions of the different interpretations of equality. To receive according to one's contribution could be considered more fair than to receive a flat-rate provision.

7. We thus follow a well-grounded critique of Esping-Andersen by feminist scholars like Orloff (1992).

8. Thus I try to reconcile Gianni (1995) (multicultural rights are new rights) and my previous point (1997) (multiculturalism is a form of pluralism and we have already experimented with it in our past). On the thesis of continuity, see Eisenberg (1995).

9. In fact internal restrictions could not include the prohibition of opting out.

10. "Contemporary liberals have become more reluctant to impose liberalism on foreign countries, but more willing to impose liberalism on indigenous minorities" (Kymlicka, 1996b).

11. According to Quentin Skinner (1996), liberalism is characterized by a definition of liberty as against slavery, subordination to other men. The core concept of liberalism according to this interpretation would be emancipation. Skinner also observes that republicanism adds the demand for a free citizen to become a law-maker to the liberal request for him to be subordinate to anything by Law. This thesis is in tune with my proposal of considering civil rights as more crucial to liberalism and political rights as more crucial to republicanism, but is rather simplified.

The very concept of representative government is liberal, though there is a difference as far as the extension of the suffrage is concerned (Zincone, 1992). Even this difference is valid if we do not take it too strictly: in fact not all republicans agree with the principle of universal suffrage. What is more, the very definition of the 'universe' in the history of republican regimes (man, soldiers, loyalty) was limited and biased.

12 If we reread parliamentary debates of liberal regimes in the past century or look at how poor people were perceived, we see that the resistance to factory laws bringing in shorter working hours and higher salaries was argued on the basis of the propensity of the working classes to spend their spare time and extra money getting drunk. "The poor were increasingly referred to by the gentry and merchants as 'savages', 'beasts' and 'incorrigibles'" (Jansson, 1988: 15).

13 "Violent forms of behaviour which tend to be socially rather than ethnically based, a tendency to the Islamization of young people, are usually fairly remote from fundamentalism" (Wieviorka, 1996c: 23).

14 These requests are supported by a cultural definition of poor regions and poor people as morally inadequate – we are facing a return to the nineteenth century with the ethnic connotation of the poor.

15 Similarly, I do not intend to deny the mere appearance of a clash of civilizations (Huntington, 1993), but I would like to suggest a different key of interpretation.

16 The idea of not contrasting interests and culture, as suggested for instance by Pizzorno (1993), comes from Hirschman's claim that the legitimization of interests should be considered a crucial cultural turn.

17 This is Kepel's thesis (1996a,b) to which I would suggest adding the resistance to cultural contempt. Social marginalization is deepened by the radical version of the culture of interests, neo-liberalism combines with neo-tribalism, to use Wieviorka's (1996b) terminology.

18 Allen Buchanan (1991) considered the refusal of rich regions to stick with the poor ones as a way of escaping a redistributive duty, and the refusal of solidarity to be morally ungrounded, but as Nadia Urbinati (1996) maintains, sympathy has always been considered a crucial element of sociability and solidarity. To withdraw sympathy is, in my opinion, a first step towards the refusal of solidarity.

19 "La culture est une conséquence de l'éthnicité et non pas un élément de définition de cette dernière. Dès lors, il devient plus aisé de concevoir que les identités ethniques puissent être maintenues en dépit du changement culturel et de la disparition des différences culturelles objectives entre les groupes" (Martiniello, 1995: 81).

20 In fact interests cannot become relevant if they do find political actors able to transform them into identities. Pizzorno thus recalls the distinctions between class and class consciousness and the role of the party in this operation, whereas Kepel's argument implies some degree of 'false consciousness' or double standards.

21 I suggest that we could follow Hirschman's (1997) suggestion of presenting the legitimization of interests as a cultural turn-around and the basis of capitalist ideology and practice. The

22   expansion of this ideology and practice produces victims and winners that are both likely to use cultural identities to resist and get rid of resistance, but there is also an ideological (religious, ecological, localistic) resistance. Instrumental and assertive logic can be combined in public action, but we can also have a clear prevalence of one or the other.

22 To date, since social scientists have mainly focused their attention on multiculturalism in society, they have also started to define typologies: at this level a distinction has been made, for instance, between *light* and *heavy* multiculturalism (Spinner-Halev, 1996) depending on (a) the level of horizontal segmentation between different groups and (b) the level of vertical legitimization of the common national identity and of the common political system by a single group. We can apply the heavy-light distinction also in our model.

23 The permeable or non-permeable nature of cultural boundaries (Bauböck, 1994a: 274) is an important feature to observe when we want to understand the impact of multiculturalism on democratic systems and the viability of our liberal ideals. The morally dubious institutional goal "equal and separate" can prove less dangerous than a conflictual integration (Dahrendorf, 1996: 102-103).

24 The comparison with animals has been considered the prototype of alienation processes where other human beings' capacity to feel and suffer are removed from the consciousness. The words used in the Bible for animals were used by the Nazis to describe Jews (Battaglia, 1988).

25 Kymlicka (1996) suggested considering the setting up of reserves for indigenous people as a federalism from above.

26 The preference given to the possession of skills and money as criteria for admittance is another indicator of the relative decay of culture when compared to interests.

27 Up to 1984 only associations where three out of five members or funding members were Belgian were allowed (Layton-Henry, 1990).

28 The federal state comprises three regions: the Flanders and Walloon districts and Brussels as a bilingual district. Additional autonomy provisions are foreseen for Dutch-, German- and French-speaking minority communities within the three regions.

29 Especially in recent studies there are some virtuous exceptions to the general tendency of underestimating European traditional multiculturalism and overestimating traditions of multiculturalism in immigration countries (Castles, 1993; Schain, 1996; Kymlicka, 1996).

30 PDS membership fell rapidly from 1,814,317 in 1976 to 1,264,790 in 1990 and was 705,540 in 1995.

31 After the 1989 'Svolta' (the ideological turn-about) that involved the definitive abandonment of the Communist creed, and the split of the party, the new PDS (Democratic Party of the Left) received 16.1% of votes and 'Rifondazione Comunista', which had opposed the turn, 5.6%. In 1994, the PDS gained 20.4% and the RC 6.0%, in 1996 21.1% and 8.6% respectively.

32 Because of increased fiscal revenues, cuts in public expenditure and economic growth, the proportion of the deficit to the GDP has decreased over the last three years. Italy's economy has entered a virtuous circle, but it has cost a lot in terms of cuts in public services and higher taxation.

33 This increased from 32% of income in 1981 to 43% in 1992, reaching a peak of 44% in 1993. The percentages decreased in 1994 (41.7%) and 1995 (41.8%) because of the growth of the GDP (Franco, 1993; *La Stampa*, 2 June 1996).

34 Dominant cleavages are those able to emerge and get organized with the right timing, since they are present in the moment in which the suffrage is extended as Rokkan (1998) has noted. These cleavages can submit to, or silence, other potential cleavages as long as the situation does not change radically (Zincone, 1992).

35 The percentage of regular church-goers dropped to 30% in the 1970s and has remained at that level (Cesareo et al., 1995; CRA-"Avvenire" Survey 1996). In the meantime, Catholics have become more independent from Church teaching and 'disloyal' to the Christian Democratic and other Catholic parties (Diamanti/Mannheimer, 1994; Mannheimer/Sani, 1994).

36 This view was shared abroad (Castles et al., 1992a). North and South Italian immigrants were classified as coming from different nations (Franzina, 1995).

37 The so-called *Bicamerale* (a joint House Committee of 70 people) discussing the reform proposed a Chamber of Guarantees (*Camera delle Garanzie*) consisting of one-third members of the Senate, one-third representatives of the Regions, and one-third members of the Commons and Districts. A subsequent amendment allowed the revision of article 59 of the *Bicamerale* project and thus produced an even more absurd solution – a Chamber of Guarantee would replace the present Senate, and would be elected with a proportional system disquietingly similar to the old electoral system of the First Republic. This same chamber would have housed (only in specific circumstances and with specific expertise) 200 members appointed by Regions and other local bodies in proportion to their population, but with a minimum quota. One seat would have been guaranteed to Aosta Valley and 2 to Molise, but Lombardy would have 32 seats. On this subject see Vassallo (1997). At the beginning of 1998, representatives of the regions and large cities presented a new proposal according to which the Senate would become representative of regions and big cities, which would enjoy high levels of autonomy.

38 On the public role of sympathy for social cohesion and cooperation in John Stuart Mill and David Hume see Urbinati (1996).

39 In February 1998, a wing of the CCD, led by Clemente Mastella, split again to join a new centre movement led by the former president of the Italian Republic, Francesco Cossiga.

40 In their income tax declarations, tax payers have an option to give 0.8% of their income tax either to the state or to one of the following religious congregations: the Catholic Church, the Waldensians, the Lutherans, the Seventh Day Adventists, the Assembly of God in Italy, and the Jewish Community.

41 There were rumours that Irene Pivetti (of the Lega Nord), then Speaker of the Chamber of Deputies, attended a special mass devoted to expiate the sacrilegious event.

42 Kymlicka (1996) observed the same phenomenon in Spain for Catalonia and in Canada for Quebec, and defined it as "asymmetrical federalism".

43 In these regions the centre-left coalition attained more than 60% of the vote.

44 Unfortunately even the Bolzano district is not homogeneous. For instance, in the city of Bolzano itself, the Italian community has a majority, which means the area will match the Elazar (1993) condition of risk in case of requests for further autonomy.
45 Also relevant to this are Decree no. 572 of 12 October 1993 and Regulation no. 362 of 4 April 1994.
46 We should recall that contracts between Italian workers and German and Belgian employers used to impose limits on the kind of jobs and the regions in which foreign labourers could be employed.
47 Restrictions to non-European Union citizens also concern the self-employed. On the other hand, exams giving access to some jobs are simplified for foreigners.
48 See the proceedings of the conference *Pensieri Meticci*, Turin, 17 May 1997.
49 Individual states can refuse non-citizens the right to run for election (art. 6, par. 2) (Schnapper, 1992: 105).
50 The Committee of Constitutional Affairs of the Chamber of Deputies took this decision on 22 September 1997.
51 Among the opposition parties, only the CCD, a small Christian Democratic splinter group, opposed the Northern League's preliminary questions.
52 Canadian and Australian governments showed some reluctance to accept Italian electoral campaigns in their territories. Such campaigning is likely to be forbidden.
53 In Turin, the local administration signed a contract in 1992 with three voluntary associations (Alma Mater, Amecu and Kantara) to have this kind of service provided. Kantara specializes in heath services.
54 Angela Lostia, CARPOS, Turin. Interview 29 May 1996.

References

Barbé, C. (1997) 'Il drastico irrobustimento dell'identitá nazionale in Italia', *Quadérni di Sociologia* 31 (I).
Barry, N. (1990) *Welfare*. Buckingham: Open University Press.
Barth, F. (1969) *Ethnic Groups and Boundaries: The Social Organisation of Culture Differences*. London and Oslo: Allen & Unwin and Forgalet.
Bartolini, S./Mair, P. (1990) *Identity, Competition, and Electoral Availability*. Cambridge: Cambridge University Press.
Bastenier, A./Dassetto, F. (1990) *Nodi conflittuali conseguenti all'insediamento definitivo delle popolazioni immigrate nei paesi europei*, in AA.VV., *Italia, Europa e nuove immigrazioni*. Turin, Fondazione Agnelli.
Bastenier, A./Dassetto, F. (1991) *Europa: nuova frontiera dell'Islam*. Roma: Ed. Lavoro.
Battaglia, L. (1988) 'Nazismo e diritti degli animali', *Biblioteca della Libertà,* XXIII (102): 65-74.

Bauböck, R. (1994a) *Transnational Citizenship. Membership and Rights in International Migration*. Aldershot: Edward Elgar.

Bauböck, R. (ed.) (1994b) *From Aliens to Citizens. Redefining the Status of Immigrants in Europe*. Aldershot: Avebury.

Betts, K. (1995) 'Immigration to Australia: a New Focus for the 1990s?', in Heckman, F./Bosswick, W. (eds.), op. cit.

Buchanan, Allen (1991) *Secession. The Morality of Political Divorce from Fort Sumter to Lithuania and Quebec*. Boulder, Co: Westview Press.

Carens, J.H. (1994) 'Cultural Adaptation and Integration. Is Quebec a Model for Europe?', in: Bauböck, Rainer (ed.), op. cit.

Cartocci, R. (1996) 'Il voto proporzionale tra squilibrio e continuità', *Rivista Italiana di Scienza Poltica* XXVI: 609-653.

Castles, S./Vasta, E./Lo Bianco, J. (1992a) 'Dall'assimilazionismo al multiculturalismo', in Castles, S./Alcorso, C./Rando, G./Vasta, E., *Italo-australiani: la popolazione di origine italiana in Australia*. Turin: Fondazione Agnelli.

Castles, S. (1992b) 'The Australian Model of Immigration and Multiculturalism: Is It Applicable to Europe?', *International Migration Review* XXVI (2): 549-567.

Castles, S./Miller, M.J. (1993) *The Age of Migration: International Population Movements in the Modern World*. London: Macmillan.

Castles, S. (1994) 'Democracy and Multicultural Citizenship. Australian Debates and their Relevance for Western Europe', in Bauböck, R. (1994b) (ed.), op. cit.

Cesareo, V./Cipriani, R./Garelli, F./Lanzetti, C./Rovati, G. (1995) *La religiosità in Italia*. Milan: Mondadori.

Costantini, L. (1994) *Dentro la Lega*. Rome: Koiné.

Cross, M./Entzinger, H. (1988) *Lost Illusions, Caribbean Minorities in Britain and the Netherlands*. London: Routledge.

Daalder, H. (1966) 'Parties, Elites and Political Development in Western Europe', pp. 43-77 in LaPalombara, J./Weiner, M. (eds.), *Political Parties and Political Development*. Princeton: Princeton University Press.

Dahrendorf, R. (1979) *Life Chances: Approaches to Social and Political Theory*. London: Weidenfeld and Nicolson.

Dahrendorf, R. (1996) 'Il multiculturalismo', in *Diari Europei*. Bari: Laterza.

Diamanti, I. (1993) *La lega*. Rome: Donzelli.

Diamanti, I. (1996a) *Il male del nord: Lega, localismo, secessione*. Rome: Donzelli.

Diamanti, I. (1996b) 'Territorio e politica: una mappa elettorale (molte Italie e molti Nord)', paper presented to the conference "Politics and Society in Italy", Italian Association of Sociology, Political Sociology Section, Turin, 8-10 May.

Diamanti, I./Mannheimer, R. (1994) *Milano a Roma*. Rome: Donzelli.

Dossier Caritas 1997, Rome, Anterem, September 1995.

Dworkin, R. (1984) 'Liberalism', in Sandel, M. (ed.), *Liberalism and its Critics*. New York: New York University Press.

Dworkin, R. (1992) 'Deux conceptions de la démocratie', in Lenoble, J./Dewandre, N. (eds.), *L'Europe au soir du siècle. Identité et démocratie*. Paris: Esprit.

Eisenberg, A. (1995) *Reconstructing Political Pluralism*. Albany: State University of New York Press.

Elazar, D. (1993) 'International and Comparative Federalism', *Political Science and Politics* XXV (4): 180-195.

Fabbrini, S. (1996) 'Lo stato non stato', paper delivered to the Italian Political Science Association Annual Conference, Urbino, 13-15 June.

Farneti, P. (1971) *Sistema Politico e Società Civile*. Turin: Giappichelli.

Fehér F./Heller, A. (1994) 'Naturalization or "Culturalization"', in Bauböck, R. (ed.), op. cit.

Ferrera, M./Piazzini, A. (1996) 'Una rivolta fiscale alle porte?', *Political Trends* 6, April.

Franco, D. (1993) *L'espansione della spesa pubblica in Italia*. Bologna: Il Mulino.

Franzina, E. (1995) *Gli Italiani al Nuovo Mondo: l'emigrazione italiana in America 1492-1942*. Milano: A. Mondadozi.

Galeotti, A.E. (1994) *La tolleranza*. Naples: Liguori.

Galli, G. (1966) *Il bipartitismo imperfetto: comunisti e democristiani in Italia*. Bologna: Il Mulino.

Gianni, M. (1994) *Les liens entre citoyenneté et démocratie sur la base du débat "Libéraux-Communautariens"*. Genève: Département de Science politique, Etudes et Recherches 26.

Gianni, M. (1995) 'Le "fait" du multiculturalisme: quelques implications concernant la théorie normative de la citoyenneté', *Revue Suisse de Science Politique* IV (1): 3-40.

Ginsburg, B.A. (1995) 'Converging Approaches to Societal Integration? Britain, France, Germany, Sweden, Italy and the United States Compared', workshop "Citizenship beyond the Nation-State: the Case of Immigrants in Western Europe", Annual Joint Session of the European Consortium for Political Research, Bordeaux, 27 April – 2 May 1995.

Habermas, J. (1994) 'Struggles for Recognition in the Democratic Constitutional State', in Gutman, A. (ed.), *Multiculturalism*. Princeton: Princeton University Press.

Heckmann, F./Bossick, W. (eds.) (1995) *Migration Policies: a Comparative Perspective*. Stuttgart: Enke.

Hirschman, A.O. (1977) *Passions and Interests*. Princeton: Princeton University Press.

Hirschman, A.O. (1994) 'Social Conflicts as Pillars of Democratic Market Society', *Political Theory* 22 (2): 203-218.

Hirschman, A.O. (1997) *Autosovversione*. Bologna: Il Mulino.

Hunningust, E. (1996) *Interests and Institutions in Western Europe*. Cambridge, Cambridge University Press.

Huntington, S.P. (1993) 'The Clash of Civilization?', *Foreign Affairs*, Summer: 22-49.

Ignazi, P. (1992) *Dal PCI al PDS*. Bologna: Il Mulino.

Ireland, P. (1994) *The Policy Challenge of Ethnic Diversity: Immigration Politics in France and Switzerland*. Cambridge: Harvard University Press.

Jansson, B.S. (1988) *The Reluctant Welfare State.* Belmont, Cal.: Wadsworth.

Kepel, G. (1996a) *A Ovest di Allah.* Palermo: Sellerio.

Kepel, G. (1996b) 'Il caso francese', paper delivered to the conference "Conflitti culturali e democrazia in Europa", Istituto Gramsci and Goethe Institut, Turin, 3-4 June.

Keyes, C. (1976) 'Towards a New Formulation of the Concept of Ethnic Groups', *Ethnicity* III: 202-213.

Kymlicka, W. (1996) *The Rights of Minority in a Liberal State.* San Domenico di Fiesole: European Forum on Citizenship.

Kymlicka, W. (1996a) *The Rights of Minority Cultures in a Liberal State.* San Domenico di Fiesole: European Forum on Citizenship, June 1996.

Kymlicka, W. (1996b) 'Minority Rights: On the Importance of Local Knowledge', *Dissent*, Summer (3): 27.

Layton-Henry, Z. (1990) 'Immigrant Associations', in Layton-Henry, Z. (ed.), *The Political Rights of Migrants Workers.* London: Sage.

Leibfried, S./Pierson, P. (1992) 'Prospect for Social Europe', *Politics and Society* XX: 333-366.

Lijphart, A. (1977) *Democracy in Plural Societies: A Comparative Exploration.* New Haven: Yale University Press.

Mannheimer, R./Sani, G. (1994) *La rivoluzione elettorale. L'Italia tra la prima e la seconda repubblica.* Milan: Anabasi.

Martiniello, M. (1995) *L'ethnicité dans les sciences sociale contemporaines*, "Que sais-je". Paris: Presse Universitaire de France.

Mongeri, M. (1996) 'Il rilancio del fisco', *Il Sole-24 ore*, 28 May.

Operti, L./Cometti, L. (1992) *Verso un'educazione interculturale.* Turin: Bollati Boringhieri.

Orloff, A. (1992) 'Gender and Social Rights of Citizenship', paper presented to the conference "Comparative Studies of Welfare State Development", Bremen, 3-6 September.

Parrillo, V. (1994) *Strangers to these Shores. Race and Ethnic Relations in the United States.* London: MacMillan (4th edition).

Pizzorno, A. (1993) 'Identità e Interesse: sulla razionalità della scelta democratica', in *Le radici della politica assoluta.* Milan: Feltrinelli.

Pizzorno, A. (1993) *Le radici della politica assoluta.* Milan: Feltrinelli.

Poinsot, M. (1993) 'Competition for Political Legitimacy at Local and National Level among Young North Africans in France', *New Community* XX (1): 79-93.

Rey, M. (1986) *Training Teachers in International Education? The Work of the Council for Cultural Cooperation (1977-1983).* Strasbourg: Council of Europe.

Rokkan, S. (1970) *Citizens, Elections, Parties.* Oslo: Universitetforlaget.

Rokkan, S. (1998) 'Nation-Building, State Formation, and Mass Politics in Europe', in Klunle, S./Urwin, D./Flora, P. (eds.), *The Theory of Stein Rokkan.* Oxford: Oxford University Press.

Salvadori, M. (1963) *Il mito del buon governo.* Turin: Einaudi.

Schain, M. (1996) 'Minorities and Incorporation in France: the State and the Dynamics of Multiculturalism', paper delivered at the Conference "Multiculturalism, Minorities and Citizenship", Florence, 18-23 April.

Schnapper, D. (1992) *L'Europe des immigrés*. Paris: Francois Bourin.

Schnapper, D. (1994) *La communauté des citoyens*. Paris: Gallimard.

Skinner, Q. (1996) paper delivered to the Conference "Libertà politica e coscienza civile. Liberalismo, comunitarismo e tradizione repubblicana", Fondazione Agnelli, Turin, 21-22 November.

Segatti, P. (1997) 'Un centro instabile eppure fermo', in Corbetta, P./Parisi, *A domanda risponde*. Bologna: Il Mulino.

Spinner-Halev, J. (1996) 'Cultural Pluralism and Partial Citizenship', conference on "Multiculturalism, Minorities and Citizenship", Citizenship Forum, Villa Schifanoia, San Domenico di Fiesole, 18-22 April.

Taylor, C. (1992) *The Sources of the Self: The Making of Modern Identity*. Cambridge: Cambridge University Press.

Taylor, C. (1992c) 'Quelle identité politique?', pp. 58-66 in Lenoble, J./Dewandre, N. (eds.), *L'Europe au soir du siécle. Identité et démocratie*. Paris: Esprit.

Taylor, C. (1994) 'The Politics of Recognition', in Gutman, A. (ed.), *Multiculturalism*. Princeton: Princeton University Press.

Urbinati, N. (1996) 'Attenti senza nazione non c'è federalismo', *Reset* III, no. 29, 11-19 June.

Vassallo, S. (1997) 'Il federalismo sedicente', *Il Mulino* XLVI: 694-708.

Veca, S. (1995) 'Sulla tolleranza', *Filosofia e Questioni pubbliche* I: 5-28.

XXI Secolo (1994) *Studie ricerche della Fondazione Agnelli*, anno IV, No. 2 (10), June.

Walzer, M. (1992) *Che cosa significa essere americani*. Padua: Marsilio.

Walzer, M. (1997) *On Toleration*. Yale: Yale University Press.

Weber, M. (1961, 1st. ed. 1922) *Economia e società*. Milan: Edizioni Comunità (1st. ed.: *Wirtschaft und Gesellschaft*. Tubingen: Mohr).

Wieviorka, M. (1996b) 'Multiculturalismo, ricerca sociale e democrazia', in Crespi, F/Segatori, R. (eds.), *Multiculturalismo e Democrazia*. Rome: Donzelli.

Wieviorka, M. (1996c) 'Cultural differences and Democracy: United States and France', conference on *Multiculturalism, Minorities and Citizenship*, "European Forum on Citizenship", San Domenico di Fiesole, 18-23 April.

Wieviorka, M. (1996a) 'Conflitti culturali, conflitti sociali e Democrazia in Europa', paper delivered to the conference "Conflitti culturali e democrazia in Europa", Istituto Gramsci and Goethe Institut, Turin, 3-4 June.

Withol de Wenden, C. (1987) *Citoyenneté, Nationalité et Immigration*. Paris: Arcantères.

Zincone, G. (1982) 'Introduction', pp. I-XVII in Zincone, G. (ed.), Report to the European Economic Community: *Decision-making Arenas Affecting Women at Work in Four European Countries*.

Zincone, G. (1992) *Da sudditi a cittadini*. Bologna: Il Mulino.

Zincone, G. (1994) *Una Schermo contro il razzismo*. Roma: Donzelli Editore.

Zincone, G. (1995) 'Immigration to Italy: Data and Policies', in Heckmann, F./Bosswick, W. (eds.), op. cit.

Zincone, G. (1997) 'The Powerful Consequences of Being too Weak. The Impact of Immigration on Democratic Regimes', *Archives Européens de Sociologie* XXXVIII: 104-138.

CHAPTER 7

Egalitarian Multiculturalism: Institutional Separation and Cultural Pluralism

Veit Bader

Processes and politics of incorporation of ethnic immigrant minorities differ widely among societal fields and countries. In order to describe, compare, and explain these varieties, we urgently need a disaggregated conceptual and analytical framework (see Bader, 1995; 1997). In this article, I will bracket descriptive and explanatory questions and focus on (a) normative criteria to evaluate multiculturalism politics and (b) an outline of egalitarian politics of incorporation which live up to the demands of practical reason.

Dominant political philosophy is afflicted by a 'terrible lack of institutional concreteness' (Unger, 1987). As a committed 'non-foundationalist' and defender of a liberal, democratic, ecological socialism I am less interested in endless repetition, subtle elaboration or deeper foundations of the two moral principles of equality and difference which, taken together, are the essential cornerstones of egalitarian multiculturalism. Instead, I intend to show what these cherished principles mean on the 'lower' levels of institutions and practices. Moral (and legal) principles of equality and difference are underdetermined. They limit the set of legitimate options: not 'anything goes' (as relativists, post-modernists and particularistic communitarians state), but they do not prescribe one best institutional and practical solution that is universally applicable in all contexts. Practical judgements have to balance moral, ethical, pragmatic and realistic arguments[1] and require much context-specific information, experience, and prudence, as neo-Aristotelians have rightly reminded us. Politics of egalitarian multiculturalism have to be differentiated. Often the answer is: 'it depends'. This, however, would be a very disappointing answer if we were unable to articulate some universal normative criteria guiding these judgements: it depends on what?

As a moral pluralist, I will recast the tensions between the moral principles of equality and difference (section 1) and stress the indeterminacy of these principles (section 2). Next, I will try to elaborate five general, normative criteria in order to evaluate existing politics of multiculturalism and to design new ones (section 3). The evaluation of politics of multiculturalism is hindered by an old, widespread, and recently fashionable sociological prejudice: that institutional separation and cultural pluralism inevitably lead to conflicts and disintegration and therefore have to be rejected even if they would be normatively preferable options. In section 4, I examine four types of incorporation using certain polities as examples representing these types. In the remaining sections I apply my criteria for the evaluation of politics of multiculturalism to the fields of education (section 5) and law (section 6) using examples from Western European states, and specifically from the Netherlands. Thereby I hope to demonstrate the tension between equality and difference, to specify my general criteria which may have remained fairly abstract for many readers, and to show how context-sensitive practical solutions may be found.

1   All Different, All Equal

During the last decades, the agreement that modern constitutions of the social, democratic, constitutional state contain two principles of morally defensible politics of incorporation is, in my view, broadening and deepening: I am referring to the principle of equality and that of recognition of difference. Both are combined in egalitarian multiculturalism (Rex, 1997: 21ff.).

Political and other philosophers tend to disagree on almost everything when it comes to foundational questions. It is my strong impression that the amount of disagreement is higher amongst them than it is in public talk and democratic action. However, even the most outspoken perfectionist and particularistic communitarian living in modern plural societies with liberal and social-democratic constitutions usually takes into account that the right to be deeply different should be recognized for all 'communities': Politics of difference have a universalistic basis at least in modern forms (see Taylor, 1994: 38 ff.). And even the most 'unreconstructed liberal' who attacks all group rights or politics of affirmative action as a betrayal of liberal principles, as absolutely detrimental or counter-productive, would claim that equal dignity of all individuals includes respect for their different individual and collective choices and their profoundly different 'private' views of the good and practical ways of life. Of course, there are still premodern communitarians around (mainly from all varieties of religious fundamentalism: Catholic, Protestant, Jewish, Muslim, Hindu) as well as strongly eurocentric, assimilationist and individualistic 'rights as shooting guns' liberals, though they are clearly – at least in political theory – a tiny and shrinking minority.

Politics of multiculturalism have been developed in many states, not only in Canada, Australia and the USA, but also in Sweden, the Netherlands and, more hesitantly, in many other European states. To a large extent, the historical differences among these countries, their diverging institutional structures, class constellations, legal, political, administrative and cultural traditions explain the different varieties of politics of multiculturalism.[2] Multiculturalism does not have the same meaning everywhere. Despite substantial differences between these politics, their rhetorical legitimation, and sometimes also their actual implementation, refers to equal integration and the recognition of cultural difference. In 1968 the British Home Secretary defined integration as involving 'not a flattening process of uniformity, but cultural diversity, coupled with equal opportunity, in an atmosphere of mutual tolerance' (quoted by Rex, 1997: 21), and the Dutch *minderheden- en allochtonenbeleid*, despite all its changes, is based on the double ends of equal participation or equal chances (*inhalen van achterstanden en gelijkwaardige participatie*) requiring indirect and often even direct forms of ethnic affirmative action and cultural fairness in a context of freedom (*culturele gelijkwaardigheid in vrijheid*), thereby explicitly rejecting 'social and cultural isolation', 'enforced complete assimilation' and 'enforced return-migration'.[3]

Many comparative social scientists criticize one-sided and unbalanced 'politics of recognition' and ask for more effective politics of equality. But in their own normative statements they underscore the equal importance of both principles.[4]

However important this agreement of 'all reasonable people' may be, it immediately fades away when it comes to two questions that indicate major areas of disagreement. Firstly, how can and should these two principles be grounded philosophically? Secondly, what do they mean when translated into institutions and practical policies? What does equality practically require in complex modern societies in general and in ethnically plural societies in particular? What does recognition of difference practically mean in different societal fields and how do these different ends relate to each other? Most reasonable people disagree seriously and passionately on all these questions.

Policies of multiculturalism have triggered an enormous amount of philosophical contributions addressing 'foundational' questions which cover the whole range of philosophical disagreements: (i) Post-modern deconstructivists claim that a politics of recognition requires that metaphysics as well as all notions of coherent identity be jettisoned. In contrast, defenders of the project of modernity claim that recognition of difference is at the roots of modern liberalism itself. For them, the recognition of all identities in modern societies as overlapping and quite fragile constructions does not imply that we need to sacrifice normative notions of coherent identities. Moreover, they claim – and this is of particular importance – that equal rights include equal rights to be as different as one wants (equality is not similitude). (ii) There are also controversial debates about the so-called 'ontological status' of groups or collectivities: Do they 'exist' or are the only existing entities individuals and their actions? (iii) Are societies, states, communities, and cultures as collective phenomena subjects of moral concern, or are the ultimate subjects of moral concern only individuals? (iv) Is the guarantee of equal human rights, if interpreted and applied in a really 'colour-blind' way, all that is required to challenge morally illegitimate economic, social or cultural inequalities or do we need (in ideal situations and in reality) group rights and policies of affirmative action? (v) If so, how should group rights and affirmative action policies be legitimated morally? Are legitimations good enough when they start from strong notions of individual autonomy and choice, arguing that in situations of severe objective (economic, social, political, cultural) inequalities, universalistic justice requires conditional, particular group rights and policies of differential treatment? Or do we need strong perfectionist legitimations that argue from the intrinsic value not only of cultural diversity, but also of the specificity of cultures conserved for future generations by means which cannot be defended on grounds of justice and individual autonomy or which openly conflict with these values?

Here I cannot discuss these deep disagreements among philosophers nor elaborate my own version of egalitarian liberalism which is based on the following intuitions: (i) strong concepts of individual autonomy and choice; (ii) choices are made in circumstances: if economic, social, legal, political and cultural circumstances were really approximately equal, specific group rights or affirmative action politics would neither be needed nor be morally defensible.[5] However, to conclude from this ideal world that, in the real world, universal 'individual human rights' would be enough is a seriously flawed argument; (iii) universalistic justice requires particular group rights and differential policies to equalize chances not only because of severe historical injustice but also because of recent and prospective severe inequalities which are the consequences of the working of institutional translations of strictly 'neutral' and 'difference-blind' principles and mechanisms. Will Kymlicka, Joseph Carens, Thomas Pogge, Allen Buchanan, Maurice Rickard, Hurst Hannum, and others have elaborated different aspects of such a philosophical position which, in my view, are convincing. Instead of reiterating these arguments or elaborating my own special version of this thematic strand, I will focus on institutions and practices, which is the second, immense area of disagreement, for two reasons: as far as I can see it has been less discussed and it has a higher practical and political relevance.

2 Indeterminacy of Equality and Difference

Many studies have shown the great variety of policies of incorporation within and across countries. Some of these policies are clearly morally indefensible (guest-worker regimes) or even morally repulsive (*apartheid* regimes), while others fall within the broad range of morally permissible varieties of liberal-democratic incorporation policies. In these matters, as in many others, there is a range of reasonable disagreement about what liberal democratic principles (like equality, recognition of cultural and religious difference, tolerance, freedom of association) require. Within that range, different states are free to adopt different institutional arrangements and practical policies.[6] This is a consequence of the well-known but not always clearly spelled-out indeterminacy of principles.

What does equality mean and require? The principle of equality forbids any prima facie unequal treatment, but as soon as one discusses criteria, it splits into many equalities: legal equality and/or economic, social, political, cultural equality; formal equality and/or procedural equality and/or material equality of results; equality of resources and/or of welfare and/or of status.[7] Living in a morally pluralistic world means that one has to find sensible compromises between conflicting equalities even on the level of principles instead of pushing consistency or parsimony to its limits. Responsive morality has to balance rights, procedures and outcomes. Complex differentiated modern societies and complex resources and rewards require differentiated and complex standards of equalities in normative philosophy.

Despite much intellectual labour in the last 20 years such a comprehensive theory of rough but complex equality is still not available. Theories of justice in the Rawlsian tradition drastically reduce the complexity of 'primary goods' and neglect problems of measurement, weighing, comparability and differential evaluation. They have rightly been criticized as theories of 'simple equality'. Theories of 'complex' (Walzer, 1983) or 'local justice' (Elster, 1992) recognize that fields, resources and rewards are not simply 'objectively given', they are always culturally interpreted and each of these cultural meanings has direct and indirect consequences for their relative evaluation or importance. However, these theories show two serious shortcomings. Firstly, they either assume a consensus of evaluations within fields, or they only register the interpretations and evaluations of the dominant elites.[8] Secondly, they have not adequately grasped, let alone solved, the huge problems of measurement and comparability of resources and rewards across fields. As a consequence, they are unable to clearly describe the cumulation of negative privileges across fields and cannot elaborate normative criteria in order to prevent globally unjust outcomes of locally just distributions. Even if it may turn out that we are unable to measure and aggregate the different resources and rewards in an exact and quantitative way, we can still make educated guesses which allow us to describe them in substantive ways. We can, for example, show how cumulative effects of discrimination and disadvantage lead to the development and stabilization of ethnic underclasses.[9]

In my view, standards of rough, qualitative, complex equality require 'differential' policies to equalize economic, social, cultural, and political chances in all situations of severe, structural inequality. The appropriate measures cannot be discussed in a general and context-free way. They depend on specific groups and their history, on the degree of inequalities, on institutional arrangements and traditions of policies of the receiving states, and so on.[10] To conclude, the first pillar of egalitarian multiculturalism requires rough equality, although much prudence, fairness, experience and context-sensitivity is needed to translate this first pillar of egalitarian multiculturalism into appropriate institutions and practical policies.

What does difference mean and require? And how far can and should it go? The philosophical foundation and meaning of difference is at least as contested as that of equality: post-modernist difference-talk and the cultural relativism of 'anything goes' compete with a deep conservationism with regard to cultural diversity, as well as with a strong perfectionism and its judgements about the 'objective' value of cultures, with weak liberal perfectionism, and with strict liberal neutrality. Bracketing this whole discussion,[11] I think that most egalitarian political liberals, however strongly they may differ with regard to the foundation of the value of individual and cultural difference(s), actually tend to agree, or at least should agree, about two crucial demarcations. First, morally legitimate differences require a principle of equal respect and concern as a firm basis. They are opposed to, and incompatible with, all old and new caste-, feudal- or 'separate-but-equal' versions of difference, where differences are based upon inequalities and where imagined or real cultural differences serve as a legitimation for inequalities.[12] Second, at least for all liberals the recognition of cultural differences and group identities can never be unqualified or unconditional. Practices of 'doing harm' to others cannot be morally tolerated, neither in relation to other ethnic groups nor in relation to internal groups (for example women) or individuals.[13]

This twofold agreement, important as it is, also indicates two major areas of tension or conflict between principles: The debate on affirmative action clearly exemplifies the first area of general disagreement among liberals; the debate on legitimate restrictions of liberties for outsiders and insiders by aboriginal communities demonstrates the second. Egalitarian liberals disagree about how to balance conflicting principles and about sensible practical directions. They also disagree about what respect of cultural differences specifically means in different societal fields, and how far cultural pluralism can and should go.

3   Normative Criteria

Before discussing a reasonable balance between equality and difference in education and law I would like to introduce five normative criteria of rough complex equality in order to evaluate the incorporation of ethnic minorities and to design fair egalitarian multicultural incorporation policies. Egalitarian liberalism, as stated above, does not require universal and unitary models of incorporation. Contested institutions and policies should be evaluated according to the following standards:

(i)   The actual degree of incorporation and of inequality in specific societal fields (see Figure 1 below).
(ii) The degrees to which institutional inclusion or separation and cultural assimilation or pluralism are free or enforced. For example, differential exclusion in guestworker – or apartheid – regimes obviously differs morally from relatively freely chosen institutional separation which is constitutionally and legally guaranteed by the freedom of association, religious and cultural expression or education.[14]
(iii) The legitimate wishes and ends of ethnic minorities and/or their elites with regard to the institutional and cultural forms of incorporation, including their own interpretation, evaluation and weighing of the importance of specific fields, activities, resources, and rewards. Ethnic minorities may differ from majorities in their evaluation of material consumption, (higher) education, expressive activities, spiritual revelation or religious salvation; they may strike a different balance between the value of work and leisure, monetary income and self-realization or prestige attached to work. These differential evaluations may also be characteristic for ordinary people compared with ethnic elites and scientists.[15] Obviously, universally acknowledged, (quasi-) objectively given evaluations and weights cannot exist. Cultural meanings, perspectives, and diverging interests cannot be overcome. However, these evaluations are neither completely subjective (like in private-preference utilitarianism) nor arbitrary. There are clearly dominant cultural evaluations in societies which must not be neglected, and resources show a degree of structural importance in societal formations which is quite resistant to diverging cultural interpretations. Ethnic minorities may value prestige or relations in networks more than money or educational skills and credentials, but like the feudal nobility they have to learn that things in capitalist market economies are different.[16]
(iv) The degree of overall rough equality or inequality. Evaluations of the importance of fields, activities, resources, and rewards may differ considerably among ethnic groups. Still, the cumulation of negative privileges typical for the societal position of ethnic underclasses is morally intolerable. I also think

that there are clear limits to acceptable trade-offs. In my view, it is morally impermissible to compensate for exploitation and oppression by (rhetorical) recognition of cultural diversity; to trade claims to material equalities for some promised equality of 'status' – even if ethnic minorities would make such 'choices'. Not only do economic, social, political and cultural inequalities empirically go hand in hand with negative collective prestige, but the kind of actually enforced choices that are involved is morally unacceptable for egalitarian liberals. Wherever such an impression emerged, the promise of a truncated version of recognition of cultural diversity in exchange for renouncing aspirations to equal economic, social, and political opportunities has discredited politics of multiculturalism.[17]

(v) The – contested – effects of institutional inclusion or separation and of cultural assimilation or pluralism on minimal social cohesion and political integration and unity (see section 4 below and Bader, 1997e).

4. Institutional Separation and Cultural Pluralism: Recipes for Conflict and Disintegration?

Problems of incorporation can be analysed along two axes, an institutional and a cultural one. If one crosstabulates institutional inclusion or separation and cultural assimilation or pluralism, one gets four different typical options of incorporation of ethnic or national minorities which can be applied to specific societal fields as well as to polities (see Figure 2). A long-standing, heavily politically biased prejudice says that institutional separation and cultural pluralism inevitably lead to disruptive conflicts and eventually to the dissolution of states and polities. This prejudice has had an astonishing revival in recent debates about multiculturalism and affirmative action, particularly in the United States.[18] In response to this newly developing, fashionable approach it is important to recall older insights from ethnic studies (see Schermerhorn, 1970) and from theories of consociationalism (see Lijphart, 1984, 1995; v. Dyke, 1995; Hannum, 1990). Institutional separation and cultural pluralism can be the only available options for relatively stable and peaceful conflict resolution under conditions of deep ethnic or national diversity. The effects of institutional separation and cultural pluralism on integration or conflict can be completely opposite ones and generally depend on two factors: firstly, whether they are relatively freely accepted by both minorities and majorities, and whether the resulting centrifugal or centripetal strategies of majorities and minorities point towards the same solution, and secondly, on the characteristics of economic, political, and socio-cultural traditions and contexts.

If we bracket contexts,[19] the following statements are theoretically plausible and empirically fairly well corroborated. Conflicts result in all cases in which centripetal strategies of institutional inclusion or cultural assimilation are enforced by majorities and resisted by minorities, as long as these strategies are felt to be enforced and minorities are able to mobilize enough resources to actually resist. Also, conflicts result in all cases in which centrifugal strategies of enforced institutional separation or rejected cultural assimilation (legally or socially enforced cultural pluralism) by majorities or states are resisted by minorities which strive for full institutional inclusion or relatively free acculturation.[20]

A prima facie moral evaluation shows that, in general, all four options may be morally legitimate, provided they are not legally or socially enforced by majorities but (more or less) freely accepted by minorities. A very rough empirical comparison of the four options with regard to cohesion and political stability or conflict and disruption of polities indicated in Figure 2, shows the following picture. Inclusion into unchanged, unitary institutions of the dominant ethnie or nation (*cell 1*) can be integrative and fairly stable when, and depending to what degree, the state and dominant majorities offer and stimulate options granting full institutional inclusion and cultural assimilation, and when those options are accepted by ethnic or national minorities (myth of the French republic or of the Melting Pot). Wherever states or majorities enforce institutional separation and cultural pluralism, this results in the development of social or legal apartheid regimes (the US-American South, the 'plantation-belt societies', the South African *Apartheidsregime*). These morally abject versions of *cell 2* can be relatively stable as long as minorities – in these cases often numerical majorities – are unable to resist effectively. Wherever states and majorities broaden the circle of ethnic (immigrant) minorities, which are defined capable of 'integrating' and being 'integrated' and assimilating and being 'assimilated', and wherever minorities accept this chance (as has been the case with the overwhelming majority of all immigrants),[21] *cell 1* can be stable even if the Melting Pot remains predominantly Anglo-Saxon.[22] Moreover, wherever minorities reject full inclusion and assimilation, as all strong national minorities commonly have done, and wherever majorities (are forced to) concede to institutional separation and cultural pluralism, the well-known cases (*cell 2*) of considerable institutional separation and cultural pluralism (combined with strong cultural assimilation within the 'pillars') develop. The Canadian Mosaic, the consociational democracies of the Netherlands (predominantly religious pillars), Belgium and Switzerland (ethnic/national pillars) have, for a long time, provided fairly stable patterns of conflict resolution. If minorities rejected cultural assimilation and states and majorities agreed to change and develop state institutions in a de facto relational neutral way, the utopia of a 'post-ethnic' and 'trans-national'

America, which Hollinger (1996) and Lind (1995) have mistaken for reality, would offer excellent conditions for stable conflict resolution (*cell 3*). If minorities could not be convinced of the presumed 'neutrality' of this model and consequently resisted full inclusion, and if majorities and minorities did allow for internal cultural pluralism, the utopia of a 'federation of nations' or a new form of national or ethnic 'consociational democracy' (*cell 4*) could be a stable and morally ideal setting for conflict resolution. As long as national minorities resist the minimal institutional inclusion (for example a common constitution, common armed forces, a common currency) required for this option to be stable, and instead keep fighting for independence and complete sovereignty, even this option would lead to endless conflicts. Determined strategies to achieve completely separate institutions are usually a reaction to enforced, all-inclusive and unitary inclusion. They will certainly 'disunite America' (Schlesinger, 1991). Wherever minorities have a strong power-base and are able to mobilize sufficient resources, these strategies are extremely difficult to counter.[23] In concluding this overly short empirical evaluation it seems clear to me that considerable institutional separation and cultural pluralism do not *per se* lead to irresolvable conflict, disintegration, and political instability as is generally assumed by the common sociological prejudice.

If one rejects the idea that options 2 and 4 are inherently unstable and disruptive, then further moral evaluation of them is necessary. To begin with, it becomes more and more obvious that we have to overcome the traditional dichotomy of, on the one side, 'Millet-systems' or pillarized polities that do not leave much individual freedom inside the pillars, and do not represent those who do not belong to any pillar, and, on the other side, a majoritarian republican model which has little respect for group rights, minority protection, legal pluralism, and fair degrees of political autonomy. From an egalitarian liberal point of view, the 'third way' of a liberal, consociational or associative democracy (option 4) seems to have two considerable advantages. Firstly, it requires much less *social* unity as a – supposed – precondition of political unity.[24] It is, therefore, not only more in line with complex modern, plural societies but also with liberal political philosophy which emphasizes individual autonomy and the variety of meaningful choices.[25] Secondly, it does not require too much *political* unity and coherence. It does not link minimal political unity to too much pre-political social and cultural unity, and it is less statist[26] and more in line with the limitation, reconstruction, and devolution of state sovereignty, which leaves more space for federal and associational autonomy. Only with difficulty does the model of a centralized, unitarian republican polity (option 3) become really, not only formally, 'ethnically neutral' on all levels and in all branches, not only with regard to rules, rights, procedures, institutions, cultures, and practices, but also with regard to recruitment for all positions, particularly leading positions in government, civil services, courts, and armed forces.[27] Projects of building a unified 'pre-political' cultural, 'post-ethnic' nation cannot easily avoid the danger of strong republican state perfectionism and paternalism as well as the danger of republican exclusionism when it comes to 'international obligations'. The resulting political culture may be very strong, but it is clearly not 'thin enough'.[28] Whether the thin common core-institutions and the thin political culture of ethnic/national associative democracy can be strong enough is the hard question advocates of option 4 have to answer, when there is a strong need for egalitarian or ecological state intervention, or when strong politics of democratic transformation are on the agenda. Option 3 is, evidently, institutionally better equipped for such policies than option 4 which gives more leeway to pluralism. Equality and difference cannot easily and universally be balanced and there is no single best model of polity for all people in all circumstances.[29]

5 Education: Between 'Assimilating' Univalent Equality and 'Disuniting' Polyvalent Plurality

Equality and plurality are both invoked in multicultural education policies, although they present themselves in different concoctions and there is considerable variance regarding legitimation, official proclamation, implementation, and practices of these policies across all Western European countries,[30] in the USA, Canada, and Australia. To combine equality and plurality may be particularly difficult and seriously contested in public education. In my short discussion I will apply the five criteria introduced above in section 3.

5.1 Inequalities in Provision and Attainment of Education

Despite all variation among ethnic groups and among states underachievement of ethnic minorities in education is a common problem faced by all immigration countries.[31] There is no consensus on how to explain this, but it seems obvious that multiple causes are at work: (temporary) migration effects; effects of class origin mediated by education of parents (particularly of mothers);[32] at least some effects of ethnic differences;[33] open or hidden ethnic and racial bias of schools as well as curricula and teaching practices, even in cases of proclaimed multiculturalism or anti-racism; concentration schools ('black schools') in run-down neighbourhoods, even in cases of compensation and enrichment programmes.[34]

Rough, complex equality requires that serious ethnic underachievement be fought. It is a remarkable sign that all West European states have developed affirmative action programmes[35] with a focus on improving competencies of students and schools to reduce ethnic inequalities. Distributional policies of facilitation ('governing by input') are dominant: different versions of additional funding (dependent on students' characteristics such as gender, nationality, class origin, mother tongue, etc.) and teacher training.[36] Direct ethnic affirmative action programmes imply a thorough categorization of target groups while indirect programmes focus on neighbourhoods and all students 'at risk' and are thereby able to avoid nasty categorization problems.[37]

5.2 Enforced versus Fairly Free Separation of School Classes or Schools

The often discussed problems of moral legitimacy of enforcement in education have to do with compulsory education (legitimate paternalism and the limits of parental discretion), and with freedom of education (see Flathman, 1996), private (religious) schools and their limits in democratic polities. Both problems are also relevant when it comes to education and ethnic minorities.[38] I would, however, like to highlight some other, less discussed problems of segregation of ethnic classes or schools in West European countries: (a) Direct legal force and more indirect (social, financial) pressure by the state can be applied for opposite ends: on the one hand, in order to avoid presumed stigmatization, to prevent the creation of poor 'black schools' and to achieve equality and integration by way of rapid assimilation.[39] On the other hand, however, a 'guestworker' regime and ideology establishes 'nationality schools', 'preparatory classes' and '*Ausländerregelklassen*' (segregated regular classes for foreign pupils) which serve the morally dubious, 'double-faced' aim to 'stimulate return migration' and to maintain higher-quality education for native students.[40] (b) Separate schools do not mean the same everywhere: poorly funded and staffed 'black schools' or 'nationality schools' in ghettos should not be confused with separate private or public schools for ethnic or national minorities which operate under conditions of rough equality.[41] (c) Separate classes or lessons (preparatory classes as well as mother-tongue instruction and bilingual lessons) can rightly be viewed from opposite angles: They can be viewed with suspicion (as disintegrating, disuniting, stigmatizing, and marginalizing),[42] or they can be praised as expressions of cultural diversity. It depends.[43] It is important to distinguish morally legitimate policies under conditions of rough equality from policies under conditions of structural inequality. The latter may require much more 'unity', legitimate legal enforcement, and stricter limits to plurality and difference as long as such plurality serves to stabilize or even promote inequalities.

5.3 Legitimate Needs and Wishes

Moral principles of liberal democracy, in my view, do not prescribe unitary public education. Freedom of education allows for private ethnic, as well as religious schools. Ethnic schools that are owned and/or controlled by ethnic communities or elites and staffed with ethnic teachers give, under conditions of rough equality and non-discrimination, considerable leeway for the legitimate wishes of particular cultures. But, like other schools, they should be under public inspection and scrutiny; they have to teach toleration and live up to minimal requirements of all education in multicultural societies (see below). If ethnic groups do not want separate institutions or cannot afford them for lack of sufficient public funding (e.g. too few numbers of students and/or low territorial concentration), they still have a strong moral claim that their legitimate wishes be respected and heard in state or other public or private schools their children are enrolled in.[44] At varying paces and with considerable time-lag all Western European states have eventually responded to ethnic immigration by providing educational policies which cover the following list:[45] (1) preparatory arrangements: orientation or transition classes, *internationale schakelklassen, opvangonderwijs, classes d'adaptation et classes d'initiation, Vorbereitungsklassen* (Fase, 1994: 121ff.); (2) the teaching of mother tongues: *onderwijs in eigen taal en cultuur (OECT)* in the Netherlands (language 1, ibid. 123 ff.); (3) the teaching of the official language(s) of the country of residence (language 2, ibid. 125 ff.); (4) intercultural education (*elkaar ontmoetend onderwijs* in Belgium, ibid. 127 ff.). But there have been and still are considerable differences. Apart from differences in constructive 'throughput' policies with regard to time schedules (e.g. how many lessons, separate from or part of the official curriculum, methods, language models, teacher involvement and training, teaching materials), the main differences have to do with (a) typical orientations; (b) levels of government and degree of coordination; (c) particular representative involvement (of political and school authorities and immigrant and ethnic communities) as well as the level of discretion.

If one tries to characterize these educational practices in terms of typical orientations and categorization, particularly the mix of egalitarian and pluralistic orientations, the following rough picture emerges (Fase, 1994: 134ff.). Separate preparatory classes for clearly targeted groups in France and the Netherlands have been mainly motivated by an egalitarian orientation, whereas German *Ausländerregelklassen* have been motivated by differential exclusivism (neither egalitarian nor really pluralist). Mother-tongue education clearly specifies target groups (without an 'inner logic' with regard to which groups and which languages). In whatever way it is carried out (hours, methods, teachers; usually separate, very few and limited 'language awareness' programmes) and funded (for example, by the governments of countries of origin), its overall orientation is pluralistic in all countries: "At national level, there is a 'permissive' attitude toward introducing specific aims that go along with the teaching of mother tongue and culture, whether it is for reasons of ethnic identity, language maintenance or otherwise" (ibid.: 135). The few examples of bilingual education are transitional (first language instrumental for second language acquisition); their aims are, therefore, mainly egalitarian, not pluralistic. The even rarer efforts to introduce official migrant languages in the wider context of conventional modern language teaching are pluralistically oriented but opportunities and participation are very limited. Intercultural education, ideally for all students of all schools (zero categorization), is highly pluralistic in orientation although its specific aims vary substantially "from better knowledge of cultures and religions (...) to reducing prejudgement and prejudice" (ibid.: 137). Anti-racist education, criticizing multicultural essentialism and difference-talk, accentuates the egalitarian perspective more directly.[46]

If one tries to characterize the predominant orientation of multicultural educational policies in a cross-national perspective along this axis, the strongest divide in Western Europe is found between Britain and Germany: Britain has a system of multicultural policies that is univalent egalitarian, i.e. reluctant towards pluralism and hesitant to tolerate special treatment of ethnic minority groups or separate classes and schools.[47] The strongest contrast is the 'polyvalent' German model: "Many incentives other than egalitarian ones have their impact on multicultural policies, and in many circumstances the frequency and intensity of special arrangements for ethnic minority pupils is high." (ibid.: 139). Its pluralism has been mainly of the differential exclusionist version and is, despite all changes, still not even minimally based on egalitarian incorporation.

A moral evaluation shows that both extremes are very questionable from a liberal-democratic point of view or, to say the least, very unattractive because they do not strike a reasonable balance between equality and difference. The 'in-between' countries could do better, but they lack more principled moral grounding and minimal consistency of their policies and strategies required for strong and successful educational politics.[48] Egalitarian multiculturalism in education is clearly still a utopia.

5.4 Schools and 'Classes'

Education plays a prominent role in the reproduction and stabilization of entrenched inequalities across all fields. There is a vicious circle of ethnic underclass formation and reproduction at work: underclass or lower working-class origin – ethnic under-achievement in education – weak labour-market position – high structural unemployment – poor housing, etc. In order to break this circle, ethnic affirmative action in education is definitely an important part of any political strategy which takes moral principles of social and liberal democracy seriously. Interestingly enough, this is generally recognized by all Western European governments, but compensation policies are extremely diverse and lack determination and effectiveness even in those countries which try harder.

5.5 Multicultural Education, Social Cohesion and Political Unity

Multicultural education is so hotly contested because education plays such a prominent part in tradition and reproduction of 'thick' culture, habits, virtues and practices in general and political culture and habits in particular. All those who regard basic cultural homogeneity in terms of ethnic and national culture or religion as crucial for social cohesion and stability and who quite traditionally want to use educational institutions (together with the armed forces) as an anvil of enforced assimilation inevitably see multicultural education as a threat (even without ethnocentristic claims to superiority of the dominant ethnic or religious culture). This argument is usually meshed with the more fashionable and defensible argument, from a liberal-democratic point of view, that multicultural education would threaten the tradition and furthering of the thin morality and political culture, habits and virtues required for minimal political unity and for stability and flourishing of liberal society and political democracy.[49] The first, strongly assimilationist model of social unity has lost much of its presumed moral plausibility in the last decades. It is not only discredited by most liberal political philosophy which tries to strictly separate the right from the good, but also by positions which critically discuss the limits of such a simple disentanglement of morality from 'ethos', and of 'thin' political culture from 'thick' ethnic culture (Kymlicka, 1995; Parekh, 1995; Carens, 1997). The second argument is morally more tricky but still can, I think, be refuted: a reformulated ideal of critical 'relational' ethnic neutrality or perhaps better of 'evenhandedness' (Carens, 1997) of the state and of liberal, social and democratic political culture requires multicultural education (Bader, 1997). If one takes that for granted here, the really hard questions only begin. For instance: What exactly is this minimally required 'hard core' of liberal-democratic political culture? Which habits, virtues and good practices exactly are meant? How should they be interpreted? How can they be stimulated and developed? Furthermore, how can all educational practices, whether in private, semi-public or public educational institutions, minimally live up to these standards?[50]

The following remarks conclude this sketchy discussion. Moral principles of liberal, social democracy limit the set of permissible options in the field of education, but they do not and cannot prescribe the morally or politically right answers which should be the subject of open democratic debate and action. Better, more sensible and fair practices of multicultural education depend upon contexts, institutional settings and policy traditions: (1) Institutions and practices of fairly developed welfare states at least soften the formation and entrenchment of ethnic underclasses if they are not able to prevent these developments. At the same time they offer opportunities for policies of indirect affirmative action in education that is preferable for many reasons.[51] (2) Educational systems differ considerably among and even within states.[52] Private educational institutions may allow for more and easier ethnic diversity but traditionally they pose two serious obstacles for democratic educational politics: potentially high levels of inequality,[53] and problems to control and enforce minimum liberal-democratic standards regarding non-discriminatory recruitment of staff and students as well as in curricula and teaching practices. It may bear repeating that all schools, including private ethnic or religious ones, have to live up to minimal requirements of multicultural education in social, democratic, and constitutional states. (3) Democratic control, inspection and effective impact on changes of curricula, materials, methods and practices of teaching should, in my view, be the litmus-test for judging institutional arrangements and traditions of 'throughput policies'. Politically, not morally, I am convinced that semi-public and public institutions imply less obstacles in this regard, particularly if developed in the direction of associative democracy in education (versus statist, over-centralized, bureaucratic and non-participatory policy traditions; versus irresponsible 'private' freedom of education).[54] However, it is still a long way to achieve co-educational public schools and egalitarian multicultural education which is really relationally neutral in all relevant regards, be it sex, gender, class, religion, or ethnicity.

6 Unitary Law and Ethnic Legal Pluralism

There may be a lot of space for legitimate moral pluralism in most fields, or so it is often said, but law itself is the field of equality and unity *per se*. This is true, from a liberal-democratic point of view and with regard to the requirement of fully equal legal, political and social rights of all long-term residents and, of course, citizens.[55] The same is true for core moral principles and their translation into central legal principles in liberal-democratic constitutions and codes of civil and criminal law. These principles define the limits of all legitimate cultural pluralism in general (see also Hirst, 1994: 68) and of legitimate legal pluralism in particular. What is at stake here is legitimate pluralism within the confines of social, democratic constitutionalism, not a new version of an Ottoman Millet-system. This, however, does not mean outright acceptance of 'the' existing legal order, as is often assumed even by critical theorists.[56] Quite the contrary, liberal democracies have to accept the challenge of deeply different cultures and check, with great scrutiny, the existing legal rules and practices for morally intolerable sexist, gendered, racist, ethnocentrist, religious elements and bias: The 'law of the land' differs considerably from the 'thin moral code' of public morality in liberal theory. In most states it is still thick or pregnant with illegitimate, even stupid ethnocentrism, particularly when it comes to unspecified general norms (what is public order, decency, etc.) and administrative, executive rulings and practices.[57]

Taking these two points for granted in this chapter, I will now direct my focus to an example of legal pluralism. Immigration and settlement of ethnic minorities from countries with a considerably different legal system and legal culture create much strain and conflict.[58] Attempts to resolve these conflicts range from a strictly egalitarian and culturally absolutely insensitive application of the law of the host-state (*lex fori*) to a far-reaching normative legal pluralism which can be at odds with moral principles of liberal democracy.[59] Examples can be taken from international private law in the Netherlands: Dutch family law and jurisdiction in relation to marriage, matrimonial regimes, divorce, alimentation, custody and visiting rights of Moroccan or mixed-nationality couples.[60] The crucial question here is which legal rules (Moroccan or Dutch or international) and which interpretations should apply depending on the nationality of the spouses and on the place where the marriage was concluded (in Morocco, at a Moroccan embassy or consulate in the Netherlands, or in Dutch territory). The formal and conventional legal sources are manifold: written (Marriage Covenant The Hague 1978, not ratified by Morocco) and unwritten international private law;[61] Moroccan family law (Book 1 of the *Muddawwana*) and Dutch family law. It is by no means always clear or binding which law has to be applied.[62] Points of conflict with regard to the conclusion of marriage are: different age requirements (in Morocco 18 for male and 15 for female spouses), different requirements of consent (in Morocco, women always need agreement by their *walī* [marriage guardian], men only below the age of majority [21]). A Muslim woman is legally – not only culturally, like in Turkey and in most Turkish communities abroad – not allowed to marry a non-Muslim man. Polygamy is allowed in principle in Morocco, though it is prohibited if unequal treatment of spouses is to be feared (art. 30 par. 1 *Muddawwana*) or if it is excluded by marriage contract.[63] With regard to divorce, Dutch law is based on *favor divortii* and on equality of the sexes, whereas Moroccan law knows three forms of divorce:

talaq (art. 44-52, 60; unilateral repudiation by the man without any need for further reasons); *khul* (mutual agreement); and *tatliq* (legal divorce upon request of the woman for one of the following reasons: neglect of obligation to provide maintenance, bodily defect, rude treatment, absence, oath of abstention).

Dutch judges regularly apply and have to apply (and sometimes even incorporate) 'foreign legal' rules which contradict the old *lex fori*: they declare marriages concluded in Morocco as valid which would not be allowed in the Netherlands, they declare polygamous marriages as legal; they accept unilateral divorces in cases that the wife explicitly or tacitly has agreed or at least appeased, etc.[64] However that may work out, there should be, in my view, clear moral limits to legal pluralism and tolerable practices: no marriages under duress; limits to enforcement of pre-arranged marriages if girls explicitly resist; no wife-beating or child-beating;[65] no acceptance of gross inequalities between the sexes in cases of divorce or custody regulations, etc.[66] Essential individual rights and exit options have to be minimally guaranteed and should never be overruled by group rights and legal pluralism.[67] Legal pluralism and group rights without such limits would indeed be a nightmare, but many fears in this regard are alarmist, specious reasoning.[68] A reasonable balance between equality and legitimate differences has to be discussed 'per legal area' (Bovens, 1993: 170, 172).

In concluding this overly short and selective discussion of education and law, I hope to have shown that fair liberal-democratic incorporation policies do not follow deductively from moral principles inherent in democratic social constitutionalism. The two leading principles of equality and difference are in conflict and cannot be easily combined. Republicans and radical democrats tend to neglect difference completely or tend to subsume difference too easily to equality. They generally opt for unitary public education and unitary law in all cases and circumstances and do not only, rightly, point to the fact that all federal or associational arrangements of institutional separation have inherent difficulties to achieve and guarantee rough equality, but also use these problems as a pretext for egalitarian arguments in order to overrule conflicting claims of pluralism. Egalitarian pluralists cannot neglect these inegalitarian tendencies, as classical liberals often did. Their 'arts of differentiation', their design of 'associative democratic institutions' has not yet presented adequate solutions. They have, however, a very strong case against simple egalitarians in pointing out that unitary institutions are only presumably neutral and that institutional separation provides better social and political conditions to achieve higher degrees of relational neutrality. Also, both strands of egalitarian liberalism have not yet found convincing answers to the serious transformational problem that policies to achieve conditions of rough equality require more unity and stronger centres which, consequently, block the development of normatively preferable institutional and cultural pluralism.

Contrary to mainstream political philosophy I am convinced that there cannot be single best solution to these problems. The best balancing of equality and plurality regarding institutional settings as well as policies differs from field to field and even inside one field from country to country or city to city. Practical political judgement has to be guided not only by moral arguments, it also has to include ethical, prudential and realistic considerations (see Bader, 1997c). It is obvious that tensions, incompatibilities and paradoxes of incorporation policies multiply if one takes issues of considered long-term self-interests of contending groups into account and if one discusses empirical consequences and side-effects of incorporation policies in different fields. It often may be the case that we are not able to do practically what we are morally required to do.

Practical judgements and political decisions have to balance these diverging arguments (all things considered) and not only require prudence but also context-specific experience and information. The most adequate solutions for these contexts (versus the illusion of the simple best or optimal solution) have to be elaborated in public democratic talk and decision-making, and cannot be dictated by practical reason. The quality of these options (the output) depends on the quality of cognitive and normative patterns, of the information and the openness to the many, 'deeply different voices' (as input) and on the quality of democratic procedures (as 'throughput'). There are clearly better and worse incorporation policies and that is all we reasonably can expect in fields where Reason with the capital R does not decide. Moral and political philosophers as well as social scientists can play a modest but important tune in this polyphonic concert of public talk, decision-making and action: as policy-advisors, as critics, and as participating citizens. They should try to prevent it from ending up in orchestrated unisons or cacophonies.

Figure 1: Fields of Incorporation

Field of:	Separate Institutions and Practices	Full Inclusion
material production	ethnic entrepreneurs, ethnic occupations, ethnic niches, ethnic sectors	general, ethnically neutral business, occupations (no legal or de facto ethnic barriers, closed shops, etc.)
health care	ethnic healing practices, ethnic hospitals	general hospitals, ethnically neutral, modern medicine
recreation	separate ethnic recreational occupations and oganizations (sports, holidays in country of origin, etc.)	ethnically neutral recreational occupations and organizations
erotics, friendship, marriage	closed ethnic, direct interaction-relations, ethnic associations, and patronage; ethnic endogamy	interethnic friendship and mating, associations etc., 'miscegenation', exogamy
social security/services	separate family, kinship, ethnic networks and organizations	full legal and actual inclusion in general, public arrangements
arts	separate artistic companies and organizations	ethnically neutral musea, theatre, film, music, dance companies and institutions
'meaning'/ religion	separate ethnic religions, priests, churches, sects or denominations	inclusion into ethnically neutral, universalistic religious associations/organizat.
science	separate ethnic research institutions	universal, ethnically neutral research institutions
education	separate ethnic schools (primary, secondary, higher education; vocational schools, adult education)	inclusions into public education (in all forms, on all levels)
information	separate ethnic media (newspapers, radio, TV, journals)	general, ethnically neutral media
politics/ administration	separate ethnic movements, SMOs, political parties (or factions); separate mechanisms and rights of ethnic representation; degree of ethnic political autonomy	general, ethnically neutral movements, SMOs, parties, administration (ethnic recruitment, promotion, high positions in civil service, etc.)
law and law enforcement	(1) degree of legal inclusion of ethnic minorities: legal and political inequalities across the board: second class citizens; (2) degree of legal pluralism: recognition of ethnic law; (3) degree of ethnic pluralism: ethnic bias of 'the' legal order, in the recruitment of judges, of police forces, etc.	(1) degree of legal inclusion of ethnic minorities: full legal and political equality in all respects; (2) degree of legal pluralism: unitary, ethnically 'neutral' law and application of jus fori in all matters; (3) degree of ethnic pluralism: ethnic neutrality of the legal order, of recruitment of judges, of police forces, etc.
external relations	exclusion of ethnic minorities from military forces, from diplomatic service, etc.	full legal and actual equality in this regard

Apart from this presentation of incorporation which is focused on institutions of 'production' and on occupations in different fields, one could distinguish a second dimension, focusing on the degree of actual use, which members of ethnic minorities make of separate or general institutions and services (e.g. in health care, recreation, social services) and a third dimension, focusing on the continuation, change, retention or loss of specific ethnic cultures in the specific fields: do they continue, change or loose ethnic feasts and recreational practices; artisanal and artistic traditions; ethnic religious beliefs, rituals and practices?

Egalitarian Multiculturalism

Figure 2: Types of Institutional and Cultural Incorporation of Ethnic/National Minorities (Polities as Examples)

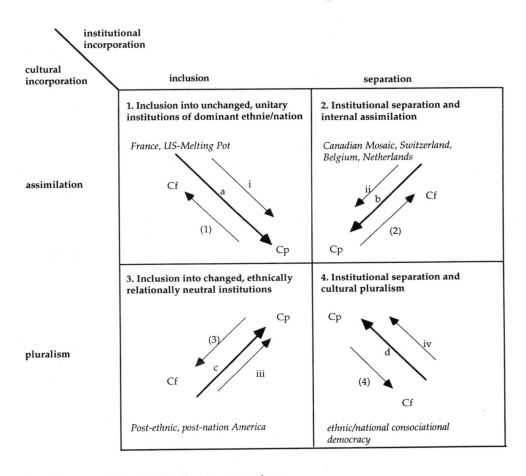

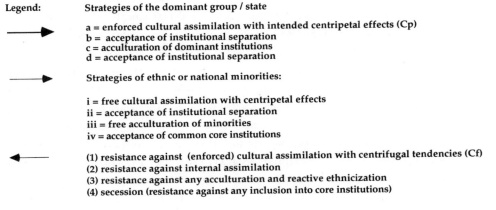

Legend: Strategies of the dominant group / state

a = enforced cultural assimilation with intended centripetal effects (Cp)
b = acceptance of institutional separation
c = acculturation of dominant institutions
d = acceptance of institutional separation

Strategies of ethnic or national minorities:

i = free cultural assimilation with centripetal effects
ii = acceptance of institutional separation
iii = free acculturation of minorities
iv = acceptance of common core institutions

(1) resistance against (enforced) cultural assimilation with centrifugal tendencies (Cf)
(2) resistance against internal assimilation
(3) resistance against any acculturation and reactive ethnicization
(4) secession (resistance against any inclusion into core institutions)

Notes

1. See Raz (1975); Habermas (1993); Bader (1997c: 176ff.).
2. For a short but concise comparative overview see Castles/Miller (1993: chapter 8).
3. See WRR (1979) and WRR (1989). See Penninx (1988), Entzinger (1984). Before the design and implementation of a new minority policy in the end of the 1970s and the early 1980s the formula has been: "integration and maintenance of the own identity" (WRR, 1979: XIV, see Penninx). The normative ends of the new policy have been (i) equal participation or equal chances, including a lot of direct and, particularly, indirect policies of affirmative action with regard to (ethnic) minorities. These policies to tackle cumulative inequalities have been argued for from a perspective of justice (WRR, 1979: XVIII ff.) and have been perceived to be a necessary precondition for the second aim (ii) 'cultural respect and equality in a context of freedom' (WRR, 1979: XX) in a multicultural society, explicitly rejecting other options like 'social and cultural isolation', 'enforced assimilation' or 'enforced return-migration'. The proposed, proclaimed and only partly realized changes in '*allochtonenbeleid*' from the late 1980s onwards do not officially reject or undermine these double aims (see WRR, 1989: 25). They still argue from justice/equality (including affirmative action (ibid.: 11, 17) to prevent an ethnically segregated society (ibid.: 55). Very roughly stated, they consist, on the one side, in shifting the balance between the two aims (giving higher priority to 'integration *vis-à-vis* cultural pluriformity and identity' (ibid.: 22f.) and, on the other side, in focusing the 'integration' or 'equality' policies on labour participation, education, vocational training and adult education, and in disconnecting cultural policies from ethnic minorities (WRR, 1989: 155). See for Canada: Juteau (1997), Jensen (1996); for important differences between Canada and the US: Kymlicka (1996, 1996b); for Australia: Castles (1997).
4. See Fraser (1995: 166f.) "The 'struggle for recognition' has become the paradigmatic form of political conflict in the late twentieth century (...) Struggles for recognition occur in a world of exacerbated material inequality (...)". Fraser sees a "new intellectual and practical task: that of developing a *critical* theory of recognition, one which identifies and defends only those versions of the politics of difference that coherently synergize with the politics of redistribution" (ibid.). See also Castles (1997: 125): "Recognizing group difference and its social meaning implies departing from the idea of all citizens as simply *equal individuals* and instead seeing them simultaneously as having *equal rights as individuals and different needs and wants as members of groups with specific characteristics and social situations.*" Four principles are pointed out: (1) taking equality of citizenship rights as a starting point; (2) recognizing that formal equality of rights does not necessarily lead to equality of respect, resources, opportunities or welfare; (3) establishing mechanisms for group representation and participation; (4) differential treatment for people with different characteristics, needs and wants. See van Dyke (1995: 42, with Owen Fiss) on an 'anti-discrimination principle' vs. a 'group disadvantage principle'. See Juteau (1997): Multiculturalism in Canada has often been presented as a politics involving the

recognition of identity (Taylor, 1994: 26f.) and the accommodation of cultural differences (Kymlicka, 1995: 10). This is not false but incomplete: Politics of recognition must involve more than the respect of *difference* if it is to move beyond the selling of illusions and achieve inclusiveness. It must extend beyond cultural recognition and encompass economic, political and social equality, on the one hand, structural pluralism on the other (108ff.). See also Hörder/Juteau (1995: 14); Fase (1994: 131); Habermas (1994: 110, 113), Bauböck (1995: 20f., 31f.).

5 The main exceptions are rights of national minorities in federalist arrangements which should be granted even under conditions of rough equality.

6 See Carens (1995: 4), Carens/Williams (1995: 14); see Bader (1997) and Carens (1997).

7 See Bader (1995b) for a more extensive treatment of dilemmas of affirmative action, where inequalities of cultural chances is explicitly not dealt with. Maurice Rickard (1994) has developed a very similar argument with regard to 'cultural protection' of different kinds of ethnic minorities and aboriginals.

8 See Walzer (1983: XIV, 4 ff.). Explicitly: Elster (1992: 4, 184, 236f., 244f.).

9 See Bader/Benschop (1989: 321), Bader (1991: 482). See recently: Sen (1992). See Bader (1995b) for a more extensive treatment, particularly for reference groups and rough proportionality. See WRR (1979: XXV; 1989: 15, 36) where the Canadian Employment Equity Act serves as a positive model. See for a critical evaluation: Kurthen (1997).

10 See Bader (1995b: Conclusions) for some general rules of thumb and a short comparison of the US American and Dutch context.

11 See Kymlicka (1989, 1990: 205-236). Raz (1986, part II).

12 See Taylor (1994: 27 ff., 37 ff.); Minow (1990: 91, 374f., 385f.).

13 See Kymlicka (1989, 1995) for these external and internal constraints.

14 Special attention should be paid to problems of opportunities and limits of free choices of kids (legitimate paternalism) and to the many forms of social coercion (up to ostracism).

15 See WRR (1979: XIII, XXXII) and Engbersen/Gabriëls (1995: 40).

16 See Bader/Benschop (1989: 155-161, 321 f.)

17 See critically: Stasioulis (1985), Juteau (1997), McAndrew/Radtke (1995), Radtke (1996). Danley's interpretation of the no-harm principle (1991: 108f.) does not seriously consider socially enforced choices.

18 Not only among journalists, but also among political scientists, historians and political philosophers. See Schlesinger (1991), Hollinger (1996), Lind (1995). Claus Offe (1997) seems to introduce this position into recent German debates.

19 Economic prosperity can, obviously, soften ethnic competition and conflict on labour-, housing-markets etc. whereas economic slump intensifies the struggle for scarce resources. Conflict resolution under conditions of zero- or negative sum games is much more difficult. See Bader (1991: 344f.) and Offe (1997). Liberal nationalism, whether republican or consociational, is evidently impossible where institutions and traditions of democratic and social constitutionalism are lacking, as in many states of Eastern Europe and most African states, where 'nasty na-

tionalism' (Walzer) dominates. In contrast, Canadian institutions and traditions could stimulate its development (see Carens, 1995: 3ff.); Kymlicka (1997: 13-46) and the same may be possible in some future European Union characterized by simultaneous reconstruction and devolution of state sovereignty. Especially if one recognizes that ethnic and national conflicts imply 'issues of rights and recognition' and cleavages of 'ideology and identity' (Offe, 1997) and cannot be reduced to 'resources' and 'interests', and if one clearly recognizes that symbolic and identity conflicts are particularly difficult to resolve (see Bader, 1991: 335) one should be more sceptical with regard to the republican unitary option. Enforced cultural assimilation and institutional inclusion are a recipe for protracted conflict and liberal democratic institutional separation and cultural pluralism can – under condition of rough, complex equality – stimulate peaceful, minimal integration.

20 See Schermerhorn (1970: 77ff). Short summary in Bader (1995: 49f.).

21 Kymlicka thinks that this is the appropriate model for ethnic immigrants who, according to him, want to participate within the mainstream of society (1996b: 112, 118f) but "want the mainstream institutions in their society to be reformed, so as to accommodate their cultural differences, and to recognize the value of their cultural heritage" (119). Quoting Modood, he points out that "the greatest psychological and political need for clarity about a common framework and national symbols comes from the minorities" because they are under constant pressure "to conform in all areas of social life, or in arbitrarily chosen areas, in order to rebut the charge of disloyalty".

22 See clear limits when it comes to blacks and indigenous peoples: Bader (1997c). Even Glazer (1996) has recognized this clearly.

23 Compare the huge differences in this regard between 'Black Africanism' in the US and Québécois separatism. See Buchanan (1991), Kymlicka (1995), Carens (1995), Rex (1994: 20ff.).

24 In his discussion of 'social unity' in a liberal, poly-ethnic or multi-nation-state Will Kymlicka not always distinguishes clearly between social unity and political unity: self-government rights need not be a 'threat to social unity' (1996b: 122) though they may be for political unity. Political unity may not need much social unity and can live with a high degree of institutional separateness, particularly in consociational democracy which may be the best institutional arrangements in which citizens in A.V. Dicey's apt phrase 'must desire union, and must not desire unity'. I agree with his critique of the traditional 'liberal' answer to the question of the required social basis of political unity: shared liberal political principles or values cannot do the job because they are common throughout the Western world, and with his critique of the 'communi-tarian' answer: 'shared ends' or a good life (ibid.: 128-131). His own, tentative answer to the question of the 'pre-political bases' of political unity: shared identities, solidarity which is grounded in cultural membership, even when this culture becomes thinner and 'thinner' (ibid.: 132) is also problematic because, as he clearly signals himself, history and culture can themselves be quite divisive, and because the problem is that the 'common culture' has to be a very

25 specific one, focused on the state (a 'political' culture) and not only respecting, but being proud of 'deep diversity' (ibid.: 134). The 'common core' of social unity would in this regard be 'diversity' which most people think is not unifying but divisive. See Bader (1997d) for a more detailed discussion of the different 'pre-political bases' of political loyalty.

25 See Flathman (1996) for tensions between individual autonomy and 'stronger' forms of participatory democracy in education from a liberal point of view.

26 And, consequently, more adequate to the anti-etatist normative intuitions shared by classical liberalism, communism and anarchism.

27 Republicans tend to neglect structural inequalities between 'majorities' and 'minorities' which are mainly responsible for the development of 'pillarization', be it 'ethnic' (as in the case of immigrant communities in the first two generations) or on religious grounds (as in the case of the Catholics in the Netherlands) or on gender criteria (as in the case of gay 'cities on the hill'). Also, they tend to neglect the importance of such power-bases in the struggle for relational ethnic/national neutrality of states.

28 See Bader (1997) for a more detailed discussion.

29 This tension becomes obvious if one compares legitimate politics under conditions of structural inequalities with politics under conditions of rough equality. The first one requires more unity and stronger centres (see Unger, 1996) but exactly these institutional forms may effectively stand in the way of the development of a rich institutional and cultural pluralism preferable under conditions of rough equality. This is one of the many paradoxes of transformation.

30 See the excellent comparative study by Fase (1994) for Western Europe (England/Wales, France, Belgium, Germany, Netherlands): (i) both principles adopted (111, 131); (ii) strain between them (102); (iii) gap between rhetoric/legitimation and practice (92, 131ff.). See also Leiprecht/ Lutz (1996); (iv) inconsistency and incoherence; see for France: 141.

31 See detailed treatments in: Fase (1994 chap. IV); Veenman (1995: 110-117) for the Netherlands. Well-known exceptions from this rule are 'Asians' in North America or Antillians in the Netherlands.

32 Most critical sociologists of education (Bourdieu, Boudon, Bowles, Dronkers, Veenman, Fase, Ganzenboom) stress the predominant, probably overwhelming impact of class/education.

33 Fase states 'that theoretical insights and empirical evidence strongly suggest, that cultural traits as such have no or very little meaning for ethnic (under)achievement in education. This does not imply, however, that the ethnic factor is of no importance in this equity debate' (159) in three respects: (i) long-term ethnic underclasses and 'lack of confidence' and 'ambition': 'sharp contrast' in this regard between the US-American setting where many black inhabitants of the inner cities have developed a strong counter-culture that rejects competition (160f.) and Western European countries where the research literature shows no signs of a lack of ambition or lack of willingness to invest in education: "Ambitions remain relatively high, despite the fact that social prospects, and unemployment figures in particular, are very alarming" (160); (ii) discontinuities between primary and secondary socialization; (iii) ethnic and racial bias of

'neutral' schools. See similarly: Veenman (1995: 113-117): Socio-economic status factors, the specific character of migration, ethnic-cultural factors, characteristics of schools have all empirical impacts, but to which degree remains open and uncertain.

[34] Again, the difference between miserably funded poor schools in the USA and positively 'discriminated' schools with high percentages of ethnic students in most Western European countries is sharp. Here, too, it is important to distinguish between unequal ethnic *'distribution'* which, of course, need not have detrimental effects, and 'ethnic *divisions*' (Fase, 1994: 155) or ethnic inequalities as one possible consequence of ethnic concentration.

[35] Fase (1994: 113f.) has constructed four models: (1) equal treatment and equal outcome, (2) equal treatment and unequal outcome, (3) unequal treatment and equal outcome, (4) unequal treatment and unequal outcome. All affirmative action policies are varieties of model (3): unequal treatment to achieve equal outcomes, criticizing 'colour-blind' and 'elitist' policy orientations and trying to combine egalitarianism with pluralism.

[36] See Fase for England and Wales (1994: 98ff): Section 11 of the Local Government Act in 1966: local education authorities can have extra grants for additional teacher payment in areas that have high proportions of ethnic minorities up to three quarters of the financial costs of multicultural teaching and policy of 'educational priority area'; for Belgium: from 1978-79 onwards 30% migrant pupils or more get extra teachers (ibid.: 93, 95); additional funds are assigned selectively according to the school's ethnic composition so as to discourage the development of 'segregated' schools: less than 30% implies a 1.7 coefficient; 30-50% a 2.0 coefficient; more than 50% 1.5. France started educational priority areas in 1981 (ibid.: 104 ff.); the Netherlands started compensation and enrichment programmes in 1974 for indigenous working-class children and enlarged the programmes since 1985 to include migrant children (extra financial resources, ranging from a 1.25 to a 1.9 coefficient for targeted pupils on the basis of criteria of class, nationality and years of residence).

[37] See for England/Wales: 'Education for all' (Swann, 1985: 392, quoted in Fase, 1994: 138): "(...) fundamental opposition to the principle of any form of separate provision which seeks to cater only for the needs of ethnic minority children since we believe that such provision merely serves to establish and confirm social barriers between groups"; see for the change in Dutch policies: *'Ceders in de tuin'* from 1992 onwards (drop in special attention for ethnic minorities in all compensation and enrichment programmes: all pupils from all uneducated families, both native and immigrant, should be targeted for special treatment; p. 163). See Veenman (1995: 127) for the development towards *'algemeen achterstandsbeleid in het onderwijs'* (a general policy to fight disadvantages in education). See Bader (1995b, §3.2) for the different modalities of affirmative action.

[38] See the ritualistic references to the Amish, Mennonites, Hutterites. Similar problems for working class kids and for some ethnic minorities, e.g. the quest for sex-segregation (for gym lessons) by some Muslim parents and groups pose no new problems, in my view, and can be treated like similar quests by other traditional denominations. No liberal moral principle prescribes

co-education (See Modood, 1993, versus Kymlicka, 1992). It depends upon what kids from a certain age themselves want and upon a lot of pragmatic arguments whether it should and can be implemented. When it comes to compulsory education of adult newcomers and/or unemployed migrant workers (see proposals in Belgium and the Netherlands: WRR, 1989: 12, 45, 156ff.; Entzinger/v.d. Zwan, 1994; Fase, 1994: 95, 111), however, 'legitimate paternalism' is clearly stretched beyond its limits.

39 In England and Wales in the 1960s it was argued that dispersal of ethnic minority children should be welcomed: "The presence of a high proportion of immigrant children in one class slows down the general routine of working and hampers the progress of the whole class, especially where the immigrants do not speak or write English fluently". In DES Circular 7/65 a bussing system was advocated, wherever the proportion of migrant children exceeded 30%. In several districts, local education authorities decided not to apply the scheme, or to apply it only partially; in the late 1970s dispersal was dropped almost all over the country for its alleged discriminatory character and stigmatizing effect on 'immigrant schools' (Fase, 1994: 98). I already referred to the Belgian differential funding system as an instrument of indirect dispersal. Progressive teachers in Amsterdam are confronted with the result of 'white flight' (first to Amsterdam-Zuid, recently to Haarlem) and with increasing ethnic self-segregation of black schools in Amsterdam-Oost. To stop these developments would require institutional measures (like strict application of neighbourhood-districts for public schools, prohibition of private schools, or a 'social bussing system') which are clearly at odds with the cherished interpretation of 'freedom of education' in the Netherlands.

40 See Fase (1994: 107ff., 122) for Germany: 'The reason for separate provision here is simply the political decision to avoid high percentages of migrant pupils and therefore low proportions of indigenous German pupils in German classrooms.'

41 Usually, immigrant ethnic minorities cannot afford separate educational institutions on a roughly equal base without considerable public subsidies and even fairly rich immigrant ethnic groups have difficulties when it comes to tertiary or higher level education (thresholds). This is one of the many important differences between 'ethnic' and 'national minorities'. "The emergence of private schools for ethnic, religious or nationality groups" deserves closer examination: If it is yet another expression of cultural and religious pluralism in modern society, there is no reason *not* to encourage such a development (...) If, however, the main incentive for such an initiative is ethnic community disappointment or resentment on what is being offered by state education in terms of quality of teaching, serious questions should be raised about multicultural practices and policies. One might expect, for instance, that the question whether mainstream education is able to find adequate responses to ethnic diversity and ethnic underachievement, is a major factor in the eventual growth and institutionalization of nationality schools in Germany, or Islamic and Hindu schools in the Netherlands" (Fase, 1994: 161). See WRR (1989: 41).

42 Whenever this is true it points to a hard problem because there are clear limits to all attempts to integrate these lessons into the curriculum for all pupils.

43   In France, the *'classes d'initiation'* and later (1973) the *'classes d'adaptation'* in secondary education have been criticized for their marginalizing effect in the 1980s when more emphasis has been given to the French language: "la langue et la culture françaises sont à la base de l'intégration scolaire, elle même au principe de la réussite sociale et professionelle" (Chevènnement in 1985).

44   See Bauböck (1998: 47) for a double asymmetry in the relationship between dominant and ethnic immigrant culture: "National cultures, however, which penetrate the public sphere and use the common institutions of the state to pass on their cultural traditions and practices, expose themselves to stronger normative constraints on how exclusive they may be. Rather than defending an illusory norm of neutrality or equality of resources for all cultures, liberal pluralists should welcome this trade-off between legitimate hegemony and legitimate exclusion." To avoid misunderstandings, I do not claim something like a primary human right to separate ethnic education or mother-tongue education nor do I claim a priority of a general right to public education. On the contrary, I think that the general moral human right to education allows for different (private, semi-public, public) institutional settings. The question which setting is the most appropriate in which context cannot be decided by moral reasons alone. I resist the temptation to present my clear preference for general, ethnically mixed, public education as a moral requirement and prefer to give all possible prudential and pragmatic political reasons for this case. These questions should be open for political talk and decisions and not closed by moral philosophy. The semantics of human rights may be highly misleading in this regard.

45   See Fase (1994: 116, 130, 157, 161f.).

46   See for a critical qualitative evaluation: Leeman (1994), see also: Leiprecht/Lutz (1996).

47   Although it should be stressed more than Fase does, that this orientation is inseparable from enforced assimilation and one-sided acculturation into English culture.

48   See the sceptical remarks for the Netherlands: Veenman (1995: 128).

49   See Fase for these 'alarmist' fears in the UK (98), Belgium(95), France (105f). The WRR (1989: 42) leaves dangerously open crucial questions: Exactly which type of unity and how much is required? Intercultural education 'would have to stimulate that despite all differences unity can develop: a primary condition for functioning together in the same society' (my translation). See critically: Bader (1997d).

50   The impact of schools and 'civic' or 'democratic education' on the development of civic and democratic habits and virtues is as overestimated by democrats and republicans (see Gutmann, 1987; Unger, 1996) as it is downplayed by libertarians and classical liberals (see Flathman's phillippika). Education to individual autonomy, respect as well as to responsible citizenship remains a difficult act of balancing.

51   See Bader (1995b: 26f.) for a comparison of the US and the Netherlands; see Fase (1994: 161f.).

52   See Fase (1994: 207ff.) for cross-national differences between European Union countries with regard to issues like: specific mix of state, public and private institutions; degree of centralization of educational policies; length of (full- or part-time) compulsory schooling, of pre-school, primary, secondary and higher-level education; vocational training.

53 See article 7.4 of the German Basic Law. See Radtke (1996). See Roberto Unger's radical proposal to fight 'social desegregation, by movement among neighbourhoods' (1996: 85) in analogy to racial desegregation.

54 Leiprecht/Lutz also stress that evaluative judgements of educational systems and practices heavily depend on specific contexts (see 1996: 8 for segregation, p. 12f. for specific power-balances in classes, schools, neighbourhoods (summarizing Leeman's findings): p. 16f. for advantages and disadvantages of private schools. See more generally for 'funding', 'standard setting' and 'inspection' in associative democracy: Hirst (1994: 24, 176). "The issue here centres on education, and the passionate commitment by liberals, democratic republicans and socialists that there be a common educational system in which, as far as possible, all citizens participate, that it should be secular and that it should promote common citizenship. These are worthy aims and it would be wholly wrong to brush them aside. An associationalist system must be more culturally and socially pluralistic than this republican model would desire; it will allow explicitly religious and other value-centred forms of education to receive public money. It creates fundamental problems about the curriculum. Can Torah schools be permitted, where children receive only a traditional Jewish education? (...) Associationalism would sharpen these questions acutely, however, since it seeks democratization through social self-governance. The central ethical principle that provides a way out of this morass is that associations are voluntary, they must be communities of *choice*, not of fate. Citizens must be at least in principle able to be informed enough to choose for themselves between different options and individuated enough to be able to choose. Education in blind conformity to given community standards thus violates the first principle (...) The fundamental principle to which associationalists and liberals together must adhere is that adult citizens do not own their children, they do not own their future lives as social beings. The public power has no interest, either in preventing the formation of identity or in peddling a multiculturalist pluralist mush as a substitute for religion and culture, but it does have an interest in ensuring individuation. That means the public power has the right to determine elements of the core curriculum in schools, to insist that schools in receipt of public funds conform to certain standards, and, in the last instance, to remove children from their parents." (ibid.: 201f.)

55 See Bader (1997c), Çinar (1995). See also WRR (1979: XXVIIff.) and WRR (1989: 29ff.) on legal status and the fight against discrimination.

56 See my critical remarks (1997: note 41) versus Habermas (1994: 125f.). Undifferentiated and uncritically also: Rex (1994: 20-22). See Fernandes Mendes (1993) who starts rather summarily with 'full respect for the laws and rules of the country' and 'public order of the law of the country' (33) but continues to show that for this legal order the new citizens still are only guests and not 'fellow lodgers who had a say in making the house-rules (...) multicultural society has had no influence on the legal order'(35). From 1990 on it is officially proclaimed policy in the Netherlands that 'the further development in the direction of a multicultural society must lead – parallel to an as equal as possible treatment of all inhabitants by the law – to a change in our legal system which has more and more to reflect the [sc. ethnic, cultural – VB] diversity of our

society' (*Nota Rechtspositie en sociale integratie minderheden*, TK 1990-91. 22138, NR. 2, p. 6, my translation).

57 See also Bovens (1993: 166, 171) for issues of 'family, religion and upbringing'. See Fernandes Mendes's list of issues: legal rules regarding funerals, ritual slaughtering, compulsory education, holidays, protection against dismissal of residents. See WRR (1989: 38) for establishment of businesses, Rutten (1988: 273f.) for licenses. See my short discussion in Bader (1997: II.4.2). Only as a result of such criticism and practical changes would positive law actually become more relationally neutral in ethnic terms.

58 There are, of course, large areas of 'co-existence' where ethnic law of groups is rather *complementary* to the law of the country: see Strijbosch (1993: 9ff.). My treatment of areas of conflict is limited to marriage and divorce. Strijbosch indicates the following main areas of friction with *criminal* law: kidnapping of girls without their consent which is known from Turkish, not from Moroccan culture (*kaçirma* not *kaçisma*) (see ibid.: 31) and clitoridectomy on the one hand, violent sanctions of cultural codes of honour, on the other hand (ibid.: 12ff.) which both are hotly debated inside ethnic groups neglecting the 'many rather trivial' but highly symbolic and sensitive conflicts like those about Sikh turbans and Islamic headscarves (ibid.: 30).

59 At stake is here not the usual sociological or anthropological 'strong' legal pluralism (see Arnaud 1994, Strijbosch 1993, von Benda-Beckman 1990; see Teubner 1993 from the perspective of law as an autopoietic system), but 'weak' pluralism discussing the normative question how we should deal with empirical legal pluralism.

60 See Rutten (1988: chap. II and IV); d'Oliveira (1995).

61 Despite all attempts towards a modern codification of international private law in the Netherlands, it is still, according to d'Oliveira "une mosaïque d'éléments hétérogènes qui ne mérite pas le nom de codification (...)" (1995a: 144).

62 See Rutten (1988: 265-267): "To the degree that an Islamic norm deviates more from a Dutch one, and the application would lead to less legitimate consequences, one can see that Dutch judges more easily tend not to apply the Islamic norm" (266, my translation). See d'Oliveira: "on constate l'existence d'un pluralisme de Méthode. A coté du modèle savignien des règles de conflits multilatérales classiques, basées sur l'égalité des ordres juridiques, on remarque des règles de protection des plus faibles, règles recherchant la loi la plus 'favorable', on retrouve des indices, déséquilibrant la neutralité de modèle classique, qui démontrent une force centripète vers la *lex fori*; le dévelopment du néo-statutisme (...): il n'y a plus de 'statut' mais des configurations variées et multiples (...)" (1995a: 145). See d'Oliveira (1985). Fons Strijbosch has drawn my attention to the fact that International Private Law and Crypto-Private International Law seem to be the only ways to make legal space for 'weak' legal pluralism. In contradiction to its name 'international', it is always 'national', in our case Dutch law and, thus, part of the *lex fori*. More exactly, the *Muddawwana* is not a formal legal source of Dutch law but of Moroccan law and Moroccan law is applied in the Netherlands.

63 'Pre-arranged marriages' are controversial (see the exchange between Modood 1993 and Kymlicka 1993). Whether 'marriage under duress', which actually always takes place to some degree between families of widely differing class- and power-position, is tolerated by *Muddawwana,* by common law and legal practice in Morocco is beyond my knowledge.

64 See for divergent interpretations and rulings: Rutten (1988: 41ff.). It is interesting to note that recent proposals for easier naturalization may worsen the legal position of Muslim women (see S. Abdus Sattar, *NRC Handelsblad*, May 1996); and that higher assimilation or acculturation may weaken the legal claims of Muslims in certain cases (see Rutten, 1988: 275).

65 Which, as indicated above, is a valid reason for divorce, according to Moroccan Law, and, by the way, is widespread in so-called 'Christian ethnic majority families' (see Carens/Williams, 1995).

66 See broader Strijbosch (1993: 16, my translation): 'Rules regarding marriage under duress, elope or abduction of women, blood revenge, feud, violence against women and clitoridectomy are beyond that border. Such rules, frustrating the autonomy and emancipation of categories of migrants, do not deserve preservation'. See Bovens (1993: 171): democracy and rule of law and guarantee of fundamental human rights.

67 For serious tensions between equal treatment of sexes and recognition of cultural differences of ethnic groups see Saharso/Verhaar (1996). See for individuality rights: Bader (1989: 26ff.). A general normative rule of tolerating ethnic law, as advocated by F. von Benda-Beckmann, may be the best, or the least worst option in case of national minorities, particularly of aboriginals. However, I agree with Strijbosch (16, 31) that such a rule is less applicable for immigrant ethnic minorities.

68 "The argument for minority rights would have allowed the creation of unequal rights for dozens of these groups (...) This argument would allow the United States to become 'Balkanized', with a crazy quilt of different jurisdictions and different languages, a jumble of different sets of rights" (Danley, 1991: 176). See Koch (1993: 153-155). There are, indeed, ways to go beyond 'the dilemma of assimilation versus segregation' (Huls/Stout [1993: 3] with Molleman's perspective of 'interactionist integration') which so long has dominated public discourse and legal paradigms.

References

Arnaud, André-Jean (1994) *Legal Pluralism and the Building of Europe*. Amsterdam.
Bader, V.M. (1989) 'Sociale Advocatuur en Mensenrechten', in Hoogeboom, T. c.s. (eds.), *Sociale Advocatuur en de Rechten van de Mens*. Nijmegen: Ars Aequi Libri.
Bader, V.M. (1991) *Kollektives Handeln*. Opladen.
Bader, V.M. (1995) *Rassismus, Ethnizität, Bürgerschaft*. Münster.
Bader, V.M. (1995a) 'Citizenship and Exclusion', *Political Theory* 23 (2): 211-246.
Bader, V.M. (1995b) 'Benign State-neutrality' vs. 'Relation Ethnic Neutrality': Part I: Dilemma's of Affirmative Action', Conference Paper Berg en Dal. Forthcoming in Turner, B. (ed.), *Citizenship Studies*, 1998.
Bader, V.M. (1997) 'The Cultural Conditions of Transnational Citizenship', forthcoming in *Political Theory*, December.
Bader, V.M. (1997a) 'Fairly Open Borders', pp. 28-61 in Bader, V.M. (ed.), op. cit.
Bader, V.M. (1997b) 'The Arts of Forecasting and Policy-Making', pp. 155-174 in Bader, V.M. (ed.), op. cit.
Bader, V.M. (1997c) 'Conclusion', pp. 175-189 in Bader, V.M. (ed.), op. cit.
Bader, V.M. (1997d) 'Institutions, Culture and Identity of Trans-National Citizenship: How Much Integration and 'Communal Spirit' is Needed?', forthcoming in Crouch, C./Eder, K. (1997).
Bader, V.M. (1997e) 'Unity, Stability and Commitment in Modern Societies and in Recent Political Philosophy', Paper to be presented at Expert Colloquium, Amsterdam, November.
Bader, V.M. (1997f) 'Incorporation of Ethnic and National Minorities: Concept, Dimensions, Fields, and Types'. Unpublished paper (Part I of 'Incorporation and Egalitarian Multiculturalism', Melbourne 1996).
Bader, V.M. (ed.) (1997) *Citizenship and Exclusion*. London: MacMillan.
Bader, V.M./Benschop, A. (1989) *Ungleichheiten*. Opladen: Leske + Budrich.
Bauböck, R. (1994) *Transnational Citizenship*. Aldershot: Edward Elgar.
Bauböck, R. (ed.) (1994) *From Aliens to Citizens. Redefining the Status of Immigrants in Europe*. Aldershot: Avebury.
Bauböck, R. (1995) 'Cultural Minority Rights for Immigrants', Conference Paper, New York, Sept.
Bauböck, R. (1996) 'Group Rights for Cultural Minorities: Justification and Constraints', Conference Paper, Firenze, April.
Bauböck, R. (1998) 'The Crossing and Blurring of Boundaries in International Migration. Challenges for Social and Political Theory' (in this volume).
Benda-Beckman, F. v. (1990) 'Rechtsanthropologie, rechtssociologie en rechtspluralisme bezien vanuit rechtsanthropologisch perspectief', *Recht der Werkelijkheid* 11 (1): 47-64.
Bovens, M.A.P. (1993) 'Babel binnen het recht. Een multidisciplinair perspectief op rechtspluralisme', pp. 159-172 in Huls/Stout (eds.), op. cit.

Buchanan, A. (1991) *Secession*. Boulder, San Francisco, Oxford: Westview Press.
Carens, J. (1995) *Is Quebec Nationalism Just*. Montreal, Kingston: McGill-Queens UP.
Carens, J. (1996) 'Immigrant Cultural Diversity and Liberal Democracy', Conference Paper, Firenze, April.
Carens, J. (1997) 'Two Conceptions of Fairness: A Response to Veit Bader', *Political Theory*, Dec.
Carens, J./Williams, M.S. (1995) 'The Rights of Islamic Minorities in Liberal Democracies: The Rhetoric of Inclusion', Paper given at Conference on "Organizing Diversity", Berg en Dal, 8-12 November.
Carens, J./Williams, M.S. (1996) 'Muslim Minorities in Liberal Democracies. The Politics of Misrecognition', in Bauböck, Rainer/Heller, Agnes/Zolberg, Aristide (eds.) *The Challenge of Diversity. Integration and Pluralism in Societies of Immigration*. Aldershot: Avebury.
Castles, S./Miller, M.J. (1993) *The Age of Migration*. MacMillan.
Castles, S. (1997) 'Multicultural Citizenship: The Australian Experience', pp. 113-138 in Bader, V.M. (ed.), op. cit.
Ceders in de tuin: Naar een nieuwe opzet van het onderwijsbeleid voor allochtone leerlingen. Delen 1 en 2. Ministerie van Onderwijs en Wetenschappen.
Çinar, D. (1995) 'From Aliens to Citizens', in Bauböck, R. (ed.), *From Aliens to Citizens*. Aldershot: Avebury.
Contourennota Integratiebeleid Etnische Minderheden. Handelingen van de Tweede Kamer, zitting 1993-94; 23684, nr. 1.
Danley, J.R. (1991) 'Liberalism, Aboriginal Rights, and Cultural Minorities', *Philosophy and Public Affairs* 20: 168-185.
Dyke, V. v. (1995) 'The Individual, the State, and Ethnic Communities in Political Theory', pp. 31-56 in Kymlicka, W. (ed.), op. cit.
Elster, J. (1992) *Local Justice*. New York: Russel Sage.
Engbersen, G./Gabriëls, R. (1995) 'Voorbij segregatie en assimilatie', pp. 15-47 in ibid. (eds.), *Sferen van integratie. Naar een gedifferentieerd allochtonenbeleid*. Meppel/Amsterdam: Boom.
Entzinger, H.B. (1984) *Het Minderhedenbeleid*. Meppel/Amsterdam: Boom.
Entzinger/v.d. Zwan (1994) *Nota: Beleidsopvolging Minderhedendebat*.
Fase, W. (1994) *Ethnic Divisions in Western European Education*. Münster/New York: Waxmann.
Fernandes Mendes, H.K. (1993) 'Integratiebeleid en multicultureel recht', pp. 31-40 in Huls/Stout (eds.), op. cit.
Flathman, R. (1996) 'Liberal versus Civic, Republican, Democratic, and other Vocational Educations', *Political Theory* 24 (1): 4-32.
Fraser, N. (1995) 'Recognition or Redistribution?', *The Journal of Political Philosophy* 3 (2): 166-180.
Glazer, N. (1996) *We Are All Multiculturalists Now*. Cambridge, Mass.: Harvard University Press.
Gutmann, A. (1987) *Democratic Education*. Princeton: Princeton UP.

Gutmann, A. (ed.) (1994) *Multiculturalism*. Princeton: Princeton UP.

Habermas, J. (1993) *Justification and Application: Remarks on Discourse Ethics*. Cambridge, Mass.: MIT Press.

Habermas, J. (1994) 'Struggles for Recognition in the Democratic Constitutional State', pp. 107-148 in Gutman, A. (ed.), op. cit.

Hammar, T. (1990) *Democracy and the Nation State*. Aldershot: Avebury.

Hannum, H. (1990) *Autonomy, Sovereignty, and Self-Determination*. Philadelphia: University of Pennsylvania Press.

Hirst, P. (1994) *Associative Democracy*. Cambridge: Polity Press.

Hörder, D./Juteau, D. (1995) 'National Models and Societal Integration. From National Culture to National Diversity', Conference Paper, Berg en Dal, November.

Hollinger, D. (1996) *Postethnic America*. New York: Basic Books.

Huls, N.J.H./Stout, H.D. (1995) 'Recht en rechtspluralisme in een mulitculturele samenleving', pp. 1-20 in ibid. (eds.), op. cit.

Huls, N.J.H./Stout, H.D. (eds.) (1993) *Recht in een multiculturele samenleving*. Zwolle.

Jenson, J. (1996) 'Citizenship Regimes: From Equity to Marketization', Paper European Forum on "Social and Political Citizenship in a World of Migration, Firenze, 22-24 February.

Juteau, D. (1997) 'Beyond Multiculturalist Citizenship. The Challenge of Pluralism in Canada', pp. 96-112 in Bader, V.M. (ed.), op. cit.

Koch, K. (1993) 'Rechtspluralisme: een politicologisch perspectief', pp. 149-158 in Hulst/Stout (eds.), op. cit.

Korver, T. (1995) 'Voor wat hoort wat', *Facta* 3 (2): 16-19.

Kurthen, Hermann (1997) 'Equity Employment as a Means of Minority Incorporation: Some Results from a 1990 Toronto Survey', pp. 273-302 in Isajiw, W.W. (ed.), *Multiculturalism in North America and Europe*. Toronto: Canadian Scholars' Press.

Kymlicka, W. (1989) *Liberalism, Community, Culture*. Oxford: OUP.

Kymlicka, W. (1989a) 'Liberal Individualism and Liberal Neutrality', *Ethics* 99: 883-905.

Kymlicka, W. (1990) *Contemporary Political Philosophy: An Introduction*. Oxford: OUP.

Kymlicka, W. (1992) 'Two Models of Pluralism and Tolerance', *Analyse und Kritik* 13: 33-56.

Kymlicka, W. (1993) 'Reply to Modood', *Analyse und Kritik* 15: 92-96.

Kymlicka, W. (1995) *Multicultural Citizenship*. Oxford: OUP.

Kymlicka, W. (1995b) (ed.) *The Rights of Minority Cultures*. Oxford: OUP.

Kymlicka, W. (1996) 'Update to *Multicultural Citizenship*', Chapter 2. Unpublished Paper, Expert Colloquium on "Citizenship and Exclusion", Amsterdam, 9-12 April.

Kymlicka, W. (1996b) 'Social Unity in a Liberal State', in *Social Philosophy and Policy Formation*.

Kymlicka, W. (1997) *States, Nations and Culture*. Assen: van Gorcum.

Leeman, Y. (1994) *Samen jong. Nederlandse jongeren en lessen over inter-etnisch samenleven en discriminatie*. Utrecht: van Arkel.

Leeman, Y./Lutz, H./Wardekken, W. (1996) 'Intercultureel Onderwijs', *Comenius* XXX.

Leiprecht, R. /Lutz, H. (1996) 'The Dutch Way: Mythos und Realität der interkulturellen Pädagogik in den Niederlanden', in Gstettner, P./ Auernheimer, G. (eds.), *Jahrbuch für Pädagogik*. Frankfurt M.

Lijphart, A. (1984) *Democracies*. New Haven/London: Yale University Press.

Lijphart, A. (1995) 'Self-Determination versus Pre-Determination of Ethnic Minorities in Power-Sharing Systems', pp. 275-287 in Kymlicka, W. (ed.), op. cit.

Lind, M. (1995) *The Next American Nation*. New York: Free Press.

McAndrew, M./Radtke, O. (1995) 'The Education of Immigrant Students: a Comparative Analysis of Policies and Outcomes in Germany and Canada', Conference Paper, Berg en Dal, October.

Minderhedennota. *Handelingen van de Tweede Kamer*, 1982-83; nr. 16102, nrs. 20, 21.

Minow, M. (1990) *Making All the Difference*. Ithaca.

Modood, T. (1993) 'Kymlicka on British Muslims', *Analyse und Kritik* 15: 87-91.

Modood, T. (1993a) 'A Rejoinder', *Analyse und Kritik* 15: 97-99.

Offe, C. (1997) 'Homogeneity and Liberal Democracy: Political Group Rights as an Answer to Conflicts of Identity?', Manuscript.

Oliveira, H.U. Jessurun d' (1985) Krypto-i.p.r. *Reeks international privaatrecht* no 17. Deventer: Kluwer.

Oliveira, H.U. Jessurun d' (1995a) 'Le droit international privé Néerlandais et les relations Maroc-Pays-Bas', *Cahiers des Droits Maghrébins* 1: 137-166.

Parekh, B. (1995) Minority Cultures and Limits of Equality, Paper given at Conference on "Organizing Diversity", Berg en Dal, 8-12 November

Penninx, R. (1988) *Minderheidsvorming en Emancipatie*. Gouda: Samson.

Radtke, F.-O. (1996) 'School Autonomy as a Mechanism for Ethnic Discrimination', Conference Paper, Melbourne, June.

Raz, J. (1975) *Practical Reason and Norms*. Hutchinson.

Raz, J. (1986) *The Morality of Freedom*. Oxford: Clarendon.

Rex, J. (1997) 'Multi-Culturalism in Europe and North America', pp. 15-34 in Isajiw, W.W. (ed.), *Multiculturalism in North America and Europe*. Toronto: Canadian Scholars' Press.

Rickard, M. (1994) 'Liberalism, Multiculturalism, and Minority Protection', *Social Theory and Practice* 20 (2): 143-170.

Rood-de Boer, M. (1993) 'Grenzen aan rechtspluralisme: een verkenning vanuit het personen, familie, en jeugdrecht', pp. 49-60 in Hulst/Stout (eds.), op. cit.

Rutten, S. (1988) *Moslims in de Nederlandse rechtspraak*. Kampen: Kok.

Saharso, W./ Verhaar, O. (1996) *Sekse, etniciteit en publieke moraal*. NWO-onderzoeksproject, Ethiek en Beleid. Amsterdam.

Schermerhorn, R.A. (1970) *Comparative Ethnic Relations: A Framework for Theory and Research*. New York.

Schlesinger, A.M. Jr. (1991) *The Disuniting of America*. New York: Norton and Company.

Sen, A. (1992) *Inequality Reconsidered*.

Stasioulis, D. (1985) 'The Antinomies of Federal Multi-Culturalism Policies and Official Practices', Paper presented at the International Symposium on Cultural Pluralism, UNESCO, Montreal.

Stolcke, V. (1995) 'Cultural Fundamentalism', *Current Anthropology* 36: 1-24.

Strijbosch, F. (1993) *Aan de Grenzen van het Rechtspluralisme. Over de sociale en juridische betekenis van migrantenrecht in Nederland.* Nijmegen.

Taylor, C. (1994) 'The Politics of Recognition', pp. 25-74 in Gutman, A. (ed.), op. cit.

Teubner, G. (1993) *Law As an Autopoietic System.* Oxford: Blackwell.

Unger, R. (1987) *Politics.* 3 vols. Cambridge.

Unger, R. (1996) *What Should Legal Analysis Become?* London: Verso.

Veenman, J. (1995) 'Integratie en het onderwijs', pp. 110-136 in Engbersen/Gabriëls (eds.), op. cit.

Walzer, M. (1983) *Spheres of Justice.*

Walzer, M. (1993) 'Exclusion, Injustice, and the Democratic State', *Dissent*, Winter: 55-64.

WRR = Wetenschappelijke Raad voor het Regeringsbeleid (1979) *Rapport 17: Ethnische Minderheden* (including: Voorstudie van Rinus Penninx). The Hague: SDU.

WRR (1989) *Rapport 36: Allochtonenbeleid.* The Hague: SDU.

WRR (1994) *Advies Beleidsopvolging Minderhedendebat* (van der Zwan/Entzinger). The Hague.

PART II

Groups, Rights and Citizenship in Multicultural Contexts

CHAPTER 8

Globalization and the Ambiguities of National Citizenship[1]

Stephen Castles

This chapter discusses the challenges to citizenship presented by globalization, international mobility of people, and growing ethnocultural diversity within countries. I will argue that basing citizenship on singular and individual membership in a nation-state is no longer adequate, since the nation-state model itself is being severely eroded. Instead, new approaches to citizenship are needed, which take account of collective identities and the fact that many people now belong to more than one society. Such reforms should be linked to measures which improve the quality of political participation by permitting more democracy in more places.

Until a few years ago, being a citizen was just a matter of common sense in the fortunate minority of the world's countries considered as democracies. Being a citizen meant having the rights to vote and to stand for political office, enjoying equality before the law, and being entitled to various government services and benefits. It also meant having the obligations to obey the laws, to pay taxes, and to defend your country. The rest of the world aspired to this model. As the President of Mongolia, Punsalmaaggiyu Orchirbat said when he visited Paris, the symbolic birthplace of the modern nation: "In 1990 we embarked on a great journey to join the common course of mankind – democracy and human rights, the market economy and economic development" (*Le Monde/Guardian Weekly* 5 May, 1996). Those were the icons of progress.

But there are signs that citizenship has become problematic in recent years. Several countries have changed their rules for access to citizenship for immigrants and other minorities. New countries emerging from the dissolving multi-ethnic states of real socialism have sought to establish appropriate rules of citizenship. Other new countries forged out of former colonies have dissolved into anarchy, due to failure to build an inclusive national identity and a stable state. Citizenship has become the focus of political and academic discourse. Various social movements claim that reforming citizenship could help solve major social problems. Why this sudden interest in something that seemed so obvious? Is it the result of changes in the political and social context? Or have we become sensitive to problems implicit in the commonsensical notion of citizenship?

The answer is both. The global context of citizenship is changing dramatically, but so is the way we perceive it. These two trends are linked: there have always been some fundamental ambiguities in the notion of citizenship, but these did not seem to matter as long as the political context appeared coherent and stable. That context was, of course, the nation-state. The current crisis of citizenship is thus closely linked with the challenges facing the nation-state model at the end of the twentieth century. These affect – in specific ways – not only the nation-states of Western Europe, but also the nation-building societies of North America and Oceania, and the new industrial countries of Asia and Latin America.

Globalization and the Nation-State

The essence of the nation-state is the institution of citizenship: the integration of all its population into the political community, and their political equality as citizens. Of course, relatively few nations match this democratic ideal. How many countries have not had a violent change in government during the twentieth century? I can only think of seven! In how many states do the people really have a choice about who forms the government and what it does? But most heads of state claim their country is democratic, and most politically-aware people aspire to this.

The European and North American nation-states that emerged from the seventeenth to the nineteenth centuries were astonishingly effective, both in internal and external terms. Their political systems facilitated the integration of diverse groups into cohesive populations and provided the conditions for capitalist industrialization. They were able to dominate and colonize the rest of the world, and to impose economic relations and cultural values which were to transform all the disparate societies and bring them into a global system. The nation-states continued the work of the great centralizing monarchies: Spain, Portugal, France and England. But they quickly transcended the absolutist model, marginalizing those countries that did not make the transition to the modern nation-state on time. Colonialism was crucial to the emerging nation-states: exploitation of the natural resources and the labour power of dominated peoples made industrialization possible. When the 'late nations' like Germany and Italy began to seek 'their place in the sun', and the colonized peoples demanded freedom, the result was the conflicts which were to lead to the most violent century in history.

This dialectic of progress and violence indicates some of the ambivalences inherent in the nation-state model. Can it work if all the societies of the world constitute themselves as nation-states and seek equality in a global system? Or is it premised on domination of weaker countries, and stigmatization and exclusion of the Other? It is vital to deconstruct the contradictions of the nation-state model, if we are to find ways of achieving more democratic types of citizenship and more equitable and peaceful international relations. However, my aim is more modest: to analyse just one aspect of the nation-state – citizenship – in the light of some of the ways in which it is being questioned and reshaped by current global transformations. In an oversimplified way, one can point to three main consequences of globalization for citizenship.

First, globalization breaks the territorial principle, the nexus between power and place. The 'national industrial society', as it evolved in the nineteenth and twentieth centuries, articulated society, state and nation in a particular form. Society referred to an economic and social system based on rational principles, within a bounded national territory. The state referred to a political system based on secular (and usually democratic) principles, capable of regulating economic and political relations. The nation referred to a 'people' defined both on the basis of belonging to the territory of the state and having a common cultural and ethnic background (Lapeyronnie et al., 1990: 258-262). Thus politics, the economy, social relations and culture were congruent in that they all took the nation-state as their main point of reference. The whole of classical sociology takes this 'national society' for granted. Even the critics of capitalism based their politics on national units: social-democratic demands for economic reform and welfare policies addressed the state; communists called for world revolution, but were organized nationally.

Today, we can observe a "decomposition of national industrial societies" (Wieviorka, 1994: 25). The dynamics of economic life transcend national borders, and have become uncontrollable for national governments. Deindustrialization of older industrial nations has led to profound economic and social changes. The nation-state is still the basic unit for welfare systems, but no government can pursue welfare policies which ignore the dictates of global markets. This alters the terms for socialist parties: even if they can get elected to power, they may have to abandon their traditional objectives and adopt economic rationalism, as the experience of the Australian Labour Party Government of 1983-96 demonstrated so vividly. Capital may appear to have won the class struggle, but this does not lead to Fukuyama's (1992) 'end of history', but rather to forms of social and political disorganization which threaten the security of the well-off and the stability of democratic states. What, then, does it mean to be a citizen, if the autonomy of the nation-state is being eroded, and the vote which one wields cannot influence key political decisions, because they are no longer made by national parliaments?

The second aspect of globalization is that it has undermined the ideology of relatively autonomous national cultures. These were always a myth, because virtually every nation-state has been made up of a number of ethnic groups, with distinct languages, traditions and histories. Homogenization is at the core of the nationalist project. The internal Other has to be made into a national before he or she can become a citizen. As Ernest Renan pointed out in 1882 in his famous discourse, 'What is a Nation' (Renan, 1992), forgetting the history of ethnic distinctiveness and the (often repressive) process of overcoming it is vital to national identity. Moreover, no frontier has ever been completely impervious to cultural influences: even Enver Hodja's Albania could not completely encapsulate itself against the influences of Western culture, as the rush to migrate to Italy after 1989 showed. All cultures are hybrids. Nonetheless, ideas of national cultural distinctiveness underpinned nation-building and patriotism.

Globalization has changed all this: rapid improvements in transport and communications have led to an unprecedented degree of cultural interchange. The industrialization of media production puts enormous pressure on national and local cultures. Dominance by global cultural factories, like Hollywood, means the diffusion of specific value systems, connected with consumerism, individualism and US lifestyles. At the same time, however, we witness a re-ethnicization of culture at a sub-national level. This trend appears as a form of resistance to both nationalization and globalization of culture. Collectivities which constitute themselves around cultural claims may be based not only on ethnicity, but also on regional location, gender, sexual preferences and lifestyles. National culture is being squeezed between the global and the local.

The third aspect is the increasing mobility of people across national borders. The period since 1945 and especially since 1980 has been marked by large-scale migrations of all kinds: temporary and permanent movements; labour migrations and refugee exoduses; individual and family flows; highly-skilled specialists and manual workers. Such migrations have led to settlement in nearly all highly-developed countries, and in many parts of the less-developed regions. Populations have become more heterogeneous and culturally diverse. Often, cultural difference and social marginalization are closely linked, creating ethnic minorities with disadvantaged and relatively isolated positions in society (Castles/Miller, 1993).

Mobility of people has always been an inherent part of modernization. Sailors, soldiers, traders, administrators and settlers were sent out to subjugate and manage the colonized Others, who were constructed through racist ideologies as inferior and threatening. As the flow of colonial profits back to the metropoles helped provide the capital for industrialization, new mass migrations started. Once internal reserves dried up, workers were pulled in across national borders: Irish to Britain; Poles and Italians to Germany, France and Switzerland; and Eastern and Southern Europeans to the USA. These migrants were, to a large extent, eventually absorbed into the national populations and their children became citizens.

Two things are new about the current migrations. The first is their sheer scale and rapidity. The speed at which new ethnic minorities have emerged has confounded policy-makers and undermined laws and practices concerned with integration and citizenship. The second is the ethnocultural characteristics of many of the immigrants: they come from areas increasingly distant – not only in kilometres but in cultural terms. They often originate in former colonies or areas of military presence of the receiving countries: North and West Africans in France; Caribbeans, Indians, Pakistanis and Bangladeshis in Britain; Mexicans, Filipinos, Koreans and Vietnamese in the USA, and so on. But many migrants come from areas where the linkages are based on more tenuous forms of economic and cultural penetration: Arabs to the USA, Southeast Asians to Japan, Chinese to virtually all developed countries. The very historical success of the Western model in dominating the Third World now questions the nation-state, because it has led to linkages which facilitate not only movement of capital and commodities, but also of people and ideas – in both directions.

Key Questions

The colonized Other is returning to the metropoles. In every city of Western Europe and North America, ethnic heterogeneity has become an inescapable reality. This Other has no shared past with the people of the receiving society. The cultural background may be very different, such as the gulf between Christian and Islamic traditions. In the case of migrants from former colonies, the culture of the Other may partially mirror that of the receiving society; yet the dialectical unity of colonizer and colonized contains a fundamental difference in experience.

This raises crucial questions:

- Can these Others be submitted to a process of acculturation (as were previous internal minorities) which will reduce them to nationals, and thus qualify them for membership in the nation-state?
- Or is such a process unthinkable in the era of globalization, with its multiple identities and diasporic communities?

- Has the pace of intermingling of ethnic groups become so rapid that there is no time for the process of forgetting different histories, which Renan saw as crucial to national identity?
- Does this mean that the nation-state and citizenship will have to be modified to fit the new reality of the collective presence of the irreducible Other in multi-ethnic societies?
- If so, what can be the characteristics of possible new forms of political belonging?
- What political action is needed to develop these new forms?

But before discussing these questions, it is necessary to turn briefly to some problems implicit in the notions of the nation-state and citizenship.

Ambiguities of Citizenship

Citizenship is one of the key institutions of contemporary societies, at the very core of both democracy and national identity. Yet it has always been ambiguous in various ways. First, it implies not only inclusion, but also exclusion: citizenship of certain types of people implies non-citizenship of others. In the Greek polis, slaves, foreigners and above all women were excluded. In the modern states which emerged in the nineteenth century, the very size of the society precluded direct democracy. Suffrage was linked to the assumption that certain categories of men were capable of rational participation in the public sphere, and of representing people dependent upon themselves (women, children, servants and employees). In a wider sense, those elected to office had to be capable of representing the social category or interest group they derived from. Citizenship was restricted to male householders, belonging to the dominant religion and ethnic group. Political movements of excluded groups (women, workers, religious minorities, indigenous peoples) have seen access to the franchise as the main instrument of their emancipation.

Today the problem of formal exclusion from citizenship applies above all to immigrants. By 1995, there were 19.4 million foreign residents in the European OECD countries, of whom only 6.7 million were European Union (EU) citizens. There were 2 million North Africans, 2.6 million Turks and 1.4 million people from former Yugoslavia (OECD, 1997: 30). Large numbers of foreign residents have actually been born in the country of residence, yet have not become citizens, due to the principle of *ius sanguinis* (nationality by descent). Even in North America and Australia, where naturalization is easier to obtain, there are quite large numbers of resident non-citizens. These are people who belong to society as workers, taxpayers and parents, and yet are denied full political participation. Even illegal immigrants may be long-term residents, but do not enjoy many basic rights. This negates the basic principle of liberal democracy that all members of society should be included as citizens.

But there is another dimension, that of de facto exclusion: in most countries there are significant groups, usually marked by race, ethnicity or being indigenous peoples, who are denied full participation as citizens. They may have the right to vote, but social, economic and cultural exclusion prevents genuine political participation. This situation is in part a reflection of the fact that the substantial meaning of citizenship itself has become extended in recent times, as civil and political rights have been joined by social rights (Marshall, 1964). Put differently, a certain level of social and economic welfare is needed before people can take advantage of formal political rights. Today it may be argued that collective cultural rights needed to be added to Marshall's triad. De facto exclusion presents new challenges for the politics of inclusion, leading to calls for 'differentiated citizenship' (Young, 1989; 1990) and 'multicultural citizenship' (Kymlicka, 1995).

A second ambiguity of citizenship concerns the relationship between rights and obligations. This is most evident in the close link between universal suffrage and universal military service. For instance, French sociologist Dominique Schnapper's important work on citizenship constantly emphasizes the notion of the 'warrior citizen' (Schnapper, 1994: 49). This link is problematic: it excludes women, who with a few exceptions (such as Israel) have not been seen as capable of defending their nation by violent means. It also implies that democratic nations can only be consolidated internally by hostility to external groups, i.e. by constructing a *Feindbild*, or concept of an enemy (see Hoffmann, 1994). Moreover, linking suffrage with conscription can be a means of exclusion of internal minorities, who may be accused of 'unclear loyalties' in the event of a conflict. A model of citizenship for a global society can hardly be based on the willingness to indulge in interstate warfare, though it might require willingness to support use of force to prevent conflict or human-rights abuses – an issue that needs careful consideration.

Both the above ambiguities are the expression of a more fundamental contradiction: that between citizenship and nationality, or between the notion of the citizen as an individual abstracted from cultural characteristics, and that of the national as a member of a community with common cultural values. In liberal theory, all citizens are meant to be free and equal persons, who as citizens are homogeneous individuals (Rawls, 1985: 232-234). This requires a separation between a person's political rights and obligations, and their membership in specific groups, based on ethnicity, religion, social class or regional location. The political sphere is one of universalism, which means equality and abstraction from cultural particularity and difference. Difference is to be restricted to the 'non public identity' (Rawls, 1985: 241).

But this conflicts with the reality of nation-state formation, in which becoming a citizen has depended on membership in a community. The nation-state is the combination of a political unit which controls a bounded territory (the state) and a national community (the nation or people) which has the power to impose its political will within those boundaries. A citizen is always also a member of a nation, a national. So citizenship is meant to be universalistic and above cultural difference, yet it exists only in the context of a nation-state, which is based on cultural specificity: on the belief in being different from other nations. Historically, this tension has been expressed in measures to incorporate minority groups into the 'national culture'. Today it is a major issue for indigenous peoples as well as for immigrants: can they only belong to the nation if they reject their own languages and traditions and conform to the dominant ones?

It is clearly vital to distinguish between the nation and the ethnic group. There are currently some 200 nation-states in the world, yet over 6,000 languages (Moynihan, 1993: 72). Language is in most cases an indicator of a cultural community and thus frequently of an ethnic group; if even a fraction of these groups were to seek to become nations, the potential for conflict would be enormous. As Moynihan (1993: 63-106) shows, there is an inherent contradiction between two basic principles of the United Nations: the principle of national sovereignty and that of self-determination of peoples.

But the essential difference between the nation and the ethnic group is not always very clear, especially in the Anglo-American literature. For instance, Seton-Watson describes a nation as "a community of people, whose members are bound together by a sense of solidarity, a common culture, a national consciousness" (Seton-Watson, 1977: 1). Walker Connor defines a nation as "a group of people who *believe* they are ancestrally related. It is the largest grouping that shares that belief" (Connor, 1991: 6, emphasis in original, quoted here from Moynihan, 1993: 1). This is very similar to widely-used definitions of ethnicity as a sense of group belonging based on ideas of common origins, history, culture, experience and values. Ethnicity is seen as 'cultural', in contradistinction to 'biological' notions of race (see Castles/Miller, 1993: 27).

The distinction between ethnic group and nation in Anglo-American interpretations is usually a practical one, based on sovereignty: An ethnic group that controls a bounded territory becomes a nation and establishes a nation-state. Factors of shared history and culture are then complemented by a common economy and legal system. Anthony Smith sums this up as follows:

> A nation can therefore be defined as a named human population sharing an historic territory, common myths and historical memories, a mass, public culture, a common economy and common legal rights and duties for all members (Smith, 1991: 14).

But since there are few homogeneous nation-states, the question is how the varying ethnic groups in a territory are to be moulded into one nation. This may take place through the forcible imposition of the culture of the dominant group on the others, for instance through prohibition of minority languages, schools and festivals, as in the case of present-day Kurds in Turkey. The process may be a more gradual and consensual one, in which groups grow together through economic and social interaction, and the development of a common language and shared institutions, such as schools, church and military service. There is a fine line between the nation based on repression and that based on historical consensus. Most have elements of both, and are open to subsequent challenge by movements of territorial minorities, as recent European history has shown.

Continental European views on the difference between nation and ethnic group have followed a rather different line, based on the well-known distinction between the *Kulturnation* (cultural nation, also known as the ethnic nation) and the *Staatsnation* (state nation, also known as the civic nation). These notions developed as ideological expressions of the struggle for dominance between Germany and France in the nineteenth century.

Germany was a backward patchwork of principalities and mini-states with absolutist rulers until the end of the eigtheenth century. Nation-state formation did not come through internal impulses, but as a reaction to conquest by the Napoleonic armies. As Habermas points out, national consciousness was not based on democratic civil liberties and popular sovereignty, but on "the romantically inspired middle-class notion of a *Kulturnation*, a nation defined by its culture" (Habermas, 1994: 146). Romanticism portrayed individuals as part of an organic whole; freedom meant not individual rights but acceptance of one's role in the greater organism. The state was the embodiment of this superior meaning, which could only be interpreted by great leaders. Democracy had no place in the model (Hoffmann, 1994: 108-130).

The French *Staatsnation*, on the other hand, developed through the democratic revolution of 1789. It was seen as being based not on common culture but on a common will, as expressed both in Rousseau's idea of the 'general will' and in Renan's famous expression of the nation as *'un plébiscite de tous les jours'* (a daily plebiscite). The implication is that citizens of a nation form a community because they constantly express the will to do so. The nation should therefore be understood as a political project capable of transcending the tension between universalism and particularism (Schnapper, 1994: 83-114). The common will creates and maintains the political unit, whatever conflicts there are within it. This idea provides the basis for a republican form of government, which should be capable of assimilating ethnic or religious minorities.

Yet the claim of transcending culture is dubious, for the French experience was actually based on linguistic homogenization, political centralization and compulsory assimilation. Shared endeavour and suffering in war were seen as the nation-building experiences par excellence. "Political nation-units are generally born in the fracas of war" (Schnapper, 1994: 45). Even Renan emphasizes alongside the principle of consent that of common history and culture (see Schnapper, 1994: 168). The republican model worked well as long as the dominant group was willing to assimilate others, and the economy was able to provide a reasonable level of social integration to all. But how well has the republican model coped with globalization and immigration of the Other? I will return to this below.

Dealing with Globalization

How should ideas and practices of citizenship be reshaped to deal with globalization and cultural diversity? Here I will discuss just two positions, which can perhaps be seen as the opposing poles in the debate. Between them lies a wide range of interpretations, to be found in a vast and still-growing body of literature. These two positions are:

- The idea that the substance of citizenship and the nation-state are changing anyway through the inexorable forces of globalization, so that little further action is needed.
- The belief that the nation-state, although weakened by internal and external contradictions, is still the only political unit capable of maintaining democratic citizenship.

The first position can be associated both with the technocratic ideas of global managerialism, and with political theories that focus on the growing role of supranational human rights norms. I will discuss the former using the work of the Japanese management expert Kenichi Ohmae, and the latter with reference to a study by Harvard sociologist Yasemin Soysal.

In his book, *The Borderless World*, Ohmae argues that a supranational power has already emerged; he calls it the Interlinked Economy (ILE), which consists of the 'Triad' (the USA, Europe and Japan), joined by new industrial economies like Taiwan, Hong Kong and Singapore.

> It has become so powerful that it has swallowed most consumers and corporations, made traditional national borders almost disappear, and pushed bureaucrats, politicians and the military towards the status of declining industries (Ohmae, 1991: xi).

This may come as something of a surprise to the officials of the EU or the generals of the Pentagon, and indeed to asylum-seekers trying to cross the borders of Fortress Europe. But this is not what Ohmae is concerned with: his borderless world applies to the transnational corporations and their executives and specialists. He is talking about what he sees as an inevitable trend:

> The policy objective for the ILE will be ensuring the free flow of information, money, goods and services as well as the free migration of people and corporations. Traditional governments will have to establish a new single framework of global governance (Ohmae, 1991: xii-xiii).

For Ohmae, the global economy is driven by the free choices of customers, which dictate a radical opening of economies. The task of government is to "ensure that its people have a good life by ensuring stable access to the best and the cheapest goods and services from anywhere in the world" (Ohmae, 1991: 12). The burgeoning flow of information is turning people into 'global citizens', who are aware of all that is happening around the world – with regard to tastes and preferences, styles of clothing, sports and lifestyles (Ohmae, 1991: 18-22). Thus Ohmae reduces the philosophical notion of the 'good life' to the right to buy the best consumer goods. Global citizenship is about reducing the role of government, in order to permit untrammelled play to the transnational corporations.

Yet Ohmae is right in claiming that much economic power has passed from states to corporations and to markets. His argument is a postnationalist one, when he claims that successful management requires abandonment of 'the headquarters mentality', and a real decentralization of decision-making to global networks. This in turn is only possible if corporations can free themselves of the national culture of their founders, and develop their own transnational culture (Ohmae, 1991: 89).

Ohmae's 'borderless world' is a comfortless place for those who believe in national autonomy. Developing countries which seek to build up their economies through protectionism are doomed to failure; they should throw open their borders to free transfers of commodities and capital, whatever the social costs (which Ohmae never mentions). The 'borderless world' is also bad news for anyone who believes in democracy. Governments are increasingly powerless, so that the right to elect them has little meaning. There are no democratic mechanisms in the global marketplaces and transnational corporations. The theme is not even discussed in

Ohmae's book – he clearly sees it as irrelevant. Ohmae's global citizen is imbued with consumerism, not democratic values.

Ohmae is an adviser to some of the world's most powerful corporations, so his views may be seen as a significant expression of the technocratic logic of advanced capital. He is pointing to real trends which contain serious threats to democratic citizenship. The analysis shows the difficulties faced by national governments, when they seek to influence the global economy. The answer can only lie in the development of democratically-elected supranational bodies with countervailing power to control economic interests at the global level.

A very different notion of 'postnational membership' is put forward in the book *Limits of Citizenship* by Yasemin Soysal. She argues that:

> A new and more universal concept of citizenship has unfolded in the post-war era, one whose organizing and legitimating principles are based on universal personhood rather than national belonging. To an increasing extent, rights and privileges once reserved for citizens of a nation are codified and expanded as personal rights, undermining the national order of citizenship (Soysal, 1994: 1).

Soysal criticizes political sociologists for remaining fixated on the nation-state as the locus for rights. Her study finds that:

> (...) the classical formal order of the nation-state and its membership is not in place. The state is no longer an autonomous and independent organization closed over a nationally defined population. Instead, we have a system of constitutionally interconnected states with a multiplicity of membership (Soysal, 1994: 163-164).

The main focus of the book is incorporation patterns of immigrants in Western Europe, and the empirical examples mainly relate to Turkish 'guestworkers' in Germany, Sweden and other countries. Soysal finds that such immigrants are being granted social, economic and political rights, without being formally admitted to citizenship. This undermines "the foundational logic of national citizenship" (1994: 2) and breaks down traditional national boundaries. The driving force in this process is "world-level pressures towards more expanded individual rights [which] have lead to the increasing incorporation of foreigners into existing membership schemes". At the same time, the extension of membership transforms the existing models, "making national citizenship less important" (1994: 29).

Soysal's analysis may be questioned on a number of grounds. Empirically, it seems to overstate the extent to which immigrants in Western European countries like Germany have gained most of the rights of citizenship without formal membership in the nation-state. In fact, immigrants are in many places still denied significant rights, and may be deported for a range of reasons. New trends towards restrictiveness and towards differentiation between various groups are evident. The causes of recent shifts towards greater rights may also be discussed. Soysal emphasizes 'world-level pressures', but it could be argued that political mobilization by immigrant groups and their allies have also played a major role in securing greater rights for minorities.

However, the main issue is Soysal's dramatic conclusion that the emergence of universal personhood is rapidly eroding the territorially bounded nation-state. In her view, this type of nation-state was the dominant form for only a fairly short time: from about the mid-nineteenth century to the mid-twentieth century. Soysal's model of 'postnational belonging' is based on universal human rights, as laid down in conventions and declarations of supranational bodies like the United Nations, which are gradually incorporated into the constitutions and laws of nation-states. Thus universal entitlements are still delivered by the nation-state, but are no longer limited by formal citizenship. The furthest-going expression of the trend is transnational citizenship within the European Union. Soysal claims:

> As an identity, national citizenship – as it is promoted, reinvented, and reified by states and other societal actors – still prevails. But in terms of its translation into rights and privileges, it is no longer a significant construction (1994: 159).

This is a perspective which seems appealing to critics of nationalism, but Soysal may be overstating the extent to which it has actually been achieved. UN and ILO conventions and the like are often not ratified by most countries, are not implemented where they are ratified, and above all are ignored by the countries where abuses are worst. The number of countries where democracy and human rights prevail is fairly small, and there are strong trends towards exclusionary nationalism and racism in many places. It seems misplaced to argue that 'postnational citizenship' is about to be achieved. Despite the globalization of economy and culture, nation-states will remain the main location of political belonging for the foreseeable future. Attempts at building transnational democracy need to take account of this fact. Some observers believe that regional political unions, above all the European Union (EU), could represent a new form of citizenship, not bound to a nation-state. Yet EU citizenship is still mainly symbolic: you can only be a EU citizen if you belong to an appropriate nation-state. Moreover, EU citizenship fails to transcend nation-state citizenship in another way: it is just as exclusionary towards foreigners. Indeed the rules for achieving free movement within the EU are concerned with keeping out and controlling the undesirable Other, especially from less-developed countries of the South and East.[2]

Let us turn now to the position that the nation-state is still the only conceivable unit for democratic citizenship, even though it is under pressure through global change. Again I will contrast a mainly economic perspective – that of Robert B. Reich – with a political sociology approach – that of Dominique Schnapper.

In his book, *The Work of Nations*, Reich (who was the US Secretary for Labour in the first Clinton administration) presents a compelling analysis of the effects of globalization:

> As almost every factor of production – money, technology, factories, and equipment – moves effortlessly across border, the very idea of a national economy is becoming meaningless (...) (Reich, 1991: 8).

The question Reich raises is whether there can be a national society in the absence of a national economy. Citing Adam Smith's *Wealth of Nations*, he argues that "the idea that the citizens of a nation shared responsibility for their economic well-being" was closely linked to the rise of the democratic nation-state (Reich, 1991: 18). As long as economic affairs were organized on national lines, there was a certain degree of common interest that transcended class divisions: successful industrial economies could pass on some of their wealth to workers through higher wages, access to consumer goods and improved welfare systems. This in turn strengthened feelings of national solidarity.

Globalization and technological change shatter the basis of national solidarity. Reich argues that class structure has been transformed through the decline of manufacturing industries in countries like the USA. Three main categories of workers now exist:

- routine production workers, the declining group of employees in manufacturing enterprises;
- in-person servers, people performing simple and repetitive tasks, such as retail sales workers, waiters and waitresses, health-care personnel and the growing army of security guards;
- 'symbolic analysts', all the problem-solving, problem-identifying and strategic-brokering activities, which require high-level skills and training (Reich, 1991: 171-184).

The first two categories are oriented towards local or national labour markets, while the symbolic analysts increasingly function in global labour markets. It is irrelevant for them whether they work for a U.S., a Japanese or a transnational company. Moreover, the symbolic analysts have a strong grip on economic power. They can ensure that their earnings grow, while the wages of the production workers and in-person servers are strictly limited. This explains the enormous growth of income inequality in the USA in the last 20 years. As real wages and working conditions fall for most of the population, symbolic analysts have been able to reduce their own rate of personal taxation. This explains the fiscal crisis of the welfare state. The wealthy one-fifth of the population, according to Reich, have effectively seceded from the rest (Reich, 1991: 282-300). They have moved into separate towns and suburbs, protected by private police. They have ceased to contribute to public expenditure, instead financing their own privatized schools, health-care systems and leisure facilities. Above all, they dominate political power and see no reason to share it with the rest of the nation. Thus politics oscillates between the 'zero-sum nationalism' of those who want to turn the clock back, and the 'impassive cosmopolitanism' of people who, as citizens of the world, may feel no particular bond with any society (Reich, 1991: 301-315).

For Reich, the only answer lies in a reassertion of national solidarity. This may be stimulated by "the inability of symbolic analysts to protect themselves, their families and their property from the depredations of a larger and ever more desperate population outside" (Reich, 1991: 303). The main factor, however, must be 'a new patriotism', founded less upon economic self-interest than 'loyalty to place'. This could be the starting point for 'a positive economic nationalism', in which each nation's citizens take responsibility for ensuring that their compatriots have full and productive lives, but also cooperate with other countries for mutual advantage. This would require a sense of national purpose, based on historical and cultural connections to a common political endeavour (Reich, 1991: 311-312). The problem with this conclusion is that it is completely voluntaristic: having demonstrated the powerful forces that are undermining the national bond, Reich postulates that these can be countered by an act of a collective will which, according to his own analysis, no longer exists.

Dominique Schnapper's book, *La Communauté des Citoyens*, was awarded the Prize of the French National Assembly in 1994 for its passionate yet rigorous defence of republican values. Schnapper asserts that the nation-state is seriously weakened:

> Today we are experiencing the weakening of civic feeling and of political bonds. There is nothing to guarantee that the modern democratic nation will in future have the capability of maintaining the social bond, as it has done in the past (...) It seems impossible for democracies to demand of their citizens to defend them with their lives. In democracy there is no longer any supreme sacrifice: the individuals and their interests have taken the place of the citizens and their ideals (Schnapper, 1995: 11).[3]

The nation-state is under external pressure through globalization and the development of supra- and infra-national units. A global political order, as represented by the UN, limits national independence and sovereignty. The need for common action to achieve collective security, to combat terrorism and to stop drug smuggling also makes inter-state cooperation essential. At the economic level, international markets and the increasing importance of global regulatory bodies like the International Monetary Fund (IMF) and The General Agreement on Tariffs and Trades (GATT) render autonomous national economic policies impossible. Administrative and legal decisions by European bodies restrict the power of national parliaments and governments. At the same time, the reassertion of local interests and cultures creates demands for regional autonomy or representation (Schnapper, 1994: 186-188).

Internally, Schnapper argues, the nation is weakened by an inherent contradiction. Democracy is based on the principle that citizens should be genuinely capable of exercising their rights of participation. This requires not just formal equality, but also a degree of real equality of socio-economic conditions. Thus the logic of democratic participation leads inevitably to a welfare state. This in turn engenders a new 'productivist-hedonist logic', which by emphasizing the interests of the individual, undermines the basic political project of the nation. People come to see the state simply as an instrument which manages the economy and distributes social benefits. *Civisme* (civic or public feeling) gets lost. There is a trend towards depoliticization, which constitutes a constant menace for democratic nations (Schnapper, 1994: 190-191).

These external and internal changes lead to a contradiction:

> (...) between the objective integration of people in a virtually global space and their social habitus, that is their feeling of collective identity, as well as their political participation, which continue to be mainly expressed at the level of the nation (Schnapper, 1994: 189).

The nation becomes degraded to a mere emotional bond, which can give a subjective meaning to people's existence. This opens the ways for a 're-ethnicization', in which people perceive themselves as members of an emotional community based on shared history and culture, rather than as political citizens who participate in a democracy. Schnapper asserts this with reference to Germany's shift from *Verfassungspatriotismus* (Habermas's term for loyalty to a constitutional political community) to a more nationalistic model after the demise of the German Democratic Republic in 1989. But she implies that the same trend applies in France, Britain and elsewhere (Schnapper, 1994: 194-196).

Peace and international cooperation appear as problems for the nation-state. "Every war or threat of war is a factor of integration" (Schnapper, 1994: 197). Now that the Soviet threat has gone, Schnapper complains of trends towards pacifism and lack of *civisme*. She observes a trend towards decline of the great public institutions – school, army, judiciary, public services – which were intended to teach the values of the nation and democracy. The depoliticization and re-ethnicization of the nation-state undermine the republican project of individual integration of immigrants and other minorities by means of common political values. This is replaced by separatist consciousness: national identity (for the majority), ethnic identities (for the minorities) and new forms of religious identity (sects, etc.) help people cope with feelings of powerlessness and disenchantment caused by the increasing rationalization, anonymity and bureaucratization of large-scale societies.

Schnapper presents a powerful analysis of the crisis of democratic citizenship, yet her critique remains problematic. Although she claims to be presenting a general argument for a political concept of the nation, her picture is clearly that of the French republican model. She is one-sided in her portrayal of the nation, emphasizing its rationality and its capacity for creating a social bond between people of differing origins. She neglects past repressions needed to homogenize ethnically diverse populations, and current racism towards immigrants and minorities. She idealizes conscription and war as means of national integration, but ignores the suffering which flowed from this notion of the warrior-citizen. She seems oblivious to the dialectic of rationality and barbarism which bedevils the history of European nations. The development of communities of warrior-soldiers armed to the teeth against external enemies, whose existence (or construction) was vital to national integration, leads inexorably to ever-more horrific wars.

The main problem is that Schnapper suggests no way of resolving the crisis of the nation-state. She explicitly rejects the notion of a multicultural society, arguing (without giving any reasons) that multiculturalism offers a merely 'magical' or apparent solution to the contradiction between the two great values of modernity: individual equality inscribed in the principle of citizenship and authenticity tied to a specific culture. In the same way, Schnapper argues that decentralization and local democracy is insufficient to unite citizens around a project which creates a common will (Schnapper, 1994: 201). In the end she states that it seems possible that the project of the democratic nation has become exhausted, but she does not offer any clear idea of a way forwards.

Conclusions

From differing perspectives, all the four authors discussed above provide convincing evidence that the model of a world based on separate nation-states and exclusive memberships is being eroded. Reich's starting-point is the economic dimensions of this shift, while Schnapper focuses on political aspects, yet both share the belief that there is no conceivable substitute for the nation-state. Reich gives an incisive critique of the increasing polarization of US society, while Schnapper presents a thorough analysis of the stresses faced by nation-states in general and by France in particular. The USA and France are widely seen as the two countries which were historically most successful in building secular political communities capable of transcending differences in religious and ethnic identity. Yet today these models of solidarity are breaking down in the face of globalization and growing cultural diversity. In the end, both Reich and Schnapper do little more than lament this while asserting the need to return to strong civic institutions and national cohesion. They cannot conceive of forms of democracy which transcend the nation-state, and can therefore offer no perspectives for dealing with the new challenges.

By contrast, Ohmae and Soysal both argue that new modes of political regulation are emerging from the process of globalization, and that the nation-state is on the way to being superseded. Ohmae stresses the economic dominance of global markets and transnational corporations, which can no longer be controlled by nation-states. His logic is that of economic determinism and depoliticization: markets and corporations are more efficient than governments in improving the quantity and quality of production and in meeting consumer needs. States are at best useful in maintaining public order and dealing with local problems; at worst they are an obstacle to efficiency, which – fortunately – can be disciplined by the power of the markets. The long-term effect of this logic would be a new form of domination completely closed to democratic control, which could exclude whole populations from economic and political participation, with appalling social, human and environmental consequences. Ohmae's 'borderless world' is a frightening dystopia, but it does have a useful side: it indicates that traditional modes of economic control and social integration through nation-states are no longer adequate. Unless we invent new institutions which address the globalization of economic power, democracy has no future.

That is where Soysal's notion of 'postnational belonging' is valuable. She argues that the extension of many citizenship rights to people who are formally non-members is based on two sets of discourses. The discourse of national sovereignty leads not only to the reinforcement of state boundaries, but also to the enhancement of the economic, social and political rights of those who do manage to cross the boundaries. The discourse of universal human rights has become a 'pervasive element of world culture' (Soysal, 1994: 7), which legitimates claims for rights and identities of persons, whether they are in their supposed ancestral homeland or not. Thus a dual logic – both internal and external – seems to be weakening the exclusiveness of nation-state belonging.

I have already argued that Soysal seems to be over-stating the effectiveness of such trends and their significance for minority groups. The global principles she postulates may be part of laws or international declarations, but the groups most in need of human rights protection may lack the financial, cultural and political resources to obtain their rights. Yet as she rightly points out: "There is no unified, homogeneous global institutional order. Instead, there is a multiplicity of discourses and modalities of legitimate action" (Soysal, 1994: 6-7). Here lies the field for action to develop new forms of social and political participation no longer fixated on nation-state boundaries. Soysal suggests that the basis for political membership may no longer be the state or allegiance to a common national ideal, but rather a shared public social space, a set of shared principles, and a common everyday praxis (1994: 166). This notion of political agency is not explored in detail, yet it could provide a useful starting-point for rethinking the location of democratic political action and organization.

The discussion on some of the old and new ambivalences of the nation-state model presented in this article indicates the need for new approaches to citizenship and political action. Such approaches must recognize both the continuing importance of the state as the single most significant focus of political belonging, and the growing salience of infra- and supranational locations of political decision-making. A theory of citizenship for a global society must therefore deal both with the question of inclusion of new groups at the state level, and the search for new forms of democratic participation at other levels.

At the individual country level, citizenship must be based on the separation between nation and state. This means a new type of state which is not constituted exclusively or mainly around the nexus of territorial, cultural and political belonging. Citizenship should no longer be based on nationality (that is on the idea of being one people with common cultural characteristics). This implies a new notion of state borders. These cannot be abolished, as distinct states will remain the rule for the foreseeable future. But borders cannot be rigid, in view of the mobility intrinsic in modernity and globalism. A notion of porous borders is required, with admission rules and rights based on people's real societal membership (compare Bauböck, 1994).

This approach would break with the outmoded norm of singular membership in a nation-state, and recognize the growing prevalence of dual or multiple membership. There must be a link between admission procedures (to the state territory and to citizenship) and the contents of citizenship. This requires differential rights and new forms of representation and participation. Citizenship should not be derived from membership of a cultural group, but from residence in a territory. Other significant links – such as origin in the territory, family bonds, economic involvement or cultural participation – should also confer citizenship rights, which may need to be differentiated according to the type of linkage.

At the local or regional level, similar contradictions are to be found. On the one hand, it is within cities that transcultural experience seems to have been most successful in creating a sense of living together that cuts across particularism. Yet it is also at the local or regional level that we find exclusionary movements that seek to exclude the Other on the basis of nostalgia for lost myths of homogeneity. There is a need for participation based not on national or cultural origins but on shared public space and a common life-world.

As for the transnational level, it is clear that countervailing power needs to be developed if there is to be any hope of democratizing and humanizing global markets and intergovernmental organizations. There is a lack of precedents here, for the emerging global arena has so far been dominated by powerful players, with the resources needed for transport and communications, as well as for the international 'projection of power' (as the almost obscene military phrase goes). New forms of global communication and networking may well provide the means for constructing new 'virtual public spaces', which will allow individuals and non-governmental organizations the means of criticizing those who hold economic and political power, and of developing new forms of public opinion. An obvious demand would be for popular representation (rather than just representation of governments) in bodies such as the United Nations or regional economic communities.

The fundamental problem at all levels is to work out new rules for conviviality, which provide not only the basis for equality but also the conditions for cross-cultural communication and the development of a new sense of community. If democracy is to be realized and enhanced, then everyone must have a political voice as a citizen, at all the levels where crucial decisions are made. Citizenship should be a political community without any claim to common cultural identity. Yet in a world of migrants, ethnic groups and diasporas, citizenship cannot be blind to cultural belonging either. Citizenship rules must start from the recognition that individuality is always formed in social and cultural contexts, and that individuals are always also members of social and cultural groups (compare Habermas, 1994). The liberal principle of abstracting from these contexts leads to a fiction of equality as citizens, which is belied by real differences in political and economic power. Democratic societies have addressed this by developing welfare states. But globalization makes it necessary to go a step further, and to develop approaches to citizenship designed to achieve individual equality, democratic participation and recognition of collective difference at all levels of political decision-making.

Notes

[1] This chapter is based on work in progress for a book being written jointly with Alastair Davidson of Monash University. I acknowledge his contribution to the ideas presented here.

[2] The example of the EU also helps to illustrate a further ambiguity. EU citizenship, with its well-known 'democratic deficit' is an example of a set of rights relating to a political unit based on the rule of law, but without full democratic participation by the citizen. The European Parliament has mainly consultative functions. Most decisions are made by the powerful bureaucracy of the European Commission, or by the Council of Ministers, who are nominated by the member states. Democratic citizenship implies the active citizen who makes laws and controls their implementation, not just the passive citizen, who obeys the laws and is protected by them.

[3] Translation by Stephen Castles.

References

Bauböck, R. (1994) 'Changing the Boundaries of Citizenship: the Inclusion of Immigrants in Democratic Polities', in Bauböck, R. (ed.), *From Aliens to Citizens*. Aldershot: Avebury.

Castles, S./Miller, M.J. (1993) *The Age of Migration: International Population Movements in the Modern World.* London: Macmillan; New York: Guilford Books.

Connor, W. (1991) 'From Tribe to Nation', *History of European Ideas* 13: 1/2.

Fukuyama, F. (1992) *The End of History and the Last Man.* London: Penguin.

Habermas, J. (1994) 'Struggles for Recognition in the Democratic Constitutional State', pp. 107-148 in Gutmann, A. (ed.), *Multiculturalism: Examining the Politics of Recognition.* Princeton NJ: Princeton University Press.

Hoffmann, L. (1994) *Das deutsche Volk und seine Feinde.* Cologne: Pappyrossa Verlag.

Kymlicka, W. (1995) *Multicultural Citizenship.* Oxford: Clarendon Press.

Lapeyronnie, D./Frybes, M./Couper, K./Joly, D. (1990) *L'Intégration des Minorités Immigrées: Etude Comparative: France – Grande Bretagne.* Paris: Agence pour le Développement des Relations Interculturelles.

Marshall, T.H. (1964) 'Citizenship and Social Class', in *Class, Citizenship and Social Development: Essays by T.H. Marshall.* New York: Anchor Books.

Moynihan, D.P. (1993) *Pandaemonium: Ethnicity in International Politics.* Oxford: Oxford University Press.

OECD (1997) *Trends in International Migration: Annual Report 1996.* Paris: OECD.

Ohmae, K. (1991) *The Borderless World.* New York: Harper Collins.

Rawls, J. (1985) 'Justice as Fairness: Political not Metaphysical', *Philosophy and Public Affairs* 14 (3): 223-251.

Reich, R.B. (1991) *The Work of Nations: a Blueprint for the Future.* London: Simon and Schuster.

Renan, E. (1992) *Qu'est-ce qu' une nation? et autres essais politiques* (introduced by J. Roman). Paris: Presses Pocket, Agora.

Schnapper, D. (1994) *La Communauté des Citoyens.* Paris: Gallimard.

Seton-Watson, H. (1977) *Nations and States.* London: Methuen.

Smith, A.D. (1991) *National Identity.* London: Penguin.

Soysal, Y.N. (1994) *Limits of Citizenship: Migrants and Postnational Membership in Europe.* Chicago and London: University of Chicago Press.

Wieviorka, M. (1994) 'Introduction', in: Wieviorka, M./Bataille, P./Couper, K./Martucelli, D./Peralva, A. (eds.), *Racisme et Xénophobie en Europe: une comparaison internationale.* Paris: La Découverte.

Young, I.M. (1989) 'Polity and Group Difference: A Critique of the Ideal of Universal Citizenship', *Ethics* 99: 250-274.

Young, I.M. (1990) *Justice and the Politics of Difference.* Princteon, N.J.: Princeton University Press.

CHAPTER 9

Cultural Pluralism and the Subversion of the 'Taken-for-Granted' World

Maria Markus

Cultural pluralism is an undisputable fact for most countries today. How particular societies and their members deal with it, however, is a different question altogether and the answer to it cannot be reduced to any singular model. Differentiation occurs not only on the level of policies but, due to the different sources of such pluralism, it also produces different responses on the level of everyday life and practices of consociates within various societies.

While the pluralism in question may, of course, refer to differently generated cultures, I am limiting myself here to cultural differentiations rooted in national/ ethnic or racial identifications only. There are at least two distinct facets of culture that are relevant here. On the one hand, there is a layer of culture which is rooted directly in the form of life into which one is born, that is, in everyday practices and relations within which initial personal identities are formed and links with others – the 'community' between the participants – are established in an unreflective way. On the other hand, there is a more abstract level of culture which consists of intellectually and reflectively generated systems of beliefs, norms, and organized traditions ('moral maps'), providing evaluative standards for different modes of life or their components. In establishing such a map, the past is not only mobilized and interpreted but also reconstructed, or even invented. This work constructs a 'collective memory' as a vital link between the given collective's past and future, thus uniting its whole as an 'imagined community'. While this certainly does not always lead to the constitution of a separate state, or to the constitution of a state at all, it may be instrumental in this process for which it provides both justification and secular legitimation and from which, in turn, it receives institutional support, facilitating the reproduction of the privileged forms of life.[1] Although there has rarely existed a nation-state composed of a single ethnic/national group,[2] various exclusionary mechanisms at work in the definition of citizenship rights and assimilationist policies often ensured the relatively homogeneous composition of nation-states. This, together with the liberal democratic principle of equality of all citizens and the subdivision of social life into public and private spheres (with the basic differences being relegated to the latter), have previously made it relatively easy to misrecognize this aspect of the nation-state and assume its basic neutrality in respect of ethnic, cultural, religious etc., differences of its citizens.

This is certainly no longer the case. Cultural identities encompassed within the borders of each state have become, as a rule, not only more pluralized and diversified but also more vocal and thus more visible.

The sources of this increased pluralization are many. They include, on the one hand, those cases when certain groups of population, although differing quite radically from the nation-forming majority in terms of concrete life practices (and often possessing separate languages or dialects), did not – at the time of the formation of the nation-state on their territory – thematize their own separate identities, that is, did not develop the second mentioned layer of culture. The factors contributing to the 'self-awakening' of these groups of population are again numerous and cannot be reduced simply to a reaction against the exclusionary policies exercized by the dominant nation *vis-à-vis* these groups, although this has often been the case. Paradoxically, the results of assimilationist policies could equally contribute to such a process: they often lead to the emergence of a stratum of 'indigenous intellectuals' as the most likely elaborators and propagators of the second mentioned type of culture and thus the heralds of the autonomous presence for the hitherto marginalized groups.[3]

A special case is constituted here by those indigenous groups whose territory has been colonized through mostly violent conquest often leading to decimation of the indigenous population, destruction of their native ways of life and cultures, and in each case to their marginalization. Furthermore, such a 'self-awakening' is often either a product or a by-product of the processes of so-called globalization or internationalization. This may emerge as a conscious strategy at 're-embedding' social institutions and relations which are increasingly separated from the local context of social interactions (Giddens, 1990), but may also be a more-or-less spontaneous response to these processes, or even – as some authors suggest (see e.g. Robertson, 1995) – constitute their organic part ('glocalization').

The other major source of such pluralization is, and always has been, the forced or voluntary migration which has recently become enormously intensified, due partly to the already mentioned processes of globalization but also, and no less importantly, to wars, famine, political oppression or emerging nationalisms.[4]

In addition, it is not only people who migrate. Boundaries and frontiers of nations and 'nation-states' are also occasionally redrawn, they also 'migrate', locating different ethnic groups within new cultural and political contexts. There is a number of historical and recent examples of such processes, some implications of which are elaborated by Rainer Bauböck (Bauböck, in this volume).[5]

These two factors, increased migration and activation of indigenous groups, bring to light an unresolved tension or even conflict between the theoretical universality of democratic citizenship and the particularity of cultural identities.

The ethical/cultural neutrality of the state as a political community which is supposed to ensure the equality of all its citizens, together with the recognition and guarantee of their individual rights as private persons to pursue different goals, to choose different lifestyles, to belong to different religious denominations, voluntary organizations and so on, constitutes one of the basic principles of liberal democracy. It has, however, never been fully realized and its interpretations have also varied considerably through history. Moreover, it has become increasingly clear in the current debates (see e.g. Taylor, 1994; Kis, 1996), such a neutrality, at least in its radical form, cannot be effectively achieved and perhaps ought not to be striven for, not without further qualification.

Why Isn't Neutrality Possible? [6]

In the most general terms, we can point firstly to the fact that the state, among other functions, has to fulfil the task of integration and coordination of society. This task requires a number of decisions in which the 'ethnic origin' of the state and its grounding in a particular culture come to the fore, even if some concessions for minority groups are introduced. For example, decisions concerning the choice of 'official language' (or even languages) of the particular country, which is necessary and which, as a rule, is quite logically defined as the language of the majority. Similarly, core decisions concerning school curricula, decisions about public holidays or recently challenged definitions of family. As the two last examples demonstrate, even such characteristics, constitutive of the very idea of a democratic state as its separation from religion, cannot be consistently realized. It is worth adding that the very division between the private and public and their concrete contents are not only culturally differentiated but are subject matters of an ongoing political contestation by different groups and movements.

Furthermore, another task of the democratic state: to ensure equality of all citizens as citizens, that is, to equalize their chances of active participation in citizenship, often demands some forms of affirmative action, or even special legislation, in respect of particular groups of citizens, that is, measures which go beyond or, in any case, differ from the general welfare policy of the state.[7]

So, while in a multicultural society the state cannot identify itself with any single ethnic group, but has to represent the political community as a whole, it also has to take into account the differences in actual conditions of equal citizenship between different groups and orient its policies towards their equalization.

All these considerations lead to the conclusion that the impartiality of the state and its desirability ought to be evaluated selectively, examining how far it contributes to the reduction of the privileged position of the majority where it is detrimental to the cultural heritage and cultural identities of other groups. For the political system ought to increase the opportunities of all citizens to participate equally in shaping the institutional/legal framework of political community as a whole without endangering individual freedom of choice.

What, However, Does This Mean Practically?

On the one hand, Stuart Hall is right to insist that the "rights of citizenship and the incommensurabilities of cultural difference both ought to be respected and that one cannot be made a condition of the other" (Hall, 1993: 360). On the other hand, however, the question arises whether in practice the exercise of citizenship can be radically divorced from the cultural 'situatedness' (location) or identification of citizens?

It is generally recognized that the exercise of democratic citizenship requires a certain degree of social cohesiveness, a certain level of social integration or solidarity, which in the nation-state has been traditionally produced by the construction of 'national culture'. If such a cohesion is indeed necessary, the question is what can possibly substitute for this type of bond in a multicultural society, encompassing not only relatively closely related but often also quite incommensurable cultures?

Different models have emerged practically or have been formulated theoretically in response to this question (Schöpflin, 1995; Tamir, 1993; Kymlicka, 1995; Kis, 1996). Apart from straightforward assimilation, which is now to a large degree compromised and cannot be openly pursued as a requirement for citizenship in democratic societies, there are different models of integration, federation or consociationalism.

One of the more challenging current theoretical propositions in this respect is J. Habermas' notion of 'constitutional patriotism' as a shared political culture of a society, separate (although not independent) from the plurality of 'lifeworld cultures' present in any given society (Habermas, 1992a, 1992b and 1994). Habermas elaborates this conception with a critical reference to the variegated conceptions of communitarianism, above all in response to Charles Taylor's interpretation of liberalism. While accepting some points of Taylor's critique of the individualistic version of citizenship, he considers the communitarian model too restrictive from the point of view of the individual, as it directly links political culture with the substantive aspirations of particular communities and demands the individual's identification with these goals. This – he argues – could lead to the 'normalizing' intervention of community, restricting the autonomy of individuals in choosing and leading their own lives.[8] In Taylor's understanding, the solidarity and cohesion of a political community is grounded in the concept of 'common good', which in a multicultural society can emerge only out of the selective 'fusion of horizons' of different cultures, or out of the equally selective[9] expansion of the horizon of the 'host culture' (Taylor, 1994: 62). In contrast, Habermas defines the cohesion and integration of political community as grounded primarily in the democratic interpretation of the constitutional principles: as a cohesion which depends upon a common political culture and not upon an ethical-cultural form of life as a whole (Habermas, 1992b: 17). Such a common political culture of deliberative democracy is based, for Habermas, on a 'formal universalism'. This is understood as a normatively grounded procedure relating to the principles and mechanisms of democratic deliberation in which citizens as individuals embedded in various cultural forms of life and/or as members of groups representing these differentiated forms confront each other to negotiate issues of common interest. Acceptance of the framework of the political culture so understood is considered to be a normative requirement for all citizens and it is safeguarded by the legal structure of the country. Such a 'political acculturation', however, does not involve, according to this conception, the necessity of giving up the person's particular cultural identification. "The same universalistic content must in each case be appropriated from out of one's own cultural form of life", says Habermas in his interview with J.M. Ferry (Habermas, 1992a: 241). Citizens are not abstract beings moving only in the political sphere. They are socialized and live within different cultural traditions and continuously redefine their identities through identification with various collectivities or communities and/or with different cultural traditions. Personal identities are thus deeply interwoven with collective identities of various sorts, including different ethnic groups, which themselves are also in a process of gradual transformation. The various cultural identifications of citizens constitute the net of 'nodal points' against which the ethical-political discourses and, with that, an interpretation and re-interpretation of their self-understanding is negotiated and renegotiated. "If the population of citizens as a whole shifts, this horizon will change as well" (Habermas, 1994: 126).

This, of course, also means that on the one hand, political culture is not static, but continually evolving and that, on the other hand, it is not only dependent upon the constituency of the political community, but itself also contributes to the process of cultural identity formation. In this latter respect at least, despite their polemic, Habermas' proposal to some degree resembles Taylor's conception. More importantly, however, it also foregrounds the gravity of problems connected to the attempts to separate, analytically and – even more so – practically, the lifeworld-embedded plural cultures and the common political culture understood as a mutual respect for basic rights. Yet, this distinction, as noted earlier, is important and consequential. Namely, if the political order is indistinguishable from the particular, cultural preferences concerning the good life, then the nation's right to restrict the intake of migrants (not only numerically, but first of all culturally), or to demand their more-or-less full acculturation, in a defence of its own integrity, would be at least understandable, however problematic it otherwise might be. If, however, the integrity of the nation can be defined primarily in terms of a shared political culture, then all that could be required from the immigrants would be "the assimilation to the way in which the autonomy of the citizens is institutionalized in the recipient society and the way the 'public use of reason' is practiced here" (Habermas, 1994: 138).

While such an uncoupling of the two forms of culture does make the prospect of maintaining a certain minimum of social integration without culturally restrictive or assimilationist policies of immigration more promising, this division is beset by its own difficulties and provokes new challenges.

These challenges are connected above all with the already-mentioned interplay between the political culture and the pluralized cultural forms of life, with the practical difficulty of separating the two. Participation in political culture requires certain resources which not all individuals and, for that matter, not all communities are in possession of. Furthermore, it also requires a degree of 'fusion of horizons', which would enable the participants to enter common deliberations. How such a fusion can be achieved and what it may encompass, are in a sense the central issues here. From this point of view two questions are particularly relevant: 'who participates' (who is in a position to participate) and 'what do those who participate bring into the common discourse'. Both are closely related to the cultures within which the initial identities of citizens are formed and which provide them with a point of reference. Ethical-political decisions are an unavoidable part of common debates, and therefore present a two-sided challenge to participants.

On the one hand, it is a challenge to those who attempt to make their entry into the already-established political culture of the country and, on the other hand, to the majority culture's self-understanding, which is reflected in this culture. This challenge – as Habermas points out – "becomes all the greater, the more profound are the religious, racial, or ethnic differences or the historical-cultural disjunctions to be bridged" (Habermas, 1994: 118). The extension of the challenge involved here, however, is not limited to variations in cultural commensurability or incommensurability. Even more crucial from this point of view is the ability and willingness of the bearers of different cultural identities to maintain the intersubjective aspect of the process of identity formation, keeping it both internally reflexive and open to external questioning. According to Habermas, it requires from different groups and individuals a recognition that culture and identity are open, historical formations and that traditions, although partly given, are (and ought to be) selectively appropriated and interpreted, and perhaps even given up, if they contradict 'one's own life-project'. It is necessary that "one be able to relativize one's own way of life *vis-à-vis* other forms of life, that one be prepared to grant strangers and others the same rights as oneself and that one does not insist on universalizing one's own identity" (Habermas, 1992a: 243, 240). This refers to majority culture as well as to endogenous minorities and migrant minorities in the diaspora. All three, although mostly for different reasons, are susceptible to essentialization of their own cultural identity and to closure which endangers the potential inclusiveness of political culture as one of the main integrative mechanisms in modern society. All three are prone, in one way or another, to conceptualize their identity as fixed and sharply delineated.

In the above-mentioned paper, Stuart Hall makes this point very emphatically: "Since cultural diversity" – writes Hall – "is, increasingly, the fate of the modern world, and ethnic absolutism a regressive feature of late-modernity, the greatest danger now arises from forms of national and cultural identity – new or old – which attempt to secure their identity by adopting closed versions of culture or community and by refusal to engage (...) with the difficult problems that arise from trying to live with difference." (Hall, 1993: 361).

While Hall refers here to such a tendency among the 'dominant white cultures', the observation is valid for the broad spectrum of cultural differentiation, although – as I have already noted – the reasons for it are quite variegated. In the case of endogenous minorities, like the Aboriginal people in Australia (whose form of life has been destroyed at its very basis) the tendency to secure identity through closure is often associated with mobilization. Aboriginal communities attempt to reorganize without being absorbed by the social structures that tend to allocate them nothing but a marginalized position. Obviously, for all minorities the common and principal reason for such a stance is a self-defensive reaction against the insensitivity or, sometimes, arrogance of the majority culture and its hegemonic position in the societies in question.

But there is yet another aspect of the minority's experience which may produce such a closure. At the beginning of this paper, I distinguished two facets of culture which underlie the cultural identities of ethnic communities: the 'pre-reflexive' (or non-reflexive) layer and the more-or-less systematized elaboration of the group's traditions, beliefs and norms. The first is grounded directly in everyday life practices, ways of doing things and arranging relationships, representing the 'taken-for-granted' social reality with its ontological security and the handed-down recipes, which are shared in the community as 'thinking-as-usual' patterns of life (Schütz, 1964). For most societies modernity has weakened this aspect of culture considerably by practically breaking up the slow flow of unnoticeable changes into more spectacular 'turning points' and ruptures, but it has survived in more traditional societies, in rural areas, in sleepy 'middletowns'. The second layer, in so far as it is explicitly elaborated, is in no sense deduced from the first, but it must somehow refer to it and legitimize it as an ethically appropriate way of life. There must be some sort of congruency between the two.

What is happening with migration or, for that matter, with the colonization of indigenous cultures, is that this 'pre-reflexive' layer is shattered and fragmented, losing its 'taken-for-granted' character. Migrants or indigenous people can, of course, try to sustain certain traditions, customs, forms of interpersonal intercourse, but these are no longer built into life conduct as a whole, which can be integrally connected to society at large. For this latter connection – as effectuated through work, through children's education, through dealings with market and bureaucracy, through 'external' social relationships – demands, as a rule, other patterns of behaviour. These are naturally the processes that set off the phenomena of so-called 'hybridization' of cultures, to the more promising aspects of which I shall return in a moment.

But hybridization does not necessarily mean 'blurring the boundaries'. It could easily mean a further 'closing off', in response to the new conditions which make the group particularly vulnerable. A type of closure may already occur at this level. Bhikhu Parekh aptly and beautifully describes such experience, which may result in cutting off the external world and creating an illusory, 'suspended' existence within the simplified and thus fragmentarily 'fundamentalized' code of rules. "There is a past, which is then ruptured and to which the present bears little relation. That leads to self-fragmentation, a painful state which one copes with by hoping that the present is only an aberration and that the future will either reconcile the past and present, or represent a happy return to the romanticized past (...) What you recreate in a new environment is never the same as what you left behind. What was a richly-nuanced body of beliefs and practices gets abbreviated into a set of abstract formulae, and a tradition degenerates into an ideology" (Bhabha/Parekh, 1989:

25). It is exactly such an 'abbreviation' that often goes on in the second layer of culture, which strives to survive without being able to reconnect or to establish its congruency with the broader spectrum of everyday life practices.

Under such conditions, the ability and willingness of the group to engage in self-reflection and self-rejuvenation is easily abandoned to the mentality of the 'besieged', when the group: "lacks the courage to critically reinterpret its fundamental principles, lest it opens the door to 'excessive' reinterpretation. It then turns its fundamentals into fundamentalism, it declares them inviolate and reduces them to a neat and easily-enforceable package of beliefs and rituals" (Bhabha/Parekh 1989: 25).

If any generalizations are here in place, it could be said that the less resourceful, the more besieged and the less confident in its future the group is, the more likely it is to mummify its past and to present it as the essence of its existence which cannot be questioned or altered.

Of course, such a 'defensive' attitude is not the only strategy employed by cultural minorities, individuals or groups, attempting to find their place in society at large. Some groups actively attempt to appropriate the new reality, to engage in common discourses and to make their own mark. In other words, not just to expose themselves passively to the spontaneous ongoing process of hybridization, facilitated grossly by such common structures as market, bureaucracy and the other institutionalized forms of intercourse, but to participate consciously in this process, turning it into mutual 'self-presentation', from which may result an expansion or even 'fusion of the horizons' enabling rational democratic debate within the political sphere.

Many migrant communities gradually develop a mode of life equally distant from both assimilation and tradition. There are some almost anecdotal cases of such blends, like the new hybrid language spoken by a small community in Victoria, Australia, which is a mixture of Italian and English, that cannot be understood either by new Italian migrants or by native English speakers (Baggio, 1989). There is also a number of other, perhaps more meaningful examples, especially in the sphere of art: popular music, film and so on. In any case, a conscious search for a better alternative than either assimilation or closure is undoubtedly emerging in a number of forms within collective ways of life and is even more widespread on the individual level. For while migration – even where voluntary – always involves pain and loss, it is also considered by many to offer a chance of a new beginning, of a more autonomous construction of the self, rendering possible a choice among cultural patterns to be selectively incorporated into their development. Or as Breytenbach puts it, despite all the feelings of loss, uncertainty and alienation, "exile is a chance, a break, an escape, a challenge (...) To be in exile is to be free to imagine or to dream a past and the future of this past" (Breytenbach, 1991: 71, 73). But he also acknowledges that it is a 'difficult craft', hoping it is also a useful one (not just for oneself), because there is no more 'homecoming'. 'The exile never returns' – he or she always remains a stranger. While there is an increasing number of strangers around us, and to be one has its own merits and functions, it is, at the same time, not an easy way to be. Bauman is right, noting : "it is not for everyone that the dismantling of constraints is experienced as liberation, for some it is experienced as loss: and what has been lost reveals itself, in retrospect, as identity" (Bauman, 1995: 149). Not everyone has the strength and the necessary resources to blend one's own identity anew.

It goes without saying that there are usually more options open to migrants than to marginalized indigenous populations in search for their place in society, mainly because in the migrants' case the voluntary aspect of their resettlement undoubtedly plays some role. In contrast, the lack of choice in the case of indigenous populations influences the shaping of relationships, for example, between the white population of Australia and the Australian Aboriginal people. The hurt is deep and the distrust widespread. Moreover, both played a mobilizing role in raising the self-consciousness and self-organization of Aboriginal people, and cultural closure has functioned here as one of the liberating instruments of these processes. The two histories of Australia were 'written' in parallel, they did not even confront, but rather ignored each other. The programme of reconciliation is an attempt to confront the 'other' history and to learn from it, but the learning is slow and new hurts are often created. Not guilt, but responsibility for the enduring consequences of the conquest have to be accepted by all non-indigenous citizens of the country today. This must not be dependent upon whether or not the Aboriginal tribes massacred each other before colonization, whether they were practicing infanticide or what their social malaises are today. But this also means that these topics ought not to be taboos either.

If it is true that the vitality of a culture depends upon its reflexivity, then this is perhaps Australia's chance on 'both sides of the fence' and therefore a common one too. For, if up to this point I was speaking about the closures created by cultural minorities, this in no way means that it is only migrants or indigenous groups that create closures in cultural encounters. Majority cultures are no less prone to be exclusionary and no less unwilling to respond to the unsettling presence of the 'stranger' with a critical examination of their own assumptions, beliefs and customs. In this case, it is not so much existential insecurity that prompts the closures, although this type of motive is often palpably present in racially motivated movements and ideologies which attempt to hide their sentiments behind 'rationalized' arguments. But the presence of strangers is unsettling and 'subversive' to these cultures above all because it often makes visible such composite elements that previously went unnoticed or unreflected upon. It is like a magnifying glass or a huge mirror in which suddenly the hidden wrinkles appear, making us aware that we are perhaps uglier (or at least look older) than we thought (or hoped). Linda Nicholson in her critical evaluation of Taylor's essay, speaks about her understanding of the 'recognition debate', according to which the 'more challenging voices are not those saying 'recognize my worth' but rather those saying, "let my presence make you aware of the limitations of what you have so far judged to be true and of worth" (Nicholson, 1996: 10). Those are exactly the voices that majority cultures often attempt to silence through their own closures created through two basic mechanisms: inclusion as assimilation and exclusion as marginalization.

Hybridization does not necessarily result in increased homogenization or cultural uniformity. It does not create a uniform mixed culture which would then become the dominant or commonly accepted one. Rather it is about the further pluralization of critical perspectives and ways of life. Hybrids constitute a 'species' in their own right. Speaking of 'displaced peoples' and 'dislocated cultures', Stuart Hall makes the point that, while "struggling in one sense at the margins of modernity, they are at the leading edge of what is destined to become the truly representative 'late-modern' experience. They are the product of the cultures of hybridity." He considers this notion essentially different from the "old internationalist grand narrative, from the superficiality of old style pluralism where no boundaries are crossed, and from the trendy nomadic voyaging of the postmodern or simplistic version of global homogenization – one damn thing after another or the difference that does not make the difference. These 'hybrids' retain strong links to and identification with the traditions and places of their 'origin' (...) They bear the traces of particular cultures, traditions, languages, systems of beliefs, texts and histories which have shaped them. But they are also obliged to come to terms with and to make something new of the cultures they inhabit, without simply assimilating to them. They are not and will never be unified culturally in the old sense, because they are inevitably the products of several interlocking histories and cultures, belonging at the same time to several 'homes' – and thus to no one particular home" (Hall, 1993: 362).

Jan Nedeveen Pieterse quotes Rowe and Schelling who, with respect to cultural forms, define hybridization as "the ways in which forms become separated from existing practices and recombine with new forms in new practices" (Pieterse, 1995: 48). Hybridization is thus not about the 'blurring of the cultural boundaries', rather it is about the crossing of these boundaries in potentially endless combinations of the new and the old. Hybrids are crossing the boundaries between minority cultures as well as between the culture of majority and that of minorities. In this way, they 'destabilize the established hierarchy of centre and margin, hegemony and minority' and perhaps, even more importantly, they contribute to the 'deterritorialization' and 'disessentialization' of the very concept of culture (ibid.: 56, 62 and 63). This latter is a crucial point for understanding the process of hybridization as providing the most appropriate basis for a democratic polity, for which the ability 'to relativize one's own lifeworld with regard to other lifeworlds' is a central one. In order to recapture this potential of the process of hybridization as the reinforcement of democratic political culture and to bring these two forms of social integration into accord, it is necessary to go beyond the spontaneity of the hybridization process and to transform it into a conscious self-reflective achievement, to move on from the hybridity of culture into a culture of hybridity. The most important result of such a transformation would be exactly such a disessentialization of the concept of identity in all its varieties, a recognition that identity is never accomplished, ready, or one-dimensional. Such a recognition would allow us to move beyond the spontaneous level of hybridization to a more reflexive one, based on autonomous choices rather than merely on the shelter of being defined by one's 'myth of origin'.

Needless to say that the issue of access to the requisite material and symbolic resources is a crucial one for this process. This includes, among others, an access to the public sphere or spaces in which this process can be played out both internally, within a particular group, and externally, between different groups. No group should feel vulnerable to the extent they can see no future other than that leading back to the past. The most important condition of doing away with a mentality of the 'besieged' is to end the siege. This of course places a special responsibility on 'majority cultures'. Only this can bring us closer to establishing a common political culture of citizenship, which would be able to utilize the whole gamut of the cultural resources of its constitutive hybrids.

Notes

[1] This is not to say that these two facets of culture exhaust the variety of meanings attached to this concept, some of which are radically divorced from, or even stand in opposition to, any ethnic/national reference.

[2] According to Walker Connor (1994), a survey of the 132 entities considered to be states in 1971, demonstrated that only slightly over 9% of these can be justifiably described as nation-states; close to a further 19%, despite containing some important minority with about 90% of more or less homogeneous population, can approximate the nation-state concept. In the largest group of almost 30%, however, the 'core nation' accounts for less than half of the population.

3   The case of the Kurds in Turkey demonstrates well the multiplicity of the possible motifs for separatist movements (see e.g. Kupchan, 1995).

4   The scope of this increase is well illustrated by Australia, where by now close to 40% of population consists of first- and second-generation migrants with 270 countries of origin. This is especially significant when we take into account that in the 1940s 90% of the Australian population was born in Australia and most migrants were from an English-speaking background. Australia, for a number of reasons, is obviously quite exceptional in this respect, but the phenomenon itself is widespread. Habermas, for example, mentions that 26% of Frankfurt's population today consists of 'foreigners' (Habermas, 1994: 144).

5   The history of the industrial belt of Lorraine in France which changed its 'nationality' and official language five times in a century is only one past example (Hobsbawm, 1996). The redistribution of the territories after the wars and after the dissolution of colonialism is another. But such phenomena are no less common today (see former Yugoslavia, former Soviet Union and so on).

6   Even in the little volume edited by Amy Gutmann (1994), there is a whole gamut of answers to this question, proposing different formulations or reformulations of this principle, see e.g. Taylor versus Walzer versus Habermas versus Appiah. Given the complexity of the issue, I can only present it here in a very simplified form.

7   In the Australian context, the recognition of Aboriginal people's native title, which is in a sense an attempt to 'integrate indigenous societies into the legal and economic structure of the country' is not 'adding' any preferential treatment for Aborigines but rather poses the issue of redressing their hitherto effected discrimination (see e.g. Patton, 1995).

8   K.A. Appiah, for example, in his contribution to the Taylor-volume (Appiah, 1994), makes some strong observations concerning the oppressive character of the ready-made scripts of behaviour for members of different communities, who often identify themselves with several such communities, and with none in the totality of their identity.

9   Taylor makes it clear that we should not create for ourselves illusions about the universal applicability of liberalism. He emphasizes that "liberalism is not a possible meeting ground for all cultures, but is the political expression of one range of cultures, and quite incompatible with other ranges (...) It shouldn't claim complete cultural neutrality. Liberalism is also a fighting creed." (Taylor, 1994: 62).

References

Appiah, K. Anthony (1994) 'Identity, Authenticity, Survival', in Taylor, Ch. et al., *Multiculturalism: Examining the Politics of Recognition*. Princeton: Princeton University Press.

Baggio, R.A. (1989) *The Shoe in my Cheese. Immigrant Family Experience*. Publ. by R.A. Baggio, Australia.

Bauman, Zygmunt (1995) 'Searching for Centre that Holds', in Featherstone, M. et al. (eds.), *Global Modernities*. London: Sage.

Bhabha, Homi/Parekh, Bhikhu (1989) 'Identities on Parade. A Conversation', *Marxism Today*, June: 23-29.

Breytenbach, Breyten (1991) 'The Long March from Hearth to Heart', *Social Research* 58 (1): 69-83.

Connor, Walker (1994) 'A Nation is a Nation, is a State, is an Ethnic Group, is a ...', in Hutchinson, J./Smith, A. D. (eds.), *Nationalism, Oxford Reader*. Oxford: Oxford University Press.

Giddens, Anthony (1990) *The Consequences of Modernity*. Cambridge: Polity Press.

Gutmann, A. (ed.) (1994) *Multiculturalism: Examining the Politics of Recognition*. Princeton: Princeton University Press.

Habermas, Jürgen (1992a) *Autonomy and Solidarity*, edited by Peter Dews, revised edition. London: Verso.

Habermas, Jürgen (1992b) 'Citizenship and National Identity', *Praxis International*. 12 (1): 1-19.

Habermas, Jürgen (1994) 'Struggles for Recognition in the Democratic Constitutional State', in Taylor, Ch. et al., op. cit.

Hall, Stuart (1993) 'Culture, Community, Nation', *Cultural Studies* 7 (3): 349-363.

Hobsbawn, E. (1996) 'Identity Politics and the Left', *New Left Review* 217.

Jordens, Ann-Mari (1995) *Redefining Australians*. Sydney: Hale and Iremonger.

Kis, János (1996) 'Beyond Nation State', *Social Research* 63 (1): 191-245.

Kupchan, Charles, A. (1995) 'Introduction: Nationalism Resurgent', in Kupchan, Ch.A. (ed.), *Nationalism and Nationalities in the New Europe*. Ithaca: Cornell University Press.

Kymlicka, Will (1995) *Multicultural Citizenship*. Oxford: Oxford University Press.

Nicholson, Linda (1996) 'To Be or not to Be: Charles Taylor and the Politics of Recognition', *Constellations* 3 (1): 1-16.

Patton, Paul (1995) 'Mabo and Australian Society', *The Australian Journal of Anthropology* 6 (1-2): 83-94.

Pieterse, Jan Nedeveen (1995) 'Globalization as Hybridization', in Featherstone, M. et al. (eds.), *Global Modernities*. London: Sage.

Robertson, Roland (1995) 'Glocalization: Time-Space and Homogeneity-Heterogeneity', in Featherstone, M. et al. (eds.), *Global Modernities*. London: Sage.

Schöpflin, George (1995) 'Nationalism and Ethnicity in Europe, East and West', in Kupchan, Ch.A. (ed.), *Nationalism and Nationalities in the New Europe*. Ithaca: Cornell University Press.

Schütz, A. (1964) *Collected Papers*, Volume 2. Edited by M. Natanson. The Hague: Martinus Nijhoff.

Tamir, Y. (1993) *Liberal Nationalism*. Princeton: Princeton University Press.

Taylor, Charles (1994) 'The Politics of Recognition', in Gutman, A. (ed.), *Multiculturalism: Examining the Politics of Recognition*. Princeton: Princeton University Press.

CHAPTER 10

Toleration as the Public Acceptance of Difference

Anna Elisabetta Galeotti

1   Introductory Remarks

Within the wide area of issues raised by multiculturalism, I have chosen to address questions of toleration/intolerance, which constitute only a small section of the multicultural agenda for a peaceful and civil coexistence of different cultures, groups, minorities in the same democratic society.

Issues of toleration emerge when representatives of minority groups claim public acceptance for their different practices, behaviour, religious and cultural symbols and rituals, acceptance which is resisted by majorities and by public officials on the ground that the differences in question oppose liberal values and contrast with the standards of liberal society. This kind of issue, which has to do with the visibility and the public presence of differences, is probably more acutely felt in Continental Europe where recent waves of immigration are seen as threatening democratic coexistence which implicitly has always been parasitic on national culture. Paradigmatic, in this respect, is the contested acceptance of the Islamic headscarf in public schools in France. However, contemporary cases on toleration arise also in the more multicultural USA: think of the controversy around the admittance of gays to the army, and of the harsh discussion over hate speech – which represents a reverse case, of non-toleration of certain majority attitudes and practices held to be offensive for minority groups.

The focus of my argument will be on this kind of issues which leaves open and untouched many questions of a multicultural society. I will argue that contemporary cases of toleration require a theory of toleration as symbolic recognition of differences, which, in turn, implies a deep revision of the standard liberal view, from which I will start my argument.

2   Setting the Problem

2.1

Questions of toleration arise whenever an individual or a group attempt to check, or to interfere with, other people's disliked or disapproved behaviour and practices which do not concern those who object to them. Conversely, they also emerge when individuals or groups resist other people's interference with, and control of, their own behaviour. Such questions acquire a political dimension when the stand-off between the two contrasting parties cannot find a spontaneous accommodation within society, either via tolerance or via repression. If neither party gives in, then the political authority is called into question in order to solve the conflict. Questions of toleration are directly political when the interfering party is the government itself or a political agent.

The liberal tradition has developed a well-defined interpretative framework and a highly refined normative doctrine to address this issue. Toleration has been implemented through the establishment of legal rights that have been constitutionally granted and firmly entrenched in the culture and practice of liberal democracy. Consequently, it is far from obvious that any politically relevant problem of toleration should arise in a liberal democracy. While the absolutist states of the sixteenth and seventeenth centuries needed to invent toleration as the solution for religious conflicts, in the world of liberal democracy this principle of toleration is generally recognized as the ethically proper way for accommodating differences about what is worth in life and how one should live. Genuine (non-trivial) cases of toleration, those which involve the political authority which is then faced with the alternative as to whether certain practices and behaviour qualify for state non-interference and/or protection, typically characterize totalitarian or authoritarian states where dissent concerning the regime's doctrine and practice can challenge the system as a whole. For any specific case of dissent, the political authority should then take a decision whether the best move is repression or toleration.

However, within liberal democracy questions of political toleration appear to be answered by the constitutional framework of the state. On the one hand, political dissent is indeed recognized as the fundamental and positive trait of democratic life whereby government is always checked by the opposition. Political dissent, thus, is not a matter for toleration, but a constitutive part of the rules of the game. On the other hand, the liberal state historically was built around an ideal of toleration that emerged during the religious conflicts of the sixteenth and seventeenth centuries. Generally speaking, the idea that differences in matters of religion, lifestyles, moral and aesthetic values and so on do not constitute a legitimate concern for politics, but rather belong to the individual's sphere of liberty, is embodied in liberal constitutions and translated into a system of rights. The inclusion of the ideal of toleration in constitutional rights, and which meant to protect individual freedom of conscience, expression and association renders toleration superfluous. If everyone is granted the right to entertain and to pursue his or her conception of the good and a corresponding lifestyle – as long as no harm to any third party is produced – the state has no right to tolerate any different forms of behaviour, ideas and morality, since it has no right to tolerate what it has no warrant to forbid in the first place.

As Thomas Paine remarked about the 1791 French Constitution, when universal rights were recognized, toleration no longer had reason to be practiced:

> The French constitution hath abolished or renounced toleration, and intoleration also, and hath established universal rights of conscience. Toleration is not the opposite of intoleration, but it is the counterfeit of it. Both are despotism. The one assumes to itself the right of withholding liberty of conscience, and the other of granting it. The one is the pope, armed with fire and faggot, and the other is the pope selling or granting indulgences. The former is Church and State, and the latter is Church and traffic (Paine, 1989: 94).

A similar understanding of the connection between toleration and despotism is implicitly made by Kant in *An Answer to the Question: What is Enlightenment?*, commenting on the attitude of Friedrich the Great about religious freedom. Kant points out that the enlightened king has acknowledged that it is his duty to refrain from any interference with the religious choices of his subjects and to grant them full liberty on this matter. Kant remarks that Friedrich has given up toleration, adopting instead the principle of freedom of thought (Kant, 1991). Thus both Kant and Paine state that the practice of toleration is always the counterpart of an arbitrary power, while the bill of rights of liberal politics provides a more proper solution for the problem, in so far as it offers a universal answer to the question of toleration.

In the world of liberal democracy infringements of toleration can occur and even be frequent. Regretful as they are, these episodes do not usually raise genuine theoretical and political problems, as the theory and the practice of toleration is generally equipped to answer them. Also cases of toleration may easily arise in everyday interactions: in relationship between neighbours, or among fellow travellers on a train, among colleagues in the workplace and so on. But these many familiar problems are not considered political issues of toleration. Thus, in a world where toleration is a shared value besides occasional infringements of the principle and besides politically irrelevant everyday-life cases, there is prima facie no room for cases genuinely engendering a theoretical and political discussion of toleration.

2.2

However, when toleration becomes an inbuilt virtue of the liberal order, issues about toleration do still arise, and not only because of our incapability to live up to the ideal. Especially in the last decade or so, non-trivial questions have often exploded and acquired a prominent position in liberal politics, engendering a corresponding theoretical interest in the topic. More assertive internal minorities and new waves of immigration in Europe, the United States and Australia are probably the cause of this recent development. The result is a more conflictual and more complex pluralistic society, for which the traditional ideal and the social practice of toleration seems to be dramatically insufficient (Losano, 1991: 7-16; Bencivenga, 1992). This may partly depend on the difficulty of implementing the principle, which is in turn due to the vagueness of its limits which have always been a matter of controversy. Yet, when the principle of toleration is infringed, or when its implementation in a given instance is a matter for discussion, liberal theory is equipped with theoretical models and arguments that in principle provide persuasive answers to any given instance. By contrast, when non-trivial questions of toleration arise, liberal toleration appears inadequate, that is insufficient, on the one hand, and too hospitable, on the other.

I intend to argue that the problem of liberal theories of toleration does not lie primarily in its normative argument but, rather, in its underlying interpretative framework. The nature of the problem is therefore more complex than liberal theory assumes. Hence, contemporary non-trivial, genuine questions are not properly grasped and consequently not satisfactorily met by liberal theory. No normative proposal can be adequate if it answers a different question different from the one that has been asked. Thus, the first task of a contemporary theory of toleration is to understand the nature of the problem anew.

3   Liberal Toleration and Contemporary Issues

3.1

Liberal theory understands the issue of toleration as produced by the disagreement and conflict around values, religion, culture and so on, a conflict which is the more serious the more pluralistic democratic societies have become. The classical theory of toleration has shown that individual liberties in matters of faith, morality and lifestyle can peacefully coexist without hindering political stability and social cohesiveness.

Within the liberal tradition, toleration has been defended as a value at various social and analytical levels. First of all, it has been presented as the political principle which traces a line between the private domain freed from state intervention and protected from a third party's invasion, and the political sphere which is indifferent and blind with reference to the many views and creeds held by its citizens. In this way, the political principle of toleration ensures the orderly display of individual liberties, on the one hand, and an equality of public treatment which is independent of religion, morality and lifestyles, on the other. Secondly, toleration is seen to be a fundamental social value of liberal society, since it allows for pluralism, individual experiments and a wide menu of options that make autonomy substantial and provide opportunities for individual self-development and meaningful choices. Finally, toleration is also presented as a moral virtue that provides individuals with moral reasons for accepting what they do not share, or even disapprove of, in others' behaviour, out of respect for the others' autonomy or integrity. The moral virtue of toleration can thus bridge the gap between the political principle and the social value of toleration, on the one hand, and private convictions and moral norms, on the other. In other words, toleration can be seen not only as a reasonable solution for the irreducible clash of values, and can be endorsed not only because it allows for social plurality and openness, but also because it is a moral virtue, at least from the point of view of all those convictions that acknowledge the respect for other people as a fundamental value.

All in all, the classical and contemporary theory of toleration provides the normative solution, at the political, social and interpersonal levels, for certain kinds of conflicts, namely those produced by the clash of religious creeds, moral values and ideological views, which are usually described as irreducible, non-adjudicative and non-negotiable. It is a case of identity conflict, yet one which can be conceptualized in terms of chosen or revisable differences, ultimately referred to individuals. The solution provided by toleration consists in acknowledging that individual choices are sovereign in certain matters where uniformity is neither possible nor necessary and perhaps not even desirable. In other words, toleration amounts to granting every citizen equal liberty concerning religious, moral and personal choices, and difference-blindness in public action and treatment.

3.2

If moral and religious conflict has been provided with such a sophisticated multi-layered normative answer, why should it still give rise to non-trivial issues within pluralistic democracy? Though attempts to limit freedom of expression and to interfere with privacy are still de facto present in liberal democratic society, in such circumstances liberal theory is not challenged and can provide soundly built arguments in favour of toleration.[1] From a theoretical viewpoint, moral, religious and ideological differences constitute the solved problem of political toleration.[2]

However, contemporary issues of toleration such as the permission of wearing Islamic headscarves in public schools, the admission of gays to the army, the ban of racist speech on campuses, seem to imply more than conflict over religious and moral differences, and cannot easily be fitted into the traditional theoretical framework. If this holds true, then contemporary issues of toleration may not find satisfactory answers in traditional liberal views. This is not because there is a problem in the normative argument, but because the interpretative framework grounding the normative theory of toleration needs to be reconceptualized.

I hold that, even if conflicting differences in the conceptions of the good or in worldviews are also present in today's most controversial cases, they are neither the only conflictual aspect, nor the most salient. Although we actually recognize such cases as cases about toleration just because they imply a disagreement about how life should be lived and why it should be lived in a particular way, what gives rise to most contemporary genuine issues of toleration are, in fact, differences linked to groups more than to individuals. This is crucial. Group differences normally have an ascriptive nature, in so far as they are not matters of choice, as in the case of classical toleration. Moreover the groups whose differences constitute issues for toleration have usually been excluded from full citizenship and from the full enjoyment of rights, either because they are latecomers on the scene, or because they were previously oppressed and/or invisible. Within the pluralism of groups, cultures and collective identities, the salient conflict does not primarily concern moral disagreement, but rather asymmetries in social standing, status, respect and social and public recognition, which then sustain ideological and cultural contrasts.[3] In other words, it is the exclusion or the unequal and incomplete inclusion of various groups into democratic citizenship which sharpens cultural differences.[4] Controversies over toleration then break out when cultural differences are publicly exhibited, implicitly claiming their presence as legitimate. These differences are perceived as such by the cultural majority because they are at odds with social standards. In the stand-off which usually follows, toleration is then usually invoked as a first step towards inclusion, as a form of public recognition of collective identity of a marginalized, oppressed or invisible group.

Thus, the members of such groups, by and large, are not simply content with toleration of their differences and culture in the private domain (which is actually already granted), but precisely claim its public acceptance. In this respect, contemporary issues around toleration have to do with a double extension of the liberal notion: first, a spatial extension from the private to the public domain, and second, a semantic extension from the negative meaning of non-interference, letting go and putting up with the positive sense of acceptance and recognition (Apel, 1997).

At a first glance, both extensions look troublesome for liberal theory and put into question the very central notion of a neutral and impartial public sphere. Yet, as I will more properly show in sections four and five below, liberal worries are misplaced in this regard, given that the notion of neutrality admits other interpretations beside public difference-blindness and secularism.

3.3

It must be remarked that the reduction of cultural and group pluralism to moral and religious pluralism is neither impossible *per se* nor theoretically illegitimate: as a matter of fact, it has already and successfully been performed just at the origin of the modern theory of toleration.[5]

After all, the religious wars following the Reformation took place among groups, churches and sects, struggling to assert their public presence, to gain public recognition and collective liberty (Sigler, 1983; Day, 1987; Gostin, 1988). The doctrine of toleration which provided the political and philosophical response to religious conflict, faced the problem by means of representing it as the struggle of irreducible religious consciences.[6] The reduction of religious identity to individual conscience, to the private forum, was successful in that it was generally accepted, probably because it appeared as the only viable alternative to persecution and to the suppression of dissenting creeds.[7]

But in contemporary democracy, physical survival and religious freedom are generally taken for granted; hence permanent and new minorities can afford to contest the traditional grounding of toleration, and claim more than equal liberty of conscience in the private sphere. As contemporary minority groups have become more assertive, their claims to the public visibility of their differences have consequently grown louder, engendering a veritable political issue (Gitlin, 1993: 172-177). However besides political reasons, there are ethical ones of fairness in that those claims should be taken seriously – as I will argue later. Hence, the reduction of the circumstances of toleration to moral conflict has now turned out to be inadequate, and not only for theoretical reasons but also for practical ones, for it is rejected by the potentially tolerated, and consequently it proves unfit to settle the stand-off.

4   Toleration and Justice

4.1

If what is really at stake in contemporary issues of toleration is equal respect, status and opportunity for groups rather than equal liberties for individuals, then such problems may be matters for justice instead of toleration. In other words, if contemporary questions of toleration cannot be answered by traditional liberal views, this would not constitute a failure of liberal theory; however, the answers would then rest on the (wrong) definition of the case as one pertaining to matters of toleration. In many cases, the answer more properly concerns distributive justice. If that is the case, then solutions for questions of toleration lie in the appropriate interplay of liberal theories of toleration and of justice.

A first possible reconceptualization of contemporary toleration issues is their inclusion into the distributive liberal paradigm (Galeotti, 1995). If moral, religious and ideological conflicts have in principle already been solved by liberal toleration, while what is still an open question are the asymmetries among social groups in terms of social status, respect, recognition, and of actual enjoyment of rights, then contemporary questions of toleration may in fact be better addressed by the appropriate specification of the liberal theory of distributive justice.

In sum, according to this viewpoint, in order to confront contemporary questions of toleration adequately, liberal theory must acknowledge that matters of distributive justice are significantly involved and that the normative theory of toleration must consequently be supplemented by the theory of distributive justice.[8]

At that point, the liberal theory of justice faces a thorny problem because the subjects of the distribution are not individuals, but groups whose members do not equally share the same disadvantages (Rae, 1981). Leaving this issue aside, the problem of toleration could be recaptured within a well-known line of inquiry of liberal thinking, that is, the distributive paradigm. The latter may be pressed hard when dealing with blocs instead of individuals, but it has already confronted the controversial issue of preferential treatments, and is in principle equipped with conceptual tools capable of dealing with differences (think, for example, of the well-known difference principle advanced by John Rawls (1971).

Equating contemporary questions of toleration to matters of justice, to be dealt with by the appropriate expansion of the distributive paradigm, would leave the normative theory of toleration intact and would avoid questioning the principle of state neutrality and the public-private divide (though the boundary can be moved). It would also avoid the risk of particular memberships and collective identities trespassing into the public domain of citizenship, which should instead remain the area of what must be shared in common, the very ground of democratic legitimacy, of the overlapping consensus, of public reasons for the liberal-democratic order to be preserved. If the distributive paradigm could be stretched out far enough to meet the problems of unequal respect, social standing, and opportunities linked to the membership in disadvantaged groups, then the liberal ideal of toleration would be properly fulfilled. On the one hand, full freedom of expression to individual and group differences in terms of religion, culture, morality and lifestyle would be granted, and, on the other, people would be freed from the burden of their differences, from the disadvantages carried along by certain memberships. From this viewpoint, John Rawls' political theory proves to be the most advanced, having attempted to solve the question of tolerance by linking it to that of distributive criteria.

4.2

Yet something escapes from the reconceptualization of issues of toleration within the liberal distributive paradigm. What liberal theory does not address is a proper and careful consideration of social differences, which are the very stuff of questions of toleration. Generally speaking, for liberal theory, all social differences, not only those of religion and culture, but also those of race and sex, are in principle equally indifferent from a political standpoint (Dworkin, 1985). They are considered differences pertaining to the sphere of personal liberty, fundamental in existential terms, yet politically irrelevant, except for the fact that some of them unfairly count as carriers of privileges or disadvantages. As sources of injustice these differences become politically relevant only from the perspective of being all equally pushed off the area that pertains to politics and public life. Political neutralization of all social differences of all kinds is indeed the final goal of the liberal theory of toleration, and in order to attain it, distributive justice may be required in the first place to balance the disadvantages carried along with some differences.

However, in this perspective social differences are considered only as disadvantages and this is probably not the best strategy for addressing the asymmetries of respect and public consideration experienced by 'different' groups. Moreover, the neutralist option characterizing this approach prevents liberal theory from understanding that not all social differences are in fact considered 'different', and that only few of them mark their bearers with a 'different' received identity. Reversing George Orwell's famous line that some are more equal than others, we find that some are also more different than others. For example, whiteness is not considered a difference and being white, like being Christian, heterosexual and so on, is not being 'different' or an 'other'. What is defined as different is in fact perceived that way from the standpoint of the majority of a society. The latter has the power to define people, cultures, languages, practices as 'different', implying that its own traits and characters are normal. And belonging to the 'normal' people or to a different group brings about something more than an unequal distribution of resources or opportunity among social groups; rather it defines the capability of being a full or a second-rate citizen.[9] In fact, from a neutralist viewpoint, all differences are equally different, and the distinction between traits, characters, behaviour, options which are perceived as 'normal', and those which are singled out as 'different' is not appreciated. But this distinction is crucial, defining inclusion and exclusion in a given society. Inclusion and exclusion here do not refer to the enjoyment of legal rights, but rather to the public consideration as members of the political and social community – a consideration applying not despite one's origin, culture, skin colour or sexual preference, but precisely given such features (Galeotti, 1994).

Being the bearer of a different identity which is socially invisible, despised or stigmatized constitutes a special barrier for becoming a functioning citizen and social actor. As I have mentioned, it is not just a matter of enjoying fewer resources and opportunities, though this is often the case; it is also a matter of having fewer capabilities for making use of them, and of having one's aspirations, expectations, and projects moulded below the threshold of those of the majority's members (Sen, 1985; Fiss, 1975-76: 107-177). If one's different collective identity is socially invisible, erased or despised, stigmatized, subjected to prejudices and stereotyping, those who are identified by it usually experience lack of confidence and of self-esteem, as well as various forms of self-hatred which, *ceteris paribus*, makes it much more difficult for them to become functioning social agents and full citizens.

If a different identity is understood as an incapability threshold for its bearers beyond actual scarcity of resources and opportunities, then this problem, which underlies questions of toleration, cannot be addressed simply by adjustments in the distributive structure of society. The distributive paradigm is designed for a fair social allocation of opportunities and resources, of rights and goods; in this case, however, what is at stake is the social (negative) perception of certain collective identities marked as different, a perception which negatively affects the chances and aspirations of the corresponding group's members. The majority's perception of social differences is politically relevant, and it is so in two senses: firstly, it constitutes a disadvantage for the bearers of difference, making it more difficult for them to command resources and opportunities; hence it causes social injustice. Secondly, it excludes minority people from certain preconditions for full participation in democratic citizenship. The feeling of shame, humiliation and self-hatred experienced in connection with one's different membership and reinforced by the required public invisibility of one's identity prevents people from developing self-respect and an adequate level of self-esteem.[10] Self-respect and a reasonable amount of self-esteem are necessary for developing one's voice and for making it heard, which in turn is the condition for enjoying rights and in general for full participation in the polity.

I hold that contemporary questions of toleration have exactly to do with these kinds of problems. Claims for toleration of differences are neither simply concerned with freedom of expression, nor primarily with compensatory redistribution for disadvantages linked to certain differences. What is at stake is neither personal liberty, nor inequality of resources, but rather the ways in which people are regarded socially and publicly, ways which can define someone as a second-rate citizen or as full member of the community. Questions of toleration are usually raised when questions of public acceptance, the protection of social differences and collective identities are at issue. These questions may be linked to permanent or new minorities who are excluded or not fully included within pluralist democratic society (Islamic communities, gays, blacks, women, immigrants and so on).

5 Reconceptualizing Toleration

5.1

So far we have established that: a) the contemporary issue of toleration concerns the majoritarian (negative) perception of minority groups, a perception which is fixed in a different collective identity that is subject to prejudices and humiliation in social life, and formally bracketed in the public sphere because of public neutrality; b) this issue is politically relevant for liberal-democratic theory, given that differences represent barriers preventing their bearers from full membership in the polity; c) neither its traditional conception of toleration nor distributive measures can satisfactorily face questions of toleration under this interpretation; d) consequently, claims to toleration raised by minority groups aim at reversing the requirement of public invisibility, implied by public difference-blindness. This reversal, however, constitutes an impossible attainment for minority members who are trapped between a received group identity that is a source of discrimination and various kinds of disadvantages which cannot be dismissed at will, on the one hand, and the required public invisibility of that very identity in the name of difference-blindness and universal citizenship, on the other. Moreover, this public blindness constitutes an unfair requirement: while minority members are required to mask their different characters, traits, and behaviour in their capacity as citizens, majority members can participate in the polity without any masking, given that their traits are not seen as a mark of any special identity, but represent normality. As such, they are perceived simply as human, and not as group attributes.

At this point, the relevant question is the following: in what sense can a revised conception of toleration, one that takes into account the circumstances just described, meet the claims of public recognition of differences which underlie issues of toleration? I argue that toleration can do the job, if it is considered in its symbolic meaning as a public gesture legitimizing the public presence of differences and of corresponding identities on the same footing as the majoritarian traits, practices and identities.

Let us consider controversial cases such as the acceptance of the Islamic headscarf in public schools, or the admission of gays to the army. In these instances, toleration means literally nothing more than granting the liberty to be and to express one's culture and identity in a given public space. In this respect there is no significant difference with classical toleration, and that is precisely why we recognize such hard contemporary cases as pertaining to matters of toleration.

An extension of classical toleration from the private sphere to the public domain characterizes contemporary cases. In the literal sense, contemporary toleration consists in an extension of personal liberty from private spheres to the public domain, an extension which is generally argued on the basis of the non-discrimination principle and of a more appropriate interpretation of neutrality. For example, in the 'headscarf affair', the principle of the secular state which grounds the argument for the prohibition of the Islamic 'hijab' did not prevent the presence of Christian and Jewish symbols at school. In a word, it has not treated secular, Christian, Jewish and Muslim students as equals, that is, it has not granted them the same consideration and respect (Galeotti, 1993: 585-605). As for the admission of gays to the army, here the principle of neutrality was clearly suspended, thus producing discriminatory effects: if homosexuals are accepted in the army, they will be treated just like anybody else of any sexual preference, hence fulfilling the neutrality principle. Contemporary non-trivial questions first of all imply a literal sense of toleration which is indeed in line with the classical liberal conception, that is, with granting non-interference with some people's behaviour and practice. What is specific in these contemporary cases are only claims for the extension of toleration into certain public domains.

Such extensions can nevertheless be perceived as problematic when it appears to contrast with the ideal of public neutrality, that is, when it is seen as not bringing down barriers and de-segregating certain groups (as the gays in the army), but, rather, as a trespassing of specific groups in the public neutral, secular sphere (as in the 'hijab' case). There is a direct answer, though, to this point that refers back to the anti-discriminatory goal underlying the neutrality ideal. If the principle of the secular state, which has represented one of the possible interpretations of public neutrality, allows some people to be treated with less than equal respect because of their religion and culture, it means that this ideal is not a good interpretation of neutrality, since it fails to attain its anti-discriminatory goals.

5.2

Before addressing the symbolic aspect of toleration though, I would like to make a further point in relation to its literal aspect in contemporary non-trivial cases. Genuine cases are not only those where public toleration of a different trait or practice linked to some minority group is at issue. There are also cases of limits to individual freedom for (generally majority) behaviour and practices, which allegedly have the effect of offending and damaging the identity and social perception of minorities or oppressed groups. The well-known controversies on hate-speech and pornography belong to this second category of contemporary questions of toleration.[11] The circumstances, as well as what is at stake, are similar for both categories: differences and collective identities linked to oppressed, marginalized or excluded groups which claim their full inclusion in liberal society via public recognition and protection of their different identities. But the actual quest for identity runs in opposite directions: in the first case, it is public toleration of one's difference; in the second case, it is non-toleration of certain (offensive) behaviour as a form of political protection for one's difference.

Whether this second claim for non-toleration is legitimate is a complex matter. At present, I only want to point out that these cases also imply a literal meaning of toleration which is continuous with the classical conception. What is at issue here are some limits to toleration with regard to individual freedom of expression, which is claimed to cause various kinds of damage, harm and offence to the members of disadvantaged, discriminated or oppressed groups. The arguments for non-toleration usually combine the classical harm principle with the principle of redress and compensation of past and persistent discrimination as a justification for a special public protection for some groups. In other words, John Stuart Mill's classical argument for limiting toleration is supplemented with an argument from distributive justice, yet applied to groups. There are actually various reasons for objecting to those arguments, but what I shall underline here is that, if they are to be satisfied, those claims literally imply some limits to toleration, that is, some regulation of freedom of expression, grounded on special justifications. Assuming the justifications can be accepted as sound, the limits of toleration would be absolutely in line with the classical liberal conception which has always recognized that toleration must be limited at the point beyond which third parties might be harmed, or else the very tolerant society would be jeopardized. Whether or not such limits can be accepted as sound is another matter which cannot be settled by considering exclusively the literal meaning of toleration.

However, this literal meaning of toleration, which I have shown to be in line with the liberal doctrine and around which most of the present discussion is engaged, especially with reference to the legitimacy of extending toleration in the public sphere and of fixing certain limits, by no means exhausts the sense of toleration in pluralistic democracy. As argued above, genuine cases of toleration do still arise in liberal democracy despite the fact that individual rights there are already granted, because what is at stake is something beyond freedom of conscience, of expression and privacy. I have outlined an alternative interpretation of the circumstances, claims and controversies characterizing contemporary questions of toleration, arguing that they are irreducible to matters of individual preferences, opinions and values. In my reading, the crucial point underlying genuine questions of toleration is the inclusion of members of minority groups into democratic citizenship through the public recognition and protection of their different excluded identities. And the public recognition of different identities can be attained by means of public toleration, if the right kind of reasons allows for its symbolic meaning to be displayed.[12]

6 The Symbolic Meaning of Toleration

6.1

The literal meaning of contemporary toleration is basically the same as in the classical conception; but, despite the fact that disputes can arise around toleration in the literal sense (its extension, its limits, etc.): conquering an extra piece of liberty or stopping someone else's alleged offensive behaviour is not the main reason why toleration is invoked and considered important by those who want their differences admitted and protected in the public space. Take the example of gays in the army – if the literal access of homosexuals to the army was the issue at stake then the compromising policy 'no one asks, no one tells' should be sufficient. However, such a policy, which is de facto tolerant, cannot be satisfactory for an oppressed minority struggling for its visibility and public acceptance, because it misses the symbolic implication of representing an official gesture or act of public recognition of that difference as legitimate. Thus, while a de facto tolerance grants the literal meaning of toleration, opening up new spaces of liberty for the tolerated, it fails completely to meet the symbolic meaning, which is actually the reason why toleration in that instance is pursued and is important. Similarly, having the Islamic headscarf tolerated in public schools in France means something more than conquering a fuller religious freedom: it actually means the public visibility of Islamic culture and identity on an equal footing with the majority's religious and cultural identities.

If the symbolic meaning of toleration in contemporary cases overcomes the literal meaning, then some consequences must be considered for redrawing a theory of toleration. First of all, it becomes crucial that toleration be backed by the right reasons. Supporting toleration for the wrong reason may destroy the possibility that its symbolic meaning becomes a form of public recognition of differences. The right reasons consist in arguments from justice, for equality of respect and dignity, stemming from a proper consideration of the circumstances and claims.

For example, in the long and ongoing controversy in France known as '*l'affaire du foulard*', after the initial prohibition of the headscarf decided by the school officials, and after the case had become political, the then socialist Minister of Education, Lionel Jospin, asked for the official opinion of the *Conseil d'Etat*. The latter took the position that religious symbols can be admitted in the public school, as long as they are not used for proselytizing and as long as they do not hinder regular teaching and order in class. Based on this opinion, the ministry allowed the headscarf at school, as a private expression of one's faith. In this way the underlying claim to public recognition of the Islamic identity was bypassed; and not by chance this compromising decision did not settle the issue. The fact is that the Islamic headscarf, in the French context, is not a quiet, private symbol of one's religion, but is a provocative and loud public statement of one's cultural identity. In this way, it was perceived by the French people who, correctly in my view, understood that the claim implied by the scarf went beyond freedom of expression and strongly resisted the symbolic meaning of the public toleration of the *hijab*. So it happened that the new conservative Ministry of Education, in autumn 1994, sent the school principals throughout the country a new directive implying the prohibition of the headscarf at school. Actually the new regulation was grounded on the very same opinion of the *Conseil d'Etat*: like most of his fellow-countrymen, Minister Bayrou considered the headscarf as a provocative sign which implied a proselytizing attitude and decreed that it should be prohibited without explicitly mentioning it. This case is paradigmatic: if the decision in favour of toleration is not backed by the right reasons, the contest is not finally settled, because, on the one hand, its relevant claims are not properly met, and, on the other, the compromising decision in principle takes side with the argument favouring prohibition, hence giving ground to the resistance against toleration. In a word, liberal toleration proves inadequate for solving contemporary cases, because it is not grounded in the right kind of reasons, as long as it refers to reasons allowing only for its literal meaning.

6.2

Secondly, if the public recognition of differences is the symbolic side-effect of the public toleration of a different behaviour, or of an aspect of a different practice, then clearly the kind of recognition involved here has nothing to do with a public appreciation of a difference or with a declaration of its value, or even its public endorsement, as the notion of public recognition is often assumed to imply (Taylor, 1993). Here, the notion of public recognition more modestly means the acceptance, hence the inclusion, of a different trait, behaviour, practice or identity in the range of the legitimate, viable, 'normal' options of the open society. It is an indirect negation of the majoritarian definition of something as different, and without questioning its actual content. In this respect the public recognition of differences, being independent from their content, is in fact compatible with public neutrality, since it requires no assessment and no evaluation of the many differences present in pluralist democracy, but rather a tendential opening up of the democratic society so as to enlarge the range of viable options, including different ones on the same footing as normal, familiar and traditional alternatives.

The reason why the symbolic meaning of toleration is so important for the settlement of genuine contemporary cases depends on a conjectural causal chain linking together the lack of public visibility of 'different' identities with the lack of public respect for their bearers and their consequent incapability to develop adequate self-esteem. Given the public invisibility of their identity and its social stigmatization, self-esteem is often pursued at the price of rejecting one's difference, thus humiliating oneself and losing self-respect. If this causal chain holds, and if the public toleration of a different trait and aspect symbolically entails the public acceptance and the legitimation of the correspondent different identity, then this very gesture will signify public respect and consideration to minority members as well as to the majority. This, in turn, should help to build up an adequate amount of self-esteem and self-respect for minority members, so that the preconditions for full citizenship could be fulfilled. If this hypothesis works,[13] then the symbolic aspect of toleration could contribute to the peaceful and respectful coexistence of the various groups inhabiting a pluralist democracy where the individual members could, in principle, be in the position of choosing the terms of their membership. Obviously, toleration will not settle all the issues raised by contemporary pluralism and by the identity conflicts underlying multiculturalism; definitely it will not provide a solution for the distributive problems implied in such conflict. Moreover, toleration will only be suitable for some groups, for some differences and for some claims. Only groups that strive for their inclusion on an equal footing with other citizens, and whose differences can be accepted by the ethical standards of liberal democracy can have their claims met, at least in part, by toleration in its symbolic meaning of public recognition. Yet, this work is not meant to answer the many problems and conflicts produced by contemporary pluralism; rather it is aimed at developing the theory of toleration so as to encompass contemporary genuine questions adequately.

7   Conclusion

In general, toleration, whether classical or contemporary, means securing freedom to express or do something that liberal society or its majority dislikes or finds itself uncomfortable with. The difference between the liberal theory of toleration and the pluralist interpretation I am proposing here lies in the reasons grounding toleration. They differ because the understanding of the circumstances for toleration differs: while the liberal theory takes into account only moral, ideological and religious conflicts, the pluralist interpretation acknowledges identity conflicts, linked to ascriptive groups, and takes the quest for public recognition of social differences as the salient feature of questions of toleration beyond moral disagreement. Such a quest underlying issues of toleration ought to be taken seriously, since it stems from the unequal conditions of social and political membership experienced by bearers of social differences. Marked by a different identity which is publicly invisible and socially stigmatized, members of minority groups generally lack the condition to be full and functioning agents on the same footing as majority people. Thus justice needs to take contemporary claims of toleration seriously. This, however, does not imply that all such claims ought to be directly satisfied and in their own terms. The different understanding of and the more complex reasons for, toleration imply, on the one hand, its extension to the public space, and, on the other hand, its symbolic meaning as public recognition, which represents a first move towards the inclusion of minority members without any requirement of assimilation.

The pluralist model of toleration I am proposing is not meant to replace the liberal theory of toleration. The latter, in its most advanced versions, actually provides persuasive solutions for the clash around values, beliefs, conceptions of the good and world views – at least in those areas where uniformity is not necessary. When there are religious, moral or metaphysical conflicts at stake, toleration in its literal sense of non-interference provides effective responses at the political, social and interpersonal levels.

However, when the issues that produce cases of toleration concern identity conflicts, and when toleration claims, put forward by minority groups, underlie a quest for public recognition of differences, then granting freedom for certain behaviour and practices – as toleration literally does – is not enough; and it does not settle the issue. And yet, it is not necessary to conclude that toleration is simply not relevant for the issues of contemporary pluralism and for identity conflicts, and that it should be substituted by distributive measures or by cultural autonomy, or some other principle. What is needed is rather a more encompassing conception of toleration, accounting for its symbolic meaning as well as for its literal sense. Public toleration symbolically means more than non-interference with certain differences: it means their public acceptance, that is, their legitimation among the viable options of a given society.

This shift modifies the overall argument leading to toleration, from the reconsideration of the circumstances and of the claims for toleration, to the reinterpretation of the grounding reasons as well. The value backing political toleration is always equal respect, in the traditional as in the revised version. But in the traditional view, equal respect is due to people's autonomy and freedom of choice; while here it is due to people's identities and ways of being. Thus the equality that political toleration is supposed to work for is not simply liberty, independently from one's convictions, but also, and especially, public standing and status, independently from one's membership. It is important to stress that here 'independently' does not mean 'despite' and 'bracketing', but, rather, 'given' one's membership, which, in its turn, is something different from 'in virtue of'. In other words, one's collective identity is neither an element to be discounted nor a reason in order to be admitted into citizenship, but a datum, a trait of the person which enters his or her definition as a citizen, just like one's family name, profession and marital status.

As mentioned above, the conception of toleration I am outlining is not equipped to dispel all the issues and conflicts of contemporary pluralism; rather its task consists in fighting the inequalities of citizen status which are consequences of membership in groups different from a society's majority. Hence toleration is appropriate only when the issue is inclusion into citizenship on equal terms for the purpose of civil coexistence under democratic institutions. It is out of place if the issue is group autonomy, cultural or social (self-)segregation or political secession from a democratic society.

Notes

1   On the recurrent problem of the enforcement of morals, see the classical debate by Lord Devlin (1959) and H.H.L. Hart (1962). More recently, on this topic, see Michael Sandel (1989) and Roland Dworkin's response (1989). Recently a moderate form of enforcement of morals has been maintained by Gerald Dworkin (1990).

2   By contrast, moral pluralism is still an open question in moral philosophy. On this aspect, see for example: Larmore (1987), Nagel (1987, 1991), Hampshire (1989), Gutmann/Thompson (1990), Gibbard (1990), Lukes (1991), Wolf (1992), Becker (1992), Wong (1992).

3   That conflicts around recognition of identities are crucial in contemporary democracy is underlined by Alessandro Pizzorno (1993: 187-203), who presents an interesting typology of social conflicts. In different ways, Charles Taylor (1993) also maintains the central role of recognition in contemporary politics.

4   That the notion of citizenship cannot be limited to its formal-legal meaning, but implies something more substantial such as the actual functioning as a citizen, and the actual enjoyment of rights is a view shared by Giovanna Zincone (1992: 187-188), by Judith Shklar (1991) and, more recently, by P. Johnston-Conover and D.D. Searing (1995).

5   That religion was a choice of the individual and that Churches were voluntary associations is the position strongly underlined by John Locke: "I say it [the church] is a free and voluntary society. Nobody is born a member of any church" (Locke, 1963: 23).

6   How such reduction was accomplished and was made use of from Thomas Hobbes to the Enlightenment is convincingly reconstructed by Reinhard Koselleck (1972). A similar view, though emerging from a different perspective, is held also by J.G.A. Pockock (1988). He maintains that the history of religious freedom between the seventeenth and the eighteenth century is a two-step process: the first step consists in the separation of State from Church and in the assertion of political independence from spiritual invasion; and the second step consists in the redefinition of religious experience as holding opinions. In this reductive redescription, the revolutionary spiritualism of many sects is transformed into the radical liberty of private conscience.

7   Moreover, such a reduction presents the further advantage of making the problem of toleration significant not only for politics, but also for moral philosophy. Thus the reasons for toleration

are not simply prudential, but derive from the immorality of coercion in matters of faith. The specific moral dimension implied in reducing of the issue of toleration to religious and moral conflict makes this understanding of toleration and pluralism so favoured among contemporary liberal theorists.

[8] John Rawls, in his *A Theory of Justice*, has indeed captured the problem of toleration within the framework of distributive justice (Rawls, 1971).

[9] The concept of capability has been advanced by Amartya Sen (1985), as a necessary supplement to the notion of acquisitions, be it resources, opportunities or goods, in order to define the individual's well-being and his or her functioning.

[10] One should mention here Rawls' inclusion of self-respect and self-esteem among the primary goods to be distributed according to his second principle of justice which pertains to social and economic inequalities (Rawls, 1971: 62; 178-179; 440-446).

[11] On these themes there is a wide literature; just as examples: on hate speech, see Altmen (1993); on pornography, see: A. Dworkin (1980), Mackinnon (1990, 1993). For the liberal side, see D. Dworkin (1993).

[12] The idea of the symbolic aspect of toleration has been given to me by Steven Lukes' (1997) comment on my work (Galeotti, 1993).

[13] Some social scientists of liberal orientation think on the contrary that any form of public recognition of differences and of collective identities will engender a dangerous process of social fragmentation and pluralistic encapsulation leading to a basic disruption of the body politic. See for example, Schlesinger (1991), Gitlin (1993), Moon (1993). Both hypotheses are so far supported only by anecdotal evidence. I do not deny that there may be a danger of fragmentation, but I think that it can be minimized if a serious politics of inclusion is carried out as soon as problems of toleration arise for all cases which can be captured by the interpretative framework I have outlined. Distributive struggles among groups, and autonomy claims of groups are questions different from those of toleration. It is part of political wisdom to be able to make distinctions between these three cases.

References

Altman, Andrew (1993) 'Liberalism and Campus Hate Speech: A Philosophical Examination', *Ethics* 103: 302-317.
Apel, Karl Otto (1997) 'Plurality of the Good? The Problem of Affirmative Tolerance in a Multicultural Society from an Ethical Point of View', *Ratio Juris* 10: 199-212.
Becker, Lawrence (1992) 'Places for Pluralism', *Ethics* 102: 707-719.
Bencivenga, Ermanno (1992) *Oltre la tolleranza*. Milano: Feltrinelli.
Day, J.P. (1987) *Liberty and Justice*. London: Croom Helm.
Dench, Geoff (1986) *Minorities in the Open Society*. London: Routledge and Kegan Paul.

Devlin, Patrick (1959) *The Enforcement of Morals.* Maccabean Lecture in Jurisprudence. Oxford: Oxford University Press.

Dworkin, Andrea (1980) *Men Possessing Women.* New York: Perigee.

Dworkin, Gerald (1990) 'Equal Respect and the Enforcement of Morals', *Social Philosophy and Policy* 7: 180-193.

Dworkin, Ronald (1985) 'Liberalism', in *A Matter of Principle.* Cambridge, Mass.: Harvard University Press.

Dworkin, Ronald (1985) 'Do We Have a Right to Pornography?', in *A Matter of Principle,* op. cit.

Dworkin, Ronald (1989) 'Liberal Community', *California Law Review* 77: 479-504.

Dworkin, Ronald (1993) 'Women and Pornography', *New York Review of Books,* October 19: 36-42.

Fiss, Owen (1975-76) 'Groups and the Equal Protection Clause', *Philosophy and Public Affairs* 5: 107-177

Galeotti, A.E. (1993) 'Citizenship and Equality: The Place for Toleration', *Political Theory* 21: 585-605.

Galeotti, A.E. (1994) 'Chador e croci della vandea', *Reset,* October.

Galeotti, A.E. (1994) *La tolleranza. Una proposta pluralista.* Napoli: Liguori.

Galeotti, A.E. (1995) 'Tolerance et justice', in Affichard, J./Foucauld, J.B. de (eds.), *Pluralisme et equité.* Paris: Esprit.

Galeotti, A.E. (1995) 'Questioni di giustizia e questioni di tolleranza', *Filosofia e questioni pubbliche* 1: 64-78.

Gibbard, Alan (1990) *Wise Choices, Apt Feelings.* Harvard University Press: Cambridge Mass.

Gitlin, Todd (1993) 'The Rise of "Identity Politics" ', *Dissent,* Spring: 172-177.

Gostin, Larry (ed.) (1988) *Civil Liberties in Conflict.* London: Routledge.

Gutmann, Amy/Thompson, Dennis (1990) 'Moral Conflict and Political Consensus', *Ethics* 101: 64-88.

Hampshire, Stuart (1989) *Innocence and Experience.* Cambridge Mass.: Harvard University Press.

Hart, H.H.L. (1962) *Law, Liberty and Morality.* Oxford: Oxford University Press.

Johnston-Conover, Pamela/Searing, Donald D. (1995) 'Citizens and Members: Dilemmas of Accommodation for Cultural Minorities', *mimeo,* Bordeaux.

Kant, Immanuel, (1991) 'Answer to the Question: What is Enlightenment?' (1783), in *Political Writings,* edited with an introduction and notes by Hans Reis, translated by H.B. Nisbet. Cambridge: Cambridge University Press.

Koselleck, Reinhard (1972) *Critica illuministica e crisi della società borghese.* Bologna: Il Mulino.

Larmore, Charles (1987) *The Patterns of Moral Complexity.* Cambridge: Cambridge University Press.

Locke, John (1963) *A Letter concerning Toleration,* ed. by Mario Montuori. The Hague: Nijhoff.

Losano, Mario G. (1991) 'Contro una società multietnica', *Micromega,* December: 7-16.

Lukes, Steven (1991) *Moral Conflict and Politics.* Oxford: Oxford University Press.

Lukes, Steven (1997) 'Toleration and Recognition', *Ratio Juris* 10: 213-222.

Mackinnon, Catherine (1990) 'Sexuality, Pornography and Method: Pleasure under Patriarchy', in Sunstein, Cass (ed.), *Toward a Feminist Theory of the State*. Chicago: Chicago University Press.

Mackinnon, Catherine (1993) *Only Words*. Cambridge, Mass.: Harvard University Press.

Moon, Donald (1993) *Constructing Community*. Princeton: Princeton University Press.

Nagel, Thomas (1987) 'Moral Conflict and Political Legitimacy', *Philosophy and Public Affairs* 16: 215-240;

Nagel, Thomas (1991) *Equality and Impartiality*. Oxford: Oxford University Press.

Paine, Thomas (1989) *The Rights of Man,* Part 1 (1791), in *Thomas Paine. Political Writings*, edited by Bruce Kuklick. Cambridge: Cambridge University Press.

Pizzorno, Alessandro (1993) *Le radici della politica assoluta*. Milano: Feltrinelli.

Pockock, J.G.A. (1988) 'Religious Freedom and the Desacralization of Politics: from the English Civil Wars to the Virginia Statute', pp. 43-73 in *The Virginia Statute for Religious Freedom*, edited by M.D. Peterson and R.C. Vaughan. Cambridge: Cambridge University Press.

Rae, Douglas (1981) *Equalities*. Cambridge, Mass.: Harvard University Press.

Rawls, John (1971) *A Theory of Justice*. Cambridge, Mass.: Harvard University Press.

Sandel, Michael (1989) 'Moral Argument and Liberal Toleration: Abortion and Homosexuality', *California Law Review* 77: 521-538.

Schlesinger, A.M. jr. (1991) *The Disuniting of America*. New York: Norton and Company.

Sen, A.K. (1985) 'Well-Being and Freedom', *Journal of Philosophy* 82: 169-221.

Shklar, Judith (1991) *American Citizenship: The Quest for Inclusion*. Cambridge, Mass.: Harvard University Press.

Sigler, Jay A. (1983) *Minority Rights. A Comparative Analysis*. London: Greenwood Press.

Taylor, Charles, (1993) 'The Politics of Recognition', in Gutman, Amy (ed.), *Multiculturalism. Examining the Politics of Recognition*. Princeton, NJ.: Princeton University Press.

Wolf, Susan (1992) 'Two Levels of Pluralism', *Ethics* 102: 785-798.

Wong, B. (1992) 'Coping with Moral Conflict and Ambiguity', *Ethics* 102: 763-784.

Young, Iris, (1990) *Justice and the Politics of Difference*. Princeton: Princeton University Press.

Zincone, Giovanna (1992) *Da sudditi a cittadini*. Bologna: Il Mulino.

CHAPTER 11

How Can Collective Rights and Liberalism Be Reconciled?[1]

Daniel M. Weinstock

The increasing frequency and urgency of claims to political autonomy and cultural protection made by cultural minorities in multinational and multi-ethnic states raises the question of the extent to which liberal theory – as well as real-world liberal constitutions – can accommodate such claims by incorporating collective provisions for minorities without thereby violating any central liberal tenets. I want to wade into the nexus of issues which this question raises in the following manner: first, I will briefly highlight those aspects of liberal theory which would seem to constitute insurmountable obstacles to any liberal theory of collective rights. Second, I will outline and assess the most systematic and rigorous attempt at showing that the conflict between liberal theory and collective rights is only apparent, and at elaborating a recognizably liberal theory of collective rights, that of Will Kymlicka. And finally, I will try to suggest certain ways in which the flaws in Kymlicka's arguments can nonetheless suggest avenues which future research in this area might follow.

I.

On the face of it, there seem to be at least three central normative commitments in liberal theory which would appear to prevent liberals from acknowledging the legitimacy of collective measures such as group rights (Arblaster, 1986; Waldron, 1993).[2] First, liberalism is committed to moral individualism, both at the justificatory and at the policy levels. With respect to the former level, liberals believe that political principles and institutions acquire legitimacy to the extent that they can be justified – at least hypothetically – to individual agents, given their individual interests and conceptions of the good life. At the level of policy, liberals are wary of governmental measures which abridge individual rights for the sake of the 'collective good'. The primary aim of liberalism, or so it has seemed to many of its most influential proponents, is to specify and secure the conditions required for individuals to be able to pursue their independently arrived at plans of life without undue governmental coercion, and in the absence of interference by other individual agents. In contrast, those who have argued for collective political measures have typically tended to attribute independent worth to groups (be they nations, ethnic groups, cultures, or nebulously defined 'communities') at least comparable to that which they attribute to individuals, and have argued that, on occasion at least, the interests of collectivities must take precedence over those of individuals. There seems to be at least *prima facie* incompatibility between liberalism's moral individualism and a recognition of collective rights which might place the priority of the individual in question.

Second, the most prominent liberal theorists have been wedded to the idea of state neutrality among groups, namely to the idea that the formulation of policy ought not to make reference to any particular conception of the good or cultural form of life. This need for governmental restraint is seen to flow from the foundational idea that a liberal state ought to manifest equal concern and respect to all its citizens (Mason, 1990: 20). The enshrinement of collective rights for some groups rather than others is seen as running foul of this fundamental egalitarian commitment. The recognition of collective rights for all groups would however give rise to what I would call the Pandora's Box problem: there are potentially a very great number of collective claims that can be made from within the civil society of a reasonably pluralistic society, and recognizing them all through special measures could balkanize it and effectively prevent governments from legislating with a view to the common good. The Pandora's Box problem could seem to suggest that neutrality is both ethically and prudentially the best option. Claims for collective rights are, however, most often premised on the idea that some differences are more different than others, that is, that certain group characteristics warrant special entitlements, exemptions from laws that hold more generally, whereas others do not. For example, those who argue for the collective rights of the *Quebecois* within the Canadian constitution hold that there is something about the *Quebecois* as a collectivity which warrants their being granted self-government rights within the Canadian Constitution which it would be inappropriate to grant to other groups within the Canadian political community, say Prince Edward Islanders or gays.

Finally, liberalism is committed to what might be called a non-teleological or procedural view of the political process. Liberals are concerned not to constrain the outcomes to which the political process gives rise, as long as that process does not curtail the area of free choice within which individuals can pursue whatever conception of the good they see fit to pursue. Were the political process thus construed to make certain forms of collective life more difficult to pursue than others, this would be so much the worse for the form of life in question. The following claim by John Rawls is typical in this respect:

> If a comprehensive conception of the good is unable to endure in a society securing the familiar equal basic liberties and mutual toleration, there is no way to preserve it consistent with democratic values as expressed by the idea of society as a fair system of cooperation among citizens viewed as free and equal. This raises, but of course does not settle, the question of whether the corresponding way of life is viable under other historical conditions, and whether its passing is to be regretted (Rawls, 1993: 198).[3]

Defenders of the cultural claims of communities can obviously not accept a purely procedural conception of the political such as this, and they have therefore argued that politics can legitimately be geared towards the pursuit of collective goods, such as the flourishing, or at the very least the survival, of cultures.

Weighty considerations apparently central to liberal theory therefore stand in the way of its ability to incorporate collective rights. I want now to turn to Will Kymlicka's important recent writings aiming to show that this incompatibility is only apparent.

II.

The most rigorous and systematic attempt to show that the incompatibility just described between liberalism and the acceptance of collective measures such as collective rights is actually only apparent can be found in Will Kymlicka's writings (Kymlicka, 1989; 1995). I want briefly to run through his principal arguments.

Kymlicka has argued that, far from it being the case that collective rights conflict with liberalism's moral individualism, the latter positively requires the former. In his view, secure cultural membership is a primary good as essential to individual well-being as are the more traditional liberal goods, such as material provision and freedom of conscience, movement, assembly, etc. This is because it is only through one's membership in a viable culture that one can develop and exercise the individual autonomy, and most specifically the ability to choose the components of an individual good life, that liberals have always privileged. To the extent that liberals have been concerned to grant individuals rights to those things that are required in order to make possible an autonomous life, they must therefore grant individuals a right to culture, which can only take the form of granting collective rights to the cultural groups to which individuals belong. Call this the autonomy argument (Kymlicka, 1989: 162-178; 1995: 82-93). However, Kymlicka is concerned that the recognition of such rights not imperil individual rights, and so he has argued that a liberal theory of collective rights can only countenance collective rights as external protections, aimed at limiting the impact on minority cultures of unrestricted interaction with other cultures, and particularly with the majority cultures within which they are embedded. It must oppose any collective claim which would require internal restrictions, that is, the curtailment of the individual rights of the members of the cultural community itself, even if such restrictions are deemed necessary for the protection of the culture. Call this the external argument (Kymlicka, 1995: 35-44).

With respect to the neutrality argument, Kymlicka has argued that the operation of the political process is in fact never neutral, and that even if it does not explicitly cite collective considerations in the formulation of policy, it will tend to privilege the majority culture to the detriment of all minority cultures. Special provisions are therefore required in order to level the playing field for the cultures existing at any one time in a society, that is to ensure that all individuals have an equal opportunity to achieve the goods of cultural membership, whatever the cultural group to which they belong. Moreover, some groups, most notably First Nations in the North American and Australasian contexts, have suffered grave injustices at the hands, or ancestors of, members of the majority culture, which make their attainment of such goods even more difficult than they already are for members of other minority cultures. Collective provisions are thus owed to them as a matter of corrective justice. Call this the equality argument (Kymlicka, 1989: 182-200; 1995: 108-115).

The autonomy argument also provides Kymlicka with a way of facing the Pandora's Box problem mentioned above. Indeed, only cultures capable of performing the function in the moral development of their members which Kymlicka envisions, namely that of contributing to their individual autonomy, merit the most thoroughgoing collective rights – primarily rights of self-government. And in Kymlicka's view, only societal cultures, that is societies having reached a high level of institutional integration, and capable of providing their members with ranges of life-options across the full range of fields of human endeavour while making clear the point of the various practices associated with these options, satisfy this condition. The upshot of this argument in Kymlicka's view is that, while national minorities and indigenous nations can legitimately be granted rights of self-government by a liberal theory of collective rights, cultures that are not in the requisite way 'societal' can only legitimately aspire to a much more limited type of collective right. For example, immigrant cultural communities can be granted 'polyethnic rights', allowing them to maintain certain aspects of their original cultures so as to ease the process of assimilation into the majority culture, but not rights of self-government. A distinction can thus be made among cultural groups as to their suitability as sites of full collective rights. The Pandora's Box problem is thus averted. Call this the societal argument (Kymlicka, 1995: 76).

Finally, liberalism's anti-teleological view of politics can be affirmed by a liberal theory of collective rights. For a liberal view of cultural protection only requires that a culture's structure be protected. Liberal cultural protection is entirely compatible with the content of a culture undergoing radical changes as a result of the free choices of its members, as long as these changes do not end up threatening the culture's essential defining characteristics, that is, changes which would lead to the disappearance of the said culture and its replacement with another. Politics can thus proceed in a fairly unconstrained manner just as it would in a liberal regime that only recognized individual rights. Call this the structural argument (Kymlicka, 1989: 166-167; Kymlicka, 1995: 101-105).

If Kymlicka's arguments are sound, he will have shown that not only is the recognition of collective rights for the purposes of cultural protection compatible with liberal theory, but that it is positively required by liberalism's individualistic premises. In the following section, I will show that the type of justification Kymlicka provides for group rights does not generate the particular distribution of such rights he envisages. I will then propose ways in which equilibrium might be restored between the justificatory base of a theory of collective rights and their distribution within a reasonably pluralistic and multicultural society.

III.

A useful way of looking at Kymlicka's work is to see him as engaged in a process of attempting to reach what Rawls has called reflective equilibrium, in which first-order intuitions about the proper way of distributing collective rights among different kinds of cultural groups are matched up with a more general ethical view, the latter providing a moral foundation for the former, the former being a confirming instance of the latter (Rawls, 1971: 48-51). The intuitions are that national and aboriginal minorities within a multinational and multiethnic state can legitimately aspire to collective rights of self-government, while immigrant communities can only legitimately be granted polyethnic rights (Kymlicka, 1995: 26-33). The more general ethical view is that liberal institutions ought to promote individual freedom and autonomy (ibid.: 80-82). What I want to show here is that the structure of the argument is out of balance in important ways.

To see this, consider first that the societal and autonomy arguments are premised upon a set of distinctions which are supposed to be co-extensive. The autonomy argument is premised on the idea that some cultures do, while others do not, promote individual autonomy. The societal argument is based on the idea that some cultural groups, given their levels of societal integration and institutional complexity, are 'societal', while others are not. The two arguments, and thus the two distinctions, are supposed to be connected in the following manner: only societal cultures possess the properties required to ensure the promotion of their members' autonomy. Finally, Kymlicka's first-order arguments about which specific groups ought to receive the most comprehensive collective rights of self-government, are built around the distinction between immigrant groups on the one hand, and national minorities, be they aboriginal or colonial, on the other. His view is that the latter, but not the former, are appropriate sites of full collective rights, as only they possess the properties required for autonomy promotion. For this conclusion not to be arbitrary, it has to connect up with the societal and autonomy arguments outlined above, and with the distinctions upon which they are based. In particular, the distinction between these types of groups would need to flow from the autonomy distinction, since it constitutes the normative ground of the whole theoretical edifice. The problem for Kymlicka is that it does not. The three distinctions fail to overlap in a number of distinct ways. And this failure of co-extension has a number of unfortunate practical consequences for Kymlicka's arguments. Let me briefly run through two, which I will refer to as the problems of inclusion and of exclusion.

First of all, it seems clear that, granted a plausible empirical assumption, the societal and autonomy distinctions fail to overlap. To see this, consider the following. There are two ways in which we could imagine that a societal culture might contribute to the autonomy of its members. First, it could do so because the content of the culture is autonomy-promoting. In other words, a culture might promote the autonomy of its members because it gives pride of place to individualistic values, such as autonomy. This hierarchy of values could manifest itself, for example, in the society's educational system, in the way in which it organizes its political life, etc. Let us say that in such a case, the contribution which the culture makes to the autonomy of its members would be direct. Second, we might imagine unintended social and psychological mechanisms such that, regardless of the specific content of the culture in question, and even in cases where the official culture of the society was quite hostile to individualistic values, the mere fact of belonging to a stable, viable culture fosters individual autonomy anyway. Let us say that in this type of case a culture contributes in an indirect manner to the autonomy of its members.

Now it is clear that, if we read Kymlicka as claiming that it is simply in virtue of being societal that a culture contributes to the autonomy of its members, his argument requires the indirect rather than the direct version of the contribution claim outlined above. Societality, as Kymlicka construes it, is a structural rather than a substantive property of groups. It thus follows that an argument which views societality as the feature through which cultures contribute to the autonomy of their members cannot place any restrictions on the content which societal cultures must have in order to perform this function. (Kymlicka is also prevented from making any such restrictions on cultural content by what I have above called the structural argument, which claims that a liberal theory of collective rights must count a culture as having been protected even when its content has undergone wholesale change and thus, in effect, that it must remain silent on all questions of cultural content.) Otherwise were he claiming that only societal cultures that also had autonomy-promoting contents actually promoted the autonomy of their members, it is unclear what work the mere fact of societality would be doing in the overall argument. At best, it would be a necessary condition of a culture's contributing to its members autonomy, as would the fact that a culture possesses autonomy-promoting contents. But if this were the case, then there would no longer be any reason, in the distribution of collective rights to different kinds of groups, to privilege societal over non-societal but autonomy-based groups. They would both possess properties which are necessary, but individually insufficient conditions of a culture being autonomy-promoting, and they would thus have an equal claim to the collective provisions which autonomy-promotion in Kymlicka's view warrants.

So the co-extension which Kymlicka's argument requires between autonomy-promotion and societality requires what I have called the indirect contribution claim. Yet this claim strikes me as implausible as an empirical hypothesis. Secure membership in a societal culture which is otherwise quite hostile to individualistic values such as autonomy might sometimes produce autonomous agents, but it is wildly optimistic to assume that it will do so reliably, and in any case when it does, it will do so, as it were, despite itself. The empirical issues which would have to be tackled in order to say with any degree of certainty that the indirect claim is false lie far beyond the reach of purely philosophical argument, and so I will state my conclusion conditionally: unless the indirect contribution claim is true, it follows that the autonomy and societal distinctions do not overlap in the manner required for Kymlicka's argument to go through. To the extent that the autonomy argument is the normative foundation for the distribution by the liberal state of comprehensive collective rights, it follows that Kymlicka has given us no reason to privilege the claims of societal over non-societal cultures.

Moreover, to the extent that the societal distinction overlaps with the first-order distinction between national and indigenous minorities on the one hand, and immigrant minorities on the other, it follows that there is no reason to privilege the former as against the latter. Immigrant communities can have cultural contents that are geared towards the promotion of autonomy, even though their lack of institutional completeness means that they lack one of the conditions necessary for the autonomous moral development of their members, while national minorities and aboriginal nations might despite their institutional completeness lack the cultural contents required to attain the same end. If we hold the view, as Kymlicka does, that the granting of collective rights to self-government must be justified by the ability of cultures to ensure the autonomy of their members, it follows that these groups all have the same, partial claim to such rights. Let me call this the problem of inclusion, to refer to the fact that, in the absence of some separate argument justifying that a priority be given to national and indigenous minorities in the distribution of collective rights, Kymlicka's arguments do not provide us with a way of including societal cultures within the ambit of collective rights that does not also end up including autonomy-promoting, but non-societal cultures.

IV.

So unless the indirect contribution claim is true, it follows that the societal and autonomy distinctions fail to overlap, and this gives rise to what I have called the problem of inclusion. Let me now suggest another reason why these two distinctions fail to overlap, which would hold even if we accepted the indirect contribution claim. Briefly stated, my claim here will be that not only does Kymlicka give us no reason to privilege national and aboriginal as opposed to immigrant cultural groups, his arguments fail to provide us with a reason to justify limiting the distribution of collective rights to ethno-cultural groups, be they national, aboriginal or immigrant. Let me explain.

Kymlicka's principal argument, as we have seen, is that community membership is a primary good because it contributes to the moral development of individuals, and more specifically to the development of their capacity for autonomous choosing. More specifically, community membership performs this function in the lives of individuals:

a) by presenting them with a range of options spanning the full range of fields of human endeavour upon which they can exercise their capacity for choice; and
b) by placing these options within a context of intelligibility which permits them to see the point internal to the practices associated with these various options (Kymlicka, 1989: 165-166).

Let's call (a) the range argument and (b) the intelligibility argument.

The range argument constitutes Kymlicka's strongest ground for limiting comprehensive collective rights to societal cultures. It is indeed quite likely that it is only in social contexts marked by institutional, cultural and social complexity that individuals will be able to draw on the broadest range of potential life plans. However, the intelligibility argument in my view calls for a finer-grained analysis. I would argue as follows: individuals belong to societal cultures not directly, as it were, but through the mediation of more local groups organized around more specific, 'local' lines, be they ethnic, religious, kinship-based, or ones defined in terms of sexual orientation, for example. In other words, societal cultures are internally differentiated, and individuals belong to such cultures through their participation in these more local groups, those voluntary and quasi-voluntary associations that make up civil society. It is indeed perhaps only through their role as citizens that individuals belong directly to a societal culture as such (Cohen/Arato, 1992; Cohen/Rogers, 1995).

This matters for Kymlicka's intelligibility argument because these more local groups contribute in an ineliminable way to making the plethora of life options made available by a societal culture intelligible to individuals. Kymlicka does not spell out the intelligibility argument in any great detail, but I think it can be made sense of in terms of two distinct claims. First, in order to be able to exercise their capacity for choice, individuals must understand the point of the various practices and life options among which they are choosing. That is, they must have a clear sense of the values that different practices realize, of their intrinsic merits, and of why one might want to pursue them. Let me call this the intrinsic claim. And second, they must also be provided with a provisional way of placing these values and the practices that are related to them in normative space. The values which different practices realize will often be incommensurable, and so in order to avoid being faced with a Buridan's Ass[4] problem, individuals will have to have some conventional way of beginning to think about them comparatively. Let me call this the comparative claim.

I would propose, as a piece of plausible armchair sociology, that what I have been calling 'local' groups contribute in an important way to making good the comparative claim implied by the intelligibility argument. Different local groups assess the options which the broader societal culture makes available to their members differently, and these evaluations matter to individuals who are trying to steer a course among the plethora of life options which a modern societal culture makes available. To the extent that what I have claimed above about individuals' membership in the societal culture being mediated by their membership in local groups is correct, it follows that the comparative perspective which individuals require in order to exercise their capacity for choice over options will at least in the first instance be provided by local group cultures rather than by the encompassing societal culture. And so even if the societal culture also issues such provisional comparative judgements, it follows that local groups at least participate in the performance of the comparative role I have been describing, which, if I am right about the way in which to understand Kymlicka's intelligibility argument, is essential in the promotion of individual autonomy. There are, moreover, normative grounds for thinking that local groups rather than the broader societal culture ought, in a pluralistic liberal polity, to perform this comparative role. Indeed it is at least plausible to claim that in a society marked by a plurality of different ways of construing the good life, the dominant culture ought not attempt to ride roughshod over the evaluations which different groups organize their communal lives around.

This means that local groups perform a task in the promotion of individual autonomy which is complementary to, but just as necessary as, that performed by societal cultures in providing individuals with a range of 'bare' options. Now the important point for my purposes is that these local groups need not be ethno-culturally defined (although they include the immigrant communities which Kymlicka sees as categorically distinct from national minorities, and thus as deserving of lesser collective rights) (Walker, 1995). Individuals, especially in large, complex modern societies, belong to a plurality of 'encompassing' groups, to borrow the term coined by Joseph Raz and Avishai Margalit, which have an impact on their identities, and more specifically on the manner in which they construe the good life in part by ranking the values and life options made available to them by the broader culture (Raz/Margalit, 1990; Margalit, 1996: 137-143). These groups are structured along all sorts of lines, including for example professional, gender, class, sexual orientation and so on. To the extent that the justification of collective rights stems in Kymlicka's framework from cultures' contributions to the specific range of tasks which go into promoting the development of autonomous individuals, these considerations give us yet another set of reasons to question Kymlicka's conclusion that comprehensive collective rights ought to be limited to societal cultures. Yet again, we are confronted with the failure of Kymlicka's autonomy and societal arguments to overlap in the manner which his overall argument requires. In effect, this is a second variant of what I have called above the problem of inclusion. Taken together, the two aspects of this problem give us reasons to question whether autonomy-promotion can justify either the priority Kymlicka ascribes to national and aboriginal minorities over immigrant minorities, or the greater importance he places on ethno-cultural minorities as opposed to groups defined along other lines.

V.

Another problem that flows for Kymlicka's first-order arguments from the failure of co-extension we have just observed is that certain groups which he is at pains to include within the circle of collective rights to self-government will run the risk of being excluded. In the North American context (and perhaps also in the Australasian one), the problem is particularly acute as far as aboriginal national minorities are concerned. Kymlicka clearly wants his arguments to have as one of their conclusions that at least some Canadian First Nations should be granted self-government rights. The problem is that the foundational status he ascribes to autonomy-promotion gives us no reason to do so. In Canada, for example, aboriginal academics and spokespersons have emphasized how different their political and social cultures are from those of the members of the majority culture. In particular, they have rejected the 'possessive individualism' which underpins much Western constitutionalism and political philosophy (Turpel, 1989-90; Tully, 1994). Many of them have argued for the legitimacy of measures which curtail the individual freedom of members for the sake of the protection of traditional ways of life. My point here is not to question the comparative ethical worths of Western and aboriginal moral schemes, but simply to point out that from the perspective of a theory which grounds collective rights in autonomy-promotion, there seems to be little reason to grant groups organized around non-individualistic moralities any such rights.

The conclusion that flows from Kymlicka's arguments is in fact even more extreme than that such aboriginal cultures ought not to be granted collective rights. An implication of his views is actually that such cultures should be encouraged to reform so as to make them more conducive to the development of their members' autonomy, and when this is not possible, that they should be assimilated into the majority culture, to the extent that the majority culture is autonomy-promoting. To see this, consider the following: Kymlicka believes that, in virtue of its importance in autonomy-promotion, cultural membership should be viewed as a primary good in the Rawlsian sense, that is, as something any rational person would want, regardless of his or her particular life plan (Kymlicka, 1989: 166).[5] As a primary good, membership in autonomy-promoting cultures thus becomes a problem of distributive justice. According to the revised Rawlsian framework Kymlicka tacitly espouses, it is something that should be distributed fairly. This means that it should be distributed in a way that does not merely reflect natural contingencies by replicating the way in which, through the work of chance, people are differentially situated with respect to the good in question (Rawls, 1971: 102). In the case of membership in autonomy-promoting cultures, this entails that individuals who have had the 'bad luck' of being born, through no fault of their own, in communities which promote more traditional or communitarian values, should, as a matter of distributive justice, benefit from redistribution aimed at offsetting the impact of natural contingencies in this area. This means that, with respect to the primary good of membership in autonomy-promoting cultures, the liberal state would be required to enact measures aimed at making it possible for members of other kinds of cultures to acquire membership in individualistic cultures, either a reformed version of their original culture, or when this is impossible, into the nearest available individualistic culture.

One obvious way out for Kymlicka would be to withdraw to what I have called the equality argument. This argument claims that minority cultures ought to be able to benefit from affirmative action measures aimed at making membership in minority cultures as viable as membership in the culture of the majority. The case for such measures would be particularly acute in the case of the indigenous cultures of North America which suffer not only from their minority status, but also from the lingering long-term effects of the injustices which have historically been visited upon them by the ancestors of some of the members of the majority.

The problem with this argument within Kymlicka's theoretical framework is that it is entirely parasitic upon the autonomy argument. Indeed, given the foundational status his arguments ascribe to autonomy, the equality argument needs to be reformulated in the following manner: autonomy-promoting minority cultures ought to be able to benefit from affirmative action measures aimed at making membership in minority cultures as viable as membership in the culture of the majority. There is no reason, from within a liberal theory premised upon the foundational value of autonomy, to ensure the equality of cultures that do not contribute to autonomy.

The upshot of the foregoing remarks is that Kymlicka's theoretical framework fails to account for and justify one of the moral intuitions he seems concerned to defend, namely that aboriginal cultures in the North American context ought to be granted the means to protect their distinct ways of life. Let me call this the problem of exclusion.

VI.

I suggested earlier that Kymlicka could usefully be seen as engaged in trying to establish reflective equilibrium between some of our considered convictions concerning the proper loci for the recognition of collective rights within a multicultural and pluralistic polity, and one of liberalism's foundational theoretical commitments, namely, the belief in the importance of individual autonomy. If the arguments of the foregoing pages have been successful, they show that the theory is out of balance in important ways: a foundational commitment to autonomy as the grounds for the recognition of collective rights to groups excludes some of the groups to which Kymlicka would want to provide the kind of cultural protection which collective rights afford, and includes some of the groups which Kymlicka thinks should not be protected from the pressures towards assimilation exercised by the majority culture (some immigrant groups, as well as some non ethno-culturally defined groups).

In this final section, I want briefly to explore some avenues which might lead us out of this impasse. Let me however first note a structural feature of our conundrum. The two problems which we have identified seem to call for mutually exclusive kinds of solutions: the problem of exclusion requires a broadening of the normative base of a theory of collective rights, one that would include not only the value of autonomy, but also other important ethical values realized by non-autonomy-promoting communities to which we think that collective rights ought to be granted. However, this kind of solution to the problem of exclusion will almost certainly exacerbate the problem of inclusion. All the groups which the narrower, autonomy-based normative foundation would have picked out would still be picked out by a broader construal of collective rights' normative grounds, as would others which realize whatever other value we decide to include therein. Conversely, tackling the problem of inclusion, for example by dropping the indirect argument and insisting that a group possess both the structural and the substantive properties required for autonomy-promotion, will make certain groups even less able than they had been under Kymlicka's theoretical dispensation to aspire to collective rights. It seems, therefore, that we will have to decide which of these two sets of problems would be least burdensome for a theory of collective rights, as it is unlikely that we will be able to eradicate both at the same time.

I want to claim that a theory of collective rights which does not address the problem of exclusion will not be of much use in radically multicultural and pluralistic societies such as our own. A theory which simply aspires to show how a liberal polity can accommodate the claims of those among its minorities which are already in the main liberal will have failed to address the principal challenge which in my view faces modern societies, which is that of determining how accommodation might be reached between a liberal majority and minorities which, while they do not affirm liberal values of individualism and autonomy, are nonetheless reasonable (in a sense to be specified below) (Barry, 1996: 154).

Addressing the problem of exclusion requires broadening the normative basis of a theory of collective rights. How might such an expansion be carried out? My suggestion is that if we try to dig deeper into the judgement according to which certain aboriginal communities ought not to be excluded from the ambit of group rights we would be likely to say that though they do not promote the autonomy of their members directly (I have left open the possibility that they do so indirectly), they nonetheless contribute to their well-being in important ways. This goes, for example, for some aboriginal First Nations which do not espouse individualistic values. The proposal that would flow from this observation, and which could serve as an alternative to the autonomy argument in the Kymlickan framework, is that group membership is a fundamental interest of individuals, enough to consider it as a primary good in the Rawlsian sense, to the extent that it contributes in some way to individual well-being.

Well-being is a notoriously difficult notion to pin down, however, but I would claim that the following is relatively uncontroversial: whether at the foundational or at a more derivative level, well-being is a pluralistic notion. It involves the realization in individuals' lives of a plurality of different values, of which it will be true to say that the pursuit of some will make the pursuit of others more difficult. In other words, whatever the specific manner in which we flesh out the notion of well-being, it will turn out that its component values will not all be jointly realizable, at least not to their fullest extents. For example, a life privileging individual autonomy and placing a high premium on individual accomplishment will probably require trade-offs with those values involved in a more community- or family-based lifestyle. Although it will be true that none of them could be realized by an individual in isolation, and thus that they will all require that individuals belong to viable groups, this fact about well-being also implies that different communities can contribute to the well-being of their members in a variety of incommensurable ways (Griffin, 1996; Nussbaum, 1995).

There are moreover reasons to prefer a well-being approach to group rights which are independent of the judgements on the distribution of such rights with which they are in equilibrium. In particular, such an approach would square more clearly than Kymlicka's autonomy-based comprehensive liberalism with the pluralistic turn which much political philosophy, both within and outside the liberal tradition, has undertaken in the last decade or so. Political philosophers in recent years have emphasized the extent to which a just society is one which treats individuals fairly not only qua holders of egoistically-defined utility functions, but also qua adherents to radically diverse conceptions of the good life. Now I propose that at least part of what explains the plurality of different plausible conceptions of the good is that they rank the various components of the pluralistic notion of 'well-being' differently.[6] So part of what treating different conceptions of the good is going to involve is treating different ways of ranking prudential values fairly. Thus, for example, a form of life which privileges the goods of community and tradition should not in a pluralistic liberal state do less well than one which privileges individualistic values, and if it does, it should not be in virtue of the fact that it contributes to the realization of values that are not as obviously individualistic as are those of the autonomy-promoting minority groups Kymlicka privileges. And thus in particular, if the latter groups are to be included within the ambit of collective rights, then all things being equal, so should the former.

The foregoing comments also give us a handle on the specific manner in which group membership must contribute to individual well-being if it is to be an appropriate locus of group rights. If what I have claimed above is right, membership in certain kinds of groups (the types of groups which Margalit and Raz term 'encompassing') matters to individuals in a way which calls for particular concern because it provides them with their way of perceiving and finding their place within the broader social world of which they are a part. Were this belonging to be endangered, individuals would literally lose their epistemic and moral bearings. It is in this sense that we can begin to flesh out the much repeated communitarian nostrum according to which 'community is constitutive of identity'. Much more work would have to be done to render this fully satisfying, and I will propose a way of thinking about the way in which the importance of membership to individual identity can be conceptualized within a liberal framework in a moment. First, however, I must attend to an objection which might plausibly be leveled at the whole idea of grounding group-differentiated tights in considerations of well-being.

An obvious objection to this view is that it will end up not only tolerating, but actively promoting unjust and authoritarian practices, for example in the treatment of women or of 'internal' minorities. Especially given the fact that the very idea of autonomous consent will be foreign to some groups which do not prioritize autonomy, it opens the door to innumerable forms of paternalistic abuse. Let me call this the oppression objection.

I want to say a number of things about this objection. Let me begin by introducing a distinction between what I would call reasonably and unreasonably non-liberal groups. A group is *reasonably* non-liberal if, (a) though it rejects the values of a comprehensive liberalism and might even structure its internal political affairs undemocratically, (b) it upholds its members basic human rights to physical and psychological security, (c) it contributes to their well-being by instantiating some combination of the values which make up the complex concept of well-being, and thus, a plausible conception of the human good life, and (d) it is broadly compatible with the rights which they possess as citizens of the larger society. A group is *unreasonably* non-liberal if (a) is true of it and at least one of (b)-(d) is false. My claim is that, though the view I am proposing might end up promoting the continued existence of non-liberal groups, it will refuse to countenance illiberal groups.

Let me now distinguish between two types of theories of minority rights. A liberal theory of minority rights sets out to determine the manner and the extent to which a liberal regime can accommodate the claims of the groups within its midst, whereas a liberal theory of rights for liberal minorities does the same, but restricts its purview to liberal minorities, or to minorities whose internal modes of organization and belief systems already incline them towards liberal values. I claim that the former type of theory is preferable to the latter for pragmatic as well as for more purely ethical reasons. The ethical reason is that it will be able to make finer-grained distinctions than the latter, and will be able to distinguish between reasonably and unreasonably non-liberal groups. All things being equal, we have reason to prefer theories which enhance rather than diminish our ethical perspicuity. The pragmatic reason is that complex modern societies obviously contain groups which do not share all of the elements of the prevailing ethos of liberal society, but which do not pose a threat to its existence, and which also provide contexts for the leading of good human lives. The unity and stability of such societies would seem to depend in part upon such groups not being relegated to the same pariah status as illiberal groups.

So a well-being based theory of minority rights is only partially vulnerable to the oppression objection. Although it will end up countenancing groups which are organized around paternalistic or otherwise undemocratic lines, it will be able to draw a principled line dividing reasonably and unreasonably non-liberal groups. There can however be no denying that such a view will also end up recognizing the claims of groups that no comprehensive liberal would want to live in. But this is an unavoidable consequence of a pluralistic liberalism which takes seriously the importance of membership to individuals, and which recognizes that that importance can not always be cashed out in terms of the value of individual autonomy.

My suggestion therefore is that we should consider a well-being rather than an autonomy-based justification of collective rights. This would allow us to re-establish equilibrium between the view that some vulnerable cultural groups which do not affirm liberal values ought, to, nonetheless, benefit from the protection afforded by collective rights and the normative basis of the theory. As already mentioned above, however, this suggestion does nothing to solve – and might actually exacerbate – the problem of inclusion discussed above. Indeed, individuals belong to a plurality of different types of associations which can reasonably be claimed to contribute to their well-being in significant ways. They are members of bird-watching groups, sports teams, unions, families, etc., and so there would seem to be no limit in principle to the groups which the view would have the state recognize in some official manner. The problem of inclusion, which is at the root of the Pandora's Box problem, which I cited earlier as the pragmatic motivation for the liberal doctrine of state neutrality, is raised again in a new, particularly acute form.

I want in closing to sketch out four arguments and sets of considerations which might be adduced to lessen this problem. The first two have to do with what I take to be features of any plausible theory of rights, be they individual or collective. Their function is to protect fundamental but vulnerable interests. Let me first touch briefly on the issue of vulnerability. Following a view like Ronald Dworkin's, rights emerge conceptually as limits upon the general presumption that political decisions ought to reflect the will of the democratic majority. These limits are justified by the fact that interests which would have to be aggregated in a purely majoritarian decision-making procedure would have to include people's 'external' preferences (that is, preferences relating to other individuals) the inclusion of which in decision-making would fail to treat those people aimed by external preferences as equals. They can also be justified however by the fact that even when democratic decision-making does not express external preferences, it can nonetheless make the fundamental interests of members of minorities difficult to realize (Dworkin, 1977).

A first restriction on the scope of a theory of collective rights thus involves the idea that their function is to protect not all interests, but rather those which might be made vulnerable in a strictly majoritarian decision-making process. A second restriction familiar to liberals is that rights are not meant to protect all interests, but rather those of our interests which can plausibly be classed as fundamental. One familiar way of cashing out this idea is in terms of Rawls' notion of 'primary goods', those goods which any rational individual wants, regardless of his or her particular plan of life. Now I agree with Kymlicka that if a liberal political philosophy is to recognize collective rights, it must be because there is something about group membership which corresponds to a primary good in the Rawlsian sense. I have, however, had occasion to criticize Kymlicka's own view of why it is that group membership ought to be considered a primary good. My suggestion that a pluralistic conception of well-being replace autonomy as the value at the basis of the theory of collective rights has however so far failed to specify the specific aspect of individual well-being to which group membership contributes, and which warrants viewing our interest in group membership as being sufficiently weighty to ground rights. Let me put forward an argument sketch that might make good this lacuna.

I start from the central liberal tenet, articulated most clearly by John Rawls, that self-respect is a fundamental good for human beings – indeed, perhaps the most important one, in so far as it is the condition of their ability to use all other basic goods. If we accept the idea that it is the state's responsibility to ensure that all its citizens possess a fair share of primary goods, it follows that the state must, *inter alia*, endeavour to provide citizens with the social bases of self-respect. In *A Theory of Justice*, Rawls maintains that self-respect involves "a person's sense of his own value, his secure conviction that his conception of his good, his plan of life, is worth carrying out", as well as "a confidence in one's ability, so far as it is within one's power, to fulfil one's intentions" (Rawls, 1971: 440). Rawls holds that such self-respect can only be ensured within associative structures: "It normally suffices that for each person there is some association (one or more) to which he belongs and within which the activities that are rational for him are publicly affirmed by others" (ibid.: 441). Rawls claims, finally, that the social bases of self-respect are sufficiently assured whenever it is true that for each individual there is at least one such association, and whenever citizens' dealings with one another respect Rawls' two principles of justice (ibid.: 441).

Although Rawls' account of the social bases of self-respect points us in the direction of an important truth about the way in which respect for persons should be embodied in a liberal polity, it is insufficient for two interrelated reasons. First, it fails to take seriously the way in which individuals' group identities can come to inform their ends. Rawls' picture of the social bases of self-respect is one in which individuals form ends which are suitable to their particular talents and aptitudes, and, though their ends might not be admired or affirmed by all other citizens, given their different talents and aptitudes, nonetheless, they can come into association with a sub-class of citizens with whom they are sufficiently in tune for their ends to get affirmed within this more limited community. But groups can be more deeply implicated than this picture suggests in the very formation of individual ends. This could be the case in at least two ways: first, as has already been argued in dealing with Kymlicka's intelligibility argument, people's ends and projects can be deeply coloured by the values of the communities to which they belong. And second, the protection and flourishing of the communities of which they are members can themselves become important projects for individuals. It often happens that people's identities are so deeply interwoven with the groups with which they identify that they could not conceive of individual ends which were not at the same time community-promotings ends.[7]

We thus have (at least) three ways in which one's community membership can be important to one's ends: first, as Rawls sees it, community matters because it can confirm us in the sense that our (in principle individually imaginable) ends are worth pursuing, and sustain us when we are unsure of our ability to realize them; second, it can colour the way in which we formulate our ends; and third, it can become a central element of our ends. Let me call these three ways in which community membership can matter to individual ends contingent, partially constitutive, and fully constitutive.

The plurality of ways in which community membership can inform our ends matters for Rawls' doctrine of the social bases of self-respect in the following way: if we accept that self-respect depends in part upon our ends being affirmed, or at least not demeaned, by our fellow citizens, then it will not be sufficient for the self-respect of those members of society for whom community membership is fully constitutive of their ends that their relations with their fellow citizens be mediated only through the two principles of justice as Rawls articulates them.[8] Rawls' view actually requires that the relation between community and ends be construed exclusively in a contingent manner: in his view, one's individually arrived-at goals are affirmed through one's participation in an association of like-minded people, and one's status as an individual end-setter is affirmed through the respect which citizens betoken to one another by viewing their relations through the lenses that the two principles of justice constitute. Nothing in the contingent view actually requires that, in addition, one's fellow citizens also affirm the community to which one belongs. But things are quite different for individuals whose ends are fully or partly constituted by their communities. For such people, being respected by their fellow citizens will require not only that they be respected as isolated individuals, but also *qua* members of the community which fully or partly constitutes their ends. In particular, the social bases of self-respect will for such individuals not be assured by a theory of justice like Rawls', which, as we have seen, views it as a matter of indifference from the point of view of justice that certain otherwise defensible collective forms of life be allowed to disappear in a regime of purely individual rights.

So my suggestion is that ensuring that citizens possess the social bases of self-respect requires in certain cases that the importance and worth of the communities to which they belong be affirmed by their fellow citizens. Now remember that this argument was invoked at this stage to counter the impression the well-being argument may have raised, to the effect that there will be no limit on the number and kind of group that will be able to claim some form of protection from the state. I now want to make its relevance for this Pandora's Box problem clear: my claim is that only those groups the non-recognition or non-protection of which would undermine citizens' self-respect can make claims of justice when, as a result of their minority status, their existence or viability is threatened. It is because certain groups contribute in a significant manner to their members' well-being, and because the ends of some individuals are identified to such an extent with the continued existence and flourishing of these groups, so that their being allowed to disappear would mean that these individuals would be unable to have their ends upheld and affirmed within the society to which they belong, and would thus be denied the social bases of self-respect, that claims made by members of vulnerable minority groups which perform these dual functions must be construed as claims of justice within a liberal framework. Now groups of which it can plausibly be claimed that they perform these dual functions are not thick on the ground, and though I think that they are not limited to the ethno-cultural groups on which most recent theories of minority rights, including Kymlicka's, have focused, they are limited in number and kind. As I have already suggested, I would as a first approximation liken the kind of group which my view would cover to Raz and Margalit's notion of an 'encompassing group', with the proviso that those aspects of their definition which unduly privilege ethno-cultural groups be removed.[9]

I will spell out the two other grounds I have for thinking that a more expansive normative foundation for collective rights will not generate too severe a Pandora's Box problem more quickly. First, a normative theory of collective rights such as the one I am proposing does not claim that the groups specified by the theory ought to claim the rights which the theory grants them, but merely that they can. In a reasonably just and tolerant society in which people are not made to feel inferior in virtue of their minority status, it is not implausible to expect that many of the potential rights which the theory would justify would go unclaimed. To borrow an argument from John Tomasi, I would say that by allowing individuals not to claim rights which they could claim, the existence in such a society of collective rights gives citizens a way of expressing solidarity with one another which would not exist in a society which did not recognize such rights (Tomasi, 1991). (However, there would be something patently unjust in denying rights to members of minority groups in societies where they were not well treated or tolerated by members of the majority on the grounds that such a recognition would give rise to an unwanted profusion of rights.)

Second, the vision of a fragmented, ghettoized society which would result from a theory of collective rights is in some measure dependent upon the kind of simplified, falsely dichotomous conception of the specific contents of the rights in question which we find in writings such as Kymlicka's. According to this vision, either groups are granted self-government rights or rights to special representation which allow them to exercise a significant degree of sovereignty over the full range of institutions and practices which make up the community's life, or they (more specifically immigrant groups) are granted mere 'polyethnic' rights, which allow them to maintain certain folkloric aspects of their native cultures whilst integrating in all other respects into the majority culture. Claiming that there is no reason in principle to restrict immigrant groups (or non-ethno-cultural minorities) to this most lowly category of collective right raises the spectre of a fractious, balkanized, splintered polity of small self-governing enclaves only if we assume that the only alternative is that they be granted self-government or special representation rights as well. But this assumption is false.

Collective rights can be tailor-made for specific groups in function of their specific needs (what areas of their collective lives does such and such a group need sovereignty over in order for their members to realize their fundamental interest in group membership?) and capacities (what kind of right can the group in question exercise, given its material and institutional capacity?). For some groups, tax exemptions or grants required for example in order to sustain media linking the members of the group together, in the case of spatially dispersed groups, will be all that will be required in order to secure the goods of community membership for their members, and all that the group could conceivably support. For others, concerned, for example, to preserve certain aspects of a traditional way of life, the requirement might be one of control over certain aspects of education. The point is simply that, given the great variety of kinds of groups present in a reasonably multicultural and pluralistic society, it is illusory to argue that they will all fit into the same mould as far as rights are concerned. The language of rights in fact covers a wide range of liberties, claims, immunities and powers, and there is no reason not to help ourselves to the full range of rights-contents which these terms denote in order to produce a more fine-grained and contextually sensitive theory of minority rights than that which a dichotomous conception such as Kymlicka's affords us.

My conclusion is that the problem of inclusion which the broadening of the normative basis of a (still recognizably liberal) theory of collective rights had threatened to exacerbate can be tamed once we realize that the interests individuals have in group membership which will warrant the attribution of rights will be limited to those interests which are vulnerable and fundamental, that the theory specifies rights which can as opposed to rights which ought to be exercised, and that the language of rights in fact covers a wide range of types of accommodations which majorities can reach with members of minorities, and which, while they stop short of full self-government or special representation rights, are nonetheless more substantive than the 'polyethnic' rights to which Kymlicka had thought that all groups which are not national minorities ought to be confined.

My general conclusion is that if we are to recognize collective rights within the framework of a liberal theory, it will be very difficult to restrict the purview of such rights to the types of groups Kymlicka identifies in his work. Whatever the normative foundation we adopt, it will cut across the first-order distinctions he sets up between ethno-cultural and non-ethno-cultural groups, as well as, within the former category, between national and aboriginal minorities on the one hand and immigrant minorities on the other.

Note the conditional form in which I have expressed this conclusion. There may be other reasons, unexplored in this paper, not to grant rights to groups. Some of the most important recent work on rights theory – Wellman (1995) and Steiner (1994) in particular – has for example claimed that ascribing rights to groups is rooted in conceptual confusion, in that rights can only be held by intentional agents, that is, individuals. There may also be weighty objections to granting rights to groups based on considerations of social unity and stability. I can obviously not consider these claims here. My point is simply to suggest that, to the extent that we ground rights in considerations of individual autonomy or well-being, it will be difficult to restrict rights to individuals, and it will also be difficult to prevent collective rights from ranging beyond the narrow category of ethno-cultural groups which have traditionally been seen as the most appropriate collective rights-holders.

Notes

[1] I would like to thank the Social Sciences and Humanities Research Council of Canada, the Fonds pour la formation de chercheurs et l'aide à la recherche of Quebec, and the Secretary of State for Citizenship and Multiculturalism for funding which made this essay possible. Drafts of the paper were presented at a conference on Immigration and Cultural Diversity at the University of Melbourne, as well as at the Université de Montreal, McGill University, the University of Auckland, the University of Waikato, Massey University, and the Australian National University. I would like to thank audiences at all these places for their helpful comments, and in particular the following people: Veit Bader, Rainer Bauböck, Peter Benson, Andrew Brien, Joseph Carens, Elisabetta Galeotti, Ian Gold, Bob Goodin, Mane Hajdin, Richard Janda, Chandran Kukathas, Loren Lomasky, Victoria Meikle, Roy Perrett, Phillip Pettit, Walter Sinnott-Armstrong, Natalie Stoljar, Shauna van Praagh. Thanks are also due to Will Kymlicka, who read and commented very thoughtfully on an early draft. Thanks finally to Vanda Taylor for translating an earlier draft into English.

[2] Specifying the minimal moral commitments of any liberal theory in a wholly satisfactory manner would obviously require much more argument than I am capable of providing here. The three

3 Compare Rawls (1975: 549) for a much harsher assessment by Rawls of what the failure to thrive in a context of just institutions reveals about a way of life.
4 Famously, Buridan's Ass stood between two equidistant and equally tempting piles of hay. Unable to make a decision, he starved to death. Though attributed to the medieval logician John Buridan, this parable appears nowhere in his extant works, and may actually have been devised as a parody of his views.
5 For Rawls' concept of primary goods, see Rawls (1971: 90-95; 1982).
6 I say that the explanation of the diversity of forms of the good is partly explained by different rankings of prudential values because part of the difference also has to do with difference in belief. The relationship between the different rankings and the different beliefs is a complex question I cannot get into here.
7 This claim does not imply the implausibly strong one that such memberships cannot be freely chosen. One chooses one's profession, but it can happen that one's sense of oneself becomes inextricably linked with the professional group with which one's choice has made one fall in.
8 I will for the purposes of this paper remain agnostic on the issue of whether this is the case for individuals whose ends are partially constituted in this manner as well.
9 But as a first approximation only. Their insistence that 'people growing up in the group acquire the group culture and possess its special traits', and that 'people do not decide to belong to an encompassing group' strikes me as arbitrarily slanted towards ethno-cultural groups. As I suggested above, people can choose as adults to belong to groups which subsequently come to inform their identities in what I have called a fully constitutive way. Think of groups organized along lines of sexual orientation (which Margalit is concerned to include among encompassing groups). People can also choose to render salient aspects of their identities which had previously not been fully constitutive in my sense. Think of the burgeoning group consciousness in many places today among the deaf and hearing-impaired. For the notion of an encompassing group, see Raz/Margalit (1990) and Margalit (1996). The quotes are taken from the latter work, pp. 138, 140.

References

Arblaster, Anthony (1986) *The Rise and Decline of Liberal Democracy*. Oxford: Basil Blackwell.
Barry, Brian (1996) 'Review of *Multicultural Citizenship*', *Ethics* 107.
Blum, Lawrence A. (1994) *Moral Perception and Particularity*. Cambridge: Cambridge University Press.
Cohen, Jean/Arato, Andrew (1992) *Civil Society and Political Theory*. Cambridge, MA.: The MIT Press.

Cohen, Joshua/Rogers, Joel (1995) *Associations and Democracy*. London: Verso.

Daniels, Norman (1996) *Justice and Justification*. Cambridge: Cambridge University Press.

Dworkin, Ronald (1977) *Taking Rights Seriously*. Cambridge, MA.: Harvard University Press.

Griffin, James (1986) *Well-Being*. Oxford: Oxford University Press.

Kymlicka, Will (1989) *Liberalism, Community and Culture*. Oxford: Oxford University Press.

Kymlicka, Will (1995) *Multicultural Citizenship*. Oxford: Oxford University Press.

Margalit, Avishai (1996) *The Decent Society*. Cambridge, MA.: Harvard University Press.

Mason, Andrew (1990) 'Autonomy, Liberalism and State Neutrality', *The Philosophical Quarterly* 40.

Norman, Wayne (forthcoming) 'Methodological Rawlsianism', *Political Studies*.

Nussbaum, Martha (1995) 'Human Capabilities, Female Human Being', in Nussbaum, M./Griffin, J. (eds.), *Women, Culture and Development*. Oxford: Oxford University Press.

Rawls, John (1971) *A Theory of Justice*. Cambridge, MA.: Harvard University Press.

Rawls, John (1975) 'Fairness to Goodness', *The Philosophical Review* 84.

Rawls, John (1982) 'Social Unity and Primary Goods', in Sen, A./Williams, B. (eds.), *Utilitarianism and Beyond*. Cambridge: Cambridge University Press.

Rawls, John (1993) *Political Liberalism*. New York: Columbia University Press.

Raz, Joseph/Margalit, Avishai (1990) 'National Self-Determination', *The Journal of Philosophy* 87.

Steiner, Hillel (1994) *An Essay on Rights*. Oxford: Blackwell.

Tomasi, John (1991) 'Individual Rights and Community Virtues', *Ethics* 101, April.

Tully, James (1994) 'Aboriginal Property and Western Theory: Recovering a Middle Ground', *Social Philosophy and Policy* 11.

Turpel, M-E. (1989-90) 'Aboriginal Peoples and the Canadian Charter: Interpretive Monopolies, Cultural Differences', *Canadian Human Rights Yearbook* 6.

Waldron, Jeremy (1993) 'Theoretical Foundations of Liberalism', in Waldron, J., *Liberal Rights*. Cambridge: Cambridge University Press.

Walker, Brian (1995) 'Une critique du nationalisme culturaliste', in Blais, F. et al. (eds.), *Libéralismes et nationalismes*. Ste. Foy: Presses de l'Université Laval.

Wellman, Carl (1995) *Real Rights*. Oxford: Oxford University Press.

CHAPTER 12

Bridging the Gap: Citizenship in Europe and Asia

Alastair Davidson

The starting point for this inquiry are certain points made by Samuel Huntington in his now notorious essay on the *Clash of Civilizations* (Huntington, 1993). The main argument of that essay was that with the end of the cold war, the real lines of division in the world would be between civilizations and that it was along such lines that dispute and war would be most likely in the twenty-first century. Within that International Relations theme and driving it was an assumption that the values of the major civilizations were so different that it was sanguine to expect them to bridge any gaps or share in common public values. He wrote:

> (...) differences among civilizations are not only real; they are basic (...) The people of different civilizations have different views on the relations between God and man, the individual and the group, the citizen and the state, parents and children, husband and wife, as well as differing views of the relative importance of rights and responsibilities, liberty and authority, equality and hierarchy. These differences are the product of centuries. They will not soon disappear. They are far more fundamental than differences among political ideologies and political regimes. Differences do not necessarily mean conflict, and conflict does not necessarily mean violence. Over the centuries, however, differences among civilizations have generated the most prolonged and most violent conflicts (Huntington, 1993: 25).

Huntington enumerates the major civilizations as Western, Confucian, Japanese, Islamic, Hindu, Slav-Orthodox, Latin American and, possibly, African.

Regardless of its merit – and his thesis has been criticized as ignorant, careless of the facts, ideological, and theoretically out of touch (Johnson, 1995: 13; Sheridan, 1995: 135; Ajami, 1993; Mahbubani, 1993; Bartley, 1993; Binyan, 1993; Rubinstein and Crocker, 1994) – it is so influential that those parts of it which refer to the citizen ('rights and responsibilities, liberty and authority, equality and hierarchy') warrant close attention.

If he is correct, then much of the projected development of democracy, human rights and citizen sovereignty forecast by international organizations (*Global Commission*, 1995) for the globalizing world of the next century will not take place. It will not take place (1) because there really are such irreconcilable differences; (2) because they *determine* what will happen in a political realm; (3) because there is no possibility of dialogue.

Even his critics concede that many of the Asian leaders and commentators tend to advance the same argument as he does. *Realpolitik* cautions us not to dismiss the weight of their views. Even if 99% of academics can drive carts and horses through his arguments, it is the Asian and Pacific leaders who will count if they act as if they were true. His views are certainly endorsed by Dr Mahathir, the Malaysian prime minister, a Muslim; by the Chinese government and the Singapore Prime Minister, the second of whom speaks as a Confucian and by many Asian commentators from Japan and from Hindu majority countries.

What unites them is the assertion that human rights, democracy and citizen sovereignty are Western values, which have either not worked, or worked less well than have those of their own civilizations (especially for their own 'peoples'). Or, in a variant of that argument, when the West demands the application of such values it is attempting a new imperialist manoeuvre designed to prevent Asian countries ever catching up. A particularly violent expression of the first view is in these lines of Goh Tok Tong, Singapore's prime minister:

> Western liberals, foreign media and human rights groups also want Singapore to be like their societies and some Singaporeans mindlessly dance to their tune. See what happened to President Gorbachev because he was beguiled by their praise. Deng Xiaoping received their condemnation. But look at China today and see what has happened to the Soviet Union. It's gone. Imploded! We must think for ourselves and decide what's good for Singapore. Above all we must stay away from policies which have brought a plague of social and economic problems to the US and Britain (cited in Sheridan, 1995: 138).

A more considered and scholarly version of the second view is in the article by Bilhari Kausikan (1993) which suggests that human rights are being used as 'an instrument of economic competition' and points to the use of the 'most-favoured-nation'-status by Clinton in US relations with China. In the World Trade Organization meetings in Singapore in December 1996 Asians frequently argued that the social clause which guaranteed minimum labour conditions was being used to limit Asian competitiveness (see also Mahathir, 1996: 27-30).

The compromise position seems to be the sort of lip-service given by Asian countries to universal human rights in the Vienna Declaration of 1993 provided they are conceded the right to apply such standards themselves on the basis of an assertion of absolute national sovereignty (HRLJ, 1993: 370-371; compare Chinese White Paper 1991 in Alston/Steiner, 1995: 233-234). This empties the notion of human rights of all content, since they are intended to exist precisely against the state.

Where the notion of the citizen is concerned, a constant theme in the Asian critique which is highly relevant to its refusal of Western standards is the notion that the latter are individualistic and adversarial where those of Asia are communitarian and consensus seeking (Kausikan, 1993). The West is doubly the loser as not only are its values non-negotiable but Asia is also able to claim a greater readiness to reach an understanding.

There can and have been a number of replies to such positions. First, and most tellingly, that the refusal of democracy, human rights and citizen sovereignty under the cloak of difference is hypocrisy by an elite of undemocratic leaders. If a democratic vote were possible the Asian masses would be in favour of such universal principles (Ghai, 1994: 5; Donnelly, 1989; Rajamoorty, 1993: 29). Indeed, the very notion of Asian values itself is a creation or fiction without popular support. Beeson, following Rodan, states, "(...) appeals to a distinctive set of Asian norms, beliefs and cultural values are, in reality, little more than ideological constructions designed to maintain authoritarian rule and legitimize a conservative political agenda" (Beeson, 1996: 43). Indeed, the same critique has been made of notions like the 'Pacific way', whose history is chiefly fiction (Lawson, 1993: 198).

There is, no doubt, substance to all these critiques but, in the absence of real democracy in most Asian countries, we cannot know how substantial one or the other view is. It is possible that the leadership does express a substantial popular consensus on values. Asian views on the nature and virtues of citizenship – even culturally redefined – are difficult to assess as there are practically no scholarly texts on citizenship available, with the notable exception of work on Singapore and other former imperial possessions. Research projects coming from Asian countries on these issues are imperative. They should come from each culture expressing itself in its own voice. Work is, of course, being done on allied areas concerned with democracy and human rights as well as with citizenship and cultural difference.

The more modest object of this essay is to start building a bridge from the 'Western' side by showing that the Asian (or indeed, Huntington's) understanding of Western values as they pertain to citizenship is a caricature. The Western notion of what it is to be a citizen has probably never been solely that of an individualistic, adversarial subject even *vis-à-vis* the state. Long since it has been developed from such a Rousseauian/Kantian ethic into one informed by the need for consensus, social conscience and mild virtues of conviviality.

The citizen of today's Western theory and practice is a human being whose values on the issues which Huntington listed (see above) are not greatly different from the caricature of the Asian ones. I suspect that when in-depth work has been done on how citizenship has developed in the countries of Asia, it will reveal not only that East and West are very close in the public solutions that they find to the threats posed by a globalizing world on the eve of the twenty-first century, but that both agree that difference is best protected by universal human rights and democracy. This has long been the position of many oppositions and minorities in Asian countries themselves.

The Great Divide

It is important to make clear that we do not wish to minimize real differences. It is also important to make clear what our argument does not assert.

It certainly assumes that human beings wish to make sense of their world to control it, whether it is natural or social. They do not wish to be tossed around by the vagaries of an indecipherable fortune and they wish to minimize risk. They, thus, favour the identification and establishment of worlds ruled by law. Socially, the first quality of citizenship is to live according to a rule of law and not of men. Modern citizenship is adamant that its object is to eliminate any arbitrariness in those laws. They wish not to be objects, and therefore victims, but subjects, and therefore free. But what procedures are needed to attain security and dignity or a sense of well-being depends on the context. There have been and clearly are different ways to attain the end to the menace of the unknown. Having a status and a role may be more reassuring in some circumstances than having autonomy. The difference between cultures thus is a difference about what we do to attain what is human.

Apart from this all that Westerners know is that there is another shore. We guess that modernization and globalization, while contradictory, are bringing those on the other shore closer to our citizen norms as they also shift those norms closer to where we are told the Other is. The two endpoints in that process of convergence provide, we hypothesize, a better place for dialogue than the two polar opposites of an individualistic, adversarial, warrior citizenry on the Western side, and a communitarian, consensual, peaceful trader subject on the Asian side.

However, the onus is on the West to make clear that a citizen, who is the basic unit of our states, is not such a selfish/unsocial individual. To do so it will have to argue on two fronts: first, against the origins of the concept of the modern citizen where the dominant quality was that of the selfish autonomous individual, and second, against the dominant economic rationalism of global capital, which has resuscitated that original minimalist notion of the citizen. In both, the abiding theme is that modern nation-state citizenship starts with the notion of a set of individuals who contract together to control their traditional patriarchal leaders. Citizenship is a revolt against the determinism of a historically transmitted order.

In its first mode it does attack the notion of a society built on familial relations; on the authority of the father (monarch); on the capacity of all men (and women implicitly) to reason and contribute to a notion of the collective good equally; and thus in the end, it challenges the notion that we have a debt to our forebears (Bobbio, 1984). By evacuating history it also evacuates difference from the citizen unit.

Its denial of history is accompanied by a determination to control it. From Kant's individual who dares to think for him- or herself to Rousseau's free person who makes the laws for himself to Marx's revolutionary who remakes what makes the Kantian individual is but a few steps for rational thought. Above all, the assertion of mind's capacity to control the world through establishing a rule of law in the face of the arbitrariness of natural and social worlds, reveals a dogged assertion of a will to power through knowledge.

So the Kantian citizen is rather like the autonomous adversarial caricature given by some Asians. The notions of earlier centuries even more so. Men wished to live without God (as authoritative truth); to end the authority of the father; to dare to think for themselves; and to establish orders based on people like them everywhere. The context of chaotic risk which they wished to control was always small and relatively homogeneous. It was a view elaborated in the tiny worlds of late eighteenth-century Europe, among intellectuals who shared basically the same value system. Once in power, these peoples did assert fiercely their right to defend their new, potentially democratic, polity based on rights – as the words *aux armes citoyens* make abundantly clear.

This quality to citizenship was central in the following century and a half. The first reason is obvious: natural law was merely an ideology on which men acted politically and on whose basis they asserted their natural or human rights (Bobbio, 1990: Introduction). The strong emphasis on the political (democratic) extraction of rights from the state in a series of revolutions against the government, which was common after 1789, meant a focus on an active citizen guided by a strong and uniform reason. Where that person fitted in was less important than his or her claim to equality in making the laws. We see this in Constant, and when de Maistre counterattacked, that it was the conservatives and reactionaries alone who defend the state, government, law and order and social peace against the refrain of the individual (Constant, 1819; de Maistre, 1992).

Precisely when the emphasis was on the active citizen and the drive was for democracy in the 100 years after 1850, we also saw the expansion of the European empires. Those peoples who were conquered and then forced to adopt Western values and later legal and political practices, could not but understand and reduplicate the 'warrior citizen' concept. It was dominant even in the minds of the peacemakers after 1919 when the doctrine of self-determination for nationalities was laboriously elaborated.

The essential quality of that experience was that of Western hypocrisy, since freedom was posited on becoming like, or adhering to, a Western communitarian culture. Other cultures – including many Asian cultures – were forced to do so.

On the other hand, while the rule of law was experienced by Asians as the rule of (their) law and thus as unfreedom, the idea of the citizen had shifted radically in the metropolis itself. It is true that the process was ambiguous. On the one hand, the hegemonic apparatuses of the state – mainly schooling and the army – were used to incorporate the working classes into what was a middle-class notion of the nation. It is, for example, emblematic that the word 'citizens' was replaced in France after 1789 by the word 'nation'. Yet, on the other hand, the very basis for a rule based on the consensus of the ruled requiring an active, thinking, participating citizen, impelled the extension of real democracy. The latter, by the 1870s, impelled a recognition that the neo-Kantian citizen was not possible without a minimum level of economic, social, educational and health rights. We see this in Mill, de Sanctis and elsewhere on the continent 80 years before Marshall wrote his famous work on citizenship (see Davidson/Castles, 1998 *forthcoming*, especially chapter 2). Marshall, of course, based his theory of citizenship on British history in which he identified three levels of citizen rights: 1) civil and legal; 2) political; and 3) social and economic rights (Marshall, 1950). Each had been exacted by agonistic or warrior citizens from the state, but the last was the product of the working class movement, and as Continental authors indicated, absolutely necessary for the first (Bobbio, 1984; Davidson, 1997).

These 'welfare state' innovations could be mistaken as a new manifestation of the Western will to dominate. Indeed, since they replaced family support for the young, aged, ill and unemployed by state support, they did seem to undermine or alter the role of the family. But there was also a little-identified shift taking place. Up to the creation of the third level of rights, citizenship had been seen as an assertion by the individual of rights as against the state. It was an affirmation of the private as something sacrosanct from public interference; and then, with the development of democracy, by acknowledging the right to draw such boundaries only in accordance with majority-supported law. This progress can clearly be seen by comparing Benjamin Constant with the later J.S. Mill. Once it was accepted that a minimum welfare threshold had to be attained – or citizens would be too busy thinking of their stomachs to think of their civic duties, which statistics showed clearly to be the case by the twentieth century (Bryce, 1909) – then the notion that citizenship required a social obligation towards those less favoured was added to the former quality. A cynic could term this an extension of interest theory as it could be seen merely as being in each individual's interest to provide the conditions for active citizenship and therefore social harmony. The same development can also be seen as a hegemonic exercise of state power.

But, what is crucial is that this could only be attained by 'bringing the state back in'. That is, in place of the attempt to minimize the state authority, and maximize the individual's autonomy, a welfare system required the expansion of the state, the recognition of authority and that the good was attained in a balance between individual autonomy and social obligation. This meant the re-introduction of history as what makes individuals different, not interchangeable abstractions. Bobbio writes perceptively that: "The state of nature was merely a doctrinal fiction which was needed to justify rights as inherent in men's nature, and as such inviolable by those who held public power, and inalienable by those who were entitled to them, and imprescribable however long they were violated or alienated; the doctrinal fiction amounted to requests for freedom which came from those who fought against the dogmatism of the Church or the authoritarianism of the state (...)" (Bobbio, 1990: 76).[1]

Third-generation rights meant however:

> (...) a passage from (...) man as Man, to specific men (...) of different social status, on the basis of different criteria for establishing difference, sex, age, physical condition, each of which shows specific difference, which do not permit equal treatment and equal protection. Woman is different from Man, a baby from an adult, the healthy from the sick, the temporarily ill from the chronically ill, the mentally ill from other sorts of sick people, the physically normal from the handicapped etc. A glance at the bills of rights which have been successively introduced internationally over the last forty years suffices to be made aware of this phenomenon: in 1952 the Convention of the Political Rights of Women; in 1959, the Declaration of the Rights of the Child; in 1971, the Declaration of

Rights of the Mentally Retarded Persons; in 1975 the Declaration of the Rights of Handicapped Persons; in 1982, the first World Assembly in Vienna on the Rights of the Aged, which proposed an action plan approved of by the United Nations on 3 December (Bobbio, 1990: 69-70).

What this highlights is the emergence of the recognition of difference and the need for respect and tolerance of difference. The notion of the universal Man who is interchangeable disappears. Its real corollary, racism, also comes under siege. In other words, the call for obligation towards different others starts to arise with the welfare state. Citizens are no longer antagonistic islands except in the voting booth, elsewhere they are unequal and must be treated unequally if justice is to be done.

The notion of duty had not been much present in assertions of rights in the West. There had been debate and allusion but no law on such issues (Rials, 1988: 166 ff.). For example, Article 6 of the Declaration which precedes the French Constitution of 24 June 1793 places a moral limit on freedom by the maxim: 'do not do to another what you would not wish done to yourself'. Article 123 states then that the Republic honours not only old-age and ill-fortune but loyalty, courage and filial piety and subjects the Constitution to all the 'virtues' (Stewart, 1963; Imbert, 1993: 4). Nor do constitutions of this century pay much attention to duties. Indeed, the fear seems always to have been that too much attention to duties in documents intended to protect the citizen from the state might give back too much power to the state. Nevertheless, in international bills of rights of post-World War II vintage, there is increasing reference to 'duties'. While we have to wait until Article 29 of the Universal Declaration before we find a reference to duties, the *Declaration of the Organization of American States* devotes Chapter II to duties as does that of the African States.

To some extent this reticence can also be explained by the dominant legal positivism among Europeans: rights mean duties. Put another way, the only rights are legal rights with corollary duties.

The Other

The starting point for nation-state citizenship was usually ethnic difference united against the state. The commons, or third estate, who had been nothing and wished to make the laws for themselves, were combinations of local difference. Indeed, French was not the national language until late in the nineteenth century, and British citizenship rules were evoked when Scots spoke Gaelic. The ethnic commons were adversarial and warlike against the state in the first stage of citizenship.

On the other hand, and this needs recalling, they also saw the market as the place where difference between themselves could be reconciled peacefully on a day to day basis. If Kant wished for people who dared to think for themselves and would make laws for themselves, thus becoming free, he also thought that one day a world citizen would evolve and that the basis for the latter would be the give and take of the market.

> (...) The commercial spirit cannot co-exist with war and it will gradually capture every people. Since, of all the forces subordinate (as means) to the state, the *force of money* seems the surest, it comes about that states feel constrained (certainly not for moral reasons) to promote a noble peace, and, wherever war threatens to break out in the world, to stop it through compromise, as if states were united in permanent alliance for that purpose (Kant, 1795: 26).

Kant's explicit belief in the fruitful conflict of the market-place would, no doubt, make Ohmae feel warm, but it is what it hides which is of interest (Ohmae, 1990). Kant believed that 'natural' differences of language and religion made any hope of centralizing homogenizing power impossible to enforce. He was therefore an early federalist – in the European, not the North American mode. That is, he thought that devolving political power to local levels would protect rights to difference. Morally, he could see no justification for the obliteration of difference.

A similar view had been coined by the earlier international lawyers, de Vitoria and Suarez, who also rejected Aristotelian communitarianism and the way its exclusiveness privileged authority (Davidson, 1996). In the latter's place they placed the Gospel, whose innate egalitarianism was the cornerstone for natural law theory. The Kantian position, despite its explicit rationalism, is thus revealed as having more to do with notions about the relation of God and Man as well as the family, than a surface or even subjective reading of Kant would suggest.

However, even if that proposition were arguable, the dilution of the Kantian position was inevitable in another way. The recognition of difference, which was incremental with the extension of Empire, or the 'discovery' of new worlds, resulted in a gradual weakening in the belief that reason or mind could dominate natural or social threats. This was the essence of the Enlightenment project whose height had been reached before the French revolution. In turn, as Western thought gradually gave up that project over the nineteenth century, and recognized the limitation to reason as mastery, it was forced into recognition that mild and convivial virtues like tolerance and compromise were needed for social survival.

The Destruction of Reason

Given the strictures of Georg Lukács about the development of an anti-Enlightenment position, it is again important to make clear what we are asserting and what we are not asserting.

The drive towards citizenship as an attempt to subject the chaotic natural and social worlds and the risks they bring by imposing some rules of law and thus predictability has already been highlighted. An attempt to understand the *ensemble* of the world's processes is thus essential to any human being who wishes to have some presence as a subject, rather than as an object buffeted by its forces. This requirement for a totalizing thought must and will always remain for any understanding of citizenship. It did so and will continue to do so.

What is at stake is the status of that thought; how it is arrived at and what effectiveness it will have. Its effectiveness affects attachment to its value system. Over the nineteenth and the twentieth century it has moved from a thick to a thin, or from a strong to a weak status. Basically, where once all those involved in the dialogue took for granted common presuppositions at a high level of generality which came from a shared life like that of the Greeks, this has become less and less the case both within nation-states and in a wider 'global' situation of the late twentieth century. Today, in states which are multicultural and multi-ethnic after failed attempts at forced homogenization or 'nation-building', there is no shared life and therefore ever fewer taken-for-granted presuppositions in any dialogue. Everything, including premises, has to be negotiated and compromises must be arrived at. Just how 'thin' this dialogue may be is best expressed by Bruce Ackerman in his notion of conversational restraint, which puts off the agenda the moral ideals which divide us. Nobody need say what they feel is affirmatively false. Dialogue is used for pragmatically productive purposes. It identifies what all political participants find not unreasonable. Anyone can raise any issue, but restraint should apply to the answers they may give legitimately to others' questions. They may see as procedures for conflict resolution only those propositions on which they may agree. Ackerman believes that his conversational restraint has at least the advantage that while every time the debate takes place the citizens may have to express many things which they think are true, they are not obliged to accept and express what is false for them. They learn to play the role of citizen, a partial role like that of a lawyer. The problem is that the area of agreement may shrink as more and more players enter the debate (Ackerman, 1989). This is reminiscent of some agonizing dinner party which is more silence than conversation as each person tries to figure out what is appropriate.

It all adds up to a massively complex and complicated world requiring endless dialogue on myriads of subjects which are only half-understood. Thus it is not easy to arrive at any position once and for all. Change forces renegotiation. There are two major ways out of the problem. The first is to return more and more to the private realm and reduce the state as a centralized body. The second and corollary process, since the state is needed, is to create more democracy in more places so that decisions can be made as close to the problem as possible and by the people most directly affected. These are typical solutions proposed by governments today in the process known as economic rationalism.

They are, however, both undermined from the outset, since the premise is difference and that means importing into the public different collective memories. It is true, and Asian commentators are justified in recalling this, that for centuries the West dealt with difference by crushing it and then forcing amnesia in hegemonic projects. It is still doing this in many places. But, overall it has been recognized that this is not a viable policy if only on interested managerial grounds (Davidson, 1997). The public/private distinction does not really hold, and public and private reasons are difficult to disentangle. In sum, the expansion of the private through the creation of more rights, typically cultural ones, and the 'subsidiarity' principle borrowed from Roman Catholic practice, may be necessary, but are not sufficient.

In order for there to be an active citizen presence, new civic virtues have had to be developed. Where for Rousseau (as for Pericles) the mark of the citizen – the citizen as warrior – was a frank and fearless defence of the sacred right of self-determination, the civic virtues of a global world, where there is a constant *face-à-face* between difference, call not only for a social conscience, but also for a mildness of manner. Citizens still must assert their equal rights as individuals on whose power 'from below' the rule of law is founded, but the emphasis shifts in the multi-faceted person from the citizen who makes the law under which life is lived, to the person who sees the ultimate value in obedience to such law. For it is through such obedience that all become equal. Another way of expressing this is to state that citizenship has seen the emphasis shift from the political assertion of right to the legal submission to it.

This shift arises and is expressed in the recognition of sovereignty as itself a religious notion, or as incorporating an immanentization of awful divine power, which can never be attained. The Nation as One and Indivisible is a renewed Godhead, allowing little role for constitutionality and the role of judges: the legislature is the sole source of power (Gauchet, 1989; Descombes).[2]

If we draw together the threads of a complicated argument, it amounts to this. The need for affirmative action led to:

(1) the recognition that citizenship was more than an individual's relation with the state. It also involved relations with other individuals;
(2) this forced an end to the abstract Man, who became men and (later) women in all their difference(s);
(3) once that was a given of citizenship, every person faced all as subjects produced differently and unable to escape that condition completely in the public realm. The public/private divide has become blurred beyond recognition.
(4) therefore, to communicate they had to replace all assumptions that what was true for one was true for all (monist received wisdom) and all values had to be ever-renegotiated compromises;
(5) this necessitated two complementary processes: (i) that public debate was like a market where bargains could be struck, not according to Cartesian rationality only, but also in a Rabelaisian hurly-burly where myriads of values found their equivalents in exchanges on a human individual scale; (ii) that the notion that the totality could be grasped in thought was impossible given the kaleidoscopic complexity of difference in combination;
(6) this ended the hubris of reason as mastery and thus the developed form of citizenship as mastery which required the warrior (Kant plus Rousseau);
(7) as the notion of mastery declined, so did that of the people as masters or sovereign, people who could control their destinies totally by understanding how it all worked in a particular domain (communitarianism);
(8) the end of sovereignty, the key notion for citizenship in the eighteenth century meant a shift in emphasis from citizen power to citizen rules;
(9) the new subordination of self to a recognition of the limits to reason added up in the context of a rule of law to a return to obedience, while recognizing that law was never merely command. Rather it required infinite consensual redefinition;
(10) but once the notion of control and dominance through reason was seen as infinitely renegotiable, all closed discourses became impossible. The very procedures which underpinned them were open to revision to meet discourses from outside(rs). The mark of civility and civic virtue became that no-one, no community, no culture, no civilization, could ever be a judge in its own cause – the very basis for thinking in such hermetically closed units had disappeared. The premise of the self-identical with itself, held together by mind, which lay behind neo-Kantian notions of citizenship, had vanished. It is this already disappearing model of citizenship which Asians wrongly accuse Westerners of believing.

Notes

1. Translation of this and following quotes from the Italian original by Alastair Davidson.
2. I am grateful to Ms Natalie Doyle for drawing my attention to the positive contribution of this French critique.

References

Ackerman, B. (1989) 'Why Dialogue?', *Journal of Philosophy* 86 (1): 5-23.
Ajami, F. (1993) 'The Summoning', *Foreign Affairs* 72 (4): 2-10.
Alston, P./Steiner, H. (eds.) *International Human Rights in Context: Law, Politics, Morals. Text and Materials*. Oxford: Clarendon Press.
Bartley, R.L. (1993) 'The Case for Optimism', *Foreign Affairs* 72 (4): 15-19.
Beeson, M. (1996) 'APEC: Nice Theory Shame about the Practice', *Australian Quarterly* 68 (2): 35-49.
Binyan, L. (1993) 'Civilization Grafting', *Foreign Affairs* 72 (4): 19-22.
Bobbio, N. (1984) *Il futuro della democrazia*. Turin: Einaudi.
Bobbio, N. (1986) *Due secoli di democrazia europea*. Perugia: University of Perugia, Department of Political Science.
Bobbio, N. (1989) *Thomas Hobbes*. Turin: Einaudi.
Bobbio, N. (1990) *L'Età dei diritti*. Turin: Einaudi.
Bobbio, N. (1990a) 'Il pensiero politico', in Barile, P. (ed.), *Piero Calamandrei*. Milan: Giuffre.
Bouamama, S. (1991) in Bouamama, S./Cordeiro, A./Roux, M., *La citoyenneté dans tous ses états. De l'immigration à la nouvelle citoyenneté*. Paris: l'Harmattan.
Bryce, J. (1909) *Promoting Citizenship*. Chicago: Houghton Mifflin.
Chan, J. (1996) 'The Task for Asians: to Discover their Own Political Morality for Human Rights', *Human Rights Dialogue* 4 (March): 5-7.
Constant, B. (1819) in Fontana, B. (ed.) (1990) *Political Writings*. Cambridge: Cambridge University Press.
de Maistre, J. (1992) *De la souveraineté du peuple. Un Anti-contrat social*. Paris: PUF.
Davidson, A. (1996) 'Expansionary Citizenship: The European Experience', Paper presented at *Globalization and Citizenship: An International Conference*, 9-11 December 1996, Geneva, UNRISD.
Davidson, A. (1996a) 'Mildness: A New Civic Virtue', *The Humanist,* May: 2-10.
Davidson, A./Castles S. (1997 forthcoming) *Globalization and Citizenship. The Citizen Who Does not Belong*. London: MacMillan.
Davidson, A. (1997) *From Subject to Citizen. Australian Citizenship in the Twentieth Century*. Cambridge: Cambridge University Press.

Donnelly, J. (1989) *Universal Human Rights in Theory and Practice.* Ithaca: Cornell University Press.

Fabricius, F. (1992) *Human Rights and European Politics. The Legal Political Status of Workers in the European Community.* Oxford: Berg.

Gauchet, M. (1989) *La Révolution des Droits de l'homme.* Paris: Gallimard.

Ghai, Y. (1994) 'Human Rights and Governance. The Asia Debate', *Australia Yearbook of International Law* 15: 5.

Global Commission (1995) *Our Global Neighbourhood. The Report of the Commission on Global Governance.* Oxford: Oxford University Press.

Harridan, H./Benoit-Rohmer, F. (1994) *The Minority Question in Europe. Towards the Creation of a Coherent European Regime.* Brussels: Centre for European Policy Studies.

Huntington, S. (1993) 'The Clash of Civilizations?', *Foreign Affairs* 72 (1): 22-50.

HRLJ (1993) *Human Rights Law Journal* 14 (9-10): 346-377.

Johnson, C. (1995) 'The Empowerment of Asia', *Australian Quarterly* 67 (2): 28-43.

Imbert, P. (1993) *Note interne sur une éventuelle déclaration des devoirs de l'homme.* Strasbourg: Council of Europe, Direction de Droits de l'Homme.

Kant, I. (1795) in Bobbio, N. (ed.) (1985) *Immanuel Kant. Per la Pace Perpetua.* Rome: Riuniti.

Kausikan, B. (1993) 'Asia's Different Standard', pp. 226-231 in Alston P./Steiner, H. (eds.) (1996), *International Human Rights in Context. Law, Politics, Morals. Text and Materials.* Oxford: Clarendon Press.

Lawson, S. (1993) 'Conceptual Issues in the Comparative Study of Regime Change and Democratization', *Comparative Politics* 24 (2): 183-205.

Mahathir, M. (1996) 'Globalization: What it Means to Small Nations', *Resurgence* 74: 27-30.

Mahbubani, K. (1993) 'The Dangers of Decadence', *Foreign Affairs* 72 (4): 10-15.

Marshall, T. H. (1950) *Citizenship and Social Class and other Essays.* Cambridge: Cambridge University Press.

Marx, K. (1975) *Early Writings.* Harmondsworth: Penguin.

Mill, J. S. (1879) in Collini, S. (ed.) (1989) *On Liberty and other Writings.* Cambridge: Cambridge University Press.

Ohmae, K. (1990) *The Borderless World. Power and Strategy in the Interlinked Economy.* New York: Harper.

Rajamoorty, T. (1993) 'A Plea for a Balanced Approach', *Third World Resurgence* 33: 29.

Reich, R. (1990) *The Work of Nations. Preparing Ourselves for 21st-Century Capitalism.* London: Simon and Schuster.

Rials, S. (1988) *La Déclaration des Droits de l'Homme et du Citoyen.* Paris: Hachette.

Rousseau, J.-J. (1971) *Oeuvres complètes,* 3 vols. Paris: Seuil.

Rubinstein, R./Crocker, J. (1994) 'Challenging Huntington', *Foreign Affairs* 96 (3): 113-128.

Schnapper, D. (1994) *La communauté des citoyens.* Paris: Gallimard.

Sheridan, G. (ed.) (1996) *Living with Dragons. Australia Confronts its Asian Destiny.* St. Leonards: Allen and Unwin.

Stewart, J. (1963) *A Documentary Survey of the French Revolution*. New York: Macmillan.
Soysal, Y. (1994) *The Limits to Citizenship. Migrants and Postnational Membership in Europe*. Chicago: Chicago University Press.

CHAPTER 13

Tensions of Citizenship in an Age of Diversity: Reflections on Territoriality, Cosmopolitanism and Symmetrical Reciprocity

John Rundell

Preface: Globalization, Nations and Citizens

In contemporary social theory, 'the dialectic of globalization' has been used as a trope to throw into relief the late twentieth century as a world caught in a tension between internationalization and regionalization in a way that has transformed the boundaries of nation-states and the relations between them. *Internationally*, these continuing and contemporary processes are economic growth through further internationalization of the division of labour and the development of global, rather than national cities, conflicts concerning democracy, solidarity and identity that have occurred in the old and newly formed states in the post-Cold War era and which have seen the involvement of international and supra-national organizations such as the UN and the European Union, and the internationalization of social problems such as damage to, and concern for, the environment, poverty, disease and crime. *Regionally*, these processes originate from increasing demographic changes, population movements and the formation of 'new' diasporas, the political dynamics between national centres and regional areas, the politicization and extension of categories of rights, and cultural diversification. As has been pointed out in a recent book by Neil Smelser, the effect of these processes may be *increased* or *decreased* sovereignty, *increased* or *decreased* military conflict or cooperation, *increased* or *decreased* cultural diversity. From this perspective, this dialectic of globalization is redrawing collective identities that can be either inward or outward looking. (In the light of the former, ethnic, sexual or gender tribes and in the light of the latter, 'new' ethnic, sexual, or gender diasporas.) Thus, a new 'map' of integration is being drawn in which the tension between society and the individual (or nation-state and citizen) is being replaced by a tension between tendencies towards regionalization and tendencies towards internationalization (Smelser, 1997; see also Bauman, 1992).

However, this post-modern sociological assessment, which views the contemporary period as one that revolves around post-nationalism, tribalism and globalization, minimizes a more complex set of configurations. The assumed current trend towards trans- or -post-nationalism is underwritten by a long history of nation-state formation. In this context, the language of modernization can be read as a metaphor for the extension and national institutionalization of some, or all of these aspects. In this way, it is more accurate to speak of a selective development and institutionalization of features that belong to *political* modernity which include democratization, the development of bounded territories and the formation of national identities, alongside the processes of globalization and regionalization. These processes of development can be viewed as selective because they are constituted as dynamics in their own right which may draw on other aspects, and which may also become privileged points of orientation by collective social actors. Furthermore, these selective political developments compete with, and even give rise to, renewed forms of selective localisms. This complex configuration means that attempts by national and transnational political and bureaucratic arrangements which aim at functional integration and systemic coordination, such as the European Union, are not so much resisted (Foucault), or result in a colonized life world (Habermas), but rather reside within a field of tensions in which conflicts are a permanent condition, and outcomes cannot be prejudged.

If one of the major themes of this volume is the blurring or even collapsing of boundaries between nation-states, then a question arises as to exactly what blurred boundaries refer to. In their contributions to this volume Rainer Bauböck and Charles Westin point to the experience of twentieth-century Western societies that have experienced large or significant migration inflows, especially in both Europe and the New Worlds of the Americas and Australasia. These migrant flows, especially in the European cases, have exposed, and indeed challenged, the ethnic core, and the way in which it has been idealized as part of the myths and identity of the receiving nations. This experience of migration and the cultural diversity that has stemmed from it has also been termed a multicultural one, or one, that can also be termed cultural hybridization: "the crossing of (...) boundaries in potentially endless combinations of the new and the old" (Markus, in this volume; see also Pieterse, 1995).

This chapter takes a different, although not unrelated, tack on these issues. Instead of invoking the metaphors of 'blurring' or 'hybridity', though, it will argue that the modern, internationally contextualized nation-state and the forms of citizenship that it is identified with are the result of the selective and competing dimensions of political modernity. These selective processes thus fracture the distinction between state and civil society through which social and political reality has been conventionally thought, and opens onto the plurality of processes and sites. Moreover, they can be given further conceptual focus and definition if approached from the vantage points of territoriality, identity, sovereignty, democracy and publicity. Thus, as has been noted by many commentators, nation-state and citizenship are sites of condensation – and here they are viewed as sites of condensation of the five processes just indicated (Habermas, 1996a, b; Nora, 1989; Heater, 1990).

In order to further elaborate, this complexity can be further drawn out in the following schematic way that suggests that each aspect itself has its own internal dimensions. In terms of the first – territoriality – the nation-state is counterpointed by a populace and communities who are defined as belonging to this nation-state, but who may also draw on other cultural and regional bases for identity (Smith, 1986; Anderson, 1983). Moreover, the idea of the sovereignty of the nation-state is informed by two counterposing traditions. In one, the command of the 'prince' (the personalization of power) is prioritized, whilst in another, it is the codification of law (juridical sovereignty). Each, though, is opposed by a tradition of civic sovereignty, which is viewed as a rulership of power based on the idea of the non-inheritable and non-transferable sanctity of 'the people' (Pocock, 1985; Baker, 1989). The democratic aspect of the nation-state, if it is at all present and this cannot be assumed, has competed between two different models of democracy, a mediated or representative one, with its counterpart of direct or unmediated democracy. Furthermore, theories of democratic practice tend to fall also into two camps, one emphasizing the procedural nature through which decisions may be reached consensually, and another one stressing the values that are articulated, and, in fact, are required as background assumptions in the course of reaching decisions democratically (Habermas, 1996a; Heller, 1985, 1991). Moreover, models of democracy and its practices assume high levels of the transparency of power and decision-making, a transparency which also assumes publicity, or the existence of a political public sphere. However, democracy and the idea of the public are not coterminous, neither historically, nor conceptually. The public itself has been subject to shifting definitions in which it is not only defined as a critico-reflexive social space for the articulation (in whatever forms) of cultural patterns and social conflict, but also as space for specific *civic* conduct. Furthermore, it has also been interpreted as a social conduit for the integration of a citizenry into democratic life, and in this light the institutional arrangements which are entered into voluntarily are emphasized from this often corporatistic point of view (Hegel, 1979; Durkheim, 1992). Alternatively, the notion of the public also shows, what might be termed, administrative slippage, where it (the public) is identified simply as a juridical-administrative-welfare apparatus which services an amorphous citizenry, the membership of which then has to be determined. This latter notion of the public is, thus, most closely allied with territorial and sovereign notions of the nation-state (Fraser, 1987; Cohen/Arato, 1992).

Thus, citizenship is a site of condensation where national and cultural or local identity, the exercise of a sovereign state's explicit power,[1] the vocabularies of participation, and publicly orientated activities, reflexivity, and conduct converge and coalesce. In other words, citizenship cannot be reduced to the democratic moment or the territorial and administrative imperatives of nation-building, and the forms of collective identity associated with this. Even together, these two aspects cannot co-extensively capture the complexity of modern citizenship. This chapter is divided into two sections in order to, nonetheless, explore some, but not all, of its aspects. The first section explores the image of the condensation of citizenship, introduced above, where the nation-state is a site for the coalescence of its different meanings. This section begins with the territorial and administrative imperatives of nation-building, before turning to other aspects concerned with sovereignty and democracy. In a second section it is argued that the sovereign and democratic aspects of the nation-state, where they exist together, require a particular cultural horizon to orient them, even in the context of their formal institutionalization in legal codes and practices. This horizon is the horizon of symmetrical reciprocity which will be explored through the work of Marcel Mauss, especially *The Gift*, and Agnes Heller, especially *A Philosophy of Morals*.

1 The Condensation of Citizenship

The territorially bound nation-state is the most universal social form in modernity, and typifies the context of modern citizenship at its rawest. As Giddens states in *Nation-state and Violence*, "the nation-state is a power container whose administrative purview corresponds exactly to its territorial delimitation" (Giddens, 1984: 172; Mann, 1986: 198). This is in marked contrast to premodern state forms, the reach of power of which only approximated boundaries that were often fluid and impossible to monitor and control because of their distance from the central organizing agency or its regional agent. Moreover, conflicts over imagined, as much as real, borders also contributed to this fluidity. Disputes occurred by those living on, or close by, instituted territorial boundaries, by the particular state in question, or by other states pursuing their own imperative of conquest and control.

Against this schematic background, and in the wake of Clausewitz, Hintze, Weber and Elias, there are three major inventions that denote the historical formation and coherence of the nation-state and the primary organizational form through which sovereignty – in both dimensions outlined above – is expressed. This historical formation includes European Absolutism in its phase of imperial reach, which is earlier and different from the later phase of nineteenth-century colonialism linked to nation-state building. The inclusion of European Absolutism in the temporal field of political modernity gives to the latter a longer history than other accounts beginning with the eighteenth century, be it the Enlightenment (Habermas), the French Revolution (Marx), or the Napoleonic proto-praetorian centralization of the French state (Foucault). The three inventions, which, to be sure, lean on prior historical forms of explicit power, are: i) the extension and rationalization of administrative apparatuses, rules of governance and articulations of explicit power; ii) the redefinition of war and thus military force neither as a *style of life* conducted by an elite, nor an arbitrary tool for conquest, but as a planned, rationalized form of social organization which is part of the nation-state's reflexive capacity to both extend its explicit power and monitor external relations within a global or internationalized context; iii) the invention of the category and notion of *territorial or national* citizenship. In this chapter, I will concentrate on the latter – the modern form of citizenship.

The nation-state is a state form that has clearly demarcated boundaries between it and neighbouring territories, and can *equate* the dimension of territorial space with the dimension of explicit power, especially in the form of state-centred or juridical sovereignty. The territorial imperative of control and conquest is supplemented and generally muted by an imperative of internal identification and monitoring by the nation-state of those who live within its borders either permanently or temporarily. Likewise, those living inside the nation-state identify as belonging to it as an ideal or imagined community (Elias, 1996; Anderson, 1983).[2] Social integration, then, occurs at the level of the nation which is viewed as a broader collectivity and basis for identity than either an ethnic core or an elite status group.

Nonetheless, an ethnic core exists which simultaneously can be *activated* as a basis for national identity and nation-building, and *subordinated* to the new form of social integration. In this context, a double and often explosive paradox occurs, whereby the ethnic community shares 'a myth of common descent and a corresponding sense of solidarity' constituted through the idea of ethnicity, whilst simultaneously subsuming this identity under a superordinate one which is also constituted through a sense of shared history, a distinctive and shared language and culture, and an association with a shared territory (Arnason, 1990: 217). This mixture of ethnic core and nation-building has been particularly explosive in two contexts. The first was the multi-ethnic nations of the Old World which emerged out of the crises and collapse of, in particular, the Austro-Hungarian and Ottoman Empires, whilst the second was the immigrant societies of the New Worlds of the Americas and Australasia, where, apart from competing and coalescing ethnic groups, there was also the confrontation by these groups, and often in a united way, with the indigenous populations. According to Anthony Smith, the ethnic and nation-building components are interdependent, although the ethnic antecedents of the modern state are a premodern feature of the nation that may come into conflict with the modern ones at any time (Arnason, 1990; Smith, 1986, 1988; Gellner, 1983; Kohn, 1967; Armstrong, 1982).

The paradox or tension between ethnicity and nation is partly resolved, or is suspended – if only for an indeterminate period – by a process of homogenization at the cultural level through *nationalism*, and at the political level through the category of *citizenship*. Citizenship is the formal and trans-communal mechanism that integrates an anonymous and even polymorphous population who inhabit the territory of a nation-state into its regulatory system. Or to put it another way, territorial, or national citizenship, in this instance, is a mechanism for the administrative control of the movement of a nation's inhabitants within and across its borders. It denotes the nation-state's preoccupation with the territory and its inhabitants over which it has jurisdiction, and includes determinations of inclusion and exclusion, entry and exit (Brubaker, 1989; Breton, 1988). Territorial-national citizenship, thus, is a point of condensation where the territorially determined nation-state, its administrative prerogatives, and its identity-securing mechanisms intersect and coalesce. In this context, territorial citizenship may also become a point where *ethnie* and the nation coincide. Thus, an accident of birth binds people to a nation's soil "on the basis of legally established criteria and procedures" (Breton, 1988: 87).

Nonetheless, a concentration on citizenship from the perspective of the territoriality of the nation-state obscures its other relevant versions. Giddens, for one, makes the useful distinction between citizenship, nationalism and sovereignty by drawing on the work of T.H. Marshall who generates a notion of citizenship as the historical accumulation of rights – firstly, civil, then political, and lastly, social ones (Giddens, 1984: 203-209; Marshall, 1950: 1-85). In contrast to Marshall, who argues that these rights of citizenship develop in a cumulative process, each dynamic of citizenship need not set the conditions nor predetermine the succeeding one, and may indeed contest the others. This means that social citizenship may not be the last type of citizenship to make its mark. Following Mann and Elias, rather than either Marshall or Giddens, in this instance, social citizenship is an internal aspect of the state's prerogative concerning the definition of who a citizen is, and by extension his/her integration into 'the infrastructural power of the state'. Whilst the British case (which Marshall views ideal-typically) presupposes a contestatory model through which social and economic rights and benefits were won and accrued by social movements, especially the labour movement and middle-class professionals, Mann and Elias argue that social citizenship was a determining characteristic of the state's own ability to integrate a citizenry 'from above'. This was also due to its capacity to levy taxation, which, in the German case, for example, specifically predated political citizenship (Mann, 1987; Elias, 1996).

Neither Giddens, nor Elias, nor Mann equate citizenship *per se* with territoriality. However, Giddens, in particular, is primarily concerned with typologies of surveillance (Held, 1989: 198). My aim, here, though, is to stress the multidimensional features of citizenship. In contrast to Giddens and Marshall, though, it is suggested here that modern citizenship can be divided into five broad types which may or may not intersect, and which may or may not be more or less totalitarian or democratic. These types are *territorial/national citizenship, public and social citizenship, sovereign citizenship, democratic citizenship* and *cosmopolitan citizenship*. Each forms an arena of contestation and conflict with the other types, as well as with the explicit power of the nation-state.[3]

The following discussion leaves to one side the otherwise important dimensions of *public and social* citizenship. In the context of a discussion concerning the blurring of local, national, and global political and cultural boundaries in the late twentieth century the most acute point of tension between the nation-state and the five modalities of citizenship occurs along the fault line between, on the one hand, the global, national and local forms of citizenship and its *sovereign* and *democratic* interpretations and practices. It is with this difference that the remainder of this section is primarily concerned. The fault line exists as a tension between particularistic perceptions and practices bound to the context of a specific nation-state and its invented nationalisms and traditions, and ones that either go beyond them, or are capable of interacting with them in an ongoing and open-ended way. According to Brubaker, the nation-state is doubly bounded by territory and membership (Brubaker, 1989: 14). From a territorial or national perspective, citizenship is a neat category – one either is or is not a member of a state. However, from sovereign and democratic perspectives, the issue of membership is more complex, especially if it is tied to questions of the multiple forms of life that constitute or intersect any nation-state, especially in a global context. In order to view the tensions involved here, it is worth revisiting the question of citizenship, but this time from the vantage points of the way it is constructed not only by territoriality, but also through the conditions of sovereignty and democracy.

A useful distinction can be made between modern citizenship and sovereignty in order to elucidate the dynamics of rulership in modernity. Citizenship in *modernity* refers not only to the ideals and activities of the citizen as a member of a political community, the image inherited from both Greek and Roman Antiquity and the medieval city, but also to the complex array of discrete phenomena that revolve around nation-state formation. This interpretation supplements the view of citizenship in the tradition of republican political philosophy that views it as having an *internal* relation to the question of rulership or sovereignty. To be sure, this conventional interpretation also belongs to the self-understanding of the eighteenth century, particularly. However, from the vantage point of the formation of nation-states a cleavage was being forged which presented its inhabitants as, *pace* Marx, people living in, or between, two worlds – citizens of a territorial state, and real, or potential, sovereigns of it (Walzer, 1974; Nisbet, 1974; Pateman, 1989).[4] In other words, and as indicated above, sovereignty was being redefined along two axes – from the vantage point of the nation-state, and from the vantage point of citizens who aspired to participate in its condition of explicit power. Each vantage point redefined the nature of rulership in a modern register. Territorial citizenship is the most recent development of the more general notion of citizenship and sits uncomfortably with its more classical origins as a more distinctly political category.

Moreover, as many writers have pointed out, especially if the French case is taken paradigmatically, a historical conflation occurs between the different aspects of nation-building, republican sovereignty *and* national citizenships. As Habermas states, "with the French Revolution, the 'nation' became the source of state sovereignty" (Habermas, 1996b: 494). In other words, in the context of the French Revolution, the administrative sovereign state that gives the law converged with nation-building that was viewed as a unified and homogeneous cultural project. Within the French case, this unified cultural project became identified with a view of sovereignty that originated from the body of '*le peuple*' (Baker, 1989: 848). As Baker goes on to say, "in the simplest of terms, national sovereignty was created when the French revolution transferred sovereign power from the crown to the nation (...) As a collective being the nation was part of a natural order, prior to all history, the ground of history" (ibid.: 850-851). This meant that the double meaning of sovereignty indicated above became fused directly with that of the nation. Baker and Habermas both point to the internal tension of this fusion in terms of the issue of sovereignty. "[O]nce sovereignty was held to be inherent in the body of the nation in this way, the danger of its alienation from the nation to the representative assembly – the threatening possibility that a particular will might be substituted for the real will of the nation – became ever present" (ibid.: 853; see Habermas, 1989: 495-496). In other words, the nation, in its primordial naturalization as the well-spring of identity and, hence, citizenship, became the source from which citizens could only be alienated and identity ruptured. The problem, then, is the subsumption of republican sovereignty by national identity and its fusion with the administrative state. A cultural horizon of the republican nation was formed which is at once viewed politically *and* primordially as the filter through which questions of social integration are solved. To challenge the cultural homogeneity of the nation is simultaneously to challenge its political will.

However, this Jacobin version of French political correctness, as it has been termed by Wieviorka, should be read as a specific instance in a more variegated and critical landscape of citizenships (Wieviorka, 1996; see also Galeotti, in this volume). Habermas, for example, points to the patterns of procedural democracy that have displaced both *ethnie* and *nation* as the primary mechanisms of social integration of a citizenship into its nation-state, at least in the West (Habermas, 1996b; Habermas, 1996c). According to him, in modern democracies questions of sovereignty and their democratic solution within the nation-state provide "a new kind of connection between persons who had been strangers to each other" (Habermas, 1996c: 284). The historical coexistence between the issues of sovereignty and democracy within the horizon of the nation-state of the European type, in Habermas's view, enables two problems to be solved simultaneously: "it established a democratic mode of legitimation on the basis of a new and more abstract form of social integration" in the form of legally mediated solidarity and procedural forms of political participation (ibid.).

To be sure, and without overlooking Habermas's recognition of the tension that exists between national and republican identities of the nation-state and its citizenry, what is of interest in this context is his insistence on the internal relation between law – juridical sovereignty – and democracy. Habermas argues that modern law is "a medium that allows for a much more abstract notion of civic or public autonomy" (1996b: 505). Modern law guarantees freedom because it is backed by a system of norms that are both coercive and positive, and it is this double feature that enables modern law to become associated with the issue of political legitimacy. "The formal properties of coercion and positivity are associated with the claim to legitimacy: the fact that norms backed by the threat of state sanction stem from the changeable decisions of a political lawmaker is linked with the expectation that these norms guarantee autonomy of all legal persons equally" (Habermas, 1996a: 447). Moreover, the medium of law and its differentiation from moral concerns enables rights to be activated by citizens in a setting that is institutionalized, and constructs and gives legitimacy to citizens as legal subjects (ibid.: 451-455). In this sense, law functions as both a guarantor and as 'transmission belt' that "simultaneously secures symmetrical relationships of reciprocal recognition between abstract bearers of individual rights" (ibid.: 448-449).

According to Habermas, this legal constitutionalism of the modern democratic state is internally buttressed by a specific form of reflexivity – democratic reflexivity – which becomes the basis upon which modern law itself is constituted. In Habermas's view, this democratic reflexivity is formulated as 'a discursively achieved agreement' in which laws and decisions are made and re-made on the basis of claims that are redeemable through practical-rational argumentation. However, it is here, at the core of his meta-theory, that a tension emerges concerning the democratic discursive proceduralism that he wishes to make the cornerstone of his theory of modern sovereign-democratic citizenship. As he is well aware, "law is not a narcissistically self-enclosed system, but is nourished by a democratic *Sittlichkeit* of enfranchised citizens and a liberal political culture that meets it halfway" (ibid.: 461). Hence, internal to the formation of a legal-democratic system is a cultural form which orientates and gives it depth. As Habermas states, "one starts with the horizontal sociation of citizens who, recognizing *one another* as equals, mutually accord rights to one another" (ibid.: 457).

This aspect of a codetermining cultural horizon is present throughout Habermas's work as a whole, and informs his writings on nationalism, sovereignty and citizenship. As he points out, in a post-metaphysical and internationally interdependent world in which collectively binding world-views have been replaced by patterns of detraditionalization, as well as pluralized contexts which themselves challenge homogeneous cultures, democratic *Sittlichkeit* provides a force for both orientation and social integration. As he says, "my suspicion is that a liberal political culture can hold together multicultural societies only if democratic citizenship pays in terms not only of liberal and political rights, but also of social and cultural rights as well (...) Democratic citizenship develops its force of social integration, that is to say it generates solidarity between strangers, if it can be recognized and appreciated as the mechanism by which the legal and material infrastructure of actually preferred forms of life is secured" (1996c: 290).

However, what occurs here is a tension between the linguistic/procedural turn in Habermas's work and a latent anthropological-cultural current that is also present. It is not the purpose to explore this tension here, but to identify and draw on it as a way of indicating a necessary background point of orientation or *horizon* through which both the formal-legal democratic culture is constituted, and a mode of sociability that is internal to this culture. The formal-legal institutionalization of democracy already presupposes some general background assumptions or prejudices (Gadamer) concerning both the conduct of political and sovereign life, and the forms of sociability through which this might be conducted. I wish to explore this horizon in the following section, not through an immanent reading of his work where such an investigation is effectively blocked, but initially through Mauss's

The Gift, and, then, the work of Agnes Heller. For each, the dialectic of mutual recognition is transposed into the more robust formulation of a horizon of symmetrical reciprocity. It is this that provides the horizon beyond homogeneous *territorial/national* citizenships and points towards a pluralist, outward looking, or what will be termed here, *cosmopolitan* citizenship. Cosmopolitan citizenship can be viewed as a supplement to sovereign and democratic citizenships, both of which may contain a tendency towards national closure at their core, as has been indicated in the case of the French conflation described above. This citizenship places the emphasize on the *real or potential mutual recognition of, and reciprocity between,* other forms of life, rather than on an *agreement* about, or between, them. This background assumption of recognition and reciprocity, which following the work of Mauss and Heller is here termed symmetrical reciprocity, may even alter the version of mutuality built into Habermas's position.

2 The Intersubjective Horizon of Political Cosmopolitan Citizenship: Symmetrical Reciprocity

Mauss's *The Gift* can be seen as a corrective to systemic approaches that not only absorb the social actor into the system, but also conceal from view the dynamics and processes of interaction between social actors through which any social system is co-constituted and brought forward.[5] Furthermore, Mauss's work demonstrates that there is a horizon of meaning to these social interactions, and that this horizon is not constituted only in linguistic terms, or rationally. Rational discourse is the end result of an imaginary horizon without which sociability can neither be entered into nor understood.[6] The trope of the gift introduces a critico-hermeneutic perspective through which his critique of modernity unfolds, a critique which is less central to the concerns of this chapter, than is the structure of reciprocity itself.[7]

Mauss's analysis of the gift relation is informed by an archaic-heroic horizon – it is, in Clausewitzian terms, a form of war by other means (Mauss, 1970: 35). In other words, his analysis, especially of the potlatch of the northwestern indigenous Americans, focuses on the agonistic and contestatory dimension of gift exchanges where "the principles of rivalry and antagonism are basic" (ibid.). Here, "essentially usurious and extravagant, [the potlatch gift relation] is above all a struggle among nobles to determine their position in the hierarchy to the ultimate benefit, if they are successful, of their own clans" (ibid.: 4-5; 35). Especially in the context of the Polynesian *kula*, defeat, if not something experienced in battle, is experienced either in the receiver's inability to repay with greater bestowal a gift, or not to repay the gift at all, the result of which is dishonour and shame. As Mauss remarks with a cross-civilizational reference, "to lose one's face is to lose one's spirit, which is truly the 'face', the dancing mask, the right to incarnate a spirit and wear an emblem or totem. It is the veritable *persona* which is at stake, and it can be lost in the potlatch just as it can be lost in the game of gift giving [generally], in war or through some error in ritual" (ibid.: 38).

However, Mauss's analysis can also be enjoined as a supplement to Habermas's more formalistic position because, unlike him, Mauss argues that although modern (economic) exchanges are saturated by utilitarianism, this neither exhausts nor completely colonizes the entire range of social interactions. This could also be said for formal democratic exchanges. According to Mauss, whilst the gift relation is constructed and analysed by means of specific civilizations – the Polynesian, northwest American – nonetheless, for him, it is not reducible to these civilizational forms alone. The gift relation is an 'empirical universal' (Heller) that denotes a common form of reciprocity – symmetrical reciprocity – where many dimensions of human life and action intersect and condense – the cognitive, the moral-ethical, the emotional. As he says, "the basis of moral action is general; it is common to societies of the highest degree of evolution, to those of the future and to those of least advancement. Here we touch bedrock. We are talking no longer in terms of law. We are talking of men and groups since it is they, society and their sentiments that are in action all the time" (ibid.: 68). In this context, the structure that Mauss gives to the gift relation can be separated, at a formal level, from the agonistic dimensions that he attributes to the potlatch. As such, it can, then, be drawn on as a model for non-violent, symmetrical reciprocity.

If we abstract from the Polynesian system of total gift-exchanges that Mauss presents, a formal structure emerges around three principle obligations: an obligation to give, to receive and to repay. This constitutes a relation of symmetrical reciprocity in which "a series of rights and duties about consuming and repaying [exists] side by side with rights and duties about giving and receiving" (ibid.: 11). Symmetrical reciprocity assumes, then, a relationship as well as reciprocity. As Heller notes, "where one party gives and the other does not receive there is no relationship. Where one party only gives and the other only receives there is a relationship but no reciprocity" (Heller, 1990: 53). Gifts are tokens of recognition that constitute a particular intersubjectivity through which social action is conducted as a form of symmetrical reciprocity. The social actor enters this relation, and thus, his/her relations with others are constituted in a particular way. Moreover, following Mauss's implicit argument, these obligations are all publicly constituted. They do not belong to a 'private language' (Mauss, 1970: 31-45). In this sense, and following Heller rather than Mauss here, actions of symmetrical reciprocity are interactions between two parties which always assume a public dimension, even if they take place within the private sphere or everyday life (Heller, 1990: 56).

In this context Agnes Heller's work can be referred to more systematically in order to extrapolate and extend Mauss's argument, and in this way also frame it in the more action-oriented manner that is implicit in it. Heller's argument combines an anthropological universality (which we have seen above) with a recognition of the historical shifts in patterns of social action. From the background of this universality Heller can address the issue of their historical transformations. She argues that even in the condition of post-traditional, multicultural and pluralized modernity, social action has not been emptied of either orientative principles or depth of meaning. Heller's recommendation is that the classical triad of matter-*paideia*-form that typifies theories of social action in the Aristotelian tradition, should be replaced by a triad of determinations-conduct-learning processes. In other words, patterns of action are not reducible to their linguistic form only, rather her triad points to the ways in which social actions are orientative principles that manifest themselves concretely. Conduct is the most important because, for her, "whereas 'form' suggests perfection, fulfillment, completeness (...) conduct is open-ended, something which goes on and on; it is the identity of being and becoming" (Heller, 1990: 67). In other words, her triad is one that emits the contingency that is a hallmark of modernity, generally.

Moreover, over and above the recognition of a contingent, post-traditional and post-metaphysical world, Heller argues that conduct also encompasses the complexity of the networks of human interactions, that are sedimented in institutions and repeated time and again in social interactions, and as such are always collective endeavours (ibid.: 67). For her, this complex condition of a form of life, and even one that is now both contingent and pluralized, continues to constitute and address the patterns of interaction and forms of meaning which are required for a form of life to have depth.

According to Heller, giving is the overarching category, and it is assumed by those who are caught in its web, to be ongoing across time and space. Gift-giving is not constituted or hampered by social or temporal boundaries. As both Mauss and Heller argue, irrespective of either their ritual or informal context, the repayment of a gift can be carried forward in time, and it is only its interruption (that is, its non-return) that throws this counterfactuality into relief. However, there are two significant differences between their analyses. In the archaic civilizations studied by Mauss all natural objects as well as social beings can be subject to gift exchanges – from shells to slaves and women. Symmetrical reciprocity refers only to reciprocity among persons of equal standing. In Mauss's analysis, the equalization is one that occurs between people usually within the same status group or hierarchical position. It is this status dimension that adds the agonistic aspect to the symmetrical reciprocity of gift-giving. However, within Heller's more reflexively modern formulation symmetrical reciprocity is constituted through the recognition of the person *qua* person, that is, men and women "recognize each other's autonomy and have respect for each other's personality" (ibid.: 67).

Secondly, within Mauss's formulation and analysis of gift-giving the dimension of shame is a central feature internal to it. However, within the context of modernity, shame, as an emotional/cultural force within the personality, is loosened as the form of sanction. An expectation of the reciprocation of a 'gift' is muted by the recognition of another's autonomy. Whilst there continues to be a sanction involved in symmetric reciprocal interactions, the sanction is mediated by the heightened sense of the values of personhood and autonomy that accompanies it. This means that an increased distance and detachment between 'gift-givers' occurs. Symmetrical reciprocity remains only an orientative principle, and its concrete form becomes more fluid and open-ended. The result of this detached form of symmetrical reciprocity is a tension between intercourse and isolation. Under these conditions of autonomy and distance between self and other, symmetrical reciprocity, then, relinquishes the presumption of automatic and *unreflective* mutuality; rather, it requires a reflective judgement – a *paideia* – through which the contingency of the intercourse, as well as its nuances, joys and disappointments can be reflected on and learnt from.

Thus, in drawing and extrapolating from Mauss's, as well as Heller's formal models, gift-giving, receiving and repaying establish a framework for a common point of reference, as well as a framework for sanctions, limits and reflective judgement. This field of symmetrical reciprocity is both serious and magnanimous, and thus provides a counter-model to cultures of both shame and mean-spirited *ressentiment*. Those who pass through the gift relation are opened by it, but in a way that enhances, rather than reduces the social actors, especially in terms of their freedom and autonomy – on both sides of the relation.

Moreover, this relation of symmetrical reciprocity cannot be separated from the highly charged and fused relation between the 'spirit' of the gift, a coexistence that Mauss, for example, analyses under the heading of the Maori *toanga*. In this context, the 'personification of things' and the 'thingification of persons' operate as forces that bind the relation of symmetrical reciprocity together. If Habermas's argument concerning the spheres of reason, and its differentiation into proper domains of rationality is followed, the archaic societies and their patterns of social relations that Mauss presents would denote a premodern conflation between nature and society (the naturalization of society and the socialization of nature) (Habermas, 1984: 48-52). Yet, Mauss's and Heller's analyses, rather than pointing towards an incomplete process of cultural differentiation, open a horizon of meaning that is the necessary, although not fully articulable, dimension through which the social relation is constituted.[8] This particular horizon of sociability is the horizon of symmetrical reciprocity which is an abstract and non-personalized, yet understood point of reference. As Mauss states, "The pattern of symmetrical and reciprocal rights is not difficult to understand if we realize that it is first and foremost a pattern of spiritual bonds (...)" (Mauss, 1970: 11). Mauss terms this horizon a contract. His point, though, is that this mode of interaction 'leans on' (Castoriadis, 1987) an irreducible *imaginary* horizon. In Heller's terms, while the conditions of giving, receiving and reciprocating are constituted according to a value horizon of freedom and autonomy, they are intersubjectively constituted and stabilized through a paradigm of symmetrical reciprocity.

Symmetrical reciprocity is also one of the many horizons to which modern forms of citizenship may be oriented. Specifically, it is the horizon to which the cosmopolitan type is oriented. Cosmopolitanism can be read in a way that emphasizes both the intersections of cultures in a context of an increased recognition and acceptance of cultural diversity. In this sense, cosmopolitanism refers not only to the *arbitrary* boundaries between cultures, but also to a transformation in both content and form that occurs once cultures interact. In this perspective, then, the issue remains not simply one of forms of social integration, hybridization and new 'civilizational' or multicultural mosaics. Rather, it concerns the *relationships* that are entered into and established between diverse cultures in either utopic or dystopic forms. As Hannerz has pointed out, "cosmopolitanism in a stricter sense includes a stance towards diversity itself, toward the co-existence of cultures in the individual experience. A more genuine cosmopolitanism is first of all *an orientation, a willingness to engage with the Other*. It is an intellectual and aesthetic stance of openness toward divergent cultural experiences, a search for contrasts rather than uniformity" (Hannerz, 1990: 239, emphasis added).

However, as Agnes Heller notes in her chapter in this volume, the *aesthetic* prioritization of diversity and interaction with others often leads to a preoccupation with the question of authenticity and thus towards the paradoxical closure of diversity, rather than its continuing openness (see also Heller, 1996: 25-42, and Waldron, 1995: 93-119). If, along with other diverse signature tunes of modernity from industrialism and techno-science to aesthetics and consumerism, national, global and local identities all claim sovereignty over the modern soul, then the issue becomes how cultures in the context of diversity remain open to the possibility of interaction, rather than close themselves off from meaningful interaction on the grounds of an imputed authenticity. The type of interaction that could be the basis for such conditions of diversity is the question that has preoccupied this chapter. It has been argued that a culture and mode of symmetrical reciprocity provides one, but not the only, stance towards such diversity. Moreover, it also provides a *boundary* to social life and interaction because of its assumption of reciprocity. In this sense, symmetrical reciprocity is open-endedness with limits.

Viewed in this way, this version of cosmopolitanism indicates two weaknesses of a dialectic of globalization. First, this dialectic blurs boundaries between nation-states in a way that decreases their prerogatives of identity and sovereignty *and* increases the likelihood of hybrid cultural forms once local, national and diasporic cultures overlap and intermingle (Hannerz, 1990: 239). However, globalization is not only synonymous with an assumed irresistible movement towards either uniformity or diversification. It also provides a context in which not only old particularisms can be reaffirmed and reconsolidated, but also new ones can form (Arnason, 1996: 52). Moreover, from the point of view of the nation-state's longevity, the ability of the nation-state to develop principles of social integration has been crucial to the narrative of its historical success as an organizational and territorial form. The key invention for this integration has been the various types of citizenship, discussed above. As Mann (1996) indicates, nation-states have not disappeared in the wake of globalization, rather they remain a continuing context in which interactions between them, their own cultural identities, the new localisms and wider global environments continue to occur. Indeed, they continue to underwrite many of these interactions (Mann, 1996: 298). Cosmopolitanism does not, then, simply refer to the idea of world citizenship or multiple citizenships brought under the umbrella of transnational or supranational entities, such as the European Union, no matter how important these arrangements might be for the relationship between, and transition from, denizen to citizen (Hammar, 1990; Brubaker, 1989). It refers to the existence of a background orientative principle of symmetrical reciprocity which exists prior to its own codification and institutionalization – to a cultural experience and a type of sociability.

Notes

1. The term explicit power is taken from C. Castoriadis and denotes the ability by social agents and institutions to "make sanction-bearing decisions about what is to be done and not to be done, that can legislate, 'execute' decisions, settle points of litigation and govern." (Castoriadis, 1995: 4).

2. Elias states in *The Germans* that "nationalism is (...) a specific phenomenon characteristic of large industrial state-societies at the level of development reached by the nineteenth and twentieth century (...) A nationalist ethos implies a sense of solidarity and obligation, not simply with regard to particular persons or a single person in a ruling position as such, but with regard to a sovereign collectivity which the individual concerned him- or herself forms with thousands or millions of others, which here and now is organized as a state (...) and the attachment to which is mediated through specific symbols (...) Collectivities which generate a nationalist ethos are structured in such a way that the individuals who form them can experience them – more specifically, their emotion-laden symbols – as representatives of themselves (...) The image of a nation experienced by an individual who forms part of that nation, therefore, is also constituent of that person's self-image" (Elias, 1996: 151).

3. Heater argues that there are six distinct traditions of citizenship – the republican, the cosmopolitan, the nationalist, the liberal, the totalitarian, and the socialist (Heater, 1990: 318). This does not rule out the traditions and world-views that are drawn on to constitute these versions. While this will be discussed below more fully in terms of sovereign and democratic citizenships, Turner (1990) draws our attention to various historical, national and cultural backgrounds, including the Christian and Islamic one, of this version.

4. This image of an internal relation informs J.G.A. Pocock's *The Machiavellian Moment* (1975), and A. MacIntyre's *After Virtue* (1985). Both authors would be critical of the modern diremption of citizenship and sovereignty.

5. An intersubjective dimension in Durkheim's work can be found in *The Elementary Forms of Religious Life* (1964), especially in the chapter on piacular rites.

6. Cf. C. Castoriadis, *The Imaginary Institution of Society*, translated by Kathleen Blamey, 1987, Cambridge, Polity Press.

7. Mauss's reflections take place within the framework of a civilizational analysis that both orients the problems and throws them into relief, as problems for modernity. In Mauss's civilizational framework, the intersection between institutional forms and personality structure does not rely on a thought experiment that divides non-state social forms from the invention of state ones, and it occurs as a nexus between forms of intersubjectivity and cultural horizons. In Mauss's view, civilization is a territorially extensive mode of relations and collective representations, which are constituted according to a horizon of reciprocity.

8. See Lévi-Strauss (1987), Dérrida (1992), Castoriadis (1987, 1993: 1-17).

References

Anderson, Benedict (1983) *Imagined Communities*. London: Verso.

Armstrong, J.A. (1982) *Nations before Nationalism*. Chapel Hill: University of North Carolina Press.

Arnason, Johann P. (1990) 'Nationalism, Globalization and Modernity', *Theory, Culture and Society* 7 (2-3): 207-236.

Arnason, Johann P. (1996) *Nation and Modernity*. Reykjavik: Nordic Summer University Press.

Baker, Keith M. (1989) 'Sovereignty', pp. 844-859 in Furet, François/Ozouf, Mona, *A Critical Dictionary of the French Revolution*. Cambridge, Mass.: The Belknap Press of Harvard University Press.

Balakrishnan, Gopal (ed.) (1996) *Mapping the Nation*. Oxford: Blackwell.

Bauman, Zygmunt (1992) 'A Sociological Theory of Postmodernity', pp. 149-162 in Beilharz, P./Robinson, G./Rundell, J. (eds.), *Between Totalitarianism and Postmodernity*. Cambridge, Mass.: MIT Press.

Breton, Raymond (1988) 'From Ethnic to Civic Nationalism: English Canada and Quebec', *Ethnic and Racial Studies* 11 (1): 85-102.

Brubaker, Rogers (1989) 'Introduction', in Brubaker, Rogers (ed.), *Immigration and the Politics of Citizenship in Europe and North America*. Lanham: University Press of America.

Castoriadis, Cornelius (1987) *The Imaginary Institution of Society*. Cambridge: Polity Press.

Castoriadis, Cornelius (1993) 'The Constitution of Society and Religion', *Thesis Eleven*, No. 35: 1-17.

Castoriadis, Cornelius (1995) 'Democracy as Procedure and Democracy as Regime', Manuscript.

Cohen, Jean/Arato, Andrew (1992) *Civil Society and Political Theory*. Cambridge, Mass: MIT Press.

Dérrida, Jaques (1992) *Given Time. I, Counterfeit Money*, trans. Peggy Kamuf. Chicago: Chicago University Press.

Durkheim, Emile (1964) *The Elementary Forms of the Religious Life*. New York: The Free Press.

Durkheim, Emile (1992) *Professional Ethics and Civic Morals*, translated by Cornelia Brookfield. London: Routledge.

Elias, Norbert (1996) *The Germans: Power Struggles and the Development of Habitus in the Nineteenth and Twentieth Centuries*, ed. Michael Schroter, trans. and preface by Eric Dunning and Stephen Mennell. Cambridge: Polity Press.

Fraser, Nancy (1987) 'Women, Welfare and the Politics of Need Interpretation', *Thesis Eleven*, No. 17: 88-106.

Gellner, E. (1983) *Nations and Nationalism*. Oxford: Blackwell.

Giddens, Anthony (1984) *Nation-state and Violence*. Cambridge: Polity Press.

Habermas, Jürgen (1984) *The Theory of Communicative Action Vol. 1*. Cambridge: Polity Press.

Habermas, Jürgen (1996a) *Between Facts and Norms*. Cambridge: Polity Press.

Habermas, Jürgen (1996b) 'Citizenship and National Identity', in *Between Facts and Norms*, op. cit.

Habermas, Jürgen (1996c) 'The European Nation-state – Its Achievements and its Limits', pp. 281-294 in Balakrishnan, op. cit.

Hammar, Tomas (1990) *Democracy and The Nation-state. Aliens, Denizens and Citizens in a World of International Migration*. London: Avebury.

Hannerz, Ulf (1990) 'Cosmopolitans and Locals in World Culture', *Theory, Culture and Society* 7 (2-3): 237-252.

Heater, Derek (1990) *Citizenship. The Civic Ideal in World History, Politics and Education*. New York: Longman.

Hegel's Philosophy of Right (1979) translated with notes by T. M. Knox. Oxford: Oxford University Press.

Held, David (1989) *Political Theory and Modern State. Essays on State, Power and Democracy*. Cambridge: Polity Press.

Heller, Agnes (1985) 'Rationality of Reason, Rationality of Intellect', in *The Power of Shame*. London: Routledge Kegan Paul.

Heller, Agnes (1990) *A Philosophy of Morals*. London: Basil Blackwell.

Heller, Agnes (1996) 'The Many Faces of Multiculturalism', in Bauböck, Rainer/Heller, Agnes/Zolberg, Aristide (eds.), *The Challenge of Diversity. Integration and Pluralism in Societies of Immigration*. Aldershot: Avebury.

Heller, Agnes/Fehér, Ferenc (1991) 'The Discourse Ethics of Habermas: Critique and Appraisal', in *The Grandeur and Twilight of Radical Universalism*. New York: Transaction Publishers.

Kohn, H. (1967) *The Idea of Nationalism*. New York: The Macmillan Company.

Lévi-Strauss, Claude (1987) *Introduction to the Work of Marcel Mauss*, translated by Felicity Baker. London: Routledge.

MacIntyre, A. (1985) *After Virtue: A Study in Moral Theory*, 2nd Edition. London: Duckworth.

Mann, Michael (1986) *The Sources of Social Power*. Cambridge: Cambridge University Press.

Mann, Michael (1987) 'Ruling Class Strategies and Citizenship', *Sociology* 21 (3): 339-354.

Mann, Michael (1996) 'Nation-states in Europe and Other Continents: Diversifying, Developing, Not Dying', in Balakrishnan, Gopal (ed.), *Mapping the Nation*, op. cit.

Marshall, T.H. (1950) *Citizenship and Social Class and Other Essays*. Cambridge: Cambridge University Press.

Mauss, Marcel (1970) *The Gift*, translated by Ian Cunnison. London: Cohen and West, Ltd.

Nisbet, R. (1974) 'Citizenship: Two Traditions', *Social Research*, Winter: 612-637.

Nora, Pierre (1989) 'Nation', pp. 742-753 in Furet, François/Ozouf, Mona (eds.), *A Critical Dictionary of the French Revolution*, op. cit.

Pateman, Carole (1989) 'The Civic Culture: A Philosophical Critique', pp. 57-102 in Almond, G.A./Verba, S., *The Civic Culture Revisited*. London: Sage.

Pieterse, Jan Nederveen (1995) 'Globalization as Hybridization', in Featherstone, Mike et al. (eds.), *Global Modernities*. London: Sage.

Pocock, J.G.A. (1975) *The Machiavellian Moment: Florentine Political Thought and the Atlantic Tradition*. Princeton, N.J.: Princeton University Press.

Pocock, J.G.A. (1985) 'Virtues, Rights and Manners: A Model for Historians of Political Thought', pp. 37-50 in *Virtue, Commerce and History, Essays on Political Thought and History, Chiefly in the Eighteenth Century*. Cambridge: Cambridge University Press.

Rundell, John (1989) 'From the Shores of Reason to the Horizon of Meaning: Some Remarks on Habermas' and Castoriadis' Theories of Culture', *Thesis Eleven*, No. 22.

Smelser, Neil (1997) *Problematics in Sociology. The Georg Simmel Lectures*. Berkeley: University of California Press.

Smith, Anthony (1986) *The Ethnic Origins of Nations*. Oxford: Blackwell.

Smith, Anthony (1988) 'The Myth of the 'Modern Nation' and the Myths of Nations', *Ethnic and Racial Studies* 11 (1), January: 1-26.

Turner, Bryan (1990) 'Outline of a Theory of Citizenship', *Sociology* 24 (2): 189-217.

Waldron, Jeremy (1995) 'Minority Cultures and the Cosmopolitan Alternative', in Kymlicka, Will (ed.), *The Rights of Minority Cultures*. Oxford: Oxford University Press.

Walzer, Michael (1974) 'Civility and Civic Virtue in Contemporary America', *Social Research*, Winter: 593-611.

Wieviorka, Michel (1996) 'Identity and Difference: Reflections on the French Non-Debate on Multiculturalism', *Thesis Eleven*, No. 47, 49-71.

CHAPTER 14

Self-Representation and the Representation of the Other

Agnes Heller

1.

The title of this chapter, which refers to representation, is ambiguous on purpose. The English (or rather Latin) word 'representation' is polysemous. In using this term I might, for example, refer to the artistic portrayal of something or somebody, of a person or a group of persons, or it might also refer to someone acting as a delegate or as a deputy for a group of persons, or someone embodying a group by his very person. There are many other sub-meanings of representation, mainly offshoots of the second kind. However, it is not just the whim of the English (or Latin) language that connects these two seemingly different referents.

The juxtaposition of hetero-representation and auto-representation that I chose as the title of this chapter, became a political, or at least a highly politicized issue in whichever of the two meanings the noun *representation* is employed. In fine arts or in literature the question arises, as to whether an author will represent the wishes, needs, thinking, behaviour, internal life of the members of the group to which he or she belongs better and truer than others do, and also better and truer than he or she would represent the life, thoughts and actions of the members of other groups. In the case of selecting, choosing, or electing a delegate the question arises whether a delegate or deputy who does not belong internally to a group can represent the needs or interests of this group. There is a further question whether the opinions and judgements of the members of a group can be represented at all. One can assert that the system of representation distorts politics by definition, and that in an authentic political life each and every member of a group should participate in decision-making directly without being represented. In the first case one makes the distinction between authentic or inauthentic representation, in the second case one rejects the possibility of an authentic representation altogether.

Although we deal with seemingly entirely different meanings of the noun *representation*, it is worth considering that the opposition of auto-representation/hetero-representation appears as an issue almost at the same time in both cases. It seems as if we were confronted with one of the dilemmas of democracy. In premodern times everyone represented his own estate – the king, the kingdom, the nobleman, the nobility, and so on. Similarly, prior to the emergence of the democratic age, the authenticity or the inauthenticity of the portrayal of members of strange and alien non-representative groups was not even raised as a question. For example, neither Shakespeare's portrayal of a Jew nor of a Moor was questioned on the ground that both the Jew and the Moor were depicted by a white Protestant Englishman as the typical representatives of their respective ethnic groups, which they were not. No one asked, whether Shakespeare, who did not know one single Jew or Moor, was entitled to portray individuals as typical representatives of the mores and behaviour of the members of those groups. For some time now, however, people have kept raising such questions. 'Uncle Tom' has become a name of abuse and a reference for the meek behaviour of the hero of the novel *Uncle Tom's Cabin*, of a hero who was portrayed by an 'other', an alien, namely by the white philanthropist Harriet Beecher Stowe, as sympathetic, attractive and good. African Americans of today would not recognize themselves in this old-fashioned representation of an honest black man. They would say, as they do, that because the representation of a black slave came from the pen of a white person, who had no idea about the inner life of black people, her portrayal of a black is therefore by definition false and phoney – in this case sentimentalized beyond recognition.

Interestingly, very similar considerations gathered momentum in the case of representation understood as delegation. In premodern times, the representatives (for example, of the Parliament) were in their very person as individuals, representing a rank or estate – for example, the estate of the nobleman, of the Church or of the civic order. In democratic times, particularly in a fully-fledged democracy with secret ballots and universal suffrage, though, the question of authenticity or inauthenticity of representation has become politicized, because it has become an issue. The deputy or member of parliament does not normally come from the group of people he represents. Moreover, it is questionable, whether anyone, even if he is a former member of a group of people, will be, in his attitudes or behaviour, his habits and needs, identical to the members of the group he formally represents. For example, within a political institution one uses a different language than is normally used by the average members of the group in their everyday reflections. More recently, and particularly in the United States, the principle of representation has assumed a new shade of meaning – it is demanded that every stratum of the population should have a share in the government in proportion to their percentage in the population at large. In the case of women, for example, because they make up 50% of the population, 50% of the politicians should be women in an ideal government. In such instances this group identity overrules political ability, qualification and so on.

This concept of representation proposed by a movement or ideology is termed by me *fundamentalism of difference*. As in all kinds of fundamentalism, its principle is that of political correctness. However, the principle of representation has already been questioned and rejected by radical universalists in its entirety from the perspective of direct democracy, fashioned on the model of the idealized Athenian polis. Direct democracy was, and still is, mostly favoured by intellectuals who rejected all kinds of political representation on philosophical grounds. Hannah Arendt and Cornelius Castoriadis, to name two such advocates of direct democracy, are convinced that there is no authentic hetero-representation, at least not in politics. Every representation is by definition hetero-representation, representation by an alien, a stranger, by another, and as such distorts opinions and fossilizes political activity.

In the case of both artistic representation and the political representation of acting as a deputy or a delegate, the same question emerges, whether or not the representation of the other by another falsifies the image, opinions, acts, needs, and wishes of others, in other words, whether there is a true kind of representation and if yes, which is the one. In what follows I will more fully and critically discuss the most radical ideas which stand for the exclusivity of self-representation. I will not discuss the other extreme that recommends qualified suffrage, because it is now out of political fashion. I will, rather, consider a kind of liberal option as a counterpart, even though I am aware that its most recent versions of formalistic liberalism make great allowances to fundamentalism on several issues, among them, the issue of representation.

2.

Who is the other? Everyone is another for another other. If the representation by another would be by definition held to be false, only autobiographies could raise claim to truth or rightness. Yet, on second thoughts, not even autobiographies would be eligible. While portraying myself I also portray others. Furthermore, when I begin to portray myself, I also alienate myself from myself to a degree. To remain identical with myself to a degree which makes portrayal impossible altogether, I must remain without a grain of self-alienation.

If one also considers that to portray requires to keep some distance from ourselves, the category of self-representation encompasses much wider territory than that of autobiography. In a novel, particularly in ones of a traditional kind, for example, one can hardly portray a person without also portraying the group characteristics of the person. If the novelist is rooted in the same milieu as her characters, the representation of the world by the novelist will resemble self-representation. One could speak about auto-representation in this wider sense, for example the case of the novels of Jane Austin, in spite of the contemptuous irony of the authoress in describing certain types of people who belong to her world yet whom she abhors. Given the commonness of their world and the strong emphasis put on certain status features, the individuals who emerge from this background are portrayed just as individuals, likable or non-likable in their own right. Moreover, in a good novel of such a type, every person can speak his/her mind. Speech also offers the single man and woman sufficient space for self-representation in a stricter, narrower sense, whether it be self-justificatory, narrative or conversational. Thus all of the characters have an opportunity to contribute to their portrayal in speaking for themselves as in a diary entry, only in a better style. This kind of novel resembles a sort of direct democracy among people of a select group, where one person convenes the meeting, during which, however, everyone can speak in turn, defending their opinions, justifying themselves and debating the issues at hand.

A more serious problem arises when a society becomes more and more heterogeneous, when entirely different social classes, ethnicities, religious denominations and other groups, who are in contact and interact with one another will be portrayed in the same story by the author of the story. Even if one presupposes that all the single members of every group are represented in a way that they can speak for themselves, defend their causes, describe their motivations, tell stories about their sufferings and joys, the suspicion still arises, that all those words are put into their mouths by the transcendental narrator who stands above them, and allegedly knows them all. However, she – the narrator – cannot know or like them equally well. We believe that the transcendental narrator gives more convincing lines to people she knows or likes best, and unconvincing ones to those whom she does not know or dislikes.

To be sure, knowing well and liking well do not always coincide. I can know my own people best without liking them best, and as such my representation, even if critical, will not put false phrases into their mouths or the mouth of the community. Alternatively, one sometimes portrays a stranger whom one hardly knows, with sympathy, yet in a way that none of their group members would recognize as their own way of speaking, thinking or acting. This is also the case in the above mentioned example of *Uncle Tom's Cabin*.

I have already pointed out that language use, or discourse, is an important issue in the debate centring around political representation, for a representative coming from a different milieu than the one represented will speak a different language. The institutions of representation, themselves, superimpose a special kind of discourse, even a jargon, on the members of those institutions. The people, for example the working people who are the ones to be represented, will perhaps not even understand the language of their Member of Parliament. This is even more so when immigrants who do not understand the mother tongue of their host country, will be represented by a Member of Parliament who, on his part, may not understand their own native tongue.

However, let me briefly return to representation in *literature*. The most radical adherents of self-representation contend that, in the portrayal of the members of other groups, particularly those of alien or strange ethnic and religious minorities, the eye of the other will not just misrepresent or falsify the other, but will portray her through the magnifying glass of his – the portrayer's – prejudices. They contend, first, that he will gather together the national or ethnic, positive and negative stereotypes about the aliens, the ones which are taken for granted in their own group or milieu, and that these will be deployed as the portrayal of the members of the groups. Alternatively, they can also act as traditional anthropologists, basing the representation of the other on external observation rather than on hear-say or personal contact. In both cases, though, prejudgements turn into prejudices almost naturally.

Similarly, in the debates conducted around *political* representation, the view is now generally held that religious groups or ethnicities should be represented exclusively by the members of their own group, optimally by men or women who come from its innermost circle. In both cases (artistic representation and representation as delegation) internal experience is contrasted to an external one, daily contact to mere observation. It is taken for granted that without sharing some internal experiences one can hardly understand the wishes, interests, and attitudes of ethnic or religious minorities, groups of a minority sexual orientation, or members of the other gender.

3.

Let me now briefly elucidate the dialectics of representation in our first case, primarily in the case of literary representation, in a pseudo-Kantian manner. Only self-representation is true. This opinion has became widespread in the recent upsurge of fundamentalist group-identity politics. Only women can represent women, only African Americans can represent African Americans, only Jews can represent Jews, only homosexuals can represent homosexuals. Naturally, the adherents of political correctness are also aware that neither ethnic nor religious groups nor homosexuals and so on, can be portrayed in hermetic isolation from other actors, and of members of other groups. A Chinese woman who writes a novel about a Chinese woman in America, will normally depict both Chinese men and non-Chinese men and women. At least in narrative genres there is no auto-representation without hetero-representation. In this case, however, so the politically correct men and women argue, the minority represents itself in contact with the members of a majority. In the works written by the members of the majority (and this is the majority literature) the authors coming from the majority will present themselves always in a more flattering light than the members of minorities. They always misrepresent minorities (women are discussed as if they were a minority). It is now high time for the minority to take revenge and to restore justice, by reversing the 'we'-'them' relationship in representation. Certainly it is still the case that a minority can live in such isolation that all shades of their culture and all kinds of characters from their rank can be portrayed without ethnic hetero-representation. This happens in several, although not all, novels and short stories by I.B. Singer. However, for the artistic success of such an undertaking, one needs Singer's incorruptible and unflattering eye. And this is exactly what is not welcomed by the adherents of self-representation.

Needless to say, the 'politically correct' position that favours self-representation and rejects all kinds of hetero-representations of members of minority groups (and of women) is fatal to all artistic practices and especially to literature. First and foremost because – as was the case with Soviet literature – it assesses works of art exclusively on the ground of their so-called content. This is irrespective of whether the hylomorphic tradition of content/form distinction makes sense in art and literature at all – a problem I cannot tackle here. The authenticity of a work is then not decided by any internal criteria of the work, but by and through a criterion external to the work. However, even apart from this most serious criticism, the political message of 'political correctness' seems to be phoney. If hetero-representation distorts the picture of the members of a group, so does self-representation, if it is willed, ideological/rhetorical and not spontaneous. We frequently understand ourselves as much through framed stereotypes as we understand others. Our prejudgements about ourselves can as frequently become distorted into prejudices as with hetero-representation. Both flattering and unflattering prejudices are prejudices. There is no essential difference between self-representation and the representation of the other as far as our inclinations towards prejudices are concerned. Both self-representation and the representation of the other can be authentic and inauthentic, true or untrue – the criterion is inapplicable and irrelevant.

To be sure, these delicate questions do not arise if we discuss the issue of self-representation and the representation of others in the mass media, including television, rather than in painting or literature. In this case, we can hardly say that the ideological demand for the exclusive auto-representation of minorities (women included) destroys the genre, as I believe is the case in fine arts or literature. However, something similar happens all the same. If the question as to who is represented and by whom becomes a pivotal issue in the mass media, the propaganda aspect of entertainment will gather momentum, and strong, ideologically motivated rhetorics will permeate all televised reports. However, didactic entertainment is not very entertaining.

It seems as if I have answered the initial question in the following way: the advocates of auto-representation are wrong. One can keep the distance necessary for the portrayal of everything, especially of characters, in both hetero-representation and auto-representation; and one can also apply stereotypes and be led by prejudices in both cases. The yardstick itself is wrong, and, perhaps, the distinction itself is also wrong.

However, maybe one could avoid fundamentalist rhetoric if one asked another, although similar, question in a different register. Instead of asking the question of which of the two kinds of representation are real, truer, more 'correct' and less prejudiced, one could ask the question whether self-representation and the representation of the other are different? Or if there is a difference, whether it makes a difference? Will it be different if a woman portrays a woman or if a man does it? Will (or can) it add to the artistic quality of a painting or of a story, that the author and the character share an essential identity which might be important for the portrayal of the character so that one could say that the person is portrayed 'from the inside', rather than on the basis of interaction or observation? One could also ask whether the possibility to write and to portray consciously, so that one emphasizes the commonness of experience and lifestyle with one's characters, adds something to, or enriches something as 'literature', if there is something that one can call 'literature'. One may also ask whether there is such a thing as 'women's literature' distinct from men's literature, or homosexual literature, distinguished from fiction written by heterosexuals, or Jewish literature? It was always taken for granted that there was French and Russian literature. Although Goethe had forged the term world literature, the latter seems to exist in the literature departments of universities alone. It is also taken as self-evident that a work of literature written in a specific language is the literature of that language. Yet this is not as simple as it seems. There is American literature and Australian and English and Irish, and also Indian literature written in English – the same language, yet not the same literature. English men and women are portrayed in novels written by Australians, Indians, Irish or Americans. Would it be absurd to distinguish already at this point between auto-representation and the representation of the other? Would it be absurd to say that, although the language is roughly the same, different life experiences distinguish one literature from another, and would it be relevant to speak of an Indian's portrayal of the life of Indians, whether in Bombay or in London, as self-representation, and about representation of the other when Englishmen portray Indians, whether in Bombay or in Oxford? Of course, authors, as almost all of us, have multiple identities, which may include multiple national or ethnic identities. It is difficult to tell whether Henry James' portrayal of Englishmen is hetero-representational or rather auto-representational. Can one maintain that his portrayal of Americans is always better, truer, or more authentic than the portrayal of Americans by an Irishman or by an Englishman, for example, George Bernard Shaw and John Galsworthy? I think not. But one can still say, that there is a difference and that this difference enriches literature. Is it true that only women can portray giving birth authentically because only women do give, or can give birth? This is sheer nonsense. Yet one can still admit that women who have given birth to children and who describe their own life experiences can portray childbirth in a different way than men usually do. Thus, although the distinction between auto-representation and hetero-representation does not yield a criterion for authenticity and truth because it does not provide a criterion for comparison, the distinction still makes sense. The multiple perspectives in representation enrich understanding and self-understanding in a hermeneutic sense.

It is interesting to see how this difference is spontaneously acknowledged. There is one case where there always remains an asymmetric reciprocity between self-presentation and the representation of the other, namely in the case of the relation between adults and children. Adults portray children. There are very few novelists who authentically portray children, and even painters paint children with an adult eye. Children are not in the position to represent themselves and the others (the adults) as they see and experience them as the representative other. Adults, though, exhibit children's drawings and paintings, not because they believe that they are 'better' paintings than those painted by adults, but because there is something in their representation about themselves and the adult world that adult drawings and paintings on children cannot match – not because they are more authentic but because they are different.

After all this had been said one could ask: is there a women's literature, a special Jewish literature or homosexual literature? I do not think that there is an unequivocal answer to this question. If, in a poem or novel, the female experience is put into the centrepoint, then this poem and novel belongs to women's literature. However, it may also belong to French or English literature, for example. Moreover, if it is also a work of high culture, that is a work that invites practically infinite interpretations, it will speak to everyone who turns towards it. But if the women's experience does not play a central role in the novel, even if it is written by a woman, I would hardly say that it belongs to women's literature, but rather to Latin American or Russian literature, and as such can also belong to high culture to which everyone may or may not have access.

4.

My question is whether this model can also serve as the model for the second – political – meaning of 'representation', that is, whether political self-representation is by definition more authentic and more just than being represented by another? Second, I am also asking whether there is a difference between self-representation and the representation of the other also in the political field, and if yes, what this difference may consist of? Finally, I am also asking whether there is something in the case of political representation that would serve as the analogy for 'high culture' and as the analogy of 'national literature'?

I came to the conclusion in the previous discussion, that to make the distinction between self-representation and hetero-representation essential for judging artworks such as painting or literature, is a gesture hostile to art. Political content cannot guide aesthetic judgement. Max Weber would say that one should not superimpose the rules of one sphere on another sphere. I would go a step further and ask, whether those rules that proved false in judging artworks are not also false in the political sphere. The connection between them is obvious. To press for the self-representation in art belongs to the strategies of political correctness, and the trend towards political correctness is essential for modern and post-modern fundamentalism. I have termed the second a fundamentalism of difference. Nowadays, it is fundamentalism based on difference that also calls for auto-representation in the field of political representation.

I cannot discuss post-modern fundamentalism in its entirety in this narrow framework, although I can enumerate some if its constituents. As with all kinds of fundamentalism, post-modern fundamentalism is based on identity politics. It differs from modernistic fundamentalism insofar as it has no universalistic ambitions, and differs from romanticism, insofar that it is not hostile towards modern science and technology. Post-modern fundamentalist movements are interested in closure, self-isolation, self-imposed apartheid rather than in world mastery. They claim to be superior, not on the ground of their universality, but on the ground of their difference. Since isolation and self-imposed apartheid are allegedly the necessary conditions of the preservation of a group identity, the declaration of identity here becomes the major political issue. Political correctness is, however, not exhausted by a mere declaration of identity; it requires the identification of all members of the group with all the issues that their ethnocracies or religious leaders have already identified as being crucial for the group's identity. Their main slogan is, just as in the case of literature or fine arts, that only self-representation is authentic, true and just. I think that this claim is also wrong.

I suggested that to regard the question of self-representation and hetero-representation as a crucial one as far as art and literature is concerned, is in itself destructive and self-destructive. I now add that the same holds true about the issue of political representation, although in a different way. If the choice between self-representation and auto-representation became the central issue in politics, and self-representation were given absolute preference as against all forms of hetero-representation, this would mean the demise of politics. Politics lives in and through the actions among citizens as citizens. However, in the case of the policy of auto-representation, no one can act in his or her capacity as a citizen, just in their capacity of being a member of one or another group. Citizens qua citizens would deal with one another in mutual and total distrust. The representatives (of a group) could never be concerned with the well-being of the city, of the body politic, but would stick exclusively to promoting the advancement of their own group. Although lobbies and parties now do this, this is not their principle; rather their practice violates it. To make this practice the principle makes politics resemble a football match where every team wants just one single thing: to win. Politics is competitive, yet it is also a collaborative and cooperative enterprise. In the case of an all-compassing acceptance of the principle of self-representation, the question of justice cannot be raised for every group claims – through its representatives – absolute rightness to its own form of life, thus rejecting the form of life of all other groups as wrong and false. This alone excludes mediation and discursive interaction altogether.

Moreover, since the politics of self-representation, as all fundamentalist politics, promotes strong, extreme rhetoric, all the prejudices become open prejudices, accepted as legitimate propaganda tools in the battle of suspicion, ruse and ruthlessness. It is always presupposed that others hold the opinions they do just because they are alien, just because they are not us, and this is why they are wrong. No one then is duty-bound to understand the other's point of view. Let me mention a few simple rhetorical devices from the menu card of identity politics in the United States. In our common European tradition that puts a premium on objectivity, if someone says that X did A because he was angry, we will not assess anger as an alleviating circumstance. Nowadays, in the United States, if someone says that X did A because he was angry, it means that he was justified doing A. Anger as a gesture of self-representation entitles a man to do things he is otherwise not entitled to do. I could also mention the Simpson case, where the selection of the jury could serve as a typical case for the system of auto-representation, this time on the judiciary. The public in the state of total mobilization by the mass media, behaved as the fans of two football teams do. The issue at stake was not justice, but which of the teams will win. Everyone wanted his team to win – no one was interested in justice. The old maxim that 'right is might' is the fundamental thesis of all the fundamentalist groups who now stand for auto-representation.

After having made the suggestion that the policy of self-representation destroys art, I added that the policy of self-representation also destroys political life. I will now go through the same steps as in my discussion about representation in art and ask: is it true, that in the case of auto-representation the interests, needs, opinions of a group are better represented than in the case of hetero-representation? Second, is it true, that auto-representation differs sometimes from hetero-representation, and that this difference can add to the richness of politics?

The very question whether a group's interests, needs, and opinions are best represented by the member of the group than by anyone else, and that the members of the group will represent the group, is fundamentalist in its conception. It presupposes that 'true' members of a group will, by definition, regard their group identity as their foremost identity, that is, if they want to be represented, they will be represented as member of this group and not in any of their other capacities. If we assume, however, that men and women have multiple identities and that one of their identities will gain preference in one situation, and the other in another, every auto-representation will be also a hetero-representation. For example, retired men can be represented by retired men, but retired men are also men of culture, and may want to be represented by men of culture. They also can be of Irish origin, and want to be represented by people of Irish origin, and so on and so forth. People are not just Hungarians, Jews, blacks, homosexuals, women and so on. If someone declares that he or she is just this or that, he or she stands already under the influence of identity politics. Ethnocracies and fundamentalist religious leaders consider men and women whose opinions diverge from theirs in several issues as traitors, they press them towards uniformity, and so do mostly their fellow group members.

I said that the call for the exclusivity of auto-representation in politics is self-destructive. But is it not justified all the same? Among other moral conflicts there can be some where there are no good choices, where self-destructive decisions are justified, for the other alternative is as bad if not worse. Cities have often been destroyed when citizens have fought for their liberty. Who was right and who was wrong: the prophet Jeremiah who implored his people to compromise with the intruding strangers, or the stubborn people who let Jerusalem be destroyed? There are tragic situations when there are no good choices. Think of a minority group which is oppressed by a majority which despises, or, alternatively, is frustrated by it. In this case one can be sure that the minority group will always be misrepresented by the majority group (and perhaps even vice versa). The call for self-representation is, then, also the call for the preservation of identity. The group will act in a fundamentalist way in the spirit of self-preservation. What is at stake here is, on the one hand, self-preservation, and, on the other hand, the destruction of the liberal-democratic political mores. Which one to choose? None of us can give a general answer. It depends. Seemingly, we could answer that even in such a case one can hold on to the proper balance between self-representation and hetero-representation and avoid fundamentalism. Unfortunately, only few, and always exceptional, individuals avoid it. The group itself, under the pressure of bad alternatives, will not be sensitive to nuances, but go in one direction without being aware of the stakes. Tragic situations exist. And no theory can get rid of them.

But tragic political situations are not frequent in already functioning liberal democracies. In a plebiscitary democracy, men and women normally understand themselves as a bundle of multiple identities. As a result, the difference between hetero-representation and auto-representation becomes smaller. It is the main tendency of modern democracies that deputies stand for issues, and that they, as well as lobbies and groups represent me in one of my identities, whilst others in another. In other words, no one represents me fully. No one single party can represent an individual fully. This is why nowadays, when citizens vote, they normally vote for the relatively better, not for the best. The principle of auto-representation, in its fundamentalist extreme version, does not only claim that there is such a thing as the best, but also tells you what it is. It is because of our multiple identities that the self-representation/auto-representation dichotomy becomes more and more chimerical. The more chimerical it becomes, the more fervently it gets promoted.

Let me return, however, to the resemblance of self-representation – and it became obvious that this is not just resemblance – to art and literature: can self-representation enrich the palette of politics with a new colour? Is there still, sometimes, a difference between self-representation and representation by the others? Does self-representation deserve our attention in this sense and can we even attach some hopes to it?

I said that modern democratic politics relativizes difference – someone represents me in one of my identities, the other in another. Yet there is an area, which can also play a role in politics, that is not about an issue, because it is somewhat more holistic. I refer to what has been called 'a way of life'. Although issues and identities become diffuse and fragmented, differing yet overlapping, there are still certain dominant ways of life which are different for all, and similar for some. It happens sometimes that voting preferences can be understood only in terms of preferences for this or that way of life. There is a modernist, easy-going, fairly cynical way of life. But there are also certain religious creeds and affiliations that promote strict mores, as well as ethnic groups with strong traditional systems of customs and a strong ethos. It is not necessary that people who share an image of a global way of life should isolate themselves from the rest and promote theirs alone. However, a way of life remains important for those who share it. If a particular way of life remains in a minority, the claim for some form of auto-representation is far from being fraudulent. This is not only because others, the outsiders who find the way of life of this group fairly strange will develop prejudices and disadvantage the members of groups they do not understand, but also because they actually do not understand them well, and, thus, can also misrepresent them. In such and similar cases auto-representation introduces difference into political life and makes it richer. Self-representation is then not the principle, it is not all encompassing; it is not the good thing one needs to contrast to the bad. But in certain cases auto-representation can supplement the general system of representation, which, on its part, cannot be described anymore in terms of auto/hetero, at least not as far as the principle of representation is concerned. Auto-representation in politics should better remain supplementary. It is not more just than hetero-representation, but, as I said, it can enrich political life, just as it enriches literature.

I mentioned at the beginning of this chapter that the principle of representation itself has been criticized and rejected by many radical thinkers. They have recommended that the system of representation be replaced altogether with direct democracy. Only they who participate in politics day by day should have a say in politics. Others should do what they like to do best – for example, write books on representation, promote their business and so on, but they should keep their hands off politics.

In my mind, this suggestion resembles too closely identity politics. It has nothing to do with fundamentalist identity politics of difference, for it is of a universalistic character. It does not promote any content, but it promotes a form, namely a form of action. Still, the model of direct democracy suggests that men and women should give absolute preference to something in life, commit themselves absolutely to this preference, a form of life. Hannah Arendt distinguishes among three forms of active life (*vita activa*). The political person gives preference to action among the three options of *vita activa*; this is her identity. Only those men and women who have committed themselves to *vita activa* against *vita contemplativa* have a right to political participation of any kind, and to action as against mere labour or creation (work). If there is no representation at all, all those who do not choose as their absolute and continuos identity politics as action, will be excluded from politics altogether.

Let us imagine a literature where there is only autobiography, painting limited to self-portrait. No one who has no capacity, wish or interest to write autobiographically or to paint herself, or to write or to paint at all, would have access to literature and/or painting. No one else but the writer and the painter could be represented in writing and painting. Direct democracy raises a similar claim. The exclusion of representation is by definition the exclusion of the representation of the other. Yet, as autobiography enriches literature and self-portraits enrich painting, so too can direct democracy supplement the systems of representation. If you identify yourself with it, you can be part of it, if not, not.

In the model case of literature, I suggested that there might be such a thing as women's literature that is also German or English or Australian literature and also belongs to high culture open to all those who are thrown into the world as strangers and who are never tired to explore the human condition.

Fundamentalist identity politics, insofar as it appears in literature or in the media, bars the way to the access of other differences, and through it also to universal meaning and concern. Literature that keeps the doors open lets books enter the avenue of universal concern. My Chinese students from Beijing have gladly discovered the resemblance between the *Story of the Stone* and *The Remembrance of Things Past*. Not because these novels portrayed something universal, but because they left the door open for everyone who was passionately interested in the human condition. The same can hold true of political representation. The alternative is not between difference and universality, between internal and external, but between closure and openness, between fundamentalism and an invitation to a voyage where we never know ahead whom we are going to meet during our journey, whether we will recognize – as once Iphigenia and Orestes did – our brothers and sisters among the strangers.

List of Contributors

Rainer Bauböck, Assistant Professor at the Institute for Advanced Studies, Department of Political Science, Vienna, and Senior Lecturer at the Universities of Vienna and Innsbruck; 1993-1996 Research Associate of the European Centre for Social Welfare Policy and Research, Vienna, Austria

Veit Bader, Professor of Sociology at the Faculty of Political and Sociocultural Sciences and Professor of Social and Political Philosophy at the Faculty of Humanities of the University of Amsterdam, The Netherlands

Eliezer Ben-Rafael, Weinberg Professor of Political Sociology, Department of Sociology, University of Tel-Aviv, Israel

Stephen Castles, Research Professor of Sociology in the Migration and Multicultural Studies Program at the Institute of Social Change & Critical Inquiry of the University of Wollongong, Australia

Alistair Davidson, Inaugural Professor of Citizenship Studies, Australian Citizenship Network, Centre for Urban and Social Research of the Swinburne University of Technology, Australia

Anna Elisabetta Galeotti, Lecturer in Political Philosophy, II Faculty of Liberal Arts and Philosophy, University of Turin, Italy

Agnes Heller, Hannah Arendt Professor of Philosophy at the New School for Social Research, New York, and Professor at the Department of Aesthetics of the ELTE University of Budapest, Hungary; 1994-1996 Member of the External Faculty of the European Centre for Social Welfare Policy and Research, Vienna, Austria

Danielle Juteau, Professeure, Département de Sociologie et Titulaire de la Chaire en Relations Ethniques, Centre d'Etudes Ethniques, Université de Montréal, Canada

Marie McAndrew, Professeure, Département d'Etudes en Education et d'Administration de l'Education et Directrice, Centre Immigration et Métropoles, Canada

Maria Markus, Senior Lecturer at the School of Sociology of the University of New South Wales, Sydney, Australia

Linda Pietrantonio, Agente de recherche, Chaire en Relations Ethniques, Université de Montréal, Canada

John Rundell, Director of the Ashworth Centre for Social Theory at the University of Melbourne, Australia

Daniel M. Weinstock, Associate Professor in the Department of Philosophy of the Université de Montréal, Canada

Charles Westin, Professor (Chair) of Migration and Ethnicity Studies, Director of the Centre for Research in International Migration and Ethnic Relations of the University of Stockholm, Sweden

Catherine Wihtol de Wenden, Directeur de Recherche au CNRS, Centre d'Etudes et de Recherches Internationales, Fondation Nationale des Sciences Politiques, Paris, France

Giovanna Zincone, Professor at the University of Turin, Department of Social Sciences, Italy